# The Art Firm

# The Art Firm

## Aesthetic Management and Metaphysical Marketing

**PIERRE GUILLET DE MONTHOUX**

*With figures by Anna Tribelhorn,*
*drawings by Pierre Guillet de Monthoux,*
*and photography by Jenny Ruther*

Stanford Business Books
An imprint of Stanford University Press
Stanford, California 2004

Stanford University Press
Stanford, California

Printed in the United States of America on acid-free, archival-quality paper

Library of Congress Cataloging-in-Publication Data

Guillet de Monthoux, Pierre, 1946–
The art firm : aesthetic management and metaphysical marketing /
Pierre Guillet de Monthoux.
p. cm.
"With figures by Anna Tribelhorn, drawings by Pierre Guillet de
Monthoux, and photography by Jenny Ruther."
Includes bibliographical references and index.
ISBN 0-8047-4813-6 (alk. paper)
1. Aesthetics. 2. Management—Philosophy. 3. Marketing. I. Title.
BH39.G852 2004
111'.85—dc21
2003007587

Designed by Andrew Ogus ■ Book Design
Typeset by Classic Typography in 9.5/14 Sabon

Original Printing 2004

Last figure below indicates year of this printing:
13   12   11   10   09   08   07   06   05   04

*to Paula*

# Contents

## Chapter 7  Art Corporations　　202

## Chapter 8  Flux Firms　　247

## Chapter 9  Postmod Performances　　269

## Chapter 10  Dionysus Inc.—Extending the Art Firm　　316

## Notes　　359

## Index　　373

====

# Preface
# Welcome to Dionysus Inc.

Imagine an art firm with faith in European philosophy, a place where art is made to work, where aesthetics is the operative management theory for the enterprise. Imagine that Fred Nietzsche has just been appointed managing director of this operation. His résumé lists an MBA earned with a man named Schopenhauer and a stint as a public relations expert for the Bayreuth Festival. Although he had some problems with Richard Wagner, CEO for the festival, the global success of the project was indisputably part of the job description for this man Nietzsche.

Imagine further that Joseph Beuys has just been appointed to lead human resource management. You know . . . he's the chap in the felt hat, the one who is lecturing in the company art space. Kant from Kaliningrad is the new and clever financial director. He's the one who came up with the revolutionary concept of aesthetic value based on consensus-credit. Rounding out Kant's department is his assistant Fred Schiller, who carries the label of management consultant/aesthetic coach.

Head of marketing is John Dewey, an American . . . although he's actually more European than American. He is a stable fellow with the ability to talk to any sort of customer. Having him do what he does so well is critical to the success of Dionysus Inc. because you have to make sure that customers don't take aesthetics the wrong way, thinking it's some sort of frightening or intimidating totalitarianism. Dewey's a democrat and can't stand the thought of people making that sort of connection. A strong suit of his is that he is well educated in philosophy and avoids connecting the operation to some banal entertainment.

While other firms manufacture materials, Dionysus Inc. turns signs and images into movies and music, or the other way round. Dewey likes to point out that art firms like this one are a kind of philosophy firm. He picked up this idea from Schopenhauer, who early recognized the market potential for metaphysics . . . given that ivory-tower eggheads no longer cater to good philosophy in their dusty, dull old universities. Nietzsche prefers to say that Dionysus Inc. provides art, although he and Dewey do not waste a lot of time quibbling over their seemingly disparate views. In a final analysis, their arguments are pretty much the same. Anyway, the point is not products and services but rather performances, for Dionysus Inc. is a high-performance art firm. Schiller likes to call the operating strategy "*Schwung*" and claims this is how the company makes art work. The Germans use the word to describe the swing between poles, and the Romantic philosophers believed that *Schwung* is born of aesthetic energy.

How I wish I could have seen Dionysus Inc. in action. But the plant tour I have just described is nothing more than a vision. It was no doubt the presence of art and aesthetics in contemporary management discourses that inspired my daydream, and therefore I concluded that the time had come to pull together studies from a quarter of a century, ideas from friends, students, and colleagues, and readings done during my academic career as a teacher in management. Questions of how aesthetics makes value and how performance in business links to performance art had become central to economy in general and the future management of creative firms in particular. My vision was about Schwung in an art firm, a new type of firm rooted in aesthetic philosophy and its special kind of metaphysics.

Schwung generates aesthetic energy in creative processes. Romantic philosophers ultimately developed a whole philosophy of aesthetics to explain what moves people and what in fact makes life swing. Very real and practical experiences, they concluded, become the seedbed for cultivating Schwung in an individual's life. If the capacity for generating this energy is possible, I wondered if it could also be managed. And if it could be, how? Further, as if in support of the conclusion of the Romantics, I recalled three of my own life experiences that had fired my curiosity and fascination with

Schwung management. I describe those experiences in detail in the first chapter before proceeding in the second, third, and fourth chapters with a crash course in the old philosophy finding new application as aesthetic theory for management. The following five chapters detail historical management cases from France, Germany, Russia, and Sweden to illustrate what it means to make art work through application of aesthetics and metaphysical marketing to practice. Finally, we travel to Italy for some good risotto and nice wine, and above all for an enlarged vision of art firms performing aesthetic value in tomorrow's new economy, where Dionysus Inc. might turn to metaphysical mainstream reality. For those interested, a bibliography of further reading can be found at the publisher's Web site: www.sup.org.

## Acknowledgments

Examples are taken from theatrical enterprises of the last two centuries in three European countries: France, Germany, and Sweden. The study of the Dramatic Theatre in Stockholm was carried out in 1973, thanks to the late Alf Sjöberg. Frank Castorf and Carl Hegemann at the Volksbühne in Berlin and Peter Wahlqvist and Elisabeth Lindfors at Stockholm's Stadsteatern helped me study their art firms in the 1990s. Marina Abramovic, Alberto Alessi, Daniel Birnbaum, Ken Friedman, Carl-Jan Grankvist, Torsten Lilja, Sven Lundh, David Neumann, Bo Nilsson, Rene Padt, Maria and Michelangelo Pistoletto, Karin Pott, Martin Rössel, Jean Sellem, Richard Stanley, Clemens Thornqvist, Hans Weil, and Robert Wilson showed me various ways of making art work.

In addition to support from my doctoral students, I got academic encouragement from Horst Albach, Thomas Bay, Ruth Bereson, Elisabeth Blanc, Dag Björkegren, Ivar Björkman, Michael Bockemühl, Gernot Böhme, Janet Borgerson, Dominique Bouchet, Simonetta Carbonaro, Armin Chodzinski, Barbara Czarniawska, Claes Dahlbeck, Albert Danielsson, Michael Dawids, Fuat Firat, Ole Fogh-Kirkeby, William Fovet, Martin Fuglsang, Bo Göranzon, Paula Guillet de Monthoux, Claes Gustafsson, Barbara Harris, Heather Höpfl, Ekkhard Kappler, Thomas Knoblauch, Bengt Kristensson-Uggla, Erik Kruse, Romain Laufer, Jacques Lebraty, Katja Lindqvist, Kenneth Macleod, Mark Markowski, Karl Erik Norrman, Gunnar Olsson, Sergei Orlov, Thomas Polesie, Rafael Ramirez, Alf Rehn, Dagmar Reichert, Willmar Sauter, Claus Otto Scharmer, Henrik Schrat, Jonathan Schroeder, Sven Erik Sjöstrand, Kaj Sköldberg, Richard Sotto, Matt Statler, Emma Stenström, Antonio Strati,

Alladi Venkatesh, Roland Vila, Charlie Wahren, Rachel Weiss, Jeanette Wetterström, and Judith Wilske. Financial support was primarily granted by the project Fields of Flow, funded by the Swedish National Bank Tercentenary Foundation, and also by Leadership of Cultural Businesses, a project funded by Humanistiskt Samhällsvetenskapliga Forskningsrådet (HSFR). Valuable help was provided by the Tavistock Institute for Human Relations in London, MTC (Market Science Institute) in Stockholm, IFL executive education in Stockholm, the Wissenschaftszentrum Berlin, IAE University of Nice Sophia-Antipolis, and the gallery Haus am Lützowplatz in Berlin. My colleagues at the School of Business at the University of Stockholm and the research students in my group ECAM (European Centre for Arts and Management), as well as colleagues of CAL (Center for Art and Leadership) at the Copenhagen Business School, have provided the intellectual environment for my work. I owe a great debt of gratitude to all who have encouraged me, informed me, and facilitated this work. Of course, I alone stand responsible for the result, *The Art Firm*.

PIERRE GUILLET DE MONTHOUX
GENÈVE, MAY 2003

# The Art Firm

# 1

Play as Aesthetic Schwung

## Points of Departure—Aesthetic Theaters

### Operating Theater

Some years ago, I spent time researching hospital waiting lists while completing a project on human suffering and anxiety. My findings were grim: six months for a hip replacement, one to two years for a heart operation, an unspecified wait for treatment of prostate cancer. As a professor of management, I dealt with my observations from the perspective of a management specialist. As a human being, however, I realized that more was going on in these situations than could possibly be explained by ordinary academic analysis. As sometimes happens, what was going on in my personal life put me in *Schwung* and compelled me to at least look at these situations from another perspective.

My own father had died recently. Tormented by cancer and catheters, he endured what seemed an inordinate delay in getting information and receiving treatment, and my memory of our last Christmas together is monopolized by scenes of his hauling himself exhausted the few short steps to his old armchair. On a night early in January, he awoke and coughed up blood. When the molelike duty doctor made his final visit at dawn, Death seemed to hover in the early mist. Father's breathing had become more and more labored, and it was only an immense exertion of will that allowed him a

1

painful sip of tea laced with honey. His next concern resulted in a resolute fumbling for the catheter bag to see if fluid was coming through. When he mistook a corner of the sheet for the pouch, it was the first time in his long illness that he showed any signs of confusion.

A few hours later in the ambulance, his eyes, wide open, screamed above the oxygen mask, and I reached for the gas tap to increase the flow. His eyes held me with their last ounce of life, until they stopped seeing me and submitted to Death. The wait for treatment had been insufferable; the wait for death, long. In one final irony, even his body had to queue up for its turn in the mortuary.

All this waiting had caused me to suffer as well. The pain of ill people marking time in their own lines, diagnosed but still waiting passively as death accelerated toward them, affected me deeply. Each passing day signified the withering away of any opportunity for even a delayed operation and improved health.

In this time of progress, wealth, and life-saving technology, people continued to suffer as arguments in the health care debate bounced back and forth like the fuzzy ball in a grotesque game of tennis. On the one hand, privatization of health care offered a solution. I myself had discovered that for a modest amount my father might theoretically have bought the operation that would have eased his suffering. I learned that the wait was not as long in the provinces as it was in Stockholm, and thirty minutes away on the other side of the Baltic Sea beds remained empty in Finland's hospitals. Of course, having this information was useless, for regulations ruled out medical care between health care jurisdictions.

One of the debate's central themes is that Sweden's public sector is too large, clumsy, and thick-skinned to be sensitive to the needs of those in its care. Like some enormous mollusk, it is withdrawing into its shell to die because it lacks both the will and the capacity to see the reality of the suffering. While people at home yearn for their operations, doctors on leave sit on their yachts, speculating about the insensitivity of the health service. Theory becomes therapy for the guilty conscience of the practitioner. Give them a private health market system, they assert, and they would operate instead of speculate.

On the other hand, others in the debate speak of poor planning and weak public leadership; the public sector needs to get a grip on its own problems, they reason. The suspicion that long waiting lists are the result of some clever budget game in which medical administrators can negotiate for *real* money is a common one. History has borne out the fact that doctors, by relying on their omnipotence as healers, have been able to procure more and more prestigious and expensive technology if they just make people wait. Imagine what would happen if they were allowed to open private clinics and apply for money directly from the National Insurance Fund. In a health service so unused to competition as the Swedish one, such a market solution would enable the doctors to charge inflated prices and shamelessly line their pockets at the expense of their consumers. Further, regional differences in the length of the waiting list would certainly not be remedied by privatization. The only cure seems to be a more effective national health organization; according to this line of argument, the solution involves stricter state control through better regulation.

In such a confrontational duel between the market and the plan, the pendulum of debate swings between extremes. As administrators, doctors, journalists, and politicians trudge through their discussions, I cannot escape mentally revisiting the scenes of my father's rampaging cancer. Like so much medical baggage, he had been transported on a conveyor belt among hospital wards, assorted treatment areas, and constantly changing faces. How our family had struggled with the medical establishment to hold this Kafkaesque world at bay! In our goal to somehow triumph over preprogrammed care regimes, we added our own personal flourishes to the prescribed routine. We added spices to his bland hospital food. We served some drops of good wine with his pasty hospital soup. We sponged him with cologne. We replaced hospital music with Schumann and trashy magazines with the Proust of his French youth.

After my father's death, as I packed my bags for a trip to Britain, I began to reflect on health care in general. Sweden has an almost exclusively state-managed health care plan, while the United States, looked upon as the source of the market solution, seems at the opposite extreme. I had the feeling that in the long run I would find Britain more interesting because of its more nearly balanced mix of private and public health care. In reality, however, I found that only a small percentage of the British population has private health insurance, and most patients with private hospital coverage are wealthy. I learned that affluent Arabs, for example, could travel to Britain and receive new heart valves in luxurious clinics, and the surgeons doing the operations in these establishments were none other than harried National Health Service doctors doing a bit of moonlighting.

During my trip, I made several visits to private clinics. One hospital had been built specifically to treat bypass patients from Norway since the Norwegians were in the process of expanding their own research and technology for heart surgery. Another facility was supported by the Dutch until the Dutch completed their own expansion.

I also discovered that the NHS is totally centralized in London; the few specialist areas receiving extra funding "earn" it only after noisy and effective lobbying. The strength of *doctor power* is fully acknowledged, and there was then talk of letting *special* inspectors check on physicians to determine whether or not they were performing their duties according to their public contract. Even though the political debate was much tougher, the two alternatives of market or plan were just the same as they were in Sweden.

Resigned to this fact, I packed my bags for the journey home, confident that my inferences were conclusive and accurate. As I was finishing my preparations, however, by sheer coincidence I stumbled upon Sir John's Eye Camp, and all of a sudden market and plan had to share the stage with a possible third alternative: aesthetics.

It was a blustery autumn afternoon on the southern coast of England, and the sea was windswept and gray. Fish-and-chip stalls hibernated in their off-season hiatus; the amusement arcades on the pier were silent reflections of their former lives. In the midst of this profile of inactivity, lights blazing through the windows of one of the Victorian hotels contributed an unusual chiaroscuro to the picture. Cars were parked outside, and the place was teeming with life. Elderly ladies and gentlemen—the men in worn tweed sports jackets, the women in loose hand-knit cardigans—made conversation as they sipped tea and ate sandwiches in the lounges overlooking the sea.

In the lobby, a group of drivers from the Royal Ambulance Corps politely escorted old ladies to the cars waiting to shuttle them to the local hospital. There, a team of doctors would be operating on hundreds of cataract patients over the course of the weekend. Sir John's Impact Foundation had just begun its first European eye camp.

Eye camps were first developed to take care of the sick in the Third World. Doctors and nurses volunteered to operate their way through the cataract waiting lists in remote Indian and Latin American towns and vil-

lages. In these far-off lands, schoolchildren gave a scrubbing to their class-
rooms and transformed them into facilities that could serve as operating
theaters. Finally, Sir John, himself blind, determined that the time had come
to bring an eye camp to England, and so he began to build his team of vol-
unteers from NHS doctors. The local health district contributed part of the
cost, and the Impact Foundation located sponsors to donate the rest.

All cataract sufferers on the local waiting list had received a letter of invitation, and they all responded that they wished to take part in the program.
Patients were to report to the hotel the day before the operation and stay
one day afterward. In addition, for a negligible fee, they could bring someone along to share their double room, since seaside hotels were usually
empty at this time of the year.

The difference between a hospital and a seaside hotel is profound, even
in the off season. Although the surgery itself was performed at the local
clinic, examinations and convalescence took place at the hotel. Institutional
protocol was avoided, and for the patients—often single, elderly, and far
from well off—the good food, the television in their room, and the opportunity to socialize in the lounges and bars clearly turned the treatment into a
treat. Nurses enjoyed working in the hotel, for they no longer had to chase
orderlies or worry about cleaning and maintenance; the hotel staff managed
all that. In addition, Sir John's team succeeded in negotiating discount rates
for medicines and equipment, and also in standing up for patient rights in
hard-fought talks with the "sharks" of the pharmaceutical industry.

Administrative procedure was simplified, and the admissions process cut
to a minimum. Many preoperative tests were done away with, to the relief
of doctors, nurses, and patients alike. In one fell swoop, the mindless routines of hospital life lost their grip. In the aesthetic theater of a good cause,
sociological habits lost their conventional power. Distanced from the institutions of economic reality, the aesthetic hospital seemed to come to life, and
the imperatives of maintenance and the demands for functionalism just
seemed part of the fabric of the building. Somewhere between the sociological and the economical, between rule and reason, Sir John had charged in
and occupied the aesthetic field that he now promoted.

All this helped me remember how I had felt when caring for my dying father and the sense of satisfaction that washed over me as I performed even
the smallest of gestures: making the bed, plumping the pillows, preparing

food, contributing to the last lingering pleasures of life. I had found myself in a state of contagious ecstasy, and I came to understand how inadequate words are to describe the way the liturgy of these small tasks had elevated my life. I praised God that I was able to serve. I met strangers in the street, held their gaze, and instigated vibrant and meaningful conversations. I was a Western *sadhu*, floating through Stockholm in my winter coat. "It must be so hard on you," said the people who could not understand, who had never experienced the comforting satisfaction of this type of caring.

In 1985, at an exhibition in Aachen, Joseph Beuys (1921–1986) described the creation of his *The Crucifixion*. His construction had gone through three stages, he related. First, he felt the figurative embodiment of the entirety of Christian experience. Following this, a feeling of paralyzing emptiness at the death of Christ came over him. Finally, a hyperactive period filled with the desire to embody the mystical power of Jesus' death consumed him. Restating an aesthetic reflection of Christ in the dry Habermasian debates of German Protestantism during the 1970s, Beuys said, "For me it was a question of showing the reality of this energy. A permanently self-reinforcing existence . . . It isn't a question of embodying or depicting an historic event. It's about making reality present."[1]

The energy surrounding my father's suffering was intense reality for me, but not in the sense of some tragic and unavoidable truth to be passively accepted, to be analyzed, or to be interpreted. On the threshold of death, life itself became intense. I was part and parcel of my existence, enveloped in a surreal feeling that I had only previously experienced in moments of euphoria in my work or in orgiastic love affairs. Through this experience outside of time, I was teleported from a mundane sociopsychological reality, the one we talk about, relate to, and compare with, into the timelessness of absolute being.

In *The Crucifixion*, Beuys displays the center of a web of energy between the two outstretched arms of the Cross, which is, interestingly enough, analogous to the health care quandary. The sculpture transmits not an idea but the feeling of harmony in dynamic balance between two poles of energy. Its Schwung moves between ideas and substance, between the sociology of work and the economy of the institution.

Back in the lobby of the English hotel once more, I saw Sir John, white stick in hand, walking between the groups of chairs. Fragile white-haired ladies came up to him, took his hands, and expressed their thanks. "He's amazing. He's doing this for us absolutely free. Even though we all went through the Blitz, nobody else cares about us. This is wonderful!"

## Lecturing Theater

The old Swedish university town of Lund marks the place where I first understood that universities are not institutions, and they are certainly not workplaces or profit centers or bureaucratic offices or factories of a knowledge industry either. Academia is an aesthetic bridge stretching between the sociological and the logical.

In the heart of Lund, a cathedral stood in a beautiful park surrounded by narrow streets in the medieval center of the city. Every house, every stone was impregnated with memories of centuries of scholars. In the midst of half-timbered buildings and majestic elms rose the medieval brick façade of Lundagård House, home of the Philosophy Department. Inside was the creaking, polished oak staircase which, legend claimed, Sweden's King Charles XI had ascended on his horse. Even though the tale of this bit of bravado was fiction—the building was a copy erected at the turn of the century—it really didn't matter. Everyone seemed to acknowledge the theatricality of academia, and they enjoyed the show. Lund's aesthetic world fueled me with the energy to write the texts that led me to the professorial chair I now hold in Stockholm.

Stockholm University was the other side of the coin. Built in the 1960s, it was designed to look like a workplace with a hint of modern factory about it. It was a post-1968 attempt to define reality by way of the ordinary. The place wanted to exist as useful and functional, and I soon observed that many students called the university their "school." To them, professors and lecturers were simply "teachers" filling up their time schedules. Lecturing teachers themselves were not performing in the lecturing theater; they took the elevator down to "the pit" to work their "shifts."

Upon landing on this assembly line, I acted on instinct. During my first week as professor, I hung pictures on the walls of my room and filled its corners with classical music from an old tape player. I launched my own little campaign to appropriate some personal aesthetic space in the university.

"But where exactly *is* the university?" a visitor to Cambridge is said to have asked a bypassing student. The Vatican apart, universities constitute some of Europe's oldest surviving institutions, many times existing "without walls." Within their disciplines, colleagues are united around the globe. The University of Stockholm pays my wages, for example, but traditions and formal recruiting procedures brought in learned peers from beyond the local sphere of influence to select me for the job. Information performed in lecture theaters is the result of international research, connected by decades-old collegial networks. Workplace democracy and other issues borrowed from the realm of factory management are fairly marginal phenomena within such research environments. The Sorbonne, Heidelberg, and Harvard all rather resemble Covent Garden, the Met, or La Scala in that they generously offer their hospitality to guest stars from the aesthetic realm of international research. Before long, my students in Stockholm would demonstrate how this perception was not merely my own romanticized vision, not merely the dreams of a hopeless idealist.

Before that happened, however, I had a nightmare one night. I was having lunch with a new colleague. During a lengthy monologue about his work, he confided that he saw himself primarily as an administrator of brown envelopes and welcomed me as an administrative colleague who would function in the same way. "Now that you've got the chair," he pointed out, "you don't have to do any more research." He had gladly exchanged the solitary toil of publishing research for what seemed to me a monotonous chairing of meetings. Although he chased official brown envelopes with great energy, the pursuit of knowledge was never his thing. In addition, a significant and time-consuming priority for him was maintaining the status quo. When I adjourned our lunch with a jaunty "Hope we're going to have fun in the future," I was met with a friendly but uncomprehending reaction. My professorial colleague utterly disapproved of the idea of academia as *fun* or *playful*. I awoke in a cold sweat just as he was thinking about sealing me into one of his brown envelopes.

My longing for play then took me to the student union, where I drank punch, handed out mock awards, and, dressed in my battered old tailcoat, gave nonsensical student speeches. My colleague's grave defense of the rules was lampooned in a student revue.

At that time, the Swedish university had become more and more vocational. Since many students worked to support themselves, they were exhausted when they got to the lecture halls. Despite this weariness, however, I sensed a growing nostalgia for old academic ideals. Students began recognizing that the university should not be a school and that tutors were different from teachers. Very soon, they would see a way to express this point of view.

Fewer and fewer staff members showed up for meetings, and those who did come gathered to eat cake together and rehash the minutes of the previous meeting. Many of the faculty members ran dynamic consultancies outside the university, and some had set up institutes where for a handsome fee they carried out analyses replicating obsolete research. Even when they were present in body, my colleagues were absent in spirit. They spoke about administration, organization, and holiday experiences; they had no doubt they were better off as well-paid consultants and businessmen than they were as learned professors. Money, not publication, was the measure of success, for money signified consultancies, which in turn signified usefulness. Their own research and competencies were used sparingly as authoritative illustrations.

An independent evaluation that criticized management education at the Swedish university attracted the attention of some members of this academic vacuum. Students, having read the report themselves and upon their own initiative, established their own quality control committee. Soon this committee had set up a development council including various luminaries from both private business and the civil public service as members. Little would come out of this, I thought, since council members seemed almost as dry and disillusioned as the staff itself. How could the kind of quality lacking in management education ever be inspired by another managerial method?

This student initiative ultimately unseated my pessimism, however, for the group proceeded to add a significant aesthetic dimension to the process of improving educational quality. Students were tired of being stationed in functional buildings, of being marked by rigid rules established years earlier. Although they were weighed down with studying and earning a living, they were still healthily rebellious and outspoken. To my surprise, the student union showed for new arrivals the 1989 movie *Dead Poets' Society,* the story of an American teacher who enchants his high school students with poetry, a piece about using aesthetic energy in teaching. In addition, the students showed a film of their own making, a short video entitled *The Good Academy,* which they had coproduced with some friends from the art school. I was astonished when I saw it.

*The Good Academy* was no send-up. On the one hand, it was not the didactic storytelling that would have come out of shameless advertising. It did not contain images of the sunny, shadowless workplaces found in the glossy marketing brochures for a majority of universities. There were no proud pictures of beautiful, stripped-pine libraries, no cozy images of coffee cups and beer cans on the grass, and no canned shots of hothouse students sitting in front of brand new computer terminals. There was not a mention of science, not even of the academic glory of Stockholm University, the Nobel Prize in Economics.

On the other hand, it was not a disguised documentary of critical theory either. It had no commercial references or public service announcements. There were no comments about classes being too large or about qualified, inspiring, or competent teachers being too few. It did not note the lack of enthusiasm for research or the dumbed-down textbooks. The ugly rooms and the alienations of student life escaped even a line in the trailer. *The Good Academy* was neither sales propaganda nor a political pamphlet, and as a result it could not be brushed aside with pompous denials. This video presentation skillfully positioned itself between nagging criticism and narrative marketing. *The Good Academy* was brought into existence, as the German poet Friedrich Schiller would have put it, between *substance* and *form*. My management students had instinctively understood how to implement an aesthetic strategy in which play, between substance and form, opens up aesthetic possibilities resulting in real quality improvement.

The star of the story was not a successful manager at work, nor was it an industrious freshman in the library. In several sublimely beautiful sequences, the film shows a ballet student at the bar, deep into her classical training. She is an artist in one of art's most difficult and demanding forms, an artist struggling with her own body under the critical gaze of her colleagues. She has been working backstage in the ballet room for years so that perhaps one single second would look better on stage, would show the beauty of her art, and would please her audience. This was how the students wanted to be seen, as beauty rooted in the truth of classical competence and hard training. This was the idea they had of a real university.

Two years after the first screening of *The Good Academy,* my workplace was once again simmering with a desire to improve. Many of the staff had returned from their extramural jobs and their high-paying consultancies. Students attended meetings and discussions, and my department experienced new life and vitality. It was the late 1980s, and I was glad to see how, albeit ever so gradually, art and artists had come to play an increasingly important part in injecting new life into moribund public and private organizations. The Stockholm students had intuitively and precociously struck the chord of a new trend in education. A decade later, the whole department moved from their factorylike enclosures into redecorated vintage brick buildings in a beautiful park on the seaside in Stockholm. The installation sculpture in the park is by the artist Charlotte Gyllenhammar, daughter of the former CEO of Volvo. Organizational behavior was taught by young assistant professors with a keen interest in both art and aesthetics. As we live in an experience economy, as future industries are to be creative industries, art and aesthetics are about to be integrated in the design of the curriculum for young managers.

## Festival Theater

One photograph in my collection shows singers taking a curtain call on the opening night of *The Marriage of Figaro* on the square in the little French village of Gattières. I recall that warm night in July 1991 when we were finally able to enjoy the fruits of four years of hard labor. From that opening night, we went on to give five performances that would have cost at least ten times our budget in the established opera market. In the pit was a professional orchestra from the Nice opera, and on stage an international cast. A director from Brussels, a conductor from Paris, and a production manager from Sweden completed the troupe. They had worked all hours of the day and night for a month to pull off this miraculous feat of art management swinging with aesthetic energy.

I get ahead of my story, though. In 1987, I bumped into two old friends, Eva and Eddy, in Nice. The meeting sparked memories of a bygone time when I sang in an amateur operatic society. Many of my friends from that time had since turned professional; I, on the other hand, had given up singing lessons and was busy writing my dissertation. The memory of those earlier times is still keen: the suggestive séances when the singing teacher, coaching you to control the uncontrollable little muscles in your throat, becomes an extension of your own being; the symbiosis between pupil and teacher; the experience of practicing, with the strange singing alchemy fusing mind and body; the dream of a career in opera for which so many give up secure jobs and sacrifice personal relationships.

I remembered how pupils became addicted to the *school* of their teacher and how easily the devotion turns into a quasi-religious faith based on a special singing method. I remembered the times of the terrible voice crises when teachers turned into therapists or became powerful shamans who could shatter the confidence of the greatest stars by a simple comment.

The day after my meeting with Eva and Eddy, the three of us sat in the shadow of the olive tree in my garden in Gattières, enjoying a Provençal collation of succulent chicken cooked with rosemary and red country wine. Later, when the rest of the town seemed to be taking its siesta, we took an afternoon walk and found ourselves in the village square, gazing in wonderment at what seemed to be an unbelievably natural festival theater. A little bar, a bakery, and a butcher shop complete with sausages and hams in the window encircled it. In the center of the scene stood a fountain, its sprays of water sparkling in the sun. By the time the clock in the church tower struck four, we all had but one thing in mind: we must have the square for our operatic performance.

The mayor, who just happened to stroll by, accepted our invitation to join us for coffee, and soon the idea took off. In a short time, other villagers became interested but were more skeptical. "Opera's so grand and expensive . . . isn't it more at home with sophisticated people in the city?" they would wonder. "Or with the snobs over there in St. Paul de Vence, where all the tourists go? Is it really possible for poor farmers like us?"

This was just the attitude Eva and Eddy wanted to change. "Had the precocious Mozart not spoken artlessly and directly to people's hearts?" they reasoned. "Had not Verdi been as popular as Yves Montand or Mick Jagger? And Wagner, with his faith in folk opera?" Over time, the big opera houses of Europe had become sadly petrified institutions, with the back stage run by the bureaucrats, and the front stage peopled by an urban elite more interested in intermission gossip than music. Opera had declined to the level of a decorative commodity, sister to the incessantly running television set in a French workman's kitchen. In the big opera houses, musicians thought about their supper, and the singers about their wages.

In addition, most European opera houses had dissolved their resident companies after World War II, and now these singers toured as international vocal consultants. Their training had become a matter of mastering a menu of ready-made parts to be marketed in auditions and assembled just-in-time. Artists flew in in the morning, rehearsed during the afternoon, delivered their arias in the evening, and caught the last plane home the same night. An audience that did not know the story of the opera by heart and had not studied the score and libretto had no chance of understanding a complex plot like that of *The Marriage of Figaro* or *Così Fan Tutte* when it was produced in such an industrial way. Unschooled newcomers believed opera to be a competition to reach high C amid a demonstration of lovely arias interspersed with bits of incomprehensible knockabout. One might even wonder if all the singers themselves knew the details of the plot they so professionally delivered on stage. The strange logic of modern production technique had shortened rehearsal time and ignored recitatives; it had turned operatic art into show-biz entertainment.

Eva and Eddy wanted to put on a performance for the villagers that they could grasp. They wanted to resuscitate the theatricality they felt belonged to real opera. They wanted to liberate an aesthetic field dominated by formal, stone-dead local institutions and a global star system of opera divas. Their persuasive strategy was unique. They did not start by making public statements or rational arguments. Like my students in Stockholm and like Sir John, they intuitively distrusted the effect of fine words or crass calculations to persuade the little village of their enterprise. Instead, they made art work.

In the spring of 1988, a small group, including the mayor, was invited to an improvised musical salon, where through the music itself Eva and Eddy persuaded them all to hold a trial concert that summer. The concert exceeded all expectations, and in July 1990 six singers and a director arrived for a month of rehearsing *The Barber of Seville* with a local pianist. Rehearsals took place outside in the heat, in public, so that the whole village could see and hear what was going on. Mornings everyone had breakfast at the bar in the square, and the artists socialized with the villagers without hesitation. On July 14, Bastille Day, they enjoyed Pistou soup together and danced merrily in the square.

The grand scheme for this production was to let the performance grow out of the village itself. The process of creation, more than the brilliance of the production, was the crucial factor, for this was to become a *Festival de Création* and not one simply inviting ready-made touring shows to perform. The village itself, its spirit and its atmosphere, would melt into the work. The houses and trees would form a natural backdrop. After the tickets were all sold out and the performances were over, their new success would pave the way for the following year's more ambitious plan: at last, perhaps, the chance to perform *Figaro* one summer evening out on the square.

An aesthetic project unprotected by stars or institutions is vulnerable and brittle. As with most of the festivals mushrooming in French villages, this one was run as a voluntary association, and exigencies constantly challenged the production. During a rehearsal for the *Barber*, we discovered that the bass did not know his part. Then extra rehearsals were needed, but the pianist had small children and could not work in the evenings. She started complaining that at least the singers were getting a holiday in the south of France, while she just had to do extra work. The director, who had been discreetly phoning around Europe for a new bass, decided to get a new pianist as well, and a musician from the village who had kindly volunteered for the project was fired. It could not have been a surprise that when the villagers later assembled to plan for the next summer's event, the future of the whole festival was put in question.

"How do you know they'll come back? They only want our sunshine, and now when it is raining, they won't come any more. Surely we have our own singers down here in Nice who could do the job cheaper. I'm starting to get tired of Eva and Eddy's thinking that we've nothing better to do than work for them, as if our village only exists for their festival."

This village unrest was reported to me over the phone while I was in Stockholm. I had been elected president of the association, and now I faced negotiating with them from afar. They decided to vote on the matter, and the secretary relayed the results to me over the phone: "Three for, one against. The festival survives another year."

The festival survived, but not without continuing aggravation. The public budget for *Figaro* was 120,000 francs according to the plan, but in February only half of it had been subscribed. Sponsors were not to be found, although auditions had already been held in Paris, Brussels, and Nice, and the cast for *Figaro* had been selected. In March, during a crisis meeting in a Montmartre bar, it was decided to carry on, regardless of budget problems.

That summer, shortly before rehearsals for *Figaro* were to begin, someone asked about the orchestra. It had been assumed that the conductor was taking care of that necessity, so everyone just shrugged and looked at everyone else. That night a local bassoonist phoned his friends, while vocal rehearsals began with piano accompaniment. Only five days before the dress rehearsal, the orchestra began to rehearse. By some miracle, the professional musicians who appeared agreed to work for next to nothing. As if that were not enough, after the performance the musicians raved about the freshness of this opera. It was so different from the opera house routine!

While problems were being solved backstage, attracting an audience was also in full swing. The performances were to bring people from all over Europe, and representatives from music schools and conservatories lined up to audition for the next summer's production. Anyone involved with music of any kind, and opera in particular, immediately understood this unique opportunity for young singers to perform the great roles long before any established theater would take a chance on them. In addition, it was a rare chance to interpret a work of art aesthetically, in a concentrated and thorough way. Here singers would not merely analyze their own parts in isolation with their singing coach, but they would go through the whole performance together, in text as well as in music, for three intense weeks. They would listen to each other and offer advice and support. They would stand together through crises and conflicts, and exchange valuable information about career opportunities. Some even planned to continue doing other projects together in the fall.

For the director and the conductor, this was an equally exceptional way of working. As professionals with flourishing careers, they were used to spending their lives commuting by plane between theaters and concert halls around the world. Several times in other venues, the conductor had performed without even meeting the director. Similarly, the director had worked on librettos without discussing the music with the conductor.

One of the things that attracted all of them was the opportunity to work on a piece of art in its entirety, and they paid for this privilege, and for their simple lodging and one meal a day, through hard work. This feeling of sufficiency held the project together and mediated the divisions that constantly threatened to break out over finances, technical shortcomings, language difficulties, and collisions of cultural values and artistic traditions. Looking at my old photograph, I remembered how everyone was spellbound after that first night, as if Mozart's music and the Beaumarchais text had miraculously melted together with the village. In the absence of better words, people kept repeating: "We've experienced a moment of magic together."

## Schiller's Schwung Strategy

When I tried to use my three experiences as management science or organizational theory, they faded into theoretical constructs and technical jargon; the energy vanished in the process of reducing experience to abstraction. What remained was a bland account of how Sir John's health project delivered good, inexpensive health care; how the student production of *The Good*

*Academy* video improved the quality of education; and how the festival in Gattières filled villagers with pride. Management scholars, who were talking about "entertainment" economies and "creative" industries, also seemed more intrigued by the unique charge and grandeur I had glimpsed in these experiences than in an academic analysis of the generalizable facts. *What was so special about this energy?* I wondered.

During the time that all this was rumbling through my mind, I was invited to teach at a German university. From the somewhat Americanized Swedish milieu of management studies, I found myself in the company of German business students who introduced me to more European management authorities. They credited Joseph Beuys, Wassily Kandinsky (1866–1944), and Friedrich Schiller (1749–1805), as well as other European artists and philosophers, with helping them understand economic energy. One student, who later wrote a book linking Schiller to strategic management,[2] invited me to join them in studying Schiller's book *On the Aesthetic Education of Man*. To the young European management students, Schiller had written about the aesthetic education of "*man-agers*"! In the philosopher-poet's statement, they saw a handy way to define the source of energy as an aesthetic play where "[n]o privilege, no autocracy of any kind, is tolerated where taste rules, and the realm of aesthetic semblance extends its sway. This realm stretches upwards to the point where reason governs with unconditioned necessity, and all that is mere matter ceases to be. It stretches downwards to the point where natural impulse reigns with blind compulsion, and form has not yet begun to appear."[3]

Who was this Schiller who sounded like a clever management consultant?

In 1788, four years before these words were written, Schiller traveled to Weimar, excited at the prospect of discussing philosophy with Johann Wolfgang von Goethe and moving in his learned circles. Because Goethe himself was on a trip to Italy, Schiller had to be content with talking to Kant's former pupil, Johann Gottfried Herder, and with conversing pleasantly with a rococo thinker called Christoph Martin Wieland. To be sure, Schiller would have been able to keep up his end of the conversation. In 1782, he had become famous overnight when his play *Die Räuber* was first performed at the theater in Mannheim. His father, Captain Schiller, had years earlier enrolled his talented son in Duke Charles Eugene's renowned breeding school for young talent, where, with military discipline, promising youths were trained for their future careers as state managers. The captivity in this enlightened college nurtured Friedrich's desire for freedom. Encouraged by a few pipes of tobacco and perhaps some wine, he performed nightly readings of his own poetry and totally captivated his classmates. When Goethe appeared as guest of honor at the academy's Examinations Feast in 1779, Schiller was beside himself with excitement.

He was eventually released from his scholastic prison, but not before he was forced to take medical exams and be recommended as a trainee doctor for the town of Stuttgart. *Die Räuber,* now finished, was to be performed for the first time in Mannheim. One evening, without permission, Schiller crossed the Württemburg border to witness the first performance of his play. Despite its success, however, Schiller was ultimately forced to creep back into service for Charles Eugene. He was completely disinterested in his work as a doctor, work characterized by his regularly prescribing overdoses of stimulants. While the town was enjoying a fireworks display one evening, Schiller fled Stuttgart for good and began many years of nomadic life. Throughout this period, his career as a poet survived because of seemingly endless energy and his passionate talent. This, combined with charm and an intoxicating spirituality, eventually persuaded Duke Charles Eugene to forgive the flight by night from his medical career.

Of course, when Schiller arrived in Weimar to talk to his idol, Goethe was nowhere to be found. He was traveling in Italy. So with the aim of using poetry to inject some life into dry historical documents, Schiller threw himself upon thick bundles in dusty archives and began rewriting history into histories. He lived frugally and dreamed of a professorial position, even though his friends could not quite see him in a dry, academic job. Schiller himself did not acknowledge any difference between artistic practice and academic theory.

Finally, on Goethe's recommendation, in 1789, the year of revolution, Schiller gained his professorship. He settled in the university town of Jena, which was in the process of becoming an incubator for German Romanticism. Johann Gottlieb Fichte was already a lecturer there, and after Schiller would come Friedrich Wilhelm Joseph von Schelling and Georg Wilhelm Friedrich Hegel.

Schiller's happiness was short-lived. First, he discovered that his position was unsalaried, which meant that his ability to care for his new wife was totally unfunded. The second blow came when he realized that his lectures were appreciated more as poetic edutainment than as academic readings.

Then, in the midst of Schiller's difficulties, fortune smiled upon him. A Danish poet alleviated his financial hardship by promising him a pension from Prince Friedrich Christian of Schleswig-Holstein Augustenburg. Instead of devoting himself to the pursuit of his art as soon as he received the money, however, he launched into studying the most recent work of Immanuel Kant (1724–1804). Schiller felt that at last he could afford to study Kant's new philosophy, and this was incredibly satisfying for him. He believed that individuals could not manage as real artists if they ignored the study of aesthetics (the management philosophy of their own trade). In 1792, after three years of concentration, he wrote twenty-seven letters thanking his benefactor, Prince Friedrich Christian. In these letters, *On the Aesthetic Education of Man,* Schiller presents a simplified version of Kant's philosophy. My students were completely right about how this work clarified the idea of economic energy. Schiller's book rendered Kant's aesthetics as a kind of strategic art management.

In the last of his aesthetic letters, Schiller wrote about the realm of art and its qualities of liberation. A careful reading of the text makes clear why Schiller, under the name of "sieur Gille,"[4] had been acclaimed an honorary Republican of France at the 1792 National Convention by no less than Georges Jacques Danton himself. But Schiller, whose patron was a prince, dreamed of a freedom other than one ending with a headless king. Freedom would not be won by storming the Bastille but by a clear strategy for an aesthetic freedom of enterprise.

Schiller opens this last letter by postulating that everyone longs for a harmonious balance between nature and culture. Such a balance may well have existed in ancient Greece, he thought, but division of labor and increasing economic alienation had long ago split the unity of mind and matter so that modern man believes he has a choice only between two evils. On the one hand is nature; on the other, morality. Nature is a slide into barbaric carnal hedonism, and morality is a road to serfdom under dogmatic tyrants. This modern dilemma grows out of the split created between these opposites by diverging drives. The sensual impulse, in German called *Stofftrieb,* seduces man into hedonism and materializes existence in time and space. *Formtrieb,* the opposite drive, results in man's building castles in the air erected by the "logic" of pure imagination. The two alternatives are then to submit to the extreme tyranny of morality or to give in to the carnal barbarity of superficial materialism. Continuing, Schiller emphasizes Kant's point that this either-or assumption

is incomplete, since a third alternative does exist between the Scylla of the mundane and the Charybdis of the possible; it is called *Spiel-trieb,* the desire to play.

Schiller urged taking the lust for play seriously; it offered a swinging bridge between form and substance. The animal kingdom offers striking examples of this. To cite just one, the dignified monarch of the beasts, the great lion king himself, is at heart a playful creature, and must like " . . . the mightiest genius . . . divest itself of its majesty and stoop in all humility to the mind of a little child."[5]

Signs of this third realm are already evident among primitive people. In the first indication of an aesthetic inclination, barbarians used to dress up and ornament themselves; even the worst tyrant had some feeling for this. Schiller wrote to his benefactor and prince that the desire for play can make the worst intellectual despot realize that he "is a free citizen, having equal rights with the noblest; and the mind, which would force the patient mass beneath the yoke of its purposes, must here first obtain its assent."[6]

The desire for play also instinctively spans the gap between body and mind, but such a bridge should neither completely blend nor totally separate the two; it is rather open to circulation between the two poles. When humans joyfully swing between the two poles, they are truly in the Schwung of things, balancing sensitively on the bridge between nature and culture, between body and soul, between form and substance.

Schiller himself lived his own life in Schwung. In a 1791 portrait of him by a contemporary, the German Romantic poet Novalis writes:

> Oh, when I now mention Schiller a mass of feelings is awakened in my bosom . . . with a form so enchanting, and yet still matter, so much of the natural and yet still nature, so much individuality and yet still general . . . so much simplicity in such richness, so much of the systematic and yet still artistic . . . so much theory and yet so much application, so much transcendental imagination followed by such method in transgression . . . so much grace with so much seriousness . . . he is in truth a unique person for whom the gods have revealed their mysteries between four eyes.[7]

Schiller provides an aesthetic escape route from the dilemma of two countervailing forces. He markets a strategic tool promising the right Schwung and claims the true purpose of art is to be an instrument for free playfulness. Art should work as Schwung. In the decadence of Rome and in fallen Athens, the gods were ridiculed and made banal, but temples and statues remain as sublime reminders of the spiritual greatness and freedom of times past. In these genuine works, artists have overcome the heavy matter of the marble. In works of art, in poetry, in sculpture, and in music, that which is unique and beneficial is released from its necessary material wrapping, torn away by Schwung, because "it must go from the magic circle of the artist pure and perfect as it came from the hands of the Creator."[8]

Schwung, the pendulum movement between form and substance, is Schiller's explanation of aesthetic play. To be sure, Schiller had a point for Sir John, the *Good Academy,* and the Evas and Eddies of the opera festival world. To Schiller, educating individuals aesthetically meant exposing them to aesthetic play, and this was best accomplished by exposing them to art. The individual would then be ready to explore, map, and cultivate the vastness between form and substance as the home of the beautiful and sublime, the broad aesthetic field in which mankind can " . . . take one step back . . . [i]n order to exchange passivity for autonomy and a passive determination for an active one. [M]an must therefore be momentarily free of all determination whatsoever and pass through a state of pure determinability." This weightless condition of Schwung, where the individual balances on the aesthetic seesaw between form and substance, positions man at a point of indifference where he "is nought."[9]

Schiller awakened my desire for a learned kind of management. He put me on the track to aesthetic play and made me really curious about how art could be made to schwung. What did other philosophers have to say?

# 2

Players in Aesthetic Philosophy

## Audience: Kant's Public

### Third-Way Philosophy

In 1793, Friedrich Schiller was ecstatic when Immanuel Kant commented favorably on his essay *Anmut und Würde*. "I can scarce describe my joy at this text coming into his hands," Schiller exclaimed, "and having such an effect."[1] In his essay, Schiller develops the thought that aesthetics can join with ethics so that art lovers act in a moral way when following the ideals of beauty. Art works ethically quite naturally, without didactic imperatives. In short, Schiller argues, art does not exist only for its own sake but can lead to both order and morality. In the same year, the second edition of Kant's successful aesthetic philosophy *Critique of Judgment,* which Schiller deemed the "bible of modern aesthetics," was marketed. Schiller was on the mark in terms of the importance of this piece; no serious attempt to grasp the modern meaning of aesthetics can ignore this basic book.

Twenty-six years before the publication of his treatise, Kant had written some "observations on the experience of Beauty and the Sublime."[2] Up to that time, the *experience* of beauty had not been regarded as serious business; the accepted belief was that this subjective response resulted from irrational, vague, and even confused feelings and emotions. In 1732, Alexander Baumgarten, one of Kant's teachers and a philosopher of the Wolffian school,

21

introduced the term *theoretical aesthetics* in the hope that he could establish a method of inquiry that by strict rational analysis of taste could account for these poetic and sensual feelings. Baumgarten's plan was to expand the realm of logic so that aesthetics could gain a rank equal to that of "serious" science.

Under Baumgarten's leadership and that of his faithful disciple Professor Meier of Halle, nicknamed "Baumgarten's little monkey,"[3] aesthetics became the fad of the day. Anyone with the least pretension to learning devoured aesthetic treatises, and countless philosophers and artists felt obliged to contribute to the flood of pamphlets and books on the subject. The premise seemed to be that even though one could not live on art alone, one could certainly write about it, and the market for books on aesthetics simply boomed. In 1764, Kant himself suggested that only someone who lacked the assured technique of an artist such as Hogarth might still find contentment in defining logical rules for beauty.[4] Kant was obviously not aware that Hogarth had emphasized the indeterminate intricacy of beauty in his own aesthetic treatise on *The Analysis of Beauty*.[5]

Kant's early work was more about prejudice than judgment. Following the conventions of his time as to beauty, Kant relates how Negroes, despite being transported by the thousands to civilized regions, had never successfully created either art or science. He points out that Canadian Indians are extremely noble, and that Arabs are proud and worthy but a little too adventurous. He also observes that the French, though graceful, had become childish from too much "womanizing." (This last opinion came to him on good authority from the Swiss scholar Rousseau.) Kant goes on, declaring that the English were loyal but reserved; the Germans were both loyal and reserved; and above all, the Germans were truly fascinated by nobility, titles, and social standing. Further, he pronounces that women were graceful and beautiful by nature, but it was men who were noble and sublime.

Such miscellaneous tidbits on taste and feeling, based more on Prussian prejudice than anthropological observation, were just that, bits of trivia, and these writings had very little in common with his later aesthetic philosophy of 1790. What was launched that year in the *Critique of Judgment* was more of a radical new way of looking at aesthetics. From that time forward, aesthetics became a special branch of modern philosophy.

Only a differentiation between beauty and the sublime makes it from these early writings to Kant's third *Critique*, which came out almost three decades after the first. It was to fill the gap between the two treatises *Critique of Pure Reason* (1781) and *Critique of Practical Reason* (1788) and became significant for bridging the two others into the grandiose Kantian system.[6]

Kant was no longer so interested in beauty as an anthropological phenomenon of taste. The purpose of a *Critique of Judgment* was to offer a philosophy for what Schiller would call the third realm. Kant labeled this new philosophy aesthetics and gave it a place of its own between science, which was covered by his first *Critique of Pure Reason,* and ethics, the subject of the second *Critique.*

## The Sublime and the Beautiful

Unlike most early books on beauty, *The Critique of Judgment*[7] is not just another entertaining catalogue of principles for what is more or less beautiful. Kant does not believe that everyday judgments obey criteria. In other words, something does not become a work of art because it is made according to special rules. Judgments of taste, notes Kant, are instead informed by an energetic authoritative drive.

The rather feeble English translation *Critique of Judgment,* from the German title, does not really do justice to the writer's intent. A more specific *Critique of the Force of Choice* or perhaps *Critique of the Energy of Decision* would better convey what Kant aimed at. An aesthetic judgment is not a matter of cool reflection or informed interpretation. It hits like a flash of lightning. It is sudden, surprising, and often overwhelming. Further, Kant believes that judgments rise from the human capacity to reach general conclusions from special aesthetic experience,[8] yet aesthetic competence has little to do with the usual modes of decision making.

Kant cites an important difference between aesthetic and logical syllogisms. A logician subsumes or ratiocinates from the rules of a general law down to the specific case at hand. Instead of thinking from the top down, however, and fitting a general rule to a specific case, aesthetic capacity helps in judgment and decision making from the bottom up. Examples of the specific are a starting point for an aesthetic judgment. From the level of everyday cases, such as individual experiences in a hospital, university, and festival, people are elevated to the level of the universal. Instead of subsuming, humans judge or reflect on matters of aesthetics on the basis of single cases only.

A consumer of art, Kant observes, is as serious when making a selection as a judge is when deciding on the fate of a suspect in court. This fact also indicates, according to Kant, that aesthetic judgment is not merely a private matter. To him, much more is at stake than personal feelings or everyday emotions. An aesthetic judgment is so serious that it would be flippant to term it merely a "matter of taste." Courtroom deliberations aim to find the truth; aesthetic judgments have precisely the same mission. It is the very fact that aesthetics is a way to find truth that qualifies it as a phenomenon worthy of philosophic consideration.

Kant developed aesthetics into a very important consideration for the public, both general and universal, for he held that all that unites and organizes individuals into a common humanity is constituted aesthetically. Therefore, it is important to be concerned about the value judgments of others and attempt to understand the aesthetic process through which an aesthetic judgment is made. To emphasize this close link between aesthetics and justice, Kant asks for its *Rechtsgrund,*[9] its legal foundation. How does aesthetic judgment form the common public sphere?

Kant suggests that two sorts of emotion accompany aesthetic judgment. The first is similar to what is experienced on a beautiful sunlit day; the second, to the moonlit night of the sublime. On the one hand is light, joy, positivity, and beauty; on the other, danger, fear, and sublime majesty. The latter emotions conjure up terror and anxiety. Then to further illustrate what his theory of aesthetic judgment is all about, Kant takes the reader on a sunlit walk through a beautiful landscape.

Look at that beautiful castle. The view is breathtaking. What do you care whether or not you are able to live there! Do not confuse what is beautiful with what is physically comfortable or crassly utilitarian. Even if the castle were merely a mirage, your experience of its beauty would remain unaffected.

And what lovely roses in the castle gardens! Why are they so beautiful? Their beauty is hardly dependent upon your physically smelling their scent. If you think they are beautiful merely because you have learned that roses are by definition beautiful, then you are far from being an aesthete. There are no rules or principles for beauty such as there are for morals and ethics and their practical application in political economy. Scholarly regularity, or *Schulgerrecht,* to use another of Kant's legalistic terms,[10] hardly guarantees the aesthetic precision of beauty. Observe the unfortunate bad artist, clutching at mannerisms and the empty phrases of artistic theory and trying to disguise the lack of vitality in his art with long, academic catalogues. No scientific methodology can elevate bad research into the truth that can only be reached by the aesthetic judgment of nature.

Consider now the joy of looking at God's natural world. Beautiful hummingbirds and parrots sweep through the graceful canopy of shady leaves, and on the long table next to the sparkling crystal carafe, the lobster presented beside other shellfish is so beautiful that the bodily requirements of hunger are replaced by the spiritual pleasure of beauty. Surely the dazzling costumes of a ball, the beautifully made-up women, and the attractively furnished salons are neither referred to as good or agreeable. They are simply beautiful. Such judgments of taste do not stem from the good or agreeable,[11] from ethics or the scientifically perceptible. Beauty assumes for Kant an intrinsic value alongside the factually agreeable and the morally good. Night falls over this beautiful operatic scenery of lobster, rose, and hummingbird, and Kant now offers the visitors to his castle an artful divertissement of exploding fireworks.

After the bright and beautiful show, Kant suggests a moonlit walk through the gothic sublime. Owls call through the gnarled, mossy trunks of the forest. A fearfully steep drop suddenly blocks the narrow path. At the bottom of the ravine, the powerful roar of a darkly turbulent river is heard. The moon is hidden by the snow-capped Alps, so high and steep that a violent avalanche could bury anything in its path at any moment. The nearness of eternity suddenly becomes overwhelming. Even the star-filled vault of the heavens no longer appears merely as a case for Newtonian celestial mechanism, for such mathematical majesty can never be scientifically grasped, only sublimely experienced. It is transformed into an endless system with its own singular purpose, a system such as was provided for botany by the discoveries of the Swede Linnaeus.

For Kant, divine nature is the definitive meaningful work of art. Sublime aesthetic experiences allow a glimpse of God's grand design in the majesty of nature. This sort of *Physikotheologie* is not disheartening but filled with dynamism and hope.[12] It inspires a spiritual force born of respect, a kind of oppositional aesthetic energy. Kant suggests that this type of sensation must be like the one experienced at the first sight of the Great Pyramid of Cheops in Egypt. In much the same way, a general must also experience the sublime feeling and courage of the population in times of war. Therefore, a general is worthy of greater aesthetic admiration than a diplomatic statesman, according to

Kant, because the latter allows his people to sink into feeble and cowardly egoism during prolonged periods of peace.[13] For Kant, the sublime, much more so than beauty, is an organizing and mobilizing force; he would whole-heartedly agree that the sublime would be a most energetic means for managing humankind.

Time after time, Kant emphasizes that the *good taste* of aesthetics must not be confused with things that either "taste good" in an epicurean sense or with the "good taste" dictated by conventional morals. If the understanding of aesthetics reduces itself to sociological or psychological observations, the philosophical point is lost. He mocks his contemporary Edmund Burke, the English empiricist who sought to explain experiences of beauty as the result of some sort of pleasant relaxation of the muscles.[14] True to Kantian form, he also rails against David Hume, who in fine Aristotelian tradition[15] denied the intrinsic value of aesthetics and sought to reduce the experience of beauty to the effect of pleasant old memories surfacing from the brain's archive of bygone experiences.[16]

An individual cannot encounter the beautiful and the sublime by merely keeping her eyes open as she wanders with and among her fellows.[17] For Kant, man has to wear many hats; in everyday business, he must be a "jolly good fellow." He cannot escape being an empirical *Homo phenomenon* of flesh and blood. In addition, modern man ought to become an "enlightened citizen," the *Homo noumenon* of humanity.

To Kant, aesthetics was necessary for enlightenment. An aesthetics education, the kind Schiller would later introduce, implies that man disciplines himself to follow the three Kantian edicts of the Enlightenment: thinking independently without preconceived prejudices, thinking logically and without contradictions, and acting with consideration of the position of his fellow human being. Enlightened knowledge comes out of the individual himself, for God resides equally in all of humankind.

The power of aesthetic judgment accounts for an enlightened ability to transcend the shortcuts of merely subjective feelings and emotions and reach the level of general objective universal humanity. Aesthetic experience that intensively involves the whole person extends into something over and above the singular, isolated person. When this happens, a sense of common meaning, a *sensus communis*,[18] is fostered. My students in Stockholm mobilized their comrades into a common quest for better education by simply showing their sublime movie; Schiller himself believed that he might overbridge form and matter with a poem. The human ability to cooperate socially and organize ourselves is, according to Kant, the result of our capacity to transcend the bounds of our own narrow ego. The private expands into the public.

In the preface of his treatise, Kant places the aesthetic energy of judgment between science, which is closely connected to beauty that draws inspiration from nature, and reason, more closely connected to spiritual sources of the sublime. Again Kant offers a triadic system, with aesthetics philosophy in its third realm. Aesthetic Schwung has turned philosophy into an elegant ballroom complete with one-two-three waltzing. In his last book, Kant even bows gently to apologize for this waltzing habit of making ideas "almost always come out threefold,"[19] as indeed this one does[20]:

| List of Mental Faculties | Cognitive Faculties | Apriori Principles | Application |
|---|---|---|---|
| Cognitive faculties | Understanding | Conformity to law | Nature |
| Feelings of pleasure or displeasure | Judgment | Finality | Art |
| Faculty of desire | Reason | Final end | Freedom[21] |

## Aesthetics for Publicity

The difference between Kant the anthropologist and Kant the aesthete is clearly discernible. Kant in the 1760s studied matters of taste by concentrating on the individual's everyday behavior, habits, and methods of affecting his or her fellows through speech, dress, and habits. Now in 1790, his curiosity has given way to enlightenment. Art has become interesting for how it makes society work.

In this perspective, Kant differentiates between the mechanical arts of technology and science and the fine arts. On the one hand are the tools for work; on the other, the toys for free play. Although this distinction between tools and toys seems rather innocent, it is problematic. The terminology invites misunderstanding. *Free* art, as opposed to the art created by necessity for wages, does not eliminate the fact that all art is composed of both play and work. A poet would be totally handicapped without spelling rules and verse forms, the tools of the trade. A painter must practice technique and could not manage without a technical understanding of color. An equestrian would qualify as foolhardy if all she tried to saddle were unbroken stallions.

That said, though technique is necessary, it is hardly sufficient. Art cannot be programmed into a system of technology. An artist who sticks rigidly to the rules and is always trying to find out what others think will never create anything of great quality. Art, like Kant's dutiful Enlightenment man, must regulate itself. Freedom is achieved through self-discipline, since the intentionality of art comes not from without but from within. Nothing reproduced to order or according to standards can be considered art. Art cannot be grasped by means of rational concepts, in the same sense that God's creation cannot be reduced merely to a formula for life.

Even though openness to persuasion in matters of taste is requisite, listening to the rhetoric of others leaves people untouched on a deeper level, for no concept can contain the actual truth of the matter. Kant emphasizes this point in his statement that it is impossible to become a doctor of art, for aesthetic judgment does not follow any clear, independent criteria. No prescription or formula exists to scientifically direct aesthetic Schwungful play, because art cannot be convincingly trapped in some sort of scientific management.

Taste then becomes a matter of eternal conflict, and from art emerges an aesthetic experience that acts as fertile soil for debate and criticism. Both beauty and sublimity are more *gegebenen* (given) than *gedachten* (thought out). A true artist follows innate natural laws of art instinctively; in works of art, as in nature, there is an almost miraculous sense of purpose.

Kant devotes the second half of his *Critique of Judgment* to this teleology. Looking at the ocean as art expands it further than just looking at it as a resource reservoir of energy or proteins. Hospitals no longer exist simply as health care factories, universities no longer function just as knowledge industries, and festivals perform as something beyond just epicurean entertainment. The snow tundra of the north is not just terrain for Lapp sledge transportation, adds Kant, for as art the tundra becomes a beautiful milky-white landscape. The heavens are no longer just a planetarium for demonstrating Newtonian celestial mechanics; art translates them into cosmic sublime and endless space. Aesthetic experience reveals nature as the ultimate work of art by the ultimate Creator. The artist's role is that of a divinely blessed medium through whom the Almighty manifests the grandeur of the scheme.

The fine arts are the expression of artistic geniality. In contrast to a lecturer who is struggling to be pedagogically useful, a poet seeks to provide opportunity for Schwung through verse. The poet is not busy representing what is in the textbook, since the art of the sculptor, the architect, the painter, the gardener, the musician, and the actor is more creative than representative. As a result, humans are not informed but rather "carried away" and in this transport gain tremendous insight.

According to Kant, who stresses the difference between artistic creation and the manufacture of useful artifacts, the purpose of fine arts is to embody Plato's pure ideas in time and space. The poet, who Kant finds represents the highest of the arts, presents symbols and allegories from his or her genius. The poet is thus no designer packaging practical function in clever concepts or illustrator materializing words in pictures. An artist depicting Jupiter's serpent with lightning in its claws puts imagination about the king of the heavens into a Schillerian Schwung (*der Einbildungskraft einen Schwung*[22]).

The artistic genius is a medium that allows nature to manage its innate *ingenium*.[23] The artist cannot alone explain how this comes about or teach others how to recreate these works of genius. Listening to master art managers describe their work is a waste of time; real learning is acquired by watching them perform. In place of rationalizing about the managerial tricks of their trade, the Warhols, the Wilsons, the Bergmans drag the audience into their most recent show.

In addition, says Kant, even if they were revealed, their tricks would tell nothing about their art. A genius attempting only to work according to learned rules becomes at best a mannered, precious fool and loses the gift. Do not forget, Kant reminds, that ingenium is like the good fairy guiding mortals along life's difficult path. How great masters still manage to impart some of their originality to their pupils is indeed, says Kant, "difficult to explain."[24] No imitable techniques or methods automatically produce classic masterpieces, nor should classics be copied or reproduced. The purpose of the masterpiece is to be an exemplary illustration and to lead pupils toward the fresh springs that gave their master inspiration. Art work provides the teaching, not the lectures by art workers. Real masterpieces, Kant insists, are never mimetic reflections, never platonically indistinct shadows of some real, perfect, or true ideal. They represent reality less than they reveal it. A work of art should be appreciated for what it is, not what it might represent. Genius is original and should not be confused with dilettantish playing for effect. Originality is always rooted in tradition; making something new requires a thorough familiarity with the old.

Kant adds a fourth characteristic, spirituality, to the three distinctives of genius (originality, exemplariness, and spontaneity). A genius must not lack the *Geist* (spirit) that has the capacity to set an observer's imagination in playful Schwung. With his work, an artist creates a field of energy that sets off this Schwung and encourages a self-generating *Gemütskräfte*.[25] It is really this spirit that turns the genius into Kant's aesthetic hero. Without knowing why, a genius solves the paradoxically insoluble antinomy.

Kant explains how a genius is able to make something that qualifies as art if it provides a solution to antinomy. Take the exclamation, "Oh, how beautiful!" It is the subjective response of an individual who has been stopped by a work of art. When someone observes the Winkelmannian archaeologist displaying his antique statue, or the Matterhorn in the morning sun, or a piece of Bauhaus furniture, or Sir John's enterprise, or *The Good Academy,* or the opera festival, and then communicates a spontaneous appreciation, it is to be taken seriously by others, because within this statement is the understanding that everyone else—the audience in the museum or fellow tourists—ought to share this aesthetic value judgment. The subjective judgment is proclaimed as if it were an objective truth.

To Kant, aesthetic judgment is never a matter of private taste alone. The individual exclamation "Oh, how beautiful!" is always, as far as it counts to Kant as an aesthetic judgment, a proposition for a general, by-everyone-accepted, truth. Nonetheless, and herein rests the antinomy, it is impossible to prove the existence of beauty in a purely logical way. It is impossible to argue the truth of taste scientifically and academically. Understandably, conflicts, quarrels, and critiques about art make it a recurrent cause of argument. To Kant, the exclamation "Oh, how beautiful!" is a call for a universal audience to agree. Aesthetic judgment sets in motion a Schwung, organizing mankind as an audience that is unified. Art works to form audiences that make up the public sphere.

The aesthetic antinomy is based on the thesis that one cannot become a doctor of taste because the position is not grounded in concepts that can be the subject of open debate.[26] This is why aesthetics and art tend to get banned when democracies become discursively defined as the political organization coordinated by rational decisions and conscious choices. For Kant, however, an enlightened human society without art and aesthetics, one only scientifically constituted as a nexus of choices and decisions, is unbearable. Kant therefore follows his thesis with his antithesis: even though the lack of rational arguments hardly constrains human beings from arguing about taste, it seems a given that aesthetics nevertheless is based upon certain disputable concepts.

Kant solves the antinomian contradiction between thesis and antithesis by introducing two definitions of the word *concept*. First, logically determined concepts are called predicates; second, indefinite concepts are universal and objective but rooted in the spiritual consciousness of every individual subjectively. *Beauty* and *the sublime* belong to the second kind, since they are not predicates; they are not names of qualities possessed by an object. For Kant, therefore, a work of art does not possess certain qualities that give it aesthetic value because concepts at play in aesthetics are of the second, indefinite kind.

In the creation of nature, God transcends the subjective and approaches the objective in much the same way that the genius makes art work. This is how very private experiences provide the dynamics of very public phenomena, how aesthetic energy forms the audiences in all sorts of public arenas such as markets, communities, or corporations. This is not irrational or the result of magic or wizardry, for it rests on what Kant calls people's supersensible capacity to judge on a transcendental level. In a way, Kant's aesthetics therefore contains a modern metaphysics, without which the markets for modern evangelists and management gurus are wide open.

In place of pseudoreligions, Kant suggests that modern art may help constitute an enlightened audience and its public space. To make something public is equal to building an audience; the spectators of a show are in fact called *le public* in French. At the end of the third *Critique*, Kant prides himself on his last philosophical tour de force: he has dragged (*hinüberziehen*[27]) aesthetics from his enlightened Königsberg study to the transcendental threshold of his Temple of Universal Truth.

## Artist: Schelling's Creator

### Aesthetics for Creativity

Kant's aesthetics is a philosophic architecture erecting a Temple of Universal Truth and holding an enlightened congregation together as a unified audience. Not long after Kant's death, young German idealists carried out a Romantic reformation that turned Kant's shrine into their Temple of Art.

Friedrich von Schelling (1775–1854), the high priest of the Romantics, seems a realistic sort for one carrying the mantle of this group of followers. Goethe's diary relates, for instance, how he was spending an evening at

Schiller's home in Jena when another Württemberg resident by the name of Schelling dropped by. Early the next morning, Goethe and Schelling met—not to dream but to carry out some optical experiments together.[28] Interestingly enough, in October of that year Schelling joined Schiller's faculty and became a Jena public professor. With this appointment, he concluded his private job as *Hofmeister* (tutor) to a young baron, in whose company he had made the traditional grand tour.

And what a grand tour it was! Master and pupil visited the modern academic theme parks of natural science, for this was no Romantic tourist trip. They went to the University of Leipzig to watch lab experiments such as Galvani's on frog legs and Lavoisier's on oxygen. They also got hooked on a current biophysical theory of development in which a certain Dr. Kielmeyer claimed he had finally discovered that "the force that brings about the growth of an individual being is the very same force of creation that has brought forth all of the organizational forms we can observe on Earth."[29]

Schelling was somewhat of a prodigy, for he was granted permission to study theology at Tübingen at the age of fifteen. It was 1790, the year of publication of Kant's third *Critique*. At this time, the lecture theater featured philosopher Fichte as an anarchistic apostle of the ego and subjectivity. Among Schelling's contacts were two somewhat older roommates, Friedrich Hölderlin and Hegel. Hölderlin went on to become a great poet of Romanticism before succumbing to insanity, and Hegel and Schelling used their theological studies to found philosophical careers as rivaling professors.

To Schelling, Hegel grew even sicker than Hölderlin. In one of his later lectures about aesthetics, Hegel not only suggested that art—for Schelling, something of primary importance to mankind—would have little importance for modern civilization[30] but he also declared art a stone-dead duck, whose faded glory it was completely pointless to reanimate. At the most, some sober modern historian might try to logically reconstruct *was die Kunst sei,* what art once upon a time had meant to people in antiquity.[31] To add insult to injury, Hegel openly suggested that Schelling, his companion of their *Sturm und Drang* youth, was always wrong about art. Art might still be pleasant, but it was interesting only from an historical perspective. Its force of Schwung was lost in the modern world; what modern society really needed was a philosophy for administrative science and managerial methods rather than aesthetics and art. Hegel now scorned Schelling's notion that "[a]rt should be the model for Science, and Science can only arise if Art first is developed,"[32] a notion they shared when the two were enthusiastic Jena students.

The youthful Hegel and the mature Hegel were two very different thinkers. When young, Hegel, Hölderlin, and Schelling fervently supported the revolutionary creed of liberty, and Hegel wrote a manifesto on German idealism. Hegel, later the pillar of Prussian state philosophy, therefore once wanted to sweep aside the mechanical apparatus of feudal state administration and do away with rules and regulations, laws, priests, and prejudices. He wanted to abolish bureaucracy and all stiff procedures in the management of human affairs. Stuffy management was to be abolished in the name of revolutionary freedom, and the force behind this revolution they believed to be aesthetic energy.

After the revolution, philosophers were to found a new and better, more natural world on the Idea that unites all the rest,

> the Idea of *beauty* taking the word in its higher Platonic sense . . .
> [T]he philosopher must possess just as much aesthetic power
> as the poet. . . . The philosophy of the spirit is an aesthetic phi-
> losophy. . . . Here it ought to become clear what it is that men
> lack, who understand no ideas—and who confess honestly
> enough that they find everything obscure as soon as it goes be-
> yond the table of contents and the index.[33]

Even though Hegel shifted his beliefs, Schelling clung to the aesthetics of his youth all his life. Hegel laid out his philosophy in numerous volumes, but Schelling claimed that real philosophy ought to be like life itself. When Hegel died in 1833, long after Hölderlin had withdrawn into his Tübingen tower of poetic madness, Schelling finally dared to speak his mind. He declared that Hegel's successful monumental work, in which he turned his back on their common youthful hope for aesthetic energy, was undeniably "monstrous."[34] Fortunately, writes Schelling, it was merely a parenthetical "episode" in the history of true philosophy.

Unfortunately, what was not mentioned was the length of this parenthesis. Karl Marx and his fanatics prolonged the episode to its bitter end in the twentieth century, and Schelling, as a consequence, actually only then got his audience back. Finally, following the postmodern criticism of Marxist modernity and the fall of the Berlin wall, modern Europeans were liberated from the most vulgar Hegelianism that long banned art and aesthetics from the academic curricula of both management and social science.

The first of Schelling's larger works, *System des transcendentalen Idealismus,* published in 1800, is built around a central chapter on art in which the writer emphasizes that art is necessary to academic philosophy, because it possesses a miraculous energy to schwung the most abstract ideas into concrete form. It makes the inconceivable conceivable. Although Kant investigated the power of judgment and how aesthetic energy organizes a public audience around art, Schelling now wanted to grasp the role of artists in making art work to mobilize its market.

Schelling deplored the fact that many good artists end up hired as inventors of economically useful discoveries. In old times, primitive barbarians demanded art for the satisfaction of physical needs. Now modern factories and workshops produced artifacts to please buyers in booming new markets. Industry transformed artists into engineers, and their materialization of ideas turned from something pure and sacred into product development and design. Realizing that art tamed to customer order runs out of aesthetic energy, Schelling declared that art must be a risky business of speculation instead of an external guarantee for pleasing the market. Aesthetic energy is generated only by inner conflict, and that process of creation cannot be administratively controlled by some artist booked as designer. Art cannot schwung on demand.

Schelling heard artists themselves account for how their inner creativity worked, and in each case, they reported functioning under high tension. They felt their powers of creativity mobilized by the challenge of an "insoluble opposition."[35] Real creativity is not a matter of intellectual problem solving, and cool calculation does not offer a solution, according to Schelling. The artist experiences the claustrophobic tension of being helplessly locked up by something resembling Kant's antinomian paradox. The act of creating makes the tension suddenly drop, and the artist, a break-out expert, escapes the antinomian bondage. The actual work of art arrogantly chops up the paradox with the Schwung of its Gordian sword. According to this pre-Freudian philosophy, Schelling's artist experiences the postcreative feeling of "immeasurable harmony" from the orgiastic suspension of that opposition. Part of bringing about the object of art has been conscious, for the artist has made skillful use of all the rules, techniques, methods, and tools of art. How-

ever, the true driving force of creation, its Schwung, says Schelling, will forever remain unconscious.

The artist has set to work driven by a subjective sensitivity to antinomian
opposition that constitutes his natural talent. Now, after the completion, he
stands before his work without comprehending how it can embody an objective truth. He has accomplished something scientifically great without
knowing how he has done it. To Schelling, as to Kant, the aesthetic quality
of art resides in its ability to convey a truth, and it follows neither the epistemological rules of rational reasoning nor the empirical modes of scientific
observation. However purposeful, considered, and articulate the artist is, he
still has to thank a higher energy for the fact that the work encapsulates an
aesthetic quality of truth that is lacking in the everyday products of craftsmen.[36] In short, Schelling contends that art is a partly conscious undertaking
by a talented artificer, but primarily it is the fruit of unconscious Schwung.
Here Schelling, the poet-philosopher, refers to his Jena colleague Schiller, the
philosopher-poet, when he accounts for this intricate mix of skills and talented intuition.[37] When Schiller wanted to inform Schelling and other philosophers about the practical conditions of art work, he sadly remarked that
"these idealistic gentlemen [philosophers such as Schelling] are far too little
concerned with practical experience . . . which of course shows that a poet
starts from the unconscious but really counts himself lucky if, with his conscious technique, he is able to fully represent his first shadowy ideas with
the same power in his finished work."[38]

The conscious part of artistic production follows the practicalities of
technique, which can be learned from theoretical study of art. For technical
art management, there are schools, tools, methods, and models. To the Romantics, no clear difference between art and science exists. Schelling compares the artist's unconscious part with the philosopher's dialectic *Kunst-
seite*.[39] Both philosopher (at that time, they were the scientists fascinated by
electrified frog legs or evolution cosmologies) and artist require technical
knowledge and logical discipline. Without the force of creative *Einbildung*,
however—without the *Kraft* of aesthetic energy—there would neither be
good philosophy nor true works of art. In no way can aesthetic Schwung be
acquired by technical training.

Aesthetic imagination should not be confused, however, with wild associations of ideas or unrestrained reproduction of sensual images. Philosophy
and art, says Schelling, are both concerned with what lies beyond the senses.

Philosophy approaches the suprasensual *ideal,* and art works as a revelation of the *real.* Schelling claims that the transcendental qualities of a work of art come as a surprise to the artist himself. The work of art is like a bolt of lightning from a clear sky, like sudden salvation, because a work of art is "the only eternal revelation, the only real miracle which, even if it occurs only once, is sufficient to give us faith in the absolute truth and reality of a Higher Power."[40]

## Creating Symbols

Schelling points out that English and French Enlightenment thinkers classified philosophical ideas on the energy of art as superstition and mystification, a predictable conclusion when empirical psychological theories are used in the analysis of art. Skeptics wanted art to belong to the domain of science, because to them science and psychology combated Catholic mysticism.

Schelling, on the other hand, had no fear of reconnecting art to religion. It was his way of filling the gap left by abandoned Catholicism. The Reformation had contributed to suppressing the connection between art and religion, and in the general revolt against the Pope poetic and lyrical readings of the Bible were dismissed as being far too Catholic. The philosophers of the Reformation lived by dry, sober interpretations of the Bible. Good everyday life was to be managed scientifically according to textual knowledge; the word was all-important, and this stern logocentricity dimmed their appreciation of art. Schelling points out that influential eighteenth-century rationalists such as Voltaire entered into a pact with reformed Christianity whereby "the Enlightenment promised to keep religion if the latter would but make itself useful."[41]

To rise above the risk of being considered a papist counterreformer, Schelling looked to the Classical pre-Christian era for guidance. This was the time when art was socially accepted on its own terms as serious reality, not as futile fantasy. To the ancient Greeks, the gods were real and involved themselves in daily life. Today, in spite of our expressed amazement at the total credence the Greeks accorded their gods, we are reminded that humanity might not have yet reached their (the Greeks') level of education where "the *ideal* is the real and is much more real than the so-called real itself."[42]

Ancient mythology does teach an important lesson: do not confuse commonsensical interpretations of the *usual* with *reality*! The usual comes out of the routine of taking the everyday for granted. To the Romantics, art and aesthetics were tools to combat a limited interpretation of human existence and enlarge its restricted scope. They thought of themselves as realists, but hardly social habitualists praising an everyday life dominated by routine habits and monotonous conditions.

Schelling is interested in the *real,* a concept much vaster and more connected not to convention and concrete facts but to truth. In antiquity, reality was poetical and philosophical. Reality meant absolute being beyond sensual proof. The gods were actually more real to the Greeks than clay pots or a wine amphora because they were absolutely real, absolutely ideal, transcendental. According to Schelling, it would be a grave mistake to interpret stories of the gods just as amusing fables. Mythology is a serious matter and definitely not entertainment; Mount Olympus was not Athenian Disneyland. It was no artifact designed to incarnate some immaterial "artifiction" in a material, everyday, banal sense. There was no point to prove the real physically true.

Mythological gods who represent universal ideas populate classical art and poetry. Each god of Greek mythology incarnates an absolute idea into a conceptual figure. Minerva, for example, represents pure strength and wisdom but consequently lacks other feminine characteristics. These gods, as conceptual figures, cannot be judged against standards of reason and nature. They belong, as Schelling puts it, to a fantasy world of "intellectual vision."[43]

A reading of Homer's poetry or Sophocles' dramas reveals that the gods act freely but within their necessary limitations, that is, morality and ethics. From an everyday perspective, the gods are different. They may limp like Hefaistos, have horns like Pan, and be randy and rude as Satyrs, but they still possess a harmonious beauty. The gods can joke, laugh, and play, but they are free from such everyday human ailments as aging and exhaustion because they were, in a word, blessed. The infinity of the universe was revealed as a natural necessity within the finite symbolic forms of the Greek gods.

In an analysis inspired by Schiller, Schelling suggests that classical art can be termed naïve in its unsophisticated simplicity. For the Greeks, mythology and the gods were realistic windows to nature, and probably the fact that poets were so good at opening those window shutters with an elegant Schwung made Plato condemn all art as merely imitation "at a third remove" in his attempt to Socratically cleanse philosophy of both myth and sophistry. Certainly the grand myth maker Homer was as dangerous a rival to the ambitious philosopher Plato as Schelling himself and even perhaps Schiller were to Professor Hegel at a later time.

Schelling believed that he was living at the beginning of the modern era where the idealism of reformed Christianity had replaced the realism of the ancient world, and he suggested that such modernity meant the arts were losing their natural naïveté. Modern art therefore expressed a sentimental nostalgia for its irrevocably bygone innocence. As Schelling confirmed, "The modern world begins when man wrests himself loose from nature, Since he does not yet have a new home, however, he feels abandoned."[44] Modern man has lost his natural paradise; he has wandered into culture, and as a cultural being, he is rootless and homeless.

Consequently, he looks back to the ideal natural world, to the Christian faith with its roots in Christ's death on the cross. For Schelling, Christ is *der letzte Gott*,[45] the only god left now that the company of ancient gods is bankrupt. Jesus is the hero of modernity, and his incarnation must be recognized as the paramount modern myth.[46] If it is insulting to the aesthetic energy of Homer to suggest his *Iliad* and *Odyssey* are nursery rhymes, it is just as blasphemous to banalize God's masterpiece, Jesus' resurrection, by calling it an allegory. At this point, Schelling urges sorting out some concepts that tend to blur the concept of art and aesthetics in everyday talk.

To Schelling, both the realistic mythology of Greece and the idealistic modern mythology of the Messiah put humanity in Schwung because these myths are true symbols, loaded with aesthetic energy. An allegory, on the other hand, is something specific that represents a universal phenomenon, just as a single judgment in court mirrors the totality of the rule of law. In the realm of justice, a specific judgment allegorically points to the universal rule. In contrast, when something universal is used to describe something specific, Schelling uses the term *schema*. Language (as well as practical rules of conduct) is schematic; it is like a tool designed for a specific use. In addition to allegories and schema, Schelling's philosophical distinctions also include images, which he does not define as bleak reflections or optical representations in a mirror; to Schelling, an image represents only itself.

Homer's poetry and the modern myth of the Resurrection are not image, allegory, or schema; they are all three at the same time. This, says Schelling, is the triple-faceted definition of symbol. They schwung, for they are symbols. The point of symbols, explains Schiller, is that they really mean nothing at all. They are negativity, a vacuum that sucks up and rearranges meaning in the zero point where aesthetic man "is nought," according to Schiller. In the symbolic, the specific is mixed with the universal, which is what happens in an allegory; concurrently, the universal fuses with the individual, as in a schema, and this creates new images. When the Schillerian pendulum schwungs between form and substance, the dualistic properties become utterly intertwined; its *Entzweiung,* its division, is dissolved on the in-between field of aesthetic play. In Schelling's words, the affirmative blends with the affirmed, or to use the linguistic terms of Saussure, so popular two centuries later, the signifying blends with the signified. This is what Schelling means when he calls symbols indifferential.[47] To him a symbol is neither a specific nor a universal sign. It creates something new, in between dualisms. This was why Kant put the third *Critique* between those of pure and practical reason, and why Schiller minted the idea of aesthetics as a play between form and substance. Schelling's Romantic aesthetic philosophy is a kind of spiritual alchemy wanting to explain this aesthetic play of symbols by which Homer's verse and Jesus' Christianity become reality that simply is; it is something in its own right, absolute being.

Schelling attempts to update mythologies for modern times. Naturally there is a difference between the symbols of the ancient world and those of Christianity. Ancient symbols are dominated by nature and being, while Christian symbols provide forms for human actions: baptism, sacrifice, and funeral. Mythology is no longer a glimpse of an omnipotent will, no longer a ray of pure light reaching earth through a cloudy sky.

Thanks to philosophers such as Immanuel Kant, the enlightened human began to rely on her own inner light. She became her own source of knowledge, a condition that in the last resort rests on her own innate divinity. In consequence, artists are now using earthly material to picture revelations of the modern mythological world. Modern mythology and representations of it are collages of historical and natural detail. Schelling would probably have accepted Warhol's Brillo boxes as well as Duchamps's ready-made urinal as indeed rude, but nevertheless catchy, illustrations of such modern mythologies. In art Schelling finds the stuff of modern mythology, and he finds it in Dante's *Inferno,* Shakespeare's *King Lear,* Cervantes' *Don Quixote,* and Goethe's *Faust.*

## The Philosophical Genius

Although Greece belonged to the past and moderns were floundering in their search for meaning, art was not dead. Contrary to what Hegel proclaimed, art was alive; further, the management of modernity needed Schelling mythology much more than Hegel methodology. Schelling was convinced that administrative art, not Hegelian administrative science, was necessary to infuse a modern public space with a vitality comparable to the ancient *agora* (marketplace) of Athens. He predicted a boom in modern myth production, calling it the true mission of art. Music, painting, sculpture, poetry, prose, and drama were all branches of this new *experience industry*.

In 1841, Schelling was at the height of his career. Hegel was dead, and Schelling had been called to fill his chair as a professor at the University of Berlin. At last, so it seemed, the old Romantic got the last word and even delivered it in the very same theater where his rationalist rival once performed to masses of young students. Schelling now had the opportunity to put philosophy back on its right Kantian tracks and search for truth in the spirit of the grand Königsbergian; he would reunite academic philosophy and art.

Schelling was indebted to Kant for making Romanticism possible.[48] In his criticism of Scottish empiricism, French *cogito ergo sum* postulations, and Wolff's insular conceptual analysis,[49] Kant made the way plain. He erected a modern version of Aristotelian categories against the dry analytical linguistic study and empirical skepticism of the 1700s.[50] He indirectly gave art a philosophical position in stressing the individual's ability to create knowledge by intuitively schwunging between reason and science.

After that, however, things degenerated. According to Schelling, Kant's pupil Fichte had unfortunately exaggerated the idea of the *subject* so much that it nearly fostered a cult of the ego. Fichte had made things worse instead of solving the real problems that remained after Kant's departure. Instead of Fichte's shedding light on Kant's mystically unexplained *Ding an sich,* his individualism succumbed to pure nihilism, a philosophy leading to an extreme egoism that legitimizes a person's dictatorship over everything outside the self. Aesthetics was turning into anarchism.

Schelling realized that this kind of doctrine easily lends support to evils such as the industrial exploitation of nature. When Fichte was dismissed as an aesthetic extremist from the university at Jena, Schelling, his former pupil, could do nothing but lament the scandal that followed. Beyond a doubt, philosophically Fichte was a heretic, for he had betrayed Kant's system. Fichte believed in nothing, not even art.

It must have been Kant's Christian background that saved the master himself from ending up in the same nihilistic cul-de-sac. Kant was convinced that an individual, as part of God's creation, was capable of creative thought. Yet, as far as Schelling was concerned, Kant himself could not account for how he was able to create.[51] Hegel also avoided this central problem, for when he addresses pure thought as an exercise of reason only he also nihilistically suggests that the creative opposite of such rationally planned thought is nothingness, emptiness, or even minus.[52] Hegel looks upon the act of creation as nonexistent, and he leaves artistry and creativity unexplained by philosophy.

Schelling, with the help of Baruch Spinoza and Gottfried Wilhelm Leibnitz, rejects this view on philosophy. Philosophy might well be a kind of science, but behind science there is always a scientist. There is always someone making science. A living, acting person is its firm ground, and this basis cannot be explained with logical constructions (form). Further, the living human does not only consist of *Stoff*[53] (matter) either. The logical empiricism of contemporary times would not have been an acceptable philosophy for Schelling, since the basis, the firm ground of existence, also consists of *Substanz* (substance), a word for *content* that Schelling borrows from Spinoza.

This content is much more than material or sensual phenomena. Its most important ingredient, substance, is akin to the extrasensual and divine content. Because of the monopoly of the church, Kant dared mention this only in passing in his dissertation on aesthetics. In modernity, the privilege was abolished, and Schelling was now determined to bring this substantial content back as a central issue of academic philosophy. In 1803, when he left his beloved Jena for a professorship at the new university in Würzburg, he specified his point of view in a manifesto for modern academic study. Pure logic is a blind alley if an individual wishes to study the substantial soil out of which all knowledge grows. The young Kant might have had a point, and maybe, after all, it was therefore not really "such a great mistake as Kant thought to combine the lifelessness of logic with an understanding of anthropology and psychology."[54]

Schelling seems to say that if the philosopher turns his back on what people really do, what really fascinates, seduces, and convinces them, then he runs the risk of locking philosophy up in a Hegelian ivory tower (or the Tübingen tower of the mad Hölderlin) and totally isolating it. Schelling asks how many poets would have succeeded in reaching a wider audience if they had merely written *Poesie über die Poesie*.[55] Successful art is not merely concerned with itself. It has content besides form and matter. What gives art an aura of truth is the fact that it concerns real life. Otherwise it would never be regarded as anything but an indulgence and entertainment. It would not be taken seriously and would have no value whatsoever but as a distraction from something else.

Therefore good art as well as good science must be in touch with not only form and matter but also the substance of content. Scientists who view nature as a lifeless Newtonian or Cartesian *Meccano* set have much to learn from artists who successfully present life in their art. In Schelling's ideal modern university, artists and philosophers unite in search of scientific truth.

Schelling occasionally called natural philosophy *identity* philosophy because it could bridge the dualistic gap between the real and the ideal.[56] Schelling had as a young man described the process of development from matter, by way of light and organic life, to a divine spirituality. As a new-age thinker of his times, he also took inspiration from medieval mystics such as Giordano Bruno and Jacob Böhme. He was convinced that the vital aesthetic energy descended from *eine Kraft eines Geistes,* a spiritual power.[57] Thus it was not possible to separate the science of nature from that of the spirit. This explains why when Michael Faraday presented his theory of electromagnetic fields in 1832 Schelling saw this as proof of his own natural philosophy.

Without reservation, the Romantics believed that they were the ones chosen to combine art and philosophy at the dawn of a new age.[58] Man and nature are a single living entity, and art bears witness to this holism. For Schelling, art is the documentation and manifestation of philosophical insight. A plant grows with inner energy to the same level of perfection that the works of Leonardo or Raphael do.[59] There can be no doubt about such artists' God-given genius; art is both true and good. Philosophy provides ideals, but art realizes the elegant truth in a neo-Platonic sense.

This message was what Schelling burned to preach from his professorial chair in Berlin in 1841. In a 1797 letter to Friedrich Schlegel (whose sister-in-law Schelling was to marry six years later), a very impressed Novalis described the young Schelling by saying, "I am most fond of him, this cosmic man, the glow of truth from his energy flows out towards infinity."[60] Now, in 1841, this cosmic professor wanted to teach a philosophy where art and science intertwined, where God engendered the artist's product as well as the output of the philosopher-scientist. This was the power to schwung the two great and incommensurable concepts, the Ideal and the Real, together. Herein lay the aesthetic miracle the Romantics worshipped in their scientific temple. By his inaugural lecture in 1841, Schelling wanted to turn the University of Berlin into a Temple of Art.

He failed miserably, perhaps because he fell into the eternal trap of boring his audience, this time by lecturing about the Greek gods. Most of the people attending Schelling's first lesson dropped out of his later lectures. His performance was obviously so bad that Søren Kierkegaard, Michael Bakunin, Friedrich Engels, and all the other faithful young Hegelians soon became worn out and walked out. Schelling's attempt to found a modern mythology on art and make aesthetics into philosophy and present himself as an academic artist never hit its mark. Kierkegaard developed existential doubts about aesthetics, Bakunin fiercely attacked modern myths such as God and the state, and Engels set off to mass-market the competing doctrine as Hegelian communism.

Theoretically, Professor Schelling may have been right, but Kant himself had pointed out that conceptual academic discourses never make art work. Schelling's theoretical claim to reveal absolute truth by means of art was far too pretentious a performance to be credible. His own stage presence obviously lacked Schwung. He himself tragically fell on the Hegelian landmine of presenting art in Berlin in dry academic lectures. Pragmatic philosophers would later understand that philosophers might be more useful to aesthetics not as artists but as critics. Fifty years later, playing that part, they turned their backs on Schelling's Temple of Art and brought art out of the Kantian Temple of Universal Truth back to people in the street.

## Critic: Dewey's Educator

### Managing Art

In 1931, the American professor of philosophy John Dewey (1859–1952) was invited to Harvard University to give a series of lectures in honor of the principal figure of American pragmatism, William James. Dewey chose to speak about aesthetics and entitled his series *Art as Experience*.[61] Dewey, to whom philosophy was education for preserving American democracy, promoted an aesthetic way of life, one which would "remove prejudice, do away with the scales that keep the eye from seeing, tear away the veils due to want and custom, perfect the power to perceive."[62] Even though his messages were not the experience economy that was to be preached from Harvard Business School three generations later, certain of his points were forerunners of this later thought pattern. Kant's aesthetics uncovered how art assembles audiences and helps constitute the public realm; Schelling focused on the symbolic Schwung whereby artists create truth. Dewey discovered that it took more than two players for art to work, more than the usual buyer/demand-seller/supply dyad of market exchange. It is his aesthetic philosophy that is a grounding for the management perspective of this book.

Management, as an American subject of education, operates with the intention of producing strategies for making people work. Thus American management has a pragmatic ring to it, one that is lacking in the strictly utilitarian British business economy, the functionalistic French *gestion* or the scholastic rationalistic kameralism of German *Betriebswirtschaftlehre*. Robert Wilson, artist, theater director, and designer, as well as an MBA himself, pinpoints what makes American management different in a minimalist Zen utterance: "Americans are interested in effects—Europeans in causes."

Dewey, as a follower of James, would indeed understand what Wilson was saying. Wilson is primarily interested in the kind of experience management that enhances aesthetic effects. Such managers, much in demand when so-called creative industries look for their aesthetic content, tend to be forgotten by experts on art management who consider the artist-audience dyad only. In this simplistic view, art management is simply the story of how outstanding things like a Mona Lisa picture or a Don Quixote book encounter their admiring audiences. It is as if an invisible hand shapes aesthetic value in making audiences demand what artists supply.

John Dewey, a realist, turned Schiller's enlightened project of aesthetic education into an American way of art management. To Dewey, the manager really responsible for making art work is a philosophical educator playing the part of an art critic who "further[s] this work, performed by the object of art."[63] He notes that most art critics neglect their real job in the aesthetic play. They either want to take on the task of the artist, as Schelling did in Berlin, or become bitter judges of art and arrogantly set themselves above the artists. Good art critics should not themselves be judgmental. It is not their role to make expert decisions and choices on behalf of either the artist or the audience. Besides, says Dewey, commenting implicitly on Kant, aesthetic judgment has as little to do with "judicial"[64] verdicts as with moral decisions; they are not applications of written and clear principles of law, ethics, or political economy. Nevertheless, bad art critics still tirelessly seek out the criteria behind which they can find authoritative cover for their cocksure suppositions. From a position of ignorance, they broadcast what Dewey calls "direct ejaculations"[65] about what they think is good or bad art. As Dewey points out, however, standards can exist only for quantities. Measurements such as the yard, the meter, or the kilo relate to physical things. Works of art can never be compared by measure, for they operate not in the realm of the relative but in that of the absolute.[66]

The history of art is full of examples of narrow-minded academic critics failing to appreciate innovative art. They lose their way in the belief that they can capture the essence of art by applying traditional standards extracted from compiled academic knowledge of previously acknowledged masterpieces. Thus contemporary critics rejected van Gogh, and the same thing nearly happened to Renoir, Cézanne, and Monet when they were threatened with expulsion from the Musée de Luxembourg in 1897.[67] When these authoritarian critics realize their mistakes, they tend to make matters worse by grasping for other superficialities. Thus the hard academic critics are catapulted, according to Dewey, from firm trust in cognitive knowledge to the belief in soft subjectivism of impressionistic perceptions. From an objectively conservative defense of principles, they switch to subjective claims of matters of taste. Just as works of art are an expression of the artist, so this type of critic believes that criticism may also be a temporary expression or whim. Through their writings, such soft critics plague their audiences with their intimate accounts, sometimes even embellishing their scribblings with biographical information and anecdotal details of the artist's personality.

In the view of these no-par critics, impressionistic artists should receive impressionistic criticism, but writing a review of Manet is not like repeating the painter's brushwork with the pen. According to Dewey, if artists were anywhere near as vague and fuzzy as subjectivist critics, there would never be any works of art. A subjective opinion is not sufficient to help manage the artist-audience relation, because art making cannot rest solely on feelings. Art (here Dewey rests on Kant's findings) is more a matter of objectification of ideals than making feelings real.

Dewey does not deny that a sociologist, psychologist, psychoanalyst, philosopher, or historian can certainly gain purely professional pleasure from art. A linguist might choose to read a novel as an example of the application of grammar. A teacher of painting might well admire Leonardo's brush strokes, and a communist activist could interpret the architecture of a château as a demonstration of power and the oppression of the masses. In the same way, a cultural economist can estimate the multiplicative effects of artistic work from a cost-benefit perspective, and a brand manager can calculate profit from design.

One should not think, however, that such learned exercises or instrumental expectations can fulfill the task of managing the aesthetic play or making art work, or even that such knowledge constitutes a good basis for educating successful art managers. Sociology or economics cannot guarantee the creativity of a successful entrepreneur or manager, just as other academic disciplines cannot guarantee aesthetically working art. Cognitive approaches to art seldom approach the prime task of an art critic, which Dewey claims is the "re-education of perception of works of art; it is auxiliary in the process, a difficult process, of learning to see and hear. . . . The individual who has an enlarged and quickened experience is one who should make for himself his own appraisal. The way to help him is through the expansion of his own experience by the work of art to which criticism is subsidiary."[68]

Such a task, such aesthetic pathfinding, cannot be accomplished by academic criticism or impressionistic journalism. A specialist of technique, the cognitive academic scholar, can only recognize what has been seen before. A paraphrasing scribbler abuses the work of art for the narcissistic purposes of her own career as pseudo-poet. These two figures lack the ability to truly manage what makes a work of art tick. They do not understand how a work of art attempts to capture new meanings and expressions of life. Such depth of understanding demands a multifaceted familiarity with many artistic traditions; it is not enough to know a few masterpieces. It demands openness to a new, personal warmth toward art. A singular reading according to any one specific theory of art never leads to good criticism, according to Dewey.

From Dewey's perspective, real artists seldom dream; they are like practical businessmen. The belief that art is illusion is one of the misunderstandings that grows out of viewing artists as impulsive daydreamers; it ignores the fact that artists are extremely goal-oriented doers, with the solid aim of accomplishing their mission. They are not subcontracted decorators; they act as entrepreneurs who love starting new projects. Their aims are not vague soft feelings; rather, they have a desire for decisive high performance. They seek risky situations far from any amateurish notion of art as relaxing entertainment or cool distraction. They have an obsession to paint, play, or write and not merely a desire to communicate with people in some general way.

This explains why real artists are not at all satisfied with merely conversing or debating about art. They are quite happy to let critics take over that task in the aesthetic play. Actually, and quite contrary to the so-called romantic creed, artists are extremely instrumental and pragmatic (not to say predatory). Everything they come across could well be a resource for their work. The most abstract wellsprings of inspiration are cleverly turned into concrete materials for construction of their piece. Real artists are not saints, either; they often come very close to their economic equivalents and are not above exploiting people. Although they may pretend otherwise, artists seem not really interested in others just for the sake of others. They are not therapists. Their primary aim is never to further the creativity of others; they want to do art themselves. By *doing* they often mean the very concrete material action by which they make completely new worlds rather than sharing experiences common to others. Matisse's *Joie de Vivre,* according to Dewey, is a motif that cannot be found in any common physical reality. For the artist, the painting itself shapes reality, for in art the physical "object, the expressed material, is not merely an accomplished purpose, but it is an object purpose from the very beginning."[69]

As a constructor of reality, the artist schwungs from the subjective to the objective. Like a Schillerian bridge over Kantian antinomy, private visions in art must lead swiftly to the production of a concrete publicity. An artist must control how to organize art work so that it resembles manufacturing. Art work is definitely not a private hobby, not a luxury afforded once the necessities of life have been scraped together. It is not something made for the artist's pleasure alone and then locked up in a drawer. Making art work is rooted in an urge, a quite basic exhibitionist addiction to expose and show off the results. Like Schelling, Dewey considers the real artist a bound Houdini struggling to break out of an antinomian cocoon to go public. Artists act, says Dewey. Further, one should not be satisfied with the definition of art given by Plato in *The Republic,* as only a primitive way of philosophizing on the third lowest step of this great ladder of wisdom that is the privileged instrument of the philosopher king. If art is captured by definition, it could die; art is action, and a pinned-down description tends to become its obituary.

Art should be interpreted instead of defined or described. It is by breathing the clear and pure air of interpretation that art stays publicly alive. Thus the work must remain unpolluted by dusty archaeological excavations, either of the artist's original forgotten intentions or of the work's true dusty historical significance. Such is the stuff of academic historians, not critics. Dewey makes clear that art criticism has little to do with scientific or intellectual activity, as little as it has to do with linguistic analysis. A linguistic definition of a word may serve as a preliminary signpost, but the real meaning of the word has to be experienced in actions undertaken by the seeing, reading, feeling, or listening of the audience. Interpretation of art should never try to substitute storytelling about art for the real encounter with art itself. Dewey compares encountering a work of art to a display of flags on a ship. Seen as art, they are not primarily signals or signs, but decorations for a ball on deck.[70] The task of critics as art managers is to open the ball to the public and invite the audience to dance surrounded by the art work.

This is Dewey's view on the management of aesthetic plays. Mastering a ceremony affords a merry Schwung to the metaphysical melody of the aesthetic waltz. For this, a critic must not elaborate a minute interpretation in the form of a complete story about art. An understanding of art can be achieved without first consciously choosing any specific interpretation.[71] In fact, although the role of the critic can sometimes be to deintellectualize the process of interpretation, his function cannot be to indicate certain properties that make an object a work of art. Such properties or criteria do not really exist, suggests Dewey, mirroring Kant's idea of art as something conceived without concepts.[72]

Critics should clarify the folly of seeing art as being purely representational. A religious painter who gives angels bodies with feathered wings is not depicting anything, not re-presenting but presenting—objectifying an ideal. Dewey gleefully cites Matisse when he thanks God for photography, for actually freeing artists from the straitjacket of representation.[73] The first task of the critic is to educate the audience in this respect. Only people with no aesthetic education whatever would reach for the wine glass in a still-life; only those with no proper introduction to art would, after the show, accuse the actor playing Hamlet of the killings.

What gives an object aesthetic value and thus makes the difference between an everyday commodity or service and a work of art cannot be totally grasped by perception. Marcel Duchamp made this point twenty years before Dewey's lecture series when he exhibited mass-produced objects in galleries. There was no visible difference between the object in the gallery and the identical product in the bathroom. Aesthetics should not be reduced to that which materially concerns the senses only, nor does it belong to the realm of subjective cognition Schiller called *form*. Something becomes art only when it *works* as such. Something relaxed and lazy remains a trivial thing forever. To become art, it has to be put to work. It has to be managed to generate aesthetic energy as art. For a pragmatist like Dewey, *artwork* is a verb. He stresses this by pointing out that

> [a]rt is a quality of doing and of what is done. Only outwardly then, can it be designated by a noun substantive. Since it adheres to the manner and content of doing, it is adjectival in nature. . . . The product of art—temple, painting, statue, and poem—is not the work of art. The work takes place when a human being co-operates with the product so that the outcome is an experience that is enjoyed because of its liberating and ordered properties.[74]

## Market Art

Aesthetics, to Dewey as to Western philosophy in the post-Kantian tradition, is much more than theories that understand intellectual meaning or explain sensual feelings. In aesthetics, the dualistic divisions of subject and object, ideal and material, rationalism and empiricism, mind and body, meaning and feeling are blurred. Dewey lays the blame for dualism on Greek philosophy. Aristotle, for example, believed that poetry and rhetoric were fine art, while the dance, music, and drama were merely physical work. Dewey questions the rationale for excluding physicality from art. Everyday speech mixes and blurs words such as *mind* and *body*. In English, *to mind* does not merely mean something intellectual or spiritual. Apart from meaning to remember, to take care of, to handle, to look out for, or to obey, all of these actions require the body and the mind to interact. In his book *Art as Experience*, Dewey wanted to offer a modern American contribution which would end this lamentable situation of split vision in which "aesthetic experience has not been trusted to generate its own concepts for interpretation of art."[75]

Although aesthetics covers an area unfit for treatment by philosophies of either perception or cognition, one must not isolate aesthetic play as something virtual or irrational, either. Though very special, the experience of art is not alien to the real social world. Although any remarkable experience of art is like a mountain top above the clouds, aesthetic alpinists should always remember that the top of every mountain always is, when it comes down to it, an elevation of the simple earthy surface. In his democratization of aesthetics, Dewey made clear that he was not seeking to put art on a pedestal and isolate it from everyday life. He doubted that art was of an eternal or religious nature. In his role as an art manager, Dewey therefore brought art out of both Kant's Temple of Universal Truth and Schelling's Temple of Art and put it squarely in the modern marketplace.

Artistic experience, though elevated, is still rooted in concrete sensuous soil and can be found in all corners of the modern community. An individual might be amazed by the acrobatics of skyscraper builders on scaffolding, by screaming fire engines in red and brass, by cool and witty jazz music, or by a funny comic strip. Dewey actually made this comment when a rat called Mortimer changed his name to Mickey and made a career marketed as a world-famous Disney cartoon character. Instead of marble Greek goddesses in the Louvre, the Italian Futurists praised the art of a Bugatti, not the art deco designer Bugatti or the sculptor of the Bugatti family but their brother the car mechanic. Duchamp, surfacing as an avant-garde name in New York, was toying with ready-mades from department stores while his two brothers quietly stayed home in France traditionally sculpting and painting. This was also the time when Sergei Pavlovitch Diaghilev, the dance experimentalist, saw the City of New York as the greatest of all modern ballets. In Germany, Walter Gropius successfully raised industry funds for his new Bauhaus school of design, aesthetically located in Goethe's Weimar, by promising industrialists that his designers would reveal the inherent beauty of standardized and mechanically produced industrial wares to new democratic mass markets. Modern art was discovered in the marketplace, where street-smart artists capitalized on avant-garde event marketing in lieu of academic training.

No wonder Dewey exclaims that everyone can be seized by aesthetic admiration of everyday things and events. Today, individuals experience everyday happenings that may introduce them to art in a casual way. There are lessons to be learned from experiences in the operating, lecturing, and festival theaters, all of them inspiring individuals to look upon society and its markets from an aesthetic perspective. From these observations, people see that markets illustrate that human life consists of a series of rolling experiences, gained from projects and activities.

John Dewey would completely agree with Adam Smith, who once postulated that a modern community is never managed by design but rather through the sedimentation of all actions undertaken in human enterprise. Art provides the wonderful capacity to take everyday experiences and vivify them, enhance them, refresh them. Art transforms the repetitive experiences of the everyday into a joyful reality for Art, with a capital *A,* and permits

Experience with a capital *E*. The joy, the pleasure, and the agreeable are all taken seriously and help develop an appreciation for the darker uplifting experiences of the sublime as well. In aesthetic experiences, gray everyday existence acquires an aura of surprising intensity.[76] It does not come out of sluggish recognition, or calm association with documented memories, or applying some methodology.

This said, it nevertheless takes management to make art work. Art's workshop must be in readiness, so to speak, although expert managers cannot prescribe the effects. The search for an immediate intense impact of artistic experience ought not lull a person into believing that art is identical to spectacular scandals and shocks. Art is not prone to be called forth by tricks such as special effects, or what Dewey calls "he-man" effects[77] (the event marketing of his time). In the narcotic rush of special effects or hard-core pornochic, sensualism is distorted into perverse sensationalism, divorced from its natural context. Dewey wants to clarify the difference between "ecstasy" and "intoxication," "erotica" and "pornography," as well as between "attraction" and "addiction"; it is the task of art management to see to that this difference is upheld. What gives experience its aesthetic value can actually be the sluggish resistance of a work of art to demands for the more spectacular. The tension between form and matter, to return once again to Schiller, is where Schwung takes place, and it arises rather by teasing than by pleasing an audience. Effects, like an instant outburst or ejaculation, a grimace, a lunge, can actually ruin aesthetic value, which has more to do with the temporal process of art at work than immediate need satisfaction.[78] Dewey would have easily understood why Hermès and Ferrari have customers who wait years for a new bag or car.

The *effect* of art may sometimes be instant, but its *experience* nevertheless takes time. The aesthetic play is no spot market for art where values jump out of a magician's hat like prices on the stock exchange. Art managers must help aesthetic plays generate their energy by making art work gently and rhythmically toward its own consummation. Dewey points out that Eugene O'Neill's plays were once criticized for being "jerky" and lacking aesthetic "retardation"[79] as "rhythmic beats of want and fulfilment, pulses of doing and being withheld from doing."[80]

Dewey explains the generation of high-tension aesthetic energy in terms going back to the biophilosophical frog legs lab of Goethe and Schelling. Dewey thus talks of aesthetic energy coming from the interaction between an organism and its environment. This mode of modeling develops from the Schillerian Schwung between two poles, with its dynamic shift of gears. Energy is exerted to effect a temporal bridge between (in Dewey's version of Schwung) the external and the internal. This is a striving for harmony where "[e]quilibrium comes about not mechanically and inertly but out of, and because of, tension."[81]

Dewey's ideas about artistic creation were most certainly inspired by the contemporary vitalistic philosophy of Henri Bergson, for one.[82] The concrete creation of art does not take place in time and space but shapes time-space. Experience of a piece of music in time extends into a sensation of spatial volume. Intensive experience of a sculpture in space likewise extends into a temporal dimension. Schwung to Dewey then becomes a matter of rhythm. The beat described by Dewey in relation to artistic experience is not the mechanical ticktock of clocks but the meaningful tam-tam messages of African drumming.[83] It is not about the mechanical reproduction of specific effects fit for studies in perceptual psychology. Art works as a rhythmic composition where the parts form a living whole.

Markets as aesthetic plays are—to use another related concept—self-organized systems. They are plays where the artist, the producer, also has the creative capacity to adopt the position of the audience, the consumer. Creation schwungs between total engagement, being inside, and the artist's capacity to keep a detached eye on the ball, like a good tennis player.[84]

Dewey warns critics who want to manage art not to confuse such a creative process with either functional design or rational planning. Art work is different from other jobs. A design engineer creates a shell protecting the components of a product, delivering an elegant form into which the matters of facture, the technical and functional parts of a product, are neatly packaged. Art is not equal to design in that respect, nor is it rational planning for attaining preconceived goals as economically and effectively as possible. An artist therefore seldom differentiates between means and ends. An artist's end results are frequently expressed in the medium used as the instrument of work. The score is the music, not just its method of notation. The colors of a painting are unified with its form, not mere instruments of coloration. As Christo Javacheff, one of the most astute art managers of the twentieth century, put it, "Art has inherent what it is."

Understandably, Dewey also believes it is impossible to capture the essence of artistic creation by close analysis of means and ends of a painter's technique, whether use of pigments, brush strokes, or sense of perspective. For that reason, the development of art, what makes a thing into a work, has little to do with utilitarian technological development. Primitive art cannot be explained as a mere lack or absence of technical capability. Technically speaking, the Egyptians could doubtless have painted three-dimensionally; they just did not want to. Douanier Rousseau might have been naïve, but he certainly was not ignorant. As a boy, Pablo Ruiz Picasso mastered the techniques of classic masters, and it took playful Picasso a lifetime of effort to unlearn academisms. This may be why artists are so reluctant to accept corporate assignments as demonstrators of the static perfection of new technologies. They do not use technology in that way. Good artists transform, destroy, or toy with technology, like Nam June Paik playing with magnets on TV sets long before video art was heard of. They delete the -*logy* and save the *techno-* they fancy. Bad artists try to make the –*logy* compensate for their lack of ideas. Most cyber, computer, and holographic artists today fall into this category of technology consumers pretending to be art producers.

A true artist searches for mastery over his medium, not vice versa. When John Dewey illustrates such aspects of the birth of an artwork, it is like reading the script of an art peep movie from 1956 called *The Mystery of Picasso,* where the French director Henri-Georges Clouzot records Picasso's work from behind a transparent canvas.

Nothing is predetermined. Picasso has no preparatory drawing. If he feels the need to trash his work, he will suddenly tear it to pieces or, as Chaim Soutine used to do, cut up the canvas in millions of mosaic pieces for a new collage version. No economic or technical considerations hold the artist from reworking the entire piece from the start.

Dewey points out that the creation of modern art is just as open to interpretation by an audience.[85] Actually the reason Soutine mutilates his canvas or Picasso smears the wet paint seems to be that they both take a step back. In the detached pose of a voyeur, the Gauloise *mégot* glued to their lips, they themselves watch their work through the eyes of their future audience. After such a pause in the act of creation, anything may happen when artists schwung back on the job, when the impressions of the external public reception mix with the private action in single details on the canvas.

The reason there are so many ugly buildings may be that modern means of production obstruct such openness, making Schwung, or what Dewey calls "retracing,'" impossible.[86] The free play of the architect to let the design and the designed, the viewed and the viewer, interact during the process of creation is nonexistent in industry. This is no abstract theoretical freedom. Retracing has to do with the concrete realities of art work. Modern artists often avoid limiting techniques (Flemish oil, al fresco, watercolor painting) since they make retracing technically difficult. They slow down the Schwung and playful freedom that allows every alteration of detail in a developing work of art to affect the outcome of the whole of the work. Classical industrial management cannot cope with Schwung, where every change of detail can lead to an entirely new finished product. A modern artist, however, is constantly aiming to reorganize and unify materials from their innate capacities, giving external form to the inspiration of a spontaneous gesture perhaps coming from deep inside. A sculptor forms a block of marble. A dancer trains the body's means of expression and struggles against material pain. Form must be immediately in touch with matter. Matter to Dewey stands for the inner content some artists may attempt to access with special psychophysical tricks for blurring the dualisms. The French poet Robert Desnos wrote surrealistic "automatic poetry" during his micronaps in the noisiest of Montparnasse bistros, while some of his colleagues indulged in "chemical experimentation" of their own.

A work of art, according to Dewey, is "organized energy,"[87] and the internal relations of its components provide this energy. Dewey expands Schiller's dynamic dualistic tensions into those of conflict and unity, frustration and fruition, impatience and hesitation, encouragement and repression, propulsion and repulsion, weight and lightness, and elevation and depression.[88] The work of art is the unification of its constituent and antagonistic parts. A chair can be functionally useful but lack the form for aesthetic experience; Dewey also suggests that it is not enough to do as functionalist Gropius did and just make visible its technical skeleton structure. This will not, whatever Gropius and Bauhaus designers may claim, produce an aesthetic form. The reason a Bugatti is a work of art is not reducible to the visibility of technical perfection. The art works of Jean Tinguely, famous for his dadaistic "doing-nothing-machines," and Panamarenko with his impractical flying machines make statements akin to Dewey's criticism of functionalism. Even technical objects may become defunct and still work as art. What makes them alive as art is aesthetics only, or as Dewey puts it, "We do not need to feel . . . that we are speaking metaphorically nor apologise for animism when we speak of a painting as alive. . . . "[89]

The totality of a living work of art lacks joints and seams, says Dewey. A work of art does not only attract and organize an audience as Kant discovered. A work of art generates each single viewer's energy. It sorts out, articulates, and concentrates his or her everyday experience. The result is an intensive and compact feeling of being alive. It would be wrong to say that a work of art conveys or mediates existence. For Dewey, art is no metaphor or media; it is existential energy. Art is the absolute thing in itself.

To experience this energy is also a sure sign that art reveals truth. Dewey does, however, reject Kant's and Schelling's project of erecting modern art museums as Temples of Art or Universal Truth. Truth according to Dewey is neither universal nor religious. William James's ground-breaking 1907 essay "Pragmatism" helps explain Dewey's view. James, in whose honor Dewey gave his aesthetic lectures, launched his own modern definition of truth. Truth is not in the intellect, as rationalists believed, nor is it to be found externally, as empiricists hoped. In his introduction to the French translation of James's book, Bergson points out that a pragmatist sees truth as an artistic invention somewhat similar to a cute little puffing engine.[90] Any joy from a new machine becomes an integrated part of everyday reality because it works and is *true,* in this restricted pragmatic sense only. Technically excellent inventions and machines often lie dormant on drawing boards, in cupboards, and in corners; like all forgotten toys, they show that usefulness is not merely a technical matter. Even a technical invention must work socially for it to become pragmatically true.

It is this sort of truth that matters in the modern era. James points out that such pragmatic truth must not be eternal or all-inclusive. Instead of being universal, it rather "grows in spots."[91] Truth is thus the name for something meaningful, in the sense that it pays to use it. At this point, James, as a good American manager, actually talks about a "cash value" of truth.[92] Truth is formed by, and itself forms, pragmatic reality, which for James, like Dewey, only exists in "human thinking."[93] It is pointless, therefore, to seek the big *T* Truth, but it can be pretty worthwhile to make small *t* truths work. James suggests that scientists, through argumentation, logic, and tests, perform such persuasion by trying to convince other scientists with their theories. They do not discover Truth; they rather invent truths.

In his James lecture, Dewey sees the practical experiments of artists in a similar fashion and uses a quotation from Shelley to describe their creative acts as "deeds that breed." James also stresses that new ideas must be connected to existing old truths and anchored in tradition in order to become new and truthful knowledge. Dewey suggests that even a new work of art, although it may occur as a bolt of lightning, requires a lengthy incubation period, and artistic experiences arise in a cultured audience through a long process of aesthetic education for which the critic-philosopher-teacher has the main responsibility. Neither art nor truth is produced overnight. As James points out: "We patch and tinker more than we renew. The novelty soaks in; it stains the ancient mass, but it is also tinged by what absorbs it. Our past apperceives and cooperates, and in the new equilibrium . . . it happens relatively seldom that the new fact is added raw."[94]

The same statement might apply to the progress of a work of art from studio to the new experiences of an art lover in the aesthetic play. Tradition is united with the new, intensely vital whole; it is open to future interpretations. This system is made to work by what Gregory Bateson later called "the pattern that connects."[95] At their point of contact, old and new melt together in the work of art, which now becomes true upon entering the consciousness of its audience. Events, shows, or fictions not organically anchored in a tradition risk remaining but short-lived and vague whims of a cranky artist.

## Aesthetics for Democracy

Art is found in many places other than the national galleries, the fancy art dealers' shops, and the private collections of rich capitalists. Dewey blames imperialistic statesmen for manipulating art shows into nationalistic events. He accuses judicial, political, and economic bureaucracies of shielding people from direct experiences of life, for impoverishing their lives by hindering aesthetic experiences. Like Marx,[96] Dewey believes that capitalists seeking monopoly power over art markets for one, and social splits by division of labor for another, seriously threaten free aesthetic play. Not only modern class barriers of industrial management have that effect, however. Plato falsely postulated that people in various roles in society were genetically preconditioned: warriors were strong-willed, merchants greedy, legislators wise. Such stereotypes need to be challenged. Dewey detests how the capitalist managers of modern economies organize citizens into "little boxes" and mental "pigeonholes." This stereotyping not only blocks the beautiful and the sublime; it is the most significant threat to modern democracy.

Good critics and their art management may remedy the harm done by industrial bureaucratic management. In 1896, Harvard professor George Santayana had already written about the aesthetics of democracy.[97] Dewey put his hope for democracy in art, since it can resist an inhumane compartmentalized society: "Art breaks through barriers that divide human beings, which are impermeable in ordinary association."[98]

Dewey dresses up Kant's idea of an aesthetic organization in democratic clothing. Art can reform society; history is full of examples of how art has been used as an organizational power.[99] How could the Christian church have persuaded people to attend Mass if it had not been spiritually embodied by artists in the objects of ritual and the art of the cult? How many kings and emperors could have ruled without communicating their power in aesthetic pomp and majesty? Surely the anxious gaze of the censor trained on the artist is ample proof of the reality of the power of aesthetics. Why waste so much time on inquisitions and controls if art did not generate this power? When Plato warned against the sophistry of poets and the myth making of artists, he probably suspected that their art was far more politically seductive and powerful than philosophy like his own.

Dewey's view on art working for democracy expands high culture toward popular culture. The democratic power of art encourages appreciation of artists such as Pieter Brueghel, the Flemish painter of popular scenes of nature and mankind, and the naïvist Douanier Rousseau. Such art leads away from ethnocentricity. To Dewey, art should be as multicultural as the United States itself. Freed from the clutching grasp of classical antiquity, art could blend European myths with Japanese or African. The more linguistic barriers were broken down, the weaker the logocentrism of art would become. Images and music would replace words. This freedom would also imply a reduction in anthropocentrism. Aesthetic experience would help override the human culture and open sensory response to universal nature. Human beings would move toward a realization that they are "citizens of this vast world beyond [them]selves, and any intense realization of its presence brings a peculiarly satisfying sense of unity in itself and with ourselves."[100]

"Cosmic" Professor Schelling would surely have appreciated this statement by Dewey, even if it does show clear signs of inspiration from Hegel. Dewey is careful, however, to distance himself from transcendental idealism. Experiences of art would first and foremost bring about a general social order by furthering communication between people, not in the sense that people will talk, speak, or discourse more but in a Kantian sense that art stimulates the imagination, making it possible for people to empathize with each other. This, in turn, furthers democracy.

Dewey is careful to guard against transcendentalism that might be rejected as superstition or mysticism. He lived in a time and place where modernism was becoming synonymous with scientific progress. When he implies the importance of *faith* in art, he is eager to emphasize that this is not primarily a matter of faith in God or demons. He prefers to refer to a more earthbound, everyday faith or trust in tune with modern postmetaphysical opinions. William James illustrated this type of worldly trust with a commercial image: "Truth lives, in fact, for the most part on a credit system. Our thoughts and beliefs 'pass' so long as nothing challenges them, just as bank-notes pass so long as nobody refuses them. But this all points to direct face-to-face verification somewhere, without which the fabric of truth collapses like a financial system with no cash bases whatever."[101]

Dewey lived in an age that saw the federal banknote monopoly replace the gold standard as the cornerstone of financial systems. He must have been aware of German sociologist Georg Simmel's notion that fiduciary money itself was modern society's most accomplished aesthetic form.[102] Dewey hoped that things would improve day by day, and that America, along with the rest of the world, would soon grow out of the infant illnesses of capitalism. The market would then turn into a genuine aesthetic play. Ugly factories, boring jobs, and poor workers who shared no joy in the rewards of production belonged to a bygone age. Dewey believed that development and science would soon become part of the shared aesthetic experience of humanity, and that the single-minded utilitarian manager straight out of the pages of Charles Dickens's *Hard Times* would disappear. Producers and consumers would come together in the participatory companies of the future, and mass-produced goods would be both beautiful and useful in a new aesthetics of consumption.[103]

Dewey even has hope for the crass businessman of the American dream. The death of the salesman only heralds the birth of a fourth character of the aesthetic play. After the audience, artist, and critic, the ugly businessman will be reborn as an art technician. Behind the dry and dull workaday façade of the businessman beats a heart of gold, a heart capable of being both seduced and seductive in aesthetic play: "I suppose that it is also true that if businessmen were the mere money grubbers they are often supposed to be by the unsympathetic outsider, business would be much less attractive than it is. In practice, it may take on the properties of a game, and even when it is socially harmful it must have an aesthetic quality to those whom it captivates."[104]

## Technician: Nietzsche's Leader

### Aesthetics for Energy

"Man now expresses himself through song and dance as the member of a higher community; he has forgotten how to walk, how to speak, and is on the brink of taking wing as he dances."[105] A Schwung of song and dance, of melody and movement, is the central theme of Friedrich Nietzsche's (1844–1900) first book, *The Birth of Tragedy*, written in 1871. Nietzsche introduces his fourth player, the technician of speed, to the aesthetic scene populated by Kant's art audience, Schelling's artistic genius, and Dewey's art critic.

In his book, Nietzsche depicts how wild, boisterous crowds in ancient Greece, garlanded with flowers, held orgiastic carnival-like plays of singing and dancing in honor of Dionysus. With immense energy, an intoxicating Schwung, such Dionysian celebrations swept aside the genteel Apollonian culture of antiquity. It was in the spirit of Apollo that Homer and other poets had created elegant sagas of man as an individual. In honor of Dionysus, individuals melted together into ecstatic crowds or audiences in which the *principii individuationis* was dissolved. Nietzsche likens this Dionysian Schwung to a kind of intoxicating speed. Apollonian art, on the one hand, may be compared to beautiful but sober daydreams living among static Doric architecture. In Dionysian sublime intoxication, the mass of humanity bubbles like a unified work of art for which no single individual artist could be made responsible.

The cool veil of Doric art was swept aside. Apollonian artists trembled with sublime fear before this chaotic aesthetic play far from their ideal of poetry: "Schiller confessed that, prior to composing, he experienced not a logically connected series of images but rather a musical mood."[106] The dynamite of Dionysian art, says Nietzsche, is that poetry does not come from the cool intellect. It grows out of a *musikalische Stimmung*,[107] a musical atmosphere as an audible phenomenon, a terrible cry out of *Urschmerze der*

*Musik,* the tragedy of music's original suffering. How could one think of an aesthetic play as a language game, as cozy storytelling? Any Apollonian poet must realize that the subjective ego could not have been at the true origin of such works of art. This true energy of art must be tapped, Dionysically, out of *dem Abgrunde des Seins,* the abyss of being. Dionysian art is salvation from whimsical and capricious egoism controlled by insignificant but destructive consciousness. This primal musical art can save the world from itself, can release it from its restrictive karma by fusing subject and object in aesthetic ecstasy. Nothing can furnish final proof of man's existence, but the Dionysian aesthetic play gives opportunity for experiencing life. As Nietzsche states, "Only as an aesthetic product can the world be justified to all eternity."[108]

In the midst of his aesthetic euphoria, Nietzsche sets up a management model for staging aesthetic plays, and he cites ancient Greek theater as a per-

fect prototype. In fact, his book reads like a management text for how Greek tragedies were produced. For example, it has been suggested that the chorus represents the Greek people witnessing the actions of their gods and heroes; but in ancient, aristocratic Hellas, Nietzsche interjects, there was no concept of a public, constitutional gathering of the people. Schlegel, the Romantic, believed that the chorus was a symbol for mod-

ern audiences. Schiller took an Enlightenment view that the chorus screens off the poetic dream of the plot from reality. Nietzsche says that both were mistaken; in original Greek tragedy, there was no difference between dream and reality. The point of its aesthetic play was to wipe out the distance between an audience and the stage by eliminating the gulf between a daydream and real experience, since in Athens Dionysian plays were not performed at night but in the daylight. Everyone participated in the action in utter seriousness; there were no passive onlookers. The tragedy, no representation of worldly drama, was a presentation of manifest reality. The theater of an Apollonian temple was a clear, beautiful procession during which the participants retained their personal identity, their *bürgerlichen Namen,*[109] but Dionysian tragedy aimed at complete "enchantment" because, as Nietzsche explains, "Enchantment is the precondition of all dramatic art."[110]

The true function of the chorus in Greek tragedy is to initiate the audience to an ecstasy that gives rise to and carries the vision of its heroic drama. The original Dionysian orgy later degenerated into bleak epic images of the Apollonian dreamplays.[111] In the Dionysian play, the chorus is a collective, creative genius. No wonder the Greek god of wine was the first hero of this original aesthetic play, and its final purpose would be that Dionysus would reveal himself in its orgiastic mystery.

Nietzsche's message to those making art work is clear. Art is not an Apollonian business where single brilliant stars perform their sober poetry to a cool audience. Even the detached Apollonian poet must acknowledge his Dionysian roots, for true art grows by the speed that is the ferment of the Dionysian sublime.

Art stopped working once artists believed themselves capable of creation without the musical support of a chorus, when the actual people concerned were no longer participating on stage. Nietzsche singles out Euripides as embodying the decline of Greek tragedy. When the playwright Euripides left the stage to sit among the audience, he became like the detached spectator at his own dramas. He was a poet who unfortunately began to think, who began to question rationally what was happening on stage. As Euripides tried to understand and elevate theater to conscious analysis, he refused to allow himself to be thrown into the action in true Dionysian fashion. This was how, according to Nietzsche, techniques of ecstasy deteriorated into calculating technologies of illusion.

A long time ago, art faded away. Its raw and powerful substance was disciplined into strict form. Design supplanted intuition. A prologue appeared, in which the roles were presented and cast, and plots were planned to keep the audience's attention. Consciousness and clarity were introduced, and what happened on the stage had to be explicable. Through this, claims Nietzsche, tragedy became domesticated and enfeebled. Poetry became the product of academic courses in creative writing, and soap opera spectacles replaced poetry. Dionysus was castrated by cognitive civilization, as thought conquered emotion.

Euripides' most prominent supporter was Socrates, the analytical philosopher whom Nietzsche makes responsible for having seduced young Plato to burn his tragedies.[112] Further, Plato then criticized the Dionysians, who were true artists, and hoped that modern intellectual philosophers would take their place. The more such intellectualism triumphed, the worse art suffered,

Nietzsche explains. From ancient Greece to modern Europe, there was a nose-dive in aesthetic development. It hit bottom with the appearance of bour-geois theater, where all energy and tension are gone. What is left is a banal plot in which the naturalistic heroes behave like vulgar Roman gladiators. The ending is a happy and banal closing, often with some deus ex machina trickery. All this is the fault of theoretical men, such as Socrates, who cut magic ties with Dionysus and reattached them to Apollo and thereby ad-ministered a deathblow to the golden age of Ancient Greece. Dionysian tragedy upheld the whole Greek state, according to Nietzsche, because it made art work for the people and link their everyday lives with mythology.

From the original position of having been able to see their existence from an eternal (position) point of view through the tragedies, *sub specie aeterni*,[113] the Greeks now tumbled into a mundanely crass everyday world. The desire for meaningful connections to art was partially satisfied by superficial ritu-als and pseudometaphysical ceremonies. Charlatans were brought in to rem-edy the lack of energy, as management consultants would be hired to resus-citate a dying business by decoding its brand genetics. This only left a feeling of emptiness, a growing nostalgia for the good old days of the gods. During the Renaissance, for example, there were attempts to revive the Greek po-etic language by opera. The recitations of the singers were invented to try to recreate ancient poetic Greek by a *stile rappresentativo*,[114] an attempt char-acterized by Nietzsche as a fiasco. Early opera declined into a technical spec-tacle full of elaborated special scenic effects, but it still lacked true aesthetic Schwung. Unfortunately, its rhythmic speeches set to music were a ludicrous sort of Renaissance rap that could not bring Dionysus back to life. Perhaps, Nietzsche posits, Martin Luther was more successful than the Renaissance opera because he had his congregation form a Dionysian psalm-singing cho-rus in church.[115] Luther seemed to understand: "Singing and dancing, man expresses himself as a member of a higher community."

## *Schwung*song Wagner

Then, suddenly, in the midst of this academic argument, Nietzsche abandons his investigation into Greek philology. His book turns from a dissertation to a clever sales brochure for contemporary art. Gone is nostalgia for old Greece; now Nietzsche proudly presents a German hero, Richard Wagner, who will finally revive true original Dionysian Hellenism in his modern music.

This was the surprising conclusion of Nietzsche's controversial book about Greek tragedy; in reality, it was a paean to the operatic art of Wagner. Through this writing, Nietzsche, recently appointed professor of philology in Basel, hurled himself out of academe into the politics of art. Nietzsche, the philosopher, turned from traditional research to devote all his energy to introducing his new discovery to a learned audience of the newly founded Bismarck Reich. Germany could learn from Greece. Only Wagner, exclaimed Nietzsche, mastered the techniques of Dionysian Schwung that could aesthetically unify Germany through "the rebirth of German myth."[116]

"Oh Fritz, Fritz, if only you could have kept yourself to your Greeks," his worried mother is supposed to have said when Nietzsche abandoned philology for his consultant position on Wagner's art management team.[117] Her concern fell on deaf ears, for Nietzsche found authoritative support in turning down Apollo and choosing Dionysus when he read in Schopenhauer that "Socratic man [had] run his course."[118]

This was a bold decision in times when mainstream German philosophy was slowly decoupling itself from art. Hegelianism dominated, and the romanticism of Schelling was outmoded. The neo-Kantians emphasized epistemological and ethical considerations rather than the aesthetics of their master. In making his commitment, Nietzsche arrogantly ignored the academic establishment and instead found inspiration in the philosophy of academic outsider Schopenhauer. It was no doubt Schopenhauer who made Nietzsche recognize the Dionysian in German music. He recommended Bach and Beethoven, and then led Nietzsche to a composer of his own discovery, Wagner.

The Schwung of music was not to be explained by historical analysis or academic musicological study; it lay in its melodies. Schopenhauer convincingly argued that truth lies in the confrontation with a melodic work of art. When the twenty-four-year-old Nietzsche, himself a reasonably good amateur composer and pianist, met the fifty-year-old Wagner in 1868, he was already fascinated by *Tristan und Isolde, Tannhäuser,* and *Die Meistersinger.* Wagner came to affect the whole of Nietzsche's work, and during several years of intense communication, Wagner was not only Nietzsche's mentor; he also became a management case for how the Dionysian *melos* would vanquish the Socratic *logos.*

Wagner was an artist whose early work was driven by political ambitions. In 1849, he stood on the barricades in Dresden, theoretically inspired to revolution by Hegelianism and practically fired up by his anarchist friend Bakunin. In the spirit of Schiller and Goethe, he wanted to create a religion of art that would suit modern statesmen. Art would become the aesthetic motor in the political life of the German people. He discussed with Ludwig of Bavaria the possibility of turning Munich into *Athens on the Isar*.[119] When attempts to establish a Wagnerian cabinet failed, he left Bavarian politics to concentrate on his own *Gesamtkunstwerk*. Instead of making art for politics, he now began making politics for art.

Munich did not become another Athens, because Bavaria did not want to be salvaged by Wagner's religion of art. He did succeed, however, in raising enough funds for an artistic enterprise of his own in the small town of Bayreuth. There he managed one of the most influential art firms of modern times, with young Nietzsche present when the foundation stone of his opera house was laid in May 1872.[120] Nietzsche enthusiastically describes how Wagner in Bayreuth was engineering an enterprise that would become a home for the cult of opera, a house where his Dionysian melodies could radiate without their power being diminished by the shortcomings of a bourgeois Apollonian theatre. Until the first festival in 1876, Nietzsche was an enthusiastic participant in the management of Wagner's enterprise. His art criticism aroused intellectual interest in it, and he identified himself with his idol to the extent that he even considered moving in with Richard and Cosima Wagner. His admiration for Bayreuth knew no bounds, and now he wanted to be backstage. Nietzsche admired how Wagner mastered the techniques of mass marketing art into popular culture, saying "Wagner's poetic ability is shown by his thinking in visible and actual facts and not in ideas; that is to say, he thinks mythically, as the people have always done."[121]

This quote not only contains a Nietzschean definition of art management, it also reveals its roots in both Schelling and Schopenhauer. Wagner's technique worked with the rhetoric of music. His songs did not convey logical meaning but rather faith and feeling. Nietzsche believed himself to have discerned something of the same emotions in the behavior of the masses during the Franco-Prussian War in 1871. It was no coincidence that Wagner was constructing Bayreuth at the same time Bismarck, with Prussian determination, was organizing the German nation. Backstage at Bayreuth, Nietzsche began to understand that a Wagner melody could serve as a march for mass mobilization, and his opinion of Wagner began to change seriously. He eventually had difficulty coming to terms with the martial undertones of Wagner's music; worse yet, he had a growing feeling that this mature artist was really an unscrupulous, calculating aesthetic entrepreneur. Perhaps Wagner was even exploiting Nietzsche for creating public relations for an aesthetic campaign of which he was the managing general? It suddenly seemed to Nietzsche that Wagner was too much a clever actor to be a sincere artist.

In addition, Nietzsche noticed growing signs of meek piety in Wagner, especially in *Parsifal*, where Nietzsche directly detected a smattering of Christianity in Wagner's work. Nietzsche mistrusted Christianity for its Socratic contribution to the fall of Dionysian art. Nietzsche, the clergyman's son, had once invoked Wagner as his modern Antichrist. The more Nietzsche discovered the calculating backstage technicality of Wagner, the more he hated him. It was as if Nietzsche did not want to admit that art had to be managed to work, that aesthetics took some planning and calculation, too. In 1888, Nietzsche schwung from love to hate. He wrote that Wagner's operas were ridiculous and false, embarrassing attempts to revive clumsy myths, full of Viking heroes rolling round the stage like *skandinavischen Untiere* (Scandinavian monsters).[122] Where he had before found strength, he began spotting flaws. The problem with Wagner was that his pessimism arose through a deficiency of spirit. Wagner was a poor aging composer in search of gods and security. He lacked the exuberant explosive power that gives rise to true rebellious Dionysian pessimism. After 1848, Wagner stopped flirting with rebels like Bakunin and abandoned the sort of pessimism that Nietzsche himself advertised in his loud, anarchistic battle cry: "I am dynamite!" Wagner was suffocating Nietzsche, who needed to take flight once again to realize his own projects. Wagner schwung from being Nietzsche's success story to becoming his mismanagement case.

Wagner never possessed true Dionysian inspiration. His work was merely a barbaric spectacle. Nietzsche no longer believed in the future for the German people in art. Art for the masses is sheer madness since it ends up in technical entertainment. Only an aristocratic elite could access pure art. Art for art's sake, never contaminated by means-ends instrumentality, was all that Nietzsche would now accept. Realizing that Wagner was a technician of Schwung, his admiration turned into bitter deception.

Nietzsche, the admiring aesthete who had grown critical of Wagner's business, became in the meantime a poetic philosopher as a result of his contact with artists. The story is a familiar one. Philosophers such as Bergson and Sartre were all Nobel laureates of literature. Sartre wrote drama; Martin

Heidegger, perhaps under the influence of Friedrich Hölderlin, would philosophize in prophetic, poetic language. The case of Wagner, with all its elements of incitement, seduction, expectation, ecstasy, suffering, disappointment, despair, and denial, reflects both Nietzsche's aesthetic infatuation and his painful sobering up in the violent field of energy surrounding art management. The experience of backstage technicalities in Bayreuth was too much for him. Nietzsche, the junkie addicted to aesthetic speed, eventually rebelled against Wagner, the pusher. In a pugnacious mood, he broke away from the psychedelic masses around Bayreuth to detoxify in a peaceful, aristocratic, Zarathustrian caste of art.

## *Schwung*dance Napoleon

Nietzsche's experience with Wagner and his interpretation of tragedy can be used to illuminate the Dionysian technicality of aesthetic plays. He mirrors the mixed feelings about the technical management of sublimely grand enterprises like running the opera house of Bayreuth. Nietzsche slowly discovered that Wagner was a general waging war on his aesthetic battlefield, that he was calculating, planning, and negotiating his own business without much consideration for the creativity or sentiments of others. Nietzsche, for example, was just expected to fulfill his duty as an officer of the staff responsible for public relations and event marketing. When Nietzsche once dared to play his own music for Wagner, Wagner is said to have heartlessly left the salon giggling with laughter.

In aesthetic philosophy one often finds references to similarities between art and war. Nietzsche, like Kant before him, often wrote about the sublimity of war in comparison to the beauty of peace. Military strategists, who have inspired strategic thought in management, also refer explicitly to their campaigns and projects as a kind of aesthetic play taking place in what they call, significantly, "theaters of war." Nietzsche's experience with Wagner may well serve as a case for highlighting his disappointment with the precise strategic technicalities of Wagner's Dionysian art management. The same aesthetic approach is actually familiar to the military strategist of the nineteenth century. What happened in Bayreuth is not so far from the action in Borodino or Austerlitz. The management case of Wagner therefore leads to consideration of the modern archetypal case of another technician of aesthetic play, Napoleon Bonaparte.

Wagner performed modern songs of *Schwung*, while Napoleon was hailed as a modern Dionysian choreographer of the sublime! Several strategy lessons originally developed from studying Napoleon have later been applied to the management of civil enterprises, although the fact that the insight such case studies convey has to do with aesthetics and art is often ignored. The most famous lesson is probably that penned by the Prussian eyewitness to "the case of Napoleon," General Carl von Clausewitz (1780–1831). In his classic work on strategy, *Vom Kriege* (published in 1832), Clausewitz reflects upon his own practical experiences in the Napoleonic Wars. In his effort to describe Napoleon's bewilderingly innovative style of war management, he looks upon strategy as art. Few today realize that Clausewitz explicitly chose an aesthetic perspective based upon secondhand knowledge of Kant's third *Critique*.[123] In a forgotten essay on the theory of art, Clausewitz proposes that all decision makers must assemble specialist knowledge to form an intelligible whole on which to base their decisions. The architecture of such a whole is, says Clausewitz, not a matter of science but *eine Kunst*.[124] Therefore a manager of a grand enterprise, like an army general, must be open to intuition. When his hunches assume "worldly, concrete form,"[125] he moves from detailed knowledge into the realm of art. Aesthetics is how he makes strategic decisions. The strategic leadership of war is therefore, for Clausewitz, not a science but an art, because "where creation and production is the object, there is the domain of art; where investigation and knowledge is the goal, there science reigns."[126]

This is not as obvious as it sounds. Clausewitz's subject—war—like Nietzsche's beloved opera, and the fields of management and business generally, had not always been looked upon philosophically as art. Campaigns of war and operatic spectacles were both considered purely practical enterprises during the Renaissance. Machiavelli's crass pieces of advice to the Italian prince were hardly a question of art and aesthetic energy but simply of political power. The prince would hire talented *condottieri* like Hawkeye, Gattemalata, or Sforza, who in return for payment would provide the professional services of their mercenaries. War was a craft and not an art. The martial entrepreneurs competed by offering various technical specialties, such as a strong cavalry or a talented longbow brigade.

The drawings and projects of Leonardo show how close craft was then to art. Elaborate craftsmanship was paramount to Renaissance opera houses; it was the ingenious inventions of the set designer that won applause. The true stars of the performance were the stage engineers and their crew, who skillfully handled stage settings as if they were sails on war vessels. One went to the opera for the special effects, and to war for its amazing technique.

As a Kantian, Clausewitz imagines war as a play, however, between the empirical materiality of craft and the analytical formality of engineering. Modern warfare was not a matter one simply outsourced to skilled condottieri subcontractors. Clausewitz also disagreed with the Enlightenment theories of war that sought to transform the practical craft of the military into tactical scientific management in true Newtonian spirit.[127] The warfare of the Enlightenment was caught in a glance as an Apollonian drama on an Italian theater stage.

Contemporary battle paintings clearly illustrate such Enlightenment thinking. In a sun-drenched valley, neatly surrounded by soft hills and taller mountains, the battle-ready armies stand in beautiful symmetrical arrangements. On a hill in the foreground stand the general and his staff in the first row, next to the regent on his throne, so like the setting at the theater before the curtain goes up. At sunrise the performance starts. When the sun goes down, the spectacle is over, and the victor declared. As in the painting, the enlightened theater of war was all supposed to take place before the eyes of an admiring audience.

This visual conception of warfare resulted in a countless number of analytical theories having been developed by Clausewitz's day. Military theorists were praised for their logical principles and methods of effective warfare. Now that war was no longer the province of mercenaries, young noblemen could be trained in academic military management. War was thus incorporated into the grand hierarchical plan of the realm. The court took care of what was previously outsourced to specialist craftsmen on the market for mercenaries. The nobility's task was to manage the troops now incorporated under the monarch.[128] From such an education in military management were developed the first methods of analyzing warfare strategy. Peaceful business schools teaching management science in the twentieth century are the rationalistic heirs of this enlightened methodology of war of royal war academies. By way of the operations research models of World War II, it became widely diffused into modern management training. When military engineering was applied to rationalize industry operations, it became a kind of chess game. From being a bloody trade, it turned into a barren field analysis; it went from technique to technology. Analyzing the case of Napoleon might also help the viewer schwung out of this dualism. War, in the Kantian tradition, belongs neither to renaissance craft nor to enlightened science. Aesthetic play takes place between matter and form.

Soldiers applied the skills of their trade in battle. Such individual craft could, as was the case in war academies, be logically analyzed and rationalized. Analysis, however, demanded well-defined single events that can be neatly observed and studied, so it was best suited to the single skirmishes and isolated encounters making up the tactical side of warfare. Clausewitz, on the other hand, suggests that overall strategy is more complex and entangled and cannot emerge out of analysis of simple events or tactical actions of practical workmanship. In addition, strategy is not reducible to martial principles. This theory hearkens back to Schiller's model of the aesthetic play, where neither the experience of materiality nor the logic of form informs the audience about how art really works.

Clausewitz discovered artwork as he experienced Napoleon's battles in person and was convinced that the business of war could not be conducted Apollonically by cool Socratic analysis. In the feudal management schools, the academies of war, the theater of action was pictured as a two-dimensional theater curtain, a flat screen on which one could draw neat geometric figures. War was fought in thoughts on the blackboard, and in this theoretical perspective attack and defense were conceived as two polar forces. Battle was looked upon as a mechanical process. As Newtonian economists calculated price as the equilibrium point between the two forces of supply and demand, so too Enlightenment military theorists believed they could predict the outcome of a battle using mathematical calculations of attack and defense vectors. Napoleon, Clausewitz's great aesthetic genius, had overturned previous concepts of war and rubbished the hopes of the theorists.

Clausewitz accounts how Napoleon transformed war into an aesthetic play: Napoleon moved quickly, with light forces. He never looked upon warfare as black ruler lines penned on a plane of white paper. A battle was not black and white designs of geometric patterns; it all took place in flesh and blood. He maneuvered through colorful three-dimensional terrain, and the concrete European landscape became an active part of his strategy of war. Clausewitz, in consequence, writes about rivers, mountains, valleys, forests, streams, shorelines, swamps, and alpine passes as if he were a landscape painter. These were no longer impassable boundaries framing a neatly delineated theater of war. The landscape became an active participant in action, because Napoleon's technique consisted in turning its site-specific elements into aesthetic players. The emperor opened up those new inanimate players by applying techniques of logistics. Conflicts were now determined by quick marches or nocturnal pursuits after the close of battle. There seemed to be little use for academic calculations suited to wars fought on flat, uniform terrain. Actually, the decision, the battle itself, became merely a small event in the overall conflict. What happened on the geometrical plane where lines crossed in a point of decision lost its previous importance. Now it was prisoners and booty taken after a battle that made all the difference. Napoleon's own fate was sealed in his Russian campaign, not by a single battle but the overall loss of two thirds of his forces on the eighty-two-day march from the Niemen to Moscow. Compared to that logistic loss in the wide winter landscape, the number of casualties in battle was almost incidental. What mattered in modern war, as in modern art, was what happened in between.

Napoleon dismantled abstract formal space and brought in concrete place. Modern war suddenly took place. Through his logistics, he also introduced concrete time into warfare. It was no longer enough to regard battles as occurring in some timeless present, like a well-organized boxing match where a neutral arbiter in the ring abstractly clocks the various rounds. The revolutionary emperor destroyed the formal etiquette of old-time wars. Symmetrical defenses no longer matched attacks. War was no longer a gallant match between gentlemen. It left the realm of cool fashion and conventional taste and moved into that of Dionysian energy. Tension, delay, acceleration, and friction are the hallmarks of war after Napoleon, in a sense like the opera after Wagner.

All of this made Clausewitz skeptical of academic decisions made without any temporal or spatial appreciation. Just as Nietzsche attacked academically distanced connoisseurs, Clausewitz condemned the military theorizing of office-bound generals and bookworms who knew all about the classics and logic but had never experienced Napoleon. They were utterly ignorant of how aesthetics made martial art work, and they were proud of their ignorance.

Nietzsche's advice was to see science as art and art as life. The same advice can be read in Clausewitz. There is a distinct Dionysian echo when Clausewitz implores generals not to forget war's fundamental "principle of destruction."[129] Generals must not shrink from "the decisive blow," and they must resist any unwillingness to take "the bloodiest way to resolution." Clausewitz regards war as the concrete application of politics, an act of the sword rather than the diplomacy of the pen. To use Nietzsche's terminology, he warns against Apollonian aesthetics that regard war as a decorative "ornamental sword." He also warns against Socratic military theorists who can conjure up painless victories with no loss of life.

Clausewitz was as little a pure romantic admirer of violence as Nietzsche was. His book was written at an avant-garde time when the use of guerrilla tactics and the hide-and-seek of partisans were becoming more widespread. Since the theater of war was no place of execution where enemies were easily slaughtered, it became necessary to promote the notion of "bloody resolution," which was much harder to accomplish than victory on the battlefield.

Modern war was much fuzzier than that of the old convention and craft. The enemy's position was unclear, and the site of any battle was unknown. Communications were difficult, and Napoleon could appear at any moment. Having a clear view of the battlefield was now just a memory of the Enlightenment. War could not be depicted and framed on a screen. Generals could see nothing and hear nothing. Perception could not work. Nonetheless, Clausewitz cautions, in a very Kantian way, that the act of command cannot rest on cognition alone; the less one can see, the more important intuitions become. The German word for intuition used by Kant was *Anschauung*, literally meaning onlooking. Rather than working as perceptive receptor of light beams in the paradigm of Newtonian optics, the eye, according to Clausewitz, seems to work as a sender of light, of *in*-sight. Clausewitz stresses the importance of a general's "inner light" and speaks of his strategic intuitions as a "coup d'oeil."[130] The leaders of military enterprises must use intuition to form a complete strategy, and this can only be effected by the mental faculty we call imagination. If great poets or painters wince at our attributing such an office to their personal goddesses, if they shrug their shoulders at the notion that a smart gamekeeper is on that account to be credited with a first-rate imagination, we readily grant that we are speaking of a similar creative capability and its employment in a truly menial office. But, however slight this service, still it must be the work of that natural gift, since if that gift is altogether wanting it would become difficult to form a clear, coherent picture of things as if they were before our eyes.[131]

In the final analysis, a general's intuition must therefore dictate his actions, even when they are in conflict with existing conventional rules and principles of logic. Clausewitz states that general principles never lead to positive doc-trines of action; at their best, they can only be a coarse checklist, because in the practice of war each task is so complex that even a Newton or an Euler would fail to analyze the problems logically.[132] In addition, logic cannot take account of material characteristics such as hate, fear, and courage, all of which arise through the enterprise of war. Clausewitz is certain that such emotions will be playing an ever-greater role in warfare after Napoleon. With Dionysian intoxicating speed, Napoleon succeeded in mobilizing the French masses into modern armies. When hired mercenaries conducted wars and the monarch ran out of money, the war was over and the condottieri moved on to their next employer. Armies then moved about like circus troupes. Their train contained not only ammunition and food but also women and children. Napoleon's modern armies, however, increased their speed and decreased their costs by seizing food and supplies from the local populace. Again, the landscape played its part. Napoleon's soldiers were now citizens of the French Republic. The revolution had set them free. This meant they no longer received payment; instead, they were working off the debt of free-dom they owed the nation. Through its national incorporation, military service turned from a burdensome cost to a rich resource; this was a duty the nation could rightly expect from every man for nothing but honor.

Both Wagner's and Napoleon's enterprises rested on aesthetic energy. Nietzsche called it Dionysian, and in Clausewitz are the signs that the same Dionysian mobilization overcame the economic barriers to larger wars; in consequence, the bellicose business boomed. Frederick the Great com-manded only thirty thousand men at the most, while Napoleon managed ten times that many. When asked what made his success, Napoleon himself gave the aesthetic answer: "to enchant the masses, you must speak to their eyes above all else."[133]

# 3

## Problems for Art Firms

### Gadamer's Art Firm

When the time came for the mass production of the industrial age to be launched on the marketplace, department stores were built on the concept of a vast theater. People were enticed by machine-age products designed to look like old crafted masterpieces. In his *Das Kapital,* Karl Marx introduced the wares of the early textile industry as Mister Coat and Miss Linen, products that performed as puppets manipulated by capitalistic strings on a shop-counter stage.

Industrial products were often displayed as unusual and attractive objects in old curiosity shop settings; early industrialists proudly presided over these marketplace museums that were fully equipped with concert halls and fine art galleries.[1] In the great retail institutions of the 1800s, such as Bon Marché in France or John Wanamaker's and Marshall Field and Co. in the United States, inventions such as tubular post systems, cash registers, electric lighting, and telephones were introduced as special theatrical effects to increase public curiosity. It was the spectacular effect of the mechanics of the department store, rather than any single product on the shelves, which charmed the consumer.

Carefully thought-out campaigns of entertainment created a carnival-like atmosphere beneath the roofs of these business theaters and featured a talented medley of goods, all stars of the mercantile production. The shows were so in tune with the rapid beat of fashions and seasons that department stores really deserved to be called *Hetztheater,* the contemporary German slang for circus.

Shopping very soon became a complete experience. After a day's entertainment in the stores, the Parisian consumer of the late 1800s could pass the evening enjoying the spectacles presented in bars or cabarets. A meal at the  Prison Cell, the Cabaret of Nothingness, or the Japanese Divan, all Paris bistros, was a complete show experience, with costumed staff acting their roles against a backdrop that could share billing with today's Disneyland.[2]

The coupling of modern marketing and museum art has an extensive history. The two connect as closely as the Schwung of bread and theater in ancient Rome, and historical record illustrates how this alliance is something that can intentionally be organized and managed. Even the Dionysian tragedy, beloved by Nietzsche for its spontaneity, was carefully managed. It was born out of religious choral works often actually performed in the agora, the Athenian marketplace. During the fifth century before Christ, these rites were performed on the southeastern slope of the Acropolis in a space dedicated to Dionysus. In 330, a permanent theater of Dionysus, with audience benches and jury chairs, was completed; it still stands in the same location today.[3]

Performances were held in conjunction with religious festivals in January and March. The March festival, known as the Great Dionysiad, was organized as a competition, with a ten-man jury deciding the winner. In these matches, three poets were called upon to read a trilogy of tragedies. Later a twelve-man chorus was added. One family contributed each chorus, and the poets cast lots to select one citizen from each family to be in charge. A choirmaster and flautist for each chorus were also selected by lottery.

During the performance, each chorus was managed by the *koryfé,* who conversed with the three male actors presenting the speaking roles of the tragedy on stage; the three were ranked respectively as the protagonist, the detragonist, and the tritagonist. In addition to these participants, actors were also chosen to perform nonspeaking roles.

The poets themselves led the rehearsals, and occasionally one would act as chorus master. All free Athenians were welcome at the performances; those who could not afford the admission fee were still allowed entrance. Each competing poet, and the actors as well, received payment from the state for their participation. What this historical data draws attention to is the intricate complexity of the organization of ancient Greek tragedy. It really required careful management to make its art work.

A naïve reading of Romanticism would conclude that art is the product of the inexplicable genius of a solitary artist, or of the equally isolated art experience of an aesthete. An even more naïve economic interpretation would include talk of supply and demand and of the production and consumption of art. Søren Kierkegaard makes light of this asocial attitude when he ironically characterizes the art consumer as a "dandy aesthete" who avoids "friendship, marriage, and livelihood" in order to escape entrapment in the "boredom" of habit.[4] Obviously, Schiller's Schwung would not have a chance without the network of players introduced by Kant, Schelling, Dewey, and Nietzsche.

The importance of social interaction to the production of art is reemphasized throughout history. Dewey's theory of aesthetics clearly stresses the social grounding of art and accentuates the fact that art arises among people. Hans Georg Gadamer (1900–2002), a student of Martin Heidegger, suggests that Kant's aesthetics bears part of the blame for the tendency to overlook socialization. The aging Kant is principally concerned with the beauty of nature, while only his youthful writings discussed taste in anthropological terms. As he matured, he carefully kept ethics, the philosophy of human relations, out of the aesthetics of his third *Kritik der Urteilskraft*. When Gadamer lays the responsibility for this oversight on Kant, as other aesthetic philosophers sometimes do, he also remarks that it might be Kant's fault that today the agricultural term *culture*, or *Kultur* in German, is used in reference to art. Kant overstressed the natural, and in consequence, forgot about what Germans call *Bildung*, education.[5]

Gadamer's reference to education, in contrast to cultivation, is akin to Schiller's view of aesthetic plays. To Schiller, Schwung does not come completely naturally or spontaneously. The artist has to provoke and manage the movement of Schwung between form and matter. At the same time, Gadamer warns against going to the other extreme and viewing art from a purely organizational perspective. In terms of discovering how aesthetic play makes art work, a Dionysian tragedy, some Disneylike experience store, or any other case of management of art and business is of little worth if it is only to focus on how the formal institution is maintained. When asked how a dramatic production is organized into art, Gadamer answered: "This much is clear: drama, and the work of art understood as drama, is not a mere schema of rules or prescribed approaches within which play can fully realize itself. The playing of the drama does not ask to be understood as satisfying a need to play, but as the coming-into-existence of the work itself."[6] What Gadamer nevertheless seems to imply is that some kind of organization must be considered to fully understand aesthetic plays. It is not enough to sum up the behaviors of the players that Kant, Schelling, Dewey, and Nietzsche helped identify, because it is not their conscious intentionality, their Socratic thought, which generates the Schwung of aesthetic play.

When aesthetic play makes art work, it performs *eine ihn übertreffende Wirklichkeit*; it makes something more real than itself.[7] Such a play has little in common with the thrill or distraction of business or computer games, or even a competitive sports game. An aesthetic play is a drama in which images are presented to an audience, images that are no mere mirroring or representation reflecting some other original. Imagination shapes values in its own right. A reflection merely shows the body to the eyes; a reproduction replaces the original, which, once it is known, extinguishes the image itself.[8] Gadamer advises casting aside the misleading metaphors of mirrors or photographic pictures and instead regarding images as one does those representations in Roman law which legitimize one person's independent actions as agent of another person.[9] Such a legal representative would never be perceived as a psychophysical clone of the principal.

Still, aesthetic plays evoke a pleasant sense of familiarity, and this raises the question of how this familiarity occurs if images of art are original and without traces in experience. A true aesthetic philosopher, Gadamer insists that this sense of awareness has nothing to do with recognition. An aesthetic play features familiar players and makes use of familiar texts or objects. The sense of the familiar, however, the aesthetic feeling, has to do with what these players and their material reveal when they interact in an aesthetic play. The outcome, the work of art, is like an elevation, an exaggeration, a surrealization aiming at what Gadamer calls the *Urbild*. An aesthetic play thus creates a surplus value by lifting the common and everyday from dull drudgery to something unique and universal. What makes art work, in other words, is a transcendental Schwung.

Gadamer, a Protestant, describes the aesthetic play as a religious cult in which both speaker and audience are uplifted by the words of the Holy Scripture. Outside the liturgy of a religion, a bible is just a big book. A church makes art work in the circle of its congregation. Gadamer thus calls his model of an aesthetic play a *Kreis,* a circle with the scriptures in its center. In the Protestant religion, Schwung thus lifts humans to truth. Gadamer refers to the sacred dimension of what is commonly understood as purely profane truth seeking: remember, he says, that the Greek word *theoria* means a "sacred collective festival" in which the theoretician takes an active part.[10] In truth-seeking festivals, the aesthetic play of a *Kreis,* one may at first lose identity, since art does not consolidate identities by mirroring everyday portraits. The artist fades from view, just like the everyday self, the curriculum vitæ of the actor, or the humdrum life of the audience. The players thus "lose themselves" in aesthetic play.

Tragedy for the Greeks was therefore an outpouring, an act of bemoaning. Only by establishing some distance from the everyday self can humans reconnect with the vibrant truth of art. The aesthetic experience can be likened to a trance, or even to an epileptic nonpresence.[11] The "attack," which Gadamer calls "*parusie,*"[12] occurs when the absolute presence of the art is revealed. In the aesthetic play, a player thus exchanges fossilized everyday self-getting and receives in return " . . . the whole of his being."[13]

Gadamer criticizes Kant's theory of aesthetics for supporting a view of pure art isolated from human affairs. Although Kant frequently refers to examples from fashion and garden or furniture design, his philosophy nevertheless encourages a feeling of superiority over the decorative and ornamental functions of art.

This said, art cannot live in isolation from human life, however. It is from everyday life that art takes its presentation of reality, and those who want to make art work have to bear this in mind, as Martin Luther did by having priests address their congregations in their native tongue and uniting congregations by means of psalmody.

*Artists* do not function as sequestered monks. The names of great artists, such as Ingmar Bergman and Andrei Tarkovsky, are not merely the names of individuals, but rather brands of teams working collectively like painters in an old Flemish art studio. In like manner, good *critics* cannot be isolated judges or censors, since according to Dewey they are pedagogues who help bridge the everyday world and art. A good critic enlivens existence through communication with the audience and with the artists themselves. Not even a *technician* can remain isolated in an aesthetic play, because the technician interprets and enriches art just as the carpenter enriches the designer's ideas; the printer, the artist's pictures; the mason, the architect's blueprint; and the musician, the composer's score. In the *Kreis* of an aesthetic play, technicians become active and transcend their purely reproductive function. Even the *audience* itself cannot be regarded merely as a passive consumer or as a calculating client in the marketplace. The audience in an aesthetic play may open itself to unexpected novelty, or it might offer distant resistance. In this way, an audience becomes active and should not be confused with the anonymous masses in the marketplace. An active audience has very little in common with the fictitious "gas cloud" that the economist model uses to describe price formation on markets.

Gadamer proposes an alternative role for the market-audience. Once captured in an aesthetic play, the market turns into an audience with desires and passions instead of demands and needs. The difference in the two characteristics is that a demand corresponds with an existing need; no one can passionately desire something that has not been presented in concrete. In the words of Umberto Eco's master, the Italian aesthetic philosopher Luigi Pareyson:

> A significant artist transcends the taste of his time because he has the capacity to create his own audience and to transmit his own original taste to it. The artist both interprets the deep needs of his own time, and pre-empts and opens up new and different epochs. These two situations are not as different as one might suppose. The existing taste of an audience is never so clearly defined that the artist's interpretation becomes superfluous. Taste must always be delivered from uncertainties and must achieve qualitative precision for it to be anticipated and represented in a process of creative revelation. In the artist's work, the audience will find a basis for its vague instincts and preferences. It will often resist innovations that are later regarded as being wholly in line with the public's deepest and most unconscious desires. It is always the market that gives way to the innovative artist. The artist usually transcends, and even destroys, a market that opposes him. The artist creates his own audience.[14]

In summary, Gadamer renders through his view of aesthetic play a model of an art firm as a theater of aesthetics, where four players interact to make art work in the center.

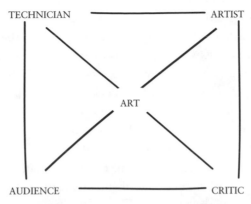

*Interaction of Four Players Making Art Work*

## The Dual Dilemma

### Totality: Imploding Art Work

At Marburg University in the 1920s, Martin Heidegger incarnated philosophy into a physical performance. Gadamer recalls how he lectured in his Alpine skiing outfit[15] at seven in the morning, a time when conventional professors were still sound asleep. Heidegger mesmerized his audience of "verheideggered" student fans. In his presence, they immediately sensed the material physicality of his philosophy; his performance simply convinced them he was right. When he lectured on Aristotle, it was as if the Greek and the Marburg professor had hybridized. This must have been the way it was when Schiller made a poetry reading of his Jena history class: philosophy physically consumed by the academic audience.

The infamous Wissenslager, a philosophy summer camp Heidegger organized in 1933, had a similar impact on students as they gathered, electrified, around their master dressed as a Lederhosened hillbilly in a Schiller-Kragen shirt. [16] Truth was performed as aesthetic play on the unexpected stages of lecture theater and campfire! His Marburg students directly experienced sublime Truth as "historical existence's own acquiescence."

Heidegger's lecture on art, delivered in Frankfurt in 1936, explains that "[h]istory means here not a sequence in time of events of whatever sort, however important. History is the transporting of a people into its appointed task as entrance into that people's endowment."[17]

To Heidegger, being a philosopher was like being a snowboarder who hits a kicker and is suddenly airborne; *es kam alles ins Rutschen.*[18] In *l'Être et le Néant*, published during the German occupation, Sartre used Heidegger's philosophy as his snowboard for political action.[19] There is no meaning, no essence, before existence, and hence existence implies action. Man *is* what he *does*—so just do it!

After the war, Heidegger turned his back on Sartre when the latter slid from existential philosophy into communist politics. Trying to overcome a hangover of his own Nazi activism, Heidegger deplored Sartre for supporting Stalin for much the same reason he himself had supported Hitler. Each was seduced by an evil force, perhaps mistaking it for sublime aesthetic energy. They were typical victims of aesthetic *totalization.* This is the first of the two eminent problems of aesthetic play; the second is its opposite: aesthetic banality.

In 1932, Ernst Jünger, one of Heidegger's admirers, wrote an essay called *Der Arbeiter.* In it, Jünger explicitly expanded upon the modern idea of art and implicitly expanded on totalization.[20] The Romantics, he concluded, were content to see art as a revelation. They never used art to transform reality. The bourgeoisie dreamed only of freedom of beauty and truth, never of becoming political and never of taking the step from pure will to its realization in power. The bourgeoisie lived, however, in an *art space,* which easily could have been turned into a *legal space,* that is, served as the constitution of the state if the will of the group had gained legitimate power.[21] Now, wrote Jünger, revolutionary times had come; he predicted total mobilization would soon be upon them. Within the year, Hitler came to power. Many, including Heidegger, then thought Hitler made art work.

Heidegger dreamed of Greek temples; Jünger, on the other hand, talked of workshops in a modern industrial landscape. Like medieval knights and monks, workers were mobilized under the modern myth of *Der Arbeiter.* The worker, *der Arbeiter,* with his party and union, wrested power from the weak and liberal bourgeoisie. Hardened by World War I, workers became foot soldiers in an aesthetic play. They are even prepared to lay down their lives and die in battle in order to reach Valhalla. In this way, soldiers and workers are the obedient organs of one all encompassing *Golem-Gestalt,* the *Arbeiter.*

Art for Jünger is the unconscious expression of this myth. Works of art become *Eigenschaft der Gestalt*, properties of the gestalt.[22] The artist, according to Jünger, is an obedient and blind tool in the interpretation of the workers of the age. In this way, the individual, intoxicated with terrifying Nietzschean sublimity, will enter completely into a collectivity.

One year later, Heidegger urged his students to swear the oath of loyalty to their new Führer. Maybe Adolf Hitler was uneducated, he said, but that matters little, since "he has such beautiful hands." In a 1933 letter to Wilhelm Furtwängler, the famous Wagnerian conductor, Joseph Goebbels, the Nazi minister of propaganda, makes clear who will be the real artists when the Third Realm of Kant toppled to a Third Reich:

> Politics is also a form of art, perhaps the highest there is. We who have had the task of shaping German politics feel ourselves to be artists. We bear the heavy responsibility of transforming the raw masses into a firm and complete image of a nation. But the task of an artist goes beyond the mere design of a whole. He is forced to create and form, and also to sweep away anything that is diseased to make a clear path for what is healthy.[23]

It was scarcely a coincidence that Heidegger published his *Origins of Art* shortly after Hitler's speech on art and architecture in an Aryan Germany[24] at Nuremberg in 1935. At that time, Heidegger still espoused the naïve hope of pessimistic philosophers that art would be able to overcome the inhumane nihilism of industrial technology. Just as Nietzsche put his faith in Wagner, so Heidegger for a while believed in Hitler. No wonder Heidegger cringed a decade later when Jean-Paul Sartre spoke admiringly of Joseph Stalin's Soviet dictatorship and existentialism as humanism.[25] They were two philosophers isolated and without premonition about the reality of concentration camps or the gulag archipelago. Aesthetics was degraded to legitimize totalitarian doctrines, and even Nietzsche's books were edited by his Nazi sister to fit propaganda purposes.

All twentieth-century dictators have abused aesthetic energy. The state became the ultimate work of art under the management of loyal party designers such as Joseph Goebbels and Albert Speer. Modern art was not simply a decorating power; it was itself the evil force by which avant-garde artists gladly became devilish demiurges.

When Benito Mussolini proclaimed the birth of the fascist movement in 1919, the futurist poet Filippo Tommaso Marinetti stood at his side.[26] Both had a background in anarchist activism. In 1909, Marinetti used the first page of *Le Figaro* to announce the birth of a new form of art. Classical art, many held, could go to hell. The statue of Nike from Samothrace could never compare with a Bugatti racing car, its exhaust glowing, its engine screaming. Senile contemplation and geriatric reflection were to be swept aside by machinery and film, the art of the future. In explosive poems, dynamic paintings, and aggressive manifestos, Marinetti and the other Futurists declared themselves Nietzschean technicians of the aesthetic speed. Anything reactionary would be crushed.

Marinetti also traveled to Russia to promote Futurism. Following the Revolution of 1918, groups of constructivists, productionists, concretists, and suprematists organized, all of them hoping to mold reality aesthetically. Their proclamations echoed the very spirit of Futurism: "We rebel against the spineless worshipping of old canvasses, old structures and old bric-a-brac, against everything which is filthy and worm-ridden and corroded by time."[27]

Marinetti was as jubilant over the Second World War as he had been over the First. As an old man in the republic of Saló, the last of the Fascists' terrible enclaves, he composed one final Futurist poem in praise of the black-clad executioners. The Italian poet and filmmaker Pier Paolo Pasolini staged a last horrible torture scene in his film *Saló* in the midst of famous futurist paintings.

The Futurism of late fascism lost the freshness of its avant-garde Schwung, with the aging Marinetti its surviving shadow. In actuality, the Futurists had lost their positive energy by the 1920s when they dissolved into an art brigade of the fascist propaganda force. Rebels were needed in the beginning, but later they were expected to conform to the movement. When the Russian avant-garde artist Kasimir Malevich was shown Marc Chagall's *Blue Horses* at the art college in Vitebsk, where Chagall had been appointed rector in 1918, Malevich fired him. Wassily Kandinsky, who became head of a state-run Soviet art institute after the revolution, was also dismissed, only to be replaced by Osip Brik, a friend of Vladimir Mayakovsky, who immediately ordered all artists to abandon art and concentrate on production. Their slogan was to be "Long live the communist expression of material constructions. . . . Art is indissolubly linked with theology, metaphysics and mysticism."[28]

Avant-garde artists revolted not only against old-fashioned academism but also against art, and they even abdicated as artists. Artists were not special. They would be workers, architects, or engineers on the great site of social construction. Soon the Russian proletcult and agitprop had turned avant-garde art into powerful design departments for Soviet propaganda. In 1920, Vladimir Tatlin designed his famous tower for the Third Internationale. Cubist-painted trains transported enthusiastic brigades of artists around the country. Filmmakers such as Sergei Mikhailovich Eisenstein set out to reengineer the thought processes of the new Soviet citizens.

In time, Vladimir Lenin began to tire of "futuristic scarecrows" that continued to resist conformity to orderly state service. Leon Trotsky asked Tatlin to kindly "reconsider his artistic position," a caution which kept Tatlin out of serious work until his death. Lenin instructed his agent Willie Münzenberg to infiltrate the capitalist West with its troublemaking leftist avant garde.[29] Agitators such as constructivist El Lissitzky or suprematist Malevich could be exported as subversive seduction to the naïve Western intelligentsia. They could exhibit freely in Berlin and Paris, as long as they stayed out of Moscow and Leningrad. The sponsor of this Western exodus of avant-garde culture, which the Nazis branded "cultural bolshevism," was the Soviet Communist Party, which kept many art celebrities on their secret payrolls.

In Germany, the same process was used when the Nazis took power. Joseph Goebbels, who had himself been an expressionistic critic, conducted a purge of avant-garde artists sympathetic to Nazism. Expressionist Emil Nolde, who had joined the Nazi party in 1920, saw his paintings censored as "degenerated." The Bauhaus school of design, to which Walter Gropius had invited Kandinsky, was radicalized by 1928, as art was slowly replaced by technique. Hannes Meyer, who with the help of activists funded by Moscow shifted the political inclination of the school to the left, had earlier replaced Gropius as its manager. Now Bauhaus architects were not to design houses but "living machines." After accomplishing this politicization, Meyer immigrated to Russia in 1930, where he swiftly shifted his artistic loyalty from the functionalism of Bauhaus to Stalin's social-realism.[30] In 1933, Bauhaus closed, although many of its designers found work under the Nazi regime.

Once they were able to access the archives of dictatorships, art historians began to offer insight into the totalization of the last century's modern art. Under political leadership, free aesthetic plays were soon frozen into monuments of totalitarian art and were staged as the return of reason and the end of infantile, irresponsible anarchism.[31] The cases of Heidegger and Sartre show how those who fought for the in-between aesthetic realm were the

first to lose their playful distance. Hitler and
Stalin took over the art management of the
play and eroded its integrity by bribing their
courtly artists with power and flattery.

   In 1934, Stalin summoned an elderly Maxim
Gorky home from ten years' exile in Mussolini's Italy and then appointed him head of
social realism. When Stalin ordered his artists
to become "the engineers of the human soul," they turned from being free
artists in aesthetic play into monks serving the sect of state art.

   Monks of the Orthodox church never signed their icons because they believed that the icons were not individual works of art but a revelation of the
Holy Spirit[32] painted according to generations of detailed instructions. Those
who stood in a St. Petersburg gallery in 1915 admiring Malevich's *Black
Square* were beyond doubt standing before a modern avant-garde icon.
Malevich intended his picture to open a window to "an absolute vacuum"[33]
where pure emotion existed.

   An icon is not a message from one person to another. For someone at
prayer, it is a window to the infinite nature of God. Malevich had replaced
God with a vacuum and purity of emotion. Not replacing the vacuum with
Joseph Stalin, however, led to the consequence of Malevich's dying poor and
forgotten. Obedient party artists became honorary members of the social-re-
alist order of academic monks. Like Hitler, Mao, and Mussolini, Stalin belongs to a Byzantine tradition of art dominated by image and icon rather
than word and text.

   The modern icons of the party—Kolkhoz farmers, Aryan youths, Soviet
cosmonauts, and Chinese party leaders—were to be portrayed realistically.
The paler the form, the clearer their eyes glowed with fanatical political
faith. In a state where the slightest sign of satire or irony led to Auschwitz
or the gulag, artistic trickery was unnecessary for conjuring up sublime terror in those viewing images of sphinxlike leaders.[34]

   *Artists* were not the only players to be locked up in the totality of the
aesthetic play. When Andrej Rubljov's 1425 icon of the Trinity was selected
as the perfect representation of the church, it was the result of several
decades of theological debate. The paramount question, "What is art?" became transformed into politico-religious censorship, and many art *critics,*

such as the literary scholar Georg Lukács, ended up as chief ideological art commissars.

In Berlin, the race aesthetician Paul Schultze-Naumburg was Nazism's absolute arbiter in artistic matters. Critics operating as Dewey had described were appointed censorious commissars, discarding autonomous artists of the avant-garde. Artists were dismissed as dreaming formalists, degenerate cultural vandals, self-willed enemies of the state, or bourgeois anarchistic romantics.

The true purpose of art was to strengthen the soul in the same way that gymnastics would build a strong body. Art turned to sports events when biennials and world exhibitions became aesthetic competitions in which the artists of the great dictatorships competed in the heroic realism of state-sponsored art.[35]

The part of the *audience* in the play also changed drastically. Works of art were no longer to be looked on or admired. A totalitarian artistic religion does not tolerate a passive audience. It demands total participation in parades and manifestations. The watchword of artists was obedience, and the ultimate aim of art was, as Jünger foresaw, total mobilization. Today they watch a parade; tomorrow, they march to the front!

The *technicians* of art were to set the play in motion. This was no longer a Schillerian pendulum Schwung, however; it became an acceleration into what Sartre called *nothingness of being* and what Heidegger simply termed *death*. To Nietzsche, the true Dionysian speed was administered by the gay science. Its purpose was a love parade rather than a military march.

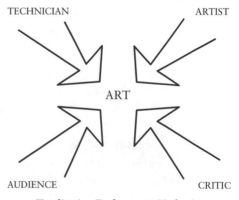

*Totalitarian Enslavement Under Art*

Totalization made society implode into a mess with no barriers between stage and auditorium,[36] a theater not worth the name, transformed as it was into a gallery of mirrors impossible to sort out.

It is said that Hitler spent the night after his victorious election designing new emblems, flags, and uniforms for party functionaries, also known as the "cadres" of totalitarian states. *Un cadre* means "a frame" in French, and indeed totalitarian art managers do their best to really frame art. Totalization means the breakdown of art work by implosion. The Schwung of free play stops where art enslaves and exploits its players. In terms of the Gadamerian model, this sad situation, where all players are sucked up into a state *Golem-Gestalt* of a cannibalizing totalitarianism, can be depicted as in the figure.

## Banality—Exploding Artwork

"But, Daddy, he's got nothing on!" piped up a small child.

"Heavens, listen to the voice of innocence!" said his father. And what the child had said was whispered from one to another."[37]

The famous youngster in Hans Christian Andersen's tale of "The Emperor's New Clothes" simply states the obvious. He is not concerned with the weaver's assurances that the cloth in the emperor's clothes was only invisible to someone who was stupid or unworthy of his social position.[38] In the eyes of the candid child, the emperor's procession goes from all-consuming pomposity to empty banality. The parade of totalitarian art builds upon lies and illusion, and this is the moral sense of Andersen's tale, the spirit of which was to be incorporated into the gentle Copenhagen Tivoli that was Walt Disney's model for his Disneyland theme parks.

When governments promoting totalitarian works of art are crushed, aesthetics indiscriminately becomes locked up in the bottom drawer of good and victorious democracies. I personally remember my own astonishment when I stumbled upon an old, tattered copy of the *Leipziger Illustrierte Zeitung* from 1944.[39] My discovery in a pile of old books in a Swedish summer cottage brutally put aesthetics back in its Nazi context. For being printed in bombed ruins just a few months before German capitulation, it was a grandiose color-illustrated Christmas magazine. Seeing the ads for new drugs from Bayer-Kreuz, increased product quality at Fried Krupp Werke or Kjellberg Autobahn Engineering gave me a real chill. Then I came upon on the first article of this journal, written by a certain Hans Georg Gadamer, professor at Leipzig University. The title was grand indeed: "Was ist der Mensch?" But I found Gadamer in shady company. His essay was printed immediately after the portrait of the Führer and it declared: "Our battle of today has high ambitions; a thousand-year culture incorporating Greece and Germany is fighting for its existence."[40]

To accentuate the point, Gadamer's text was illustrated by a dark drawing of two stern Waffen SS mounting the guard for a bleak Madonna in a *Nacht und Nebel* landscape of European ruins. The picture "Um die Kultur Europas" (For Europe's Culture) was signed by an army artist, SS-Kriegberichter Berner.

This strikingly demonstrates how aesthetic philosophy was framed by fascism. After Hitler's *Götterdämmerung,* it took more than a decade for academics to venture into the cellars of aesthetic philosophy. During the Cold War, the occupation forces of form and matter colonized aesthetic space in theoretical and practical ways. With Bertrand Russell and Karl Popper as its principal proponents, logical empiricism suppressed any attempt by aesthetics to regain its ontological status; aesthetics was equated with totalitarianism. The battle had been fought in the name of open democratic society. Totalitarian art imploded, and its ship of false "Truth" sank with its dark demons on board.

"Truth" as the basis of art was no longer credible. Nobody trusted Heidegger until, in 1958, Gadamer added " . . . *und Methode*" to the title of his treatise on *Wahrheit* (*Truth and Method*) and reintroduced aesthetic philosophy as a democratic hermeneutic acceptable in times of Donald Duck, Coca-Cola, and sticky bubble gum. I still recall the cry of "Schokolade und Zigaretten" by beggars in tattered army uniforms at Flensburg's railway station in 1952 when I journeyed to Paris in my childhood. They heralded a consumer culture of a democratic world forever ruled—everyone loved to believe—by childlike honesty and candid innocence. As in Andersen's fairy tale, everyone was so relieved that right-wing totalitarian art had been unmasked. People must have had the same feeling when the Berlin wall tumbled down on left-wing totalitarianism. Never again was art to be made to work for a social utopia. The political production of art was definitely dead, and in its place a consumer culture took off. Heidegger was forgotten, and aesthetics jumped out of the totalitarian frying pan into the fire of banality— the second fundamental problem for art management.

Schiller talked about the drive to play that is rooted in the minds of little children. Bauhaus professor Kandinsky sought spirituality and Malevich made an icon of nihilism, but the wunderkind of academic art, Pablo Picasso, struggled—all the more so as he got older—to regain joyful childlike spontaneity in the creation of his art. The dadaists beatified the author Alfred Jarry as their apostle of childlike expression. Jarry's legendary monster, King Ubu, was created around 1890 as a satire on a teacher while Jarry was still at school. Nonsense and noise, confusion and drivel were the weapons of dadaism and of Jarry's own mock science, "pataphysics." It was a science of exception, in the spirit of which avant-garde artists praised puerile practical jokes and scandalous spontaneity. Jarry's hero, the childish tyrant Ubu, soon became the dadaist icon of modernity. Ubu was the inflated, abominable, infliction-obsessed spirit of torment who felt sorry for himself and remorselessly executed everyone who did not want him to become King of Poland.

Ubu has certain characteristics reminiscent of the idol of modern economics, the joyful entrepreneur, the troublemaker of a businessman who was supposed to create the economic foundations of a democratic society. He was a slob who picked his nose and caused trouble for profitable companies. John Maynard Keynes sees this modern managerial hero as a foolhardy explorer who heedlessly throws himself into risky, childish ventures.[41] Keynes contended that had an entrepreneur been capable of making mature calculations, he would never have dared set off on all his projects. He is the self-made man, as uneducated as a pesky youngster is. He has no money and cannot hold down a respectable job. In truth, he is neither a capitalist nor a worker. He belongs to a third middle class of economic agents situated precisely on what Schiller called the "point of nothingness" in the aesthetic play.

The more one reads of business entrepreneurs, the more one comes to think that Peter Pan and Pippi Longstocking will have to join business in order to escape growing up. Entrepreneurs are *puers,* rascals whose shameless destructive nature is defended by Joseph Schumpeter and other indulgent economists from the time of the early 1900s. In the chaos or mess they make, there is a powerful Schwung that gives birth to the profitable art called business.

No doubt the avant-garde generated entrepreneurial arrogance, boldness, and aggression. Its advocates speculated wildly in new art forms, many of which thrived in economic environments. After being rejected by the directors of public art galleries, Eduard Manet, Gustave Courbet, and Auguste Rodin displayed their work among industrial products at the World Exhibitions. The grand new department stores were equipped with show rooms and galleries. Even the managerial love of system and measurement can be found in avant-garde circles.

From 1910 on, the artists of Rue Lamarck and Rue Ravignan in Montmartre began experimenting with mathematical ideas of the fourth dimension. Fernand Leger, Marcel Duchamp, Juan Gris, Pablo Picasso, and Georges Braque were all fascinated by experiments in non-Euclidian geometry,[42] and Picasso and Braque discovered cubism through analytical speculation. They recycled newspaper clippings and commercial advertisements in their pictures, and posters and catalogues became artistic manna. By way of the collage, advertising teamed up with art. Marcel Duchamp signed and exhibited a bottle rack purchased from the still existent department store BHV. The ready-mades of Duchamp came out of childish pun but nevertheless today serve as a case for how utilitarian products get value-added branded by symbolic signature. Futurist Fortunato Depero designed typefaces for products. Sonia Delaunay's clock posters or Magritte's advertisements—sold to the press via his company *Studio Dongo*—are other examples of the proximity of avant-garde art to business. Industrious art historians have also uncovered a 1915 advertisement for a hair lotion made by the Bergman perfumery in Zurich; the name of the product was *dada*. Through Tristan Tzara's avant-garde movement this ad lives on—as art.

The avant-garde route to banality started as a revolt against frozen social forms and seriously boring academic totalitarianism. The Polish avant-garde writer Witold Gombrowicz, whose cult classic, the 1937 novel *Ferdydurke*, is a celebration of banal immaturity, perhaps best articulates this childish

spirit. To Gombrowicz, mature, academic pedantry is sheer totalitarian torture. Gravity makes people assume horrible masks. Form and style become
aesthetic prisons of collective terror. This global totalization of seriousness
robbed individuals of their individualism. The ego no longer belongs to a
person but is merely a socially warped snout, a grimace. To Gombrowicz,
there is no reasonable way out. If people fight totalization actively by critically analyzing it, the attention given to it will completely devour them. The
only way out is to capitulate to immaturity, to regress to childishness.

Gombrowicz himself preferred to associate with puerile youths in rowdy
cafés. He avoided anything mature, anything accomplished. He liked to play
chess, as Duchamp did. He also liked young, irresponsible boys. He hated
real artists and Art with a capital *A*. Spontaneity was the only salvation.

When the war broke out, Gombrowicz jumped off a ship in Argentina. A
socially deformed person can only save himself and adopt an impulsive, irrational lifestyle if, accidentally:

> on leaving his study, he chanced on a child, an adolescent, a girl,
> or a semi-cultivated person, he would cease to find him or her
> boring, and no longer pat these people protectively, didactically,
> and pedagogically on the back while talking down to them in a
> superior manner; on the contrary, in a holy fit of trembling he
> would start groaning and roaring, and would perhaps even fall
> on his knees before them. Instead of shunning immaturity and
> shutting himself off in what are called coteries, he would realize
> that a truly universal style is a style born slowly and gradually in
> contact with human beings of different social conditions, age,
> education, and stages of development.[43]

Childishness becomes a hope of escaping the struc-
tural prison by accident. Sigmund Freud pointed out
that the *puer* humans worship is actually not a real
child; it is rather a Dionysian creature wrapped in the
myth of the lost power of fantasy, of bodies and their
suppressed sexuality, of passions and lust, of suppressed
and silenced pain. Picasso, the world-renowned adherent of childishness, pointed out that he was not seeking
maturity but existence. "I am astonished at how people
misuse the term development; I do not develop—I am," he exclaimed.

Having tried to escape state totalitarianism, the grown-up plays at being a child and risks ending up in a corporate prison of banality. Corporate culture of the West has often been declared "infantocratic."[44] Childish enthusiasm is the key to corporate careers. The infantile manager throws himself into one project after another with the same immense appetite. An infant has no memory, however. Business infants dress themselves in their ridiculous brand-embossed company caps and join in the singing at company events. Their faces light up as soon as they hear words like *ice cream, options,* or *profit.* This is what is termed the experience or entertainment economy. Working life Disney-style means everyone has a part to play; everyone is cast for the events. No one merely works anymore. There are no parents, just bosses, who are more violently infantile and who bully the other kids. Leering foolishly, they play doctors and nurses with the girls at conventions. Today King Ubu forgets about becoming king of Poland; instead he aspires to be CEO. For super-infants, there are said to be discrete "infantilist shops" in all the major business centers, where you can buy rompers and nappies for adults.[45] Business infants behave foolishly in the office and squabble in board meetings, but they can also freak out in their desperation at the illusion of the play; they have to watch because their playmates might swap their toys for real serial-killing guns; they might swap fun for freaked-out hostile takeovers.

The infantile jungle of the New York economic world inspired Andy Warhol to make his art work as a continuous celebrity campaign. Half a century earlier, Duchamp had moved from Paris to New York, where he admired the adventurous rascals of economic enterprises. Maybe those *puers* inspired Duchamp to quit art, start playing chess full-time, and become leisure artists without art work. Warhol completed Duchamp's project to dissolve art in the aesthetic play. He exhibited cans of soup and packets of soap powder. His art became a celebration of consumption; it became *business art.* Warhol and other pop artists worked like disciplined salesmen, producing their own durables out of everyday supermarket products.

The avant-garde in this tradition becomes increasingly focused on social organization, what sociologist Howard Becker calls art worlds.[46] The case of my friend Rick is an illustration of one of these unique art worlds. Rick went to an English art college, where he met Jeff, who was then working on his dissertation in philosophy. Over time, Jeff has written long essays in the catalogues for Rick's shows. Wherever Rick happens to be, Jeff sends him essays and books he thinks Rick might be interested in. At the moment, Rick is in Australia, where he has moved with his girlfriend. Here Rick has met Bud, an art critic, and Don, who is involved in aesthetic research.

Rick originally lived in New York and had several shows there. After a gallery owner whom he met died, he moved to Paris and was about to move to Berlin with an "interesting" woman who kept him awake at night and out of bars during the day. At least he was sober.

Rick had no driver's license and drove around rubbish dumps in an uninsured car bought from the earnings of his recent show. Seventy percent of what he received went toward the catalogue, and the rest was spent on other costs. The rusty car was all he could get with what was left. He could not afford paints or canvases. The rent on his studio was overdue, and gallery owners were taking advantage of him. Perhaps he could have sold some of his stuff, but he did not really want to. What he did want was to put on more shows.

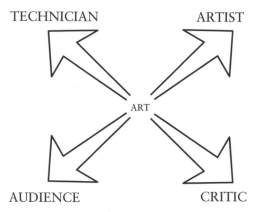

The Big Banality Bang

Rick's stuff is short-lived. It is recorded in catalogues, on slides, and in videos of his best performances. Without a penny, he set up the latest one at one of the city's best galleries. Together with Bud, he persuaded gallery owners to show the opening live on television. Since Bud invited Jeff to give a talk at the opening, he was on television as well. Rick's girlfriends dressed up in black and white and simulated an embassy party.

Everything hung by a very fine thread. The television company could have backed out, the technicians could have gotten bored, the people on the art scene might not even have turned up, and the gallery owner might not have let them use his facilities. Amazingly, however, everything worked out fine, and the next day Rick moved on to his next project.

Smiling, joking, fixing, phoning, smoking, drinking, grabbing every opportunity, Rick moves on. All day long, he organizes his own art world, taking a breathless journey in a rusty, uninsured car with no driver's license and gasoline on credit. The slightest mistake, the slightest wrong move, and it could all collapse. The German artist Joseph Beuys understood this vulnerability when he said that architecture, sculpture, painting, music, poetry, and dance were classical forms of art, but we today sculpt social organizations. The extended definition of art does not only apply to the traditional activities of artists; an expanded definition of art is itself a vehicle moving toward change.[47]

Such aesthetic plays are indeed fragile. Rick used to talk a lot about the painter Jean-Michel Basquiat, a Warhol discovery who died of an overdose. The threat of collapse and disappearance into pure banality become a constant part of these worlds. Rick, for example, finally ended up some kind of art dealer!

In Warhol's ghostwritten diaries are encountered a nirvana of superficiality, drunken and camp vacuity, and cocktail gossip.[48] It is an everlasting ringing of telephones, a constant stream of taxi receipts—all of it banality carefully accounted for. The infantile artist's total emptiness is manifested in Candy Andy's surgically enhanced glowing face/façade, in a hollow Barbie body floating around the culture clubs of Manhattan, as an autistic kitsch plankton swimming in the sewer of business aquariums. These artists are passive observers of a lifelong navel-gazing project. Art is out of work. It has exploded, delivering no content . . . only contexts, gossip, and relations.

Such is the problem of banality. The *artist* is nothing more than a topic of conversation. The *critic* is a gossip columnist, the *audience* is made up of narcissists, and the *technician* is an event marketer. Everyone talks about everyone else. Anyone who can have an exhibition catalogue printed is an artist. The emptier the gallery, the thicker the catalogue. The absence of art turns aesthetic plays into society games. Nobody cares for art, but everyone speaks of culture. In this superficial dream society, the sociology of storytelling supplants aesthetic philosophy. In the big banality bang, art has exploded and then evaporated so that only the organizational context remains. Who cares if the emperor is naked anyway?

# 4

## Metaphysics—Marketing of Art Firms

### Schopenhauer's Business of Being

Once Richard Wagner set up Bayreuth, Nietzsche's take on the operation was that aesthetic play had turned into playing at aesthetics. When he was forced to acknowledge that Wagner was actually managing his art settlement like a business, the admission totally unnerved him. Further, the better Wagner's business went, the more contrary Nietzsche became. He dreamed of art as complete spontaneity and could never accept that it might require management, what he called "transcendental counterfeit" or "theatrocratic bluff," to make art work.

In contemporary culture, the encroachment of business into areas of art and aesthetics is readily apparent as marketers feature Picasso promoting cars and computers, Louise Bourgeois advertising designer chairs, and David Bowie playing the part of Andy Warhol on the silver screen. Art has been fused with commercial reality, and the art firm, today's bastard child of Greek tragedy, is obviously here to stay.

Europe was well prepared for the art-firm market, because philosophers from Kant to Dewey had constructed the conceptual foundation necessary for this type of business operating as a Gadamerian aesthetic play in an art firm.

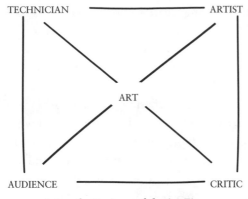

*Art as the Business of the Art Firm*

The special competence of art-firm players is to make art work in a philosophical way that implies more than just a vague idea that business can perhaps have something to do with aesthetics.

Since the 1700s, when Adam Smith introduced his economic theory, business has been understood as focused on detecting, triggering, and meeting demand for goods and services. Demand, in the political economy tradition of moral philosophy, represents the natural need for reasonable and useful goods. The value of goods and services is explained as either the amount of work put into its manufacture (the so-called labor value theory of physiocrats and later Marxians) or the usefulness perceived by the individual buyer (the theory of subjective value launched by Scottish philosophers such as Smith). These two dominant economic theories claim that value exchanged for money in markets is rooted in either the objective production process or the subjective buyer judgment. The art firm realizes a potential third way of determining value: a philosophical aesthetic way.

According to business historians, much early industrialization resulted from unexpected booms in the market for frivolous things, including fashionable garments and playful toys. Smith's *Theory of Moral Sentiments*, published in 1759, sets in place the philosophical footing for his treatise on *The Wealth of Nations,* which appeared in 1776. Luxury markets blossom, concludes Smith, because "[w]e are . . . charmed with the beauty of that accommodation which reigns in the palaces and economy of the great; and admire how every thing is adapted to promote their ease, to prevent their wants, to gratify their wishes, and to amuse and entertain their most frivolous desires."[1] Smith realized that what actually made up the "wealth of nations" was something other than harsh physical realities and sensible utilities. The something that made the manufacturers and workshops tick had to do with "charm" and "beauty," and in the long run it did more than just explain the demand for private goods. Smith further contends that "the same principle, the same love of system, the same regard to the beauty of order, of art and contrivance, frequently serves to recommend those institutions which tend to promote public welfare. . . . They make part of the great system of government, and the wheels of political machines seem to move with more harmony and ease by means of them."[2]

This contention—that desire for beauty and charm motivates the modern consumer as well as the modern citizen—begs the determination of what kind of value awakens this desire. Smith avoids trying to make the determination, instead suggesting that "it" has to do with something grand and important; but his "pleasure principle" is hardly presented as a third alternative! His use of the word *machines* in the explanation perhaps indicates why he failed to follow up on this interesting intuition, since a mechanistic outlook derailed his trip up the philosophical track.

Smith admired Newton's new science and wanted to formulate his own social mechanics of human behavior. Newton's mechanics offered explanation for patterns in the planetary system, and Smith wanted to present explanation for the patterns in mankind's worldly affairs. Ever since, the Newtonian ideal has marked Anglo-Saxon economic approaches to modernity. Using a price mechanism to measure the value of goods that attract consumers is Newtonian, and Newtonian social theory defines the value of human beings in terms of the approval of their actions by their fellow men.

To replicate the way that Newtonian markets are value mechanisms for goods, Smith began looking at communities as similar value mechanisms for human action. Newton's world is a vanity fair where values emerge through clever exchange in economic transactions and social interactions. Newtonian values are always relative; to a Newtonian, absolute value is a recondite area that bears close watching. To be sure, in the Newtonian tradition, deeper causes are never the business of the modern social scientist or economist.

Smith never denied the importance of absolutes, but in the Newtonian tradition he refrained from including them in scientific analysis. Causes were, as Newton pointed out, "occult qualities supposed from the specific forms," with which science, occupied only with stating "active principles" and "general laws," should not bother. Absolutes had to do with the "man within," an individual's moral compass, or the "natural price" of wares that was a deeply rooted intrinsic value that science had only to accept while explaining the market price that was relevant to other goods.

In other words, modern scientific man should then stay away from metaphysics, since Newtonians do not allow a third aesthetic realm placed between the object and the subject. Kant, the founder of aesthetic philosophy, questioned David Hume, a person he otherwise admired, about his Newtonian blindness toward a deeper philosophy. Hume's friend Adam Smith offered no explanation either. Skepticism about absolute causes and deeper reasons unfortunately also blocked the way to aesthetic philosophy for the majority of Newtonians. This is why Anglo-Saxon economics and social sciences realize the importance of beauty, without ever embarking on the philosophy of aesthetics.

On the continent, meanwhile, the work of Arthur Schopenhauer (1788–1860), Nietzsche's and Wagner's management professor, provides this missing link between philosophy and worldly affairs as business. Schopenhauer held that the most important demand rests on desire not for material pleasure or social approval but for the real philosophy of metaphysics. Schopenhauer was born into a wealthy Hamburg merchant family; he was even christened Arthur because the name seemed international and well suited to a successful trader. Arthur's career path was supposed to have led to taking over his father's business; contrary to expectations, however, though Arthur began in business he ended up in philosophy.

Schopenhauer was born into a Schillerian tension of opposite poles. His father was a businessman, very focused on matters of fact, and mother was an art lover, fond of form and fiction. As a boy, Schopenhauer felt a passion for art, especially theater, but this desire was difficult to satisfy in the business environment of Hamburg. To add to his plight, his mother thought him such a drag that she never welcomed him in witty Weimar for long periods.[3] After enduring an accounting class to pacify his father and enjoying an all-expense-paid trip to Italy, courtesy of his father, Schopenhauer made up his mind to devote his life to philosophy.

Schopenhauer made his decision driven by a desire to reflect upon Kant's already immensely popular Enlightenment philosophy. Kant had circulated the fascinating idea that modern man must himself shape his world from a mix of the two poles of his being: the physical and natural Homo phenomenon and the morally responsible and cultural Homo noumenon. Kant's critical philosophy was not the usual diet of desiccated fare; he did not believe in cementing eternal and divine truths. Kant offered emancipation through reflection upon an individual's own world-making capabilities.

By the time Schopenhauer began his career as a philosopher, the Kantian torch had been picked up by Kant's pupil Fichte, who lured Schopenhauer away from Göttingen in 1811 to attend instead the new Berlin University. There Schopenhauer had an unpleasant Fichte experience similar to Schelling's. Fichte's lectures were immensely popular academic shows; his auditorium really amounted to a lecture theater. Thus instead of finding a philosopher in search of truth, Schopenhauer encountered an edutainment star striving only to market himself by scandal (*"Aufsehen zur Beförderung seiner persönlichen Zweche).*"[4] The university had become a theater dominated by the stardom of a public professor who swept the philosophical question of world making under the carpet. In the process, Fichte confused and abused Kant's popularity by dressing it in the vulgar entertainment Schopenhauer condemned as "Hokuspokus" and "Wischiwaschi" triviality.

What especially irritated Schopenhauer, who knew his Kant verbatim, was that Fichte, the academic stage-strutter, promoted his career by claiming the world springs out of subjectivity.[5] Never could it be said that Kant advocated such a subjective value theory. He was hardly a virtual reality guru; he was never a pure idealist of the Bishop Berkeley sort,[6] and nothing in his writings could support a view of the world as an anarchistic castle in the air of individual fancy. Unfortunately, Fichte's subjectivist misinterpretation of Kant would soon serve as the "starting point for the even worse insanity of the clumsy and unspiritual Hegel."[7] Whereas Fichte overemphasized the subject and its forms of thought, Hegel swung to the opposite objectivistic position.

Hegel acquired Fichte's Berlin professorship in 1818, at the time when young Dr. Schopenhauer was working on *Die Welt als Wille und Vorstellung* (The World as Will and Idea). Few people came to Schopenhauer's Berlin public lectures, since a neighboring hall was crammed with students preferring to listen to their idol, Professor Hegel. Hegel was an advisor to the Prussian government, and his "philosophy of reason" was politically correct for young bureaucratic upstarts. Schopenhauer shared Schelling's view on Hegelianism as a form of rationalism pretending to grasp existence by means of concepts. In the Kantian tradition, however, Schopenhauer held that the real world cannot be conceived in concepts.[8] Concepts are only words used to cement social constructs such as corporations and bureaucracies, which survive thanks to linguistic discourses and rational planning. Concepts make up organizational order by means of convention and habit, because they take on meaning only by association when a signifier is hooked up to the signified. Conceptualizations are political tools of sophists, who let associated meanings drift together in metaphors. All this is good for administrative science and may work temporarily, but it should not be mistaken for real philosophy; it does not contain essential knowledge since it is entirely rooted in cognition by learned association. Such a metaphor connects words already familiar with things that are known in themselves. Conceptualization helps transfer old ideas to new places without ever seriously exploring them.

In other words, Schopenhauer did not regard associative discursive learning as real truth making. Since the conceptual language developed in Hegel's philosophy seemed to provide Prussian bureaucrats with the managerial jargon they needed, if it had any value at all, according to Schopenhauer, it helped organize the state. Hegel escaped the great existential questions by reducing philosophy to discussing the world in historical terms of times, epochs, phases, and stages, all of which provided Prussians, as they would later Marxians, with a common, seemingly solid ideology allowing states, parties, or classes to interact.

Looking to their future, Berlin students saw Hegel as a positive factor in reaching their career goals, much the same way students today attend business school in order to make a career rather than to search for truth. Hegel's jargon, similar to that used by any good contemporary management consultant, facilitated organizational processes such as *Durchführung* (execution of actions), *Bewahrung* (registration of decisions), *Vorhalten* (fixation of principles), and *Widerstand* (resisted spontaneous actions that might threaten public order). Unfortunately, while it acquired political correctness, the true Kantian spirit of philosophy became hopelessly lost in Fichtean-Hegelian degeneration. Real philosophy had to be rediscovered!

Schopenhauer deplored the fact that Hegel's philosophy of history had been reduced to storytelling mounted on a treadmill of endless questions such as *when?* and *why?* A real philosopher would only ask *what?*[9] Schopenhauer was not alone in his criticism, either. Plato himself realized this universal risk to real philosophy, and Plato's dialogues were themselves an ingenious strategy to avoid reducing philosophy to a grand narrative. The dialogues were designed to frustrate anyone seeking fluent answers, those answers where causes in the past and effects in the future are nicely threaded onto a string, like fine pearls. Schopenhauer maintained that the important thing is not what is to come or what has been, but rather *being* and *presence* in the world. The true philosopher should not care as much about the *why*—causes and effects so dear to Newtonians—as about the *when*—problems central to Hegelians. The main task for real philosophy is to point at the source, the "*Quelle*,"[10] of aesthetic energy for desire-driven actions.

## Aesthetic Production—
## Embodying the Thing-in-Itself

To Smith, the Presbyterian minister turned Newtonian, the increasing roles of beauty and charm made room for individual subjective feelings in modern society. Kant's aesthetics, however, claimed that when art was made to work, modernity became objectively conceivable although explicit concepts were lacking. Schopenhauer offers further precision. For him, aesthetic modernity is strictly a business of being. As a young man, he had Dionysian aesthetic experiences, and it is no wonder that the young Nietzsche was grateful to Schopenhauer, whom he idolized as much as he had Wagner, for teaching him the philosophical objective implications of subjective ecstatic feelings.[11]

In manufacturing his own interpretation of Kant, the one he missed so much at the university, Schopenhauer located the Dionysian source of aesthetic energy between the sensual and reasonable to the Schillerian aesthetic play between form and matter.[12] The world is real as the product of sensual and sound world making, far from the Fichtean virtuality of an "insubstantial dream" (*wesenloser Traum*) or the Hegelian "ghostly abstraction" (*gespensterhaftes Luftgebilde*).[13] The moment of truth, when the objective essence of being is subjectively experienced, fills man with energy; it is aesthetically attractive and desirable. Herein lies the answer to the question of what aesthetic value is. It is what makes the world real. This metaphysical manufacturing process operates so that "these images do not drift past us, entirely alien and meaningless, as they must otherwise do, but speak to us directly, are understood, and acquire an interest which involves our whole being."[14]

Schopenhauer's 1819 treatise *The World as Will and Idea* focused on this manufacturing process. Kant had minted a term for the essence of the world: *das Ding an Sich,* or the thing in itself. The world exists, as common things do. Existence might, however, seem virtual and imaginary since its essence, *the world in itself,* can never be known from within. Schopenhauer now added what he considered to be his own great philosophical contribution to what Kant had claimed. How could a thing in itself, the essence of being, be so touching? How can it convince anyone of its concrete reality? It certainly did not signal its existence from outside or gain its reality through some hypnotic brainwashing! No, reality touches humans directly, immediately, without any mediating filtering by cognition or perception.

Unfortunately, says Schopenhauer, Kant overlooked the precise way in which humans make their world real. Kant simply forgot that no philosophy, no world making, is possible without the philosopher's own inner direct experience in the only existential *Ding an Sich* ever attainable to human beings, their own embodied life. Kant forgot himself as an embodied living being. One reason for this oversight may be that Kant was eager to install Homo sapiens in a divine category of reason, totally removed from the animals. Schopenhauer conceded that humans differed from the lower beasts because although an individual's head (*Kopf*) was physiologically connected to the bottom (*Rumpf*), it was still separate.[15] On the other hand, this was no reason to join rationalist philosophers who regarded the human being as an eggheaded "winged cherub without a body."[16] Without a body, of course, no one could ever experience the world as being, not even Professor Immanuel Kant from Königsberg.

The discovery of the importance of the body for modern metaphysics determined not only Schopenhauer's philosophy but also, through it, the European market for art as a market for metaphysics. The transcendent experience of the world was directly incorporated and incarnated in human life. As such, it became the business of aesthetic experience that philosophy could only understand if it accepted this fundamental embodiment.

After Hegel, however, such real philosophy was no longer taught in universities, and this change may well explain why Schelling's Berlin lectures failed. Modern metaphysics after Hegel and Newton had to be supplied by art firms instead of academia. Art firm production is equal to philosophizing by this mix of mind and body that forms a third aesthetics entity beyond material observation and mental thought. This aesthetic entity to Schopenhauer is the gateway to "knowledge of quite a special kind"[17] ("*Erkenntnis ganz eigener Ar*")[18] of the thing in itself he called the *Will.*

Schopenhauer saw bodies as the objectification of will and illustrated the incarnation with animals, plants, and stones to show how physical elements such as teeth, extremities, or genitals are extensions of this will. At the top of the pyramid of life is the jewel of creation: man, with his ability to reason. It is here that the triumph of will is most evident.

No doubt Schopenhauer's concept of will has little to do with the intention or desire usually thought of in connection with the word. The will, as he conceives it, cannot be regarded as an inner cause for outer effect in the Newtonian mode. To Schopenhauer, individuals are, for instance, the subjective tenants of the bodily "Will of the World," and at this point his Eastern inspiration glimmers. As a youth, he was influenced by the Indian imports of the German Romantics, and each evening, when he was an old man, he would read extracts of the books of his youth.

Hinduism gave a balance to Kant's finely tuned analysis of rational philosophy. By combining Hindu cosmology with Plato's philosophy, Schopenhauer sought to create an antidote to the academic, bureaucratic buffoonery of Berlin. Indian philosophy explored a world in which man dwells, yet simultaneously the world dwells in man as well. Bodily life is the key to such knowledge. Kant ought himself to have realized that his own body was his immediate source of knowledge of the thing in itself. This immediate corporeal knowledge, unthinkable for philosophers fixated upon the intellect only, was what Schopenhauer called the will. When a human being moves, he or she is immediately conscious of the fact that the body and the will are one and the same phenomenon. To those who lack this wisdom, the world turns to a dualism of either matter or form. Schopenhauer was sure that for these people the world loses its glow, aura, and attraction. The world ceases to be when art ceases to work. The experience of will is an aesthetic one and therefore works, as Kant pointed out, without concepts and logics. It has more to do with insight than knowledge, and this permits understanding of why Schopenhauer concentrated on vision even as intellectuals in Berlin focused on thinking.

Schopenhauer had special meaning for the terms intuition and insight. The former, *Anschauung,* was highly regarded by followers of Johann Wolfgang Goethe in Weimar; Schopenhauer's mother, Johanna, had introduced her gifted son[19] to these thinkers. Goethe, who had been decorated with the French Légion d'honneur, cultivated *le bel esprit* in the tradition of the best French salons. In Weimar, just as in Versailles, weighty conversation was conducted with an elegant lightness of touch. Pedants and bookworms were excluded, because authentic knowledge presupposed a receptive spirit of playfulness. True knowledge was defined by the verb *savoir,* a French mixture of feeling and intuition.[20] In Goethe's Weimar, delicacy and elegance—and no dry theoretical reasoning—were incorporated in his salon. Here Schopenhauer encountered the antithesis of the arrogant Hegelianism that he would later ridicule in the biting irony and elegant sarcasm also so characteristic of the aphorisms of his receptive disciple Nietzsche.

Goethe had read Schopenhauer's dissertation and paid particular attention to a section about color theory. In 1813, the men began a scientific dialogue and conducted optical experiments together. Both were motivated by the desire to falsify Newton's findings on the subject of vision. Three years earlier, Goethe had published his own work on the theory of colors. In it he launched a polemical attack on Newton's theory that colors had their origin in light. Goethe believed that color did not come from the outside, from light alone. Color was the result of a creative dialogue between light and the eye, a possibility altogether overlooked by Newton, who preferred to keep inner cause out of science. Goethe speculated that Newton might have meant the eye sees forms that are then colored by the spectrum of light, but this would have meant that humans simply impart reason and formal thinking to the colorful "mess" of nature. If this were Newton's theory, Goethe thought him mistaken, for even though it might sound strange, the eye cannot perceive forms.[21] Goethe's eye did not register forms or shapes but merely perceived objects through light, shadow, and color (*Hell, Dunkel, und Farbe*), constituting only the act of perception; seeing had to be explained in a much more profound way, making use of art.

According to Goethe, mere light ought not be confused with the design or depiction of insight. The latter is closer to painting: "And so we construct the visible world from these three [light, shadow, and color] and, through this, make it possible for the painting on the canvas to present a visual world that is far more complete than the real one."[22] For Goethe, insight was an act of painting that showed nature far better than Newtonian light alone could account for. He made no distinction between man and nature, since man was a part of nature. Newton's scientific system of optics, in which external rays of light cause the perception of color within the eye, amputates part of the natural system. Goethe developed an intricate theory of how external light stimulates the inner, organic development of the eye. External light and human sight developed in tandem, so that "an inner light meets the external."[23] Thus he transformed what Newton considered a scientific physical optical effect into an aesthetic act.

Goethe could not definitely prove that he was right, but he used the paintings of the masters for support. Schopenhauer, like Goethe, believed that not even the most theoretical truth could be formally proven true. Truth is itself a matter of insight, of vision; even Euclid's geometry is based upon insight, though translated into the logical jargon of formal proof in order to diffuse its absolute truth and communicate the insight.[24] Scientific discourse and its formulas are like words; they are empty containers that have to be filled with content. Therefore, the communication of truth, its diffusion to others, should not be interpreted as the production of absolute truth.

## Aesthetic Consumption— Contemplating the Thing-in-Itself

Goethe himself had traveled to Italy, the home of light and painting, in an attempt to capture truth on canvas. Then, after several unsuccessful attempts to become a painter, he returned to his northern home to write about vision instead of trying to paint it. For Newtonians, who accepted only formal proof, the result was another beautiful text totally lacking scientific value. On the other hand, to the two fellows in Weimar the fact that art works was indication enough of its value as truth. Before their paths diverged, Goethe gave Schopenhauer authoritative support for his belief that intuition was superior to thought in making the world as will and idea.

In German, *Vorstellung* is much better translated into the theatrically flavored word "representation" than "idea." Schopenhauer lost faith in universities where professors wasted time and energy communicating proof instead of showing how truth came about. While scolding the limitations of academic philosophy, he pointed to the immense possibilities of existential philosophy, the market in which art firms had an outstanding opportunity to carry out the Kantian philosophical legacy. The Berlin of the 1820s, where he had failed to attract an audience, was a place of talentless spectacle. The New Berlin University quickly developed into a popular vocational school for students eager for a career and more interested in café society and well-paying jobs than in the Kantian thing-in-itself. Hegel loudly proclaimed the death of art and used his lectures to praise not aesthetic energy but political power built upon reason. This, Schopenhauer derided as pure nonsensical idealism.[25] His inability to attract a crowd was symptomatic of a time when, during the day, state professors would lecture in the universities and, in the evenings, the same crowd would flock to see cheap melodramas and vulgar burlesques in the theaters.

Schopenhauer believed that public education had degenerated into dry formalism and complacent materialism. A man of means, he was not dependent on a state university position. Fulminating against the masses and the career bureaucrats, he retreated in semiretirement to Frankfurt-am-Main. In the morning he would read *The Times* and then write. After a little music, he would dine at his table in the *Englischer Hof.* Then, following a visit to the theater, he would get into bed with a book of Vedic philosophy.

When religion lost its power, science was reduced to bad Newtonianism, and universities were converted to cadre schools for Hegelian formalists. To Schopenhauer, the only way of philosophizing that remained was art, so he argued for the transformation of Kant's all-too-logical workshop into a philosophical artist's studio. As for himself, all he wanted to be was an independent philosopher-artist whose research would work "like a beautiful, living painting with correct lighting and shadows, controlled tone, accomplished harmony of colors; against which the efforts of academics will seem like a great palette full of bright colors, ordered systematically but still without harmony, context or meaning."[26]

True enlightenment could never survive without reflection on being, without metaphysics, without true philosophy. The contemporary philosopher loyal to her calling simply has to escape academies and take refuge in art. She is an artist that represents the will by making art work as objectification of that same will. The Hegels and the Newtons have hopelessly polluted the everyday world with false philosophy and simplistic science. In India, there might still be a place for gurus and sadhus; in Western modernity, little room is left for the spontaneous and free philosophizing so characteristic of ancient Greece and the banks of the Ganges.

Modern men and women, the *Fabriksware der Natur,* a standardized product[27] programmed by causal and conceptual thinking, need intensive care to again become human. It is the artists who administer the intensive care that awakens the lust for absolute platonic ideas. In the West, only art can liberate mankind from this enslavement of the will, this *Sklavendienst des Willens*.[28] The sole therapy is to regain wisdom by contemplating the will in the form of art. This is the consumption of art that art firms cater to.

This reasoning displays Schopenhauer's conclusion that the modern business of art is philosophical. The new philosophers are artists producing art for the aesthetic consumption called contemplation. The holy men and sadhus of India were masters in the art of such contemplation. In Europe, the modern explorers of will were instead the artists, geniuses whose entire consciousness was filled by the will, according to Schopenhauer. In modern Europe, only artists can mirror the will as a "pure subject of knowing,"[29] *"reines Subjekt des Erkennens."*[30] Art works as a representation that "repeats or reproduces the eternal Ideas grasped through pure contemplation. Ideas are the essential and abiding element in the phenomena of the world; and accordingly to the material in which it reproduces, it is sculpture, painting, poetry or music. Its one source is knowledge of Ideas; its one main aim the communication of this knowledge."[31]

Finally, Schopenhauer embarks on a criticism of art from the standpoint of its ability to provide pure contemplative food, an art cleansed of cognitive or sensuous distortions, an art that can brings humans back to the third realm. Art can be made to work on the huge market for play and metaphysics left empty after logic and science have retreated to their respective realms of form and matter. True masterpieces, he notes, possess the remarkable ability to liberate those who were enslaved by causality of the will.

Beauty makes individuals forget both time and space; they become mere subjects of knowledge, unaware of will, pain, or even time. Sublimity achieved its aesthetic effect through the element of surprise. Contemplation now needed to be carefully prepared to avoid anything that could cause sensual stimulation. In Schopenhauer's view, art genre and form possessed its own capacity to embody ideas. The art best suited for philosophizing had to be carefully selected and singled out from other pieces having too much cognitive form or sensuous matter to provide good metaphysical material.

In Schopenhauer's view, disparate artistic forms possessed their own capacity to embody ideas. Paintings therefore ought not show nakedness or filled goblets, things that might summon baser instincts in the viewer. At the most, a flower or fruit could be used. The stone of a building could, by way of its construction techniques, embody ideas of weight, solidity, height, and light. The wealth of ideas within the architecture or construction was, how-

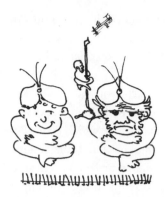

ever, supplanted by the building's overall functionalism as a useful object. Paintings of landscapes, animals, and portraits were, then, better vehicles to carry ideas and ideals than houses. If the painter toned down the temporal and spatial aspects of the costumes and décor in the work and instead concentrated on presenting universal themes, a medium of purer contemplation could also be offered. Schopenhauer suggested, for example, that Flemish painting, with its predisposition toward simple, everyday environments, often had high philosophical value.

The purpose of art was to encourage contemplation through the conscious representation of ideas. Processes of thought and conceptual analysis might block contemplation. According to Schopenhauer, a poet who used allegories, for example, was engaged in a process of conceptualization that had little to offer philosophical art, since allegories were symbols cognitively associated with something other than the thing itself. The value of such artists as Poussin and Correggio lay not in their allegorical use of symbols but in the picture itself they created. Symbols were conceptualized hieroglyphs and lacked the capacity to transmit ideas or encourage contemplative reflection.[32] Schopenhauer therefore wanted to remove anything connected with conceptualization, reason, and nominalism from art. Anything connected with language belonged to abstract thought; reflection could only be stimulated by images. Further, this became more complicated when the symbols were visual, as happened when laurel leaves symbolized honor, the cross Christianity, and the palm leaf victory. The meaning of such symbols depended upon conventions and common agreements that connected the signifier with the signified; aesthetic value and reflection had nothing to do with symbolism of this sort.

Although visual art may have had its origins beyond conceptualization, this could not be the case with poetry, whose materials were merely words. Despite this, a poet could attempt to use images as an illustration, claimed Schopenhauer. Cervantes describes sleep as "a mantle to cover man," Swift conjured up fantastic imagery in *Gulliver's Travels,* and Plato himself uses the cave as an image for purely abstract thought. A poet escaped rational philosophy, and a gifted historian such as Schiller avoided the constraints of causal chronology because they knew how to "precipitate, as it were, the concrete, the individual, the perceptible idea, out of the abstract and transparent universality of the concepts."[33]

When properly used, both language and visual art could be cleansed of this abstract conceptualization. This was what happened when a text was read out loud, or a song sung. Singing was the means by which lyrics became part of general human experience, and choral works and folk singing produced aesthetic value as a result. Poetry became an artistic representation when it was performed as drama on stage, because the dramatization of tragedy presented sorrow without recourse to symbolism as the universality of fate was depicted upon the stage.

Schopenhauer believed music to be the superior art form; it depended on neither words nor images. Composers possessed the gift of transmitting wisdom untainted by reason and intellectualization. An inspired composer was like a sleepwalker venturing into the aesthetic realm of the thing in itself. Music, in contrast to other forms of art, was not a repetition or a representation of an idea as it was seen by a contemplative genius. Music was not an idea of the will; it *was* the will, according to Schopenhauer's lyrical thesis. Musical harmony *was* organic nature. Melody *was* the development of ideas. This art was absolute and immediate—perfect for modern metaphysicians!

An art firm was a metaphysical theater where art was staged and presented for philosophical purposes by sweeping the disturbing detritus of formal thought and material senses from the representational stage. Only then could Plato's ideas become real. A common misinterpretation of Plato, according to Schopenhauer, suggested that Plato thought little of art as philosophy.[34] Plato wrote that a carpenter was acting honorably in creating a table, but that an artist who then made a painting of the table was an illusionist and deceiver, for how could a painting of a table claim to be a table? Schopenhauer asserted that the purpose of modern immediate art was not to represent tables, beds, or other material things. Art should reveal ideas, by making the invisible visible. Schopenhauer pointed out that what Plato called a "table" was a generally accepted description, another simple word in the relative commerce of communication, an abstract conceptualization working as packaging, and therefore in itself not an idea at all.[35] Using the term *table* just puts a tag or label on a hidden absolute value, the table as viewed by the artist. In actuality, Plato was probably merely dismissing false conceptual artists and not those artist-philosophers who represented ideas of the will. Plato scolded those who lured poor hungry birds to peck the grapes on a painting, and Homer, who pretends to give rational advice to politicians through poetry. Schopenhauer seems certain that if Plato were here today, he would attack methodical scientists and analytical language philosophers, not true artists. Had he lived in modern times, Plato would rather have placed the artists at the top of his system, craftsmen in the middle, and academic analytical philosophers simply trading and bartering with empty concepts on the lowest step of the ladder of truth, since will is revealed by consuming art in contemplation.

The person who begins contemplating soon becomes so inspired as to stop running after material things and formal social recognition. Form and matter become secondary; what is central in art is the content in between. Schopenhauer had high hopes for a modern business of being, where art firms undertake aesthetic embodiment and contemplation. This would make even the great Plato grateful to all art managers for making art work as the "unconscious exercise in metaphysics in which the mind does not know that it is philosophizing."[36]

# 5

## Avant-Garde Enterprises

### Cases of Aesthetic Management

#### Wagner's Bayreuth Brand

Richard Wagner (1813–1883) grew tired of the banality of operatic show biz. He had been a conductor long enough to observe that most singers were virtuosos for hire, glad to shoot for high C as long as they were paid enough to do it. He publicly deplored the fact that spectacular *Opernklingklang* no longer served the Greek muses but was instead attendant to Mercury, the Roman god of thieves and merchants. As far as he was concerned, "The public art of Greece was real art, whereas [contemporary art was] an artificial craft."[1] Stages were factories of skilled technicians trying to outdo each other with special effects. It was as if the artists and the critics had dropped out of the aesthetic play, and now only technicians and audience counted at all. A strategic plan, inspired by Schopenhauer, motivated Wagner to come up with his own art brand, called Bayreuth. His mission statement for the project: to search for improved metaphysical excellence.

Instead of quality, a reign of quantitative productivity resulted in an *Alltagstheater,* a humdrum production where each audience expected some flashy new offering for its enjoyment. Participation in this entertainment-by-demand was the price the actor or singer paid to become employed by a rich duke's mass-producing repertory company. In only a few exceptions, such as

110

at the court theater of the Duke of Sachsen-Meiningen, was an attempt made to improve quality by strict discipline and almost military planning. In the vast majority of cases, spectacular companies lacked any type of quality management.

Wagner allied himself with a notable crowd of critics, including E.T.A. Hoffman, Franz Liszt, and Carl Maria von Weber, people who also realized that organizational change was needed in theaters to make art work again. As they sought to bring about a rebirth of aesthetic plays, their critical analysis focused on managerial issues. Art was dead in spectacular show biz, Wagner proclaimed in 1851; technological innovations in special stage effects had been abused in the hunt for audience approval.[2]

Richard Wagner knew his theater industry inside out. As a conductor in Riga and Dresden, he had struggled against the feudal routines and indolence of run-down court theaters. As a young idealist, he had been deeply disappointed in most of the theatrical experience enterprises he encountered, because they were often slovenly productions, mere conveyor-belt presentations of imported goods. The majority of foreign operas were performed in poor translations and sloppy adaptations from the French or Italian. When musicians and singers were reduced to being eyewash for the audience and required to come up with a constant supply of new presentations, they reacted by falling back into a dull nostalgia for old traditions.

One option was available to these harried performers: hit stardom as soon as possible in order to get off this merry-go-round. To this end, actors and singers flirted wantonly with the audience. Arias especially gave stars a way to ingratiate themselves with the audience, while the dialogue in between amounted to batches of throw-away lines. Technical skills and powerful solo performances became the competitive edge and the only means for artists to maintain some sort of individual dignity under the pressures of a factory system.

Stars were the only ones granted leave from permanent employment so as to tour and earn a lucrative second income. Only a diva whose supporters were clearly audible in the theaters, squares, and taverns had the power to refuse certain roles and thus influence the repertoire. The star system offered a way off the treadmill of cultural spectacle, a place where other participants were looked at as grunt workers, much like the cast toiling in the Mickey Mouse routines of today's Disneyland theme park. It is easy to see why one of the protegés of Gustav III, the eighteenth-century Swedish theater king, accepted an offer to join the king's theater company only upon the explicit condition that he be regarded not "as an actor, but as an amateur of these spectacles."[3]

In terms of Gadamer's model, theatrical production put such an overwhelming emphasis on the technician-audience side that in Riga, Dresden, Munich, and Zürich Wagner sought managerial methods to somehow counterbalance this frenzy of cheap entertainment. During the 1840s, he proposed the establishment of "original theatre," and then, during the 1850s, of "exemplary theatre." His final solution for banality and imbalance became his "festival," which worked—again in terms of the art firm model—at restoring art by strengthening the positions and links between artist and critics.

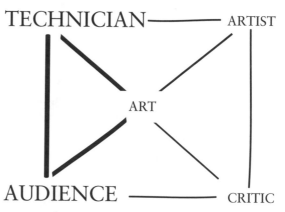

*When Entertainment Dominates the Art Firm*

Wagner's enterprise gained strength only when—with much help from his in-house critic Nietzsche—he based his managerial agenda on the Schopenhauerian ideas he had discovered in the 1840s. Schopenhauer became Wagner's management guru, helping him conceptualize how he wanted art to work for philosophical contemplation rather than just as a diversion. In early reports on what he then labeled "original theatre," Wagner suggested thinning out the number of works by Spontini and Rossini in a standard repertoire. He hoped to limit the predominance of Italian-content imports by encouraging original works in German. Next he proposed what he called "exemplary theatre" (featuring mostly his own work!). Wagner also suggested the replacement of court theaters with nonprofit theaters administered by public authorities who would set quality standards for the theatrical trade. He believed that if theatrical production were no longer the responsibility of the Royal Prussian Art Academy, the state would have to serve as benchmark for art by public theaters. Otherwise, he felt, it would turn into a spectacular profit-oriented *Gewerbe-betriebe,*[4] operations that were like secondhand outlets trading on license in ready-made plays without any fresh investment in product development.

In the early 1860s, Wagner dreamed of renting a theater in Paris to conduct an international market test of his exemplary theater. Parisian theater was then a hectic and profitable industry. On the Boulevard du Temple, commonly known as the "Boulevard du Crime" because of all the bloody melodramas performed there, at least ten big theaters aimed at a mass audience. The façades of these theaters boasted balconies upon which costumed actors would parade as advertisements for current productions. The stalls were full of middle-class citizens eager for entertainment, and higher up in the gods sat the working-class crowds, hungering for distraction. Such auditoriums no longer mirrored a feudal system full of drowsy court bureaucrats and strutting officers; instead, these audiences now had a hard day's work behind them and came in search of recreation and relaxation. Theaters had evolved by moving away from the feudal order of art and wit, where the difference between the connoisseurs/critics in the audience and the amateurs/artists on stage was scarcely visible.

On Boulevard du Crime, this alliance between artists and critics, which Wagner now wanted to restore to modern bourgeois guise, was therefore broken; these theaters were markets for mass-produced melodrama where stage technicians delivered their services to an anonymous audience. A despondent theater critic of the 1830s wrote that "this is a total disaster: factory production has taken over; a play is made as you manufacture a dress."[5] Theaters were factories, and feudal *haute couture* turned into popular *prêt à porter*. Crowds of extras lined up by the stage doors for the night shift, and agencies could provide whatever was required in characters. Wagner himself remarked that these cheap extras were used as sections of human scenery.

In an arrangement managed by theatrical agents, successful Parisian plays were packaged and sold to the provinces. Like today's franchised musicals, the deal included text, music, costume sketches, and set designs. In an effort to educate the middle class to become good theatrical consumers, toy shops merchandized the shows by featuring model theaters with accompanying scripts, settings, and paper dolls. As a result, provincial families making up the market for touring shows were well prepared for visits from these theatrical companies. The agents helped the companies supply actors from their manpower registers; of course, the companies preferred stars from the capital to attract a big audience. As the wages of the stars increased, the residue available to pay the other actors decreased. By the middle of the 1800s, the European theater market Wagner wanted to innovate with his art enterprise was dominated by the star system and its connected managerial problems.

Deteriorating court theaters, with their run-of-the-mill production processes, became Wagner's first target in his criticism of quality. The time was right. The abolition of feudal privileges during the French Revolution had made room for the creation of a private experience industry such as that of the Boulevard du Crime in Paris. Further, royal theaters had been stripped of their monopoly to perform the plays of both living and dead dramatists.

After the Revolution, the playwrights themselves began assuming economic responsibility for the performance of their plays. Absence of efficient copyright laws fostered a competitive spirit, where authors sometimes felt driven to establish their own theatrical enterprises to guarantee income, rapidly exploiting their scripts before others did. To camouflage a weak text, they invested in technical equipment for creating visually attractive images on stage. Gas lights and image projectors were installed. The famous playwright Guilbert de Pixérécourt, for example, excelled in technical effects and advanced lighting in his own Parisian melodrama theater. Next door, Cirque Olympique audiences could enjoy accurately reproduced Napoleonic battle scenes and displays of high-tech illusions. Paris was a Las Vegas long before Vegas built its Paris.

It was not only backstage technology that was developed, either. Out front, "claques" and "ticklers" technically manipulated the audience. Claques were planted to bring on cheers and applause, and ticklers were to anticipate and detonate the audience's laughter by their own well-timed small explosions of mirth. For their services, claques and ticklers usually got paid in theater tickets. In Paris, claques made extra cash by capitalizing on their "earnings" through the infamous "gutter Venus," who usually stood posted next to a Boulevard du Crime gutter and sold last-minute tickets for them on secret commission. Theater-lovers too poor to afford tickets now attended shows on secret invitation of a particular actor or the director and in return supported the fan group planted in the audience. This technical manipulation of audiences by claques and ticklers, who many times actually provoked hysteria in the audience, was severely criticized. In this show-biz setting, they were clever Nietzschean technicians of speed, but what happened in these theaters was what happens in today's sports arenas; the havoc created by these Dionysian hooligans was totally beyond control.

In addition to Wagner's critical assessment of show business, his painful experience when his opera *Tannhäuser* was performed at the Paris Opera in 1861 definitely triggered his view of art as an entrepreneurial task. Before this Paris experience, he felt that the business was rotten because the aesthetic play had degenerated to a banal technician-audience dyad. After the experience, he was convinced that he himself had to single-handedly improve the situation by reinforcing the critic-artist link. Only as an entrepreneur could he make art work.

Wagner went to Paris, like a European moviemaker to Hollywood, full of great expectations. At a gala reception held by Count Metternich, he was introduced to Napoléon III's new prime minister, Count Walewsky, who assured him that *Tannhäuser* would be a great success. All of Paris admired Wagner's music, and they *all,* Walewsky emphasized, looked forward to the nice second act ballet.

Wagner could not understand the minister's remark; there was no such ballet in the second act. The minister insisted, however. Success would be guaranteed as long as Wagner included a nice piece of ballet in the second act.[6] Furthermore, Petipa, the famous balletmaster, was placed at Wagner's disposal, and Napoléon III himself would pick up the tab for bringing beautiful ballerinas from St. Petersburg and London.

When Wagner pointed out that he already had a ballet sequence in the *first* act of his opera, habitués informed him that the most important steady members of the audience would not have finished dining at the Jockey Club by then and that he had better adapt himself to their habits. After a fine dinner together, those gentlemen were accustomed to picking out available female companionship for a gallant *chambre séparée* supper later. When this scenario happened, Wagner was under the spell of Schopenhauer's art management gospel, and having carefully studied *Die Welt als Wille und Vorstellung*, he adamantly insisted he was an artist-philosopher and not a pimp. Metaphysics, not call-girl promotion, was his calling.

From then on, for some odd reason, Wagner began meeting with harsh resistance from the management of the Paris Opera House. Slowly he lost control over his project. The conductor he was assigned was sloppy, and Wagner himself had to mark time for the orchestra. He could not find any male extras or money for costumes for the poor ballet students who were ordered to dance his intermezzo in the first act. In addition, in the whole of Paris, it was impossible to find the twelve French horns he needed. Then, when the administration of the Opera wanted to squeeze the latest experimental saxophone into the performance, Wagner came close to canceling *Tannhäuser* altogether. Even the threat of cancellation was powerless, though. The management would not let him withdraw the score or even replace the incompetent conductor. The most he was permitted was a few extra rehearsals—provided he did not go over budget.

Time was running out. The extra rehearsals threatened to kill any spontaneity in the performances, and initial enthusiasm for the project degenerated into rampant disenchantment. The whole project was quickly becoming a fiasco. Niemann, one of the singers concerned about his reputation, demanded score revisions that Wagner would not agree to. At the same time, Wagner's patrons and benefactors were arriving from near and far to witness their protegé's definitive breakthrough. These connoisseur-critics had high expectations for their artist; Monsieur Chandon, one of these patrons, arrived with a crate of his finest champagne with which to celebrate the performance.

Wagner also discovered that when it came to getting seats for the performance, members of Napoléon's imperial court took precedence, and the remaining seats had already been reserved for regular subscribers to the Opera. How the mood of Wagner's admirers deteriorated when they understood that he would not even be able to give them good seats in return for years of patience and support!

The mediocre premiere disintegrated into a complete catastrophe by the second performance. During Act II, a loud chorus of whistling was heard from the boxes. "Ce sont les Jockeys, nous sommes perdus," Director Royer of the Imperial Opera muttered in despair. Indeed, as was their habit, the gentlemen of the club had finally arrived for the second act—and indeed, they were expecting to see their own brand of entertainment. Instead of ballet tutus and leotards, however, they were presented with a crowd of hearty knights on stage. In accordance with their privileged tradition, the gentlemen decided to join the mood of the audience and began to whistle loudly through their hollow box keys. It made little difference that members of Napoléon's court had tried in advance to secure a fair hearing for the artistic innovations of *Tannhäuser*. The Jockeys tolerated no change in their normal routine.

The third and final performance took place on a Sunday, so as not to further disturb regular operagoers. Now that the scandal was obvious, Wagner chose to stay home. Niemann and the other singers, in a last-ditch attempt to save their professional hides, ignored Wagner's instructions altogether. The song to the evening star firmly embedded in the plot of the drama was performed from the proscenium and directed straight at the audience. During the chorus of booing, Niemann shrugged his shoulders and pointed an accusing finger toward the box where the composer usually sat. Of course, the box was empty.

*Tannhäuser* was forced back into the spectacular form of banality Wagner had struggled to avoid, and the experience taught him a clear, though painful, management lesson. No old factory like the Paris Opera would ever voluntarily open up to aesthetic play. As long as he insisted on producing philosophy and offering contemplation to his consumers, he had to enter into the business of being, by founding an art firm completely under his own managerial control.

After this debacle in Paris, Wagner split his time between composition and his new project, the establishment of his art enterprise. "Set up committee," he began in his concisely written 1869 description of how to proceed. "Organize subscription of underwritten shares. Management solely in my hands. Can appoint myself chairman if I wish. Financial management: the committee and the representatives of shareholders. Careful planning and control of budget."[7]

When Ludwig II of Bavaria, Wagner's great patron who had already built himself a private Venus Grotto for intimate Wagner concerts, wanted to have *The Ring* performed in Munich, Wagner was still stressed by his *Tannhäuser* fears about spectacles. He truly believed it would be as bad to be a jewel in the crown of Bavarian royalty as to be an audience magnet for some greedy theater manager. Therefore his enterprise had to become a true Dionysian festival in the countryside, far from the capital and its capitalists. Wagner also politely but firmly declined invitations from spa towns on the lookout for attractive entertainment for their guests. His art firm needed to be free from the influence of both commerce and politics. Art could be neither bought nor sold; it could only be generously bestowed as a gift.

To this end, Wagner needed three hundred thousand talers, and when not one of his patrons offered support, he tried to sell shares on the open market . . . with no assurance of revenue. Construction of the theater in Bayreuth was delayed for three years; by 1873, only 490 shares had been sold. Once again, it was King Ludwig who came to the rescue by offering a hundred thousand talers as security on the loan that finally permitted the opening of the festival in 1876. Wagner proudly remained a true art entrepreneur; he alone was responsible for the debt, the final repayment of which was made by his descendants in 1913.[8]

Not much remained of Wagner's original intention to invite connoisseurs and art-loving students from the universities to a free festival in Bayreuth. In the end, he was forced into the Schopenhauerian business of being and had to sell all but fifty of the tickets on the open market. The final cost of construction in Bayreuth was 945,000 talers, and the first performances of *The Ring of the Niebelung* cost 180,000. The Kaiser himself attended the gala premiere, and the Bavarian court orchestra performed under the direction of Ludwig's favorite conductor, Hermann Levi. Ludwig had provided the orchestra and its Jewish conductor on the express condition that Richard Wagner and wife, Cosima, would put an end to their embarrassing anti-Semitism. Over a concentrated period of four days, the Bayreuth enterprise finally performed *The Ring* to Wagner's stipulations. After the premiere, he is reported to have said, "In the future it will be up to you, dear members of the audience, if you want to have any art at all."[9] Wagner's own presentation of the performances echoed Arthur Schopenhauer's philosophy:

> These performances must be regarded as a feast of art to which I invite friends of my art from near and far. These feasts have a different character than normal theatre performances. The relationship between theatre and audience is different because now it is no longer a matter of approval or disapproval as in the modern theatrical game of luck. It is a matter of fulfilling the goals that I have set for my work of art. It is a matter of how these goals have been reached, whether or not it has indeed been worthwhile to attain them.[10]

The differences between show biz and the art enterprise were clear. In the regular business of entertainment, a show was modeled on scripts and scores. Conscientious workers, and occasionally individual virtuosi, recreated the play on stage. In an art firm, on the other hand, neither scores nor scripts were originals to be slavishly copied; rather, they stated philosophical problems that could only be solved in direct interaction of audience and performer. Wagner actually refers to this direct immediate process as *Unternehmen,* which *"nichts mehr mit unserem heutigen Theater zu tun habe."*[11] That an enterprise had nothing to do with normal theater meant creation in place of reproduction, and it demanded thorough practical preparation. Wagner believed that opera was drama, and that the performers ought to learn acting skills in "stylistic schools."

In addition, the audience was expected to behave differently than the Jockeys of Paris had. As an integral part of his art firm marketing, Wagner wrote and lectured in order to educate—in Schiller's spirit—a new audience open to Schopenhauerian contemplation. He wove actual themes into his German operas[12] to activate this openness. To stimulate his audience, he integrated trendy philosophies of popular thinkers, such as Ludwig Feuerbach. Wagner had a good feeling for philosophical fashion, having joined, in the Revolution of 1848, the barricades of Dresden in the company of Bakunin the revolutionary anarchist. After their first meeting, Wagner had immediately enrolled Nietzsche as the young philosophical trendsetter of his management team for his Bayreuth business.

Wagner skillfully combined Hellenism and the ideas of ancient theater with the living medieval theatrical traditions of Oberammergau, where the audience actively participated in the mystery plays. He addressed his audience not as customers or clients but as "guests" and select "lovers of art." In building his ideal audience among his followers and benefactors, he mobilized fan clubs, his "Wagner societies," by calls in the press. Ever since his early success with the opera *Rienzi,* he knew the value of marketing for public success.

Through the establishment of his art enterprise, Wagner's audience developed from an anonymous open market to a progressively more exclusive circle of friends. After his marriage to the conservative and aristocratic Cosima Liszt, daughter of the great pianist and former wife of conductor Hans von Bülow, Wagner turned his back on mass marketing. The old days—when he would plan a rebel opera about Jesus with Bakunin, based on the text "hang him, execute him, fire, fire"—were definitely gone.[13]

Bayreuth was fenced off from the street and its mass audience, since it targeted groups carefully prepared to join in Wagner's metaphysical meditations. At Bayreuth, artists, aware of their philosophical mission, would encounter a collected, contemplative audience, prepared by a thorough familiarity with the score and other Wagner writings before they began their pilgrimage to the Bavarian village. This was especially important because Wagner installed electric lighting in order to darken the auditorium, and the dimness would prohibit any score consulting during the performance. The journey itself, the meetings with other Wagnerians, and the Spartan accommodations were all connected to the art enterprise and contributed to a sense of heightened expectation. Art had to work as a total experience.

This intellectual conditioning was not all of the preparation for the audience, either. Just as the performers put on makeup and costumes and warmed up their voices, so too the audience was expected to dress up, be well perfumed and coiffured, and be seated behind locked doors in the festival hall designed as a Dionysus amphitheater. During the week of the festival, plenty of opportunities existed to discuss the experience at length at improvised seminars held in local taverns. Obviously, the procession to the opera was a formal affair and certainly not a case of rushing directly from work with a head full of everyday concerns and dressed in everyday clothing. Nor was it like spending the evening sitting in a box with a supply of chilled champagne and gossiping about other members of the audience one glimpsed through opera glasses. Schopenhauerian contemplation was conditioned by shut doors, dimmed light, and an orchestra pit hidden under the stage to make the contact between artists and audience as direct and immediate as Schopenhauer had wished.

Wagner was adamant that this was a case of art in the singular, not arts in the plural. Spectacles—with their marketing hype, carnival processions, fairground attractions, and show-stopping numbers—consisted of a collage of disparate arts. According to Wagner, though, the result of piling arts one on top of the other was as disappointing as being in "a picture gallery . . . listening to the reading of a novel by Goethe in the midst of a display of statues, and, on top of this, having a Beethoven symphony played as background music."[14]

Schopenhauer maintained that art had little in common with the experience economy of lazy impulsive shopping in a mall of physical pleasures and excitements. Spectacular zapping was to be avoided, and to achieve this "[we must] make up our minds, and instead of behaving like children on the marketplace, attracted by whatever passes, then vainly the clear line of our being will flatten out to a space where we run around in zigzags, leaping about, accomplishing nothing."[15]

Wagner wanted to make his art—in the singular—work as a *Gesamt-kunstwerk*. Patchwork arts, in contrast to philosophical art, existed to give external stimulation to the eyes and ears. Making art work was, in Wagner's words, to embed the audience "in the midst of the work itself," so that it would no longer be possible to regard art dispassionately as the result of skilled technical ability. His opera, his work of art, took the place of the Holy Scripture in Gadamer's hermeneutic *Kreis* of aesthetic play. Wagner wanted art to work as Schopenhauerian philosophizing. It should bridge matter and form and perform a *Gefühlswerdung des Verstandes,* the emotionalization of reason. His Dionysian renaissance resulted in performances producing an aesthetic surplus over its mere raw materials, its text and image. In the footsteps of Richard Wagner, the pioneer of the modern art enterprise, a number of European projecteers joined the business of being. Not surprisingly, many such avant-gardists worked in Paris, the nineteenth-century experience economy capital par excellence.

## Théâtre Libre—Antoine's Naturalist Project

The nature of Parisian show biz changed dramatically within one year of Wagner's *Tannhäuser* fiasco. Count Haussmann's 1862 architectural plans for modernization of the capital entailed the destruction of the theatrical quarter around the Boulevard du Crime. This demolition of the concentration of mass theaters caused considerable bourgeois relief. Theaters were class melting pots that easily whipped up political winds.

In place of the mass theaters came the carefully planned commercial city of light, with its ostentatious opera house at the end of a new luxurious shopping boulevard called l'Avenue de l'Opéra. The shows on stage were replaced by commercial performances in every deluxe boutique. In the theater, one paid at the entrance; now payment was made at the counter at the end of a seductive shopping performance. While modern merchants created new forms of mass spectacle in big department stores, theater directors became traders that launched new projects as old companies went bankrupt. The conveyor-belt system of popular theater continued, but in a more standardized frenzy. A great supply of *pièces bien faites,* fast-moving, soap operalike entertainment, provided a standard entertainment that featured the brightest stars of the day. People knew precisely what they were getting, in the same sense that the Jockeys expected their routine of beautiful girls in the second act ballet. *Les spectacles* were proving so effortlessly successful that theater directors could claim in all seriousness that Paris really only needed a couple of mass-producing playwrights. The well-oiled machinery of a slightly boring business stage was all set for an innovative aesthetic pioneer to make an appearance.

In 1887, like a bolt out of the blue, André Antoine (1858–1943) struck the spectacle industry with his new enterprise. Antoine, who in 1906 went on to become an established director of the grand Odéon Theatre, joined the industry by chance, as many young hackers or musicians do today. He came to theater through the main entrance, not the backstage door. As a boy, he was obsessed with the stage, but because he was poor, he found himself in the claque, cheering "spontaneously" in return for free tickets.

Antoine's first job in a bookstore awakened his interest in literature. He also took acting lessons, although he failed the entrance exam for the *conservatoire,* perhaps due to lack of connections and letters of recommendation. He finally made it onto the stage as an extra, where he was able to study the techniques of the most successful actors. After work in an office of the Parisian gasworks, he would walk with a colleague up to the Montmartre hill, which was once the home of anarchist heroes of the 1871 Paris commune. Across the boulevard at the Place Pigalle, they would climb up the steep Rue des Martyrs into one of the rare parts of the capital spared Baron Hausmann's modernization. Here lived a mélange of bourgeois established artists in newly built stone houses alongside poor bohemian painters in cheap rundown shacks. Near the entrance to the Place des Abbesses, they would be greeted by Old Krauss, a former soldier, whose enthusiasm for the theater had led him to found his own amateur theatrical society, the Cercle Gaulois.[16] The group rehearsed every evening to perform for their friends and acquaintances once a month. Antoine brought a new intensity with him when he joined the group; to him, theater was serious business, not just a relaxing hobby.

When the Cercle Pigalle, a neighboring theatrical club whose members were more upper-middle-class, managed to persuade the famous theater critic Sarcey to write about them, Antoine's competitive spirit immediately kicked in. He persuaded his comrades at the Cercle Gaulois that they too could entice the critics by finding well-known authors who had written previously unperformed plays that would be hot because of their political actuality. Antoine was right; by 1887, the amateurs had built up a small network of playwrights, some of whom proved to be influential journalists as well. One Monsieur Byl provided contacts to the circle of the Goncourt brothers, and then to the great Émile Zola. A program of four single-act plays was planned, one of them written by Zola himself. Zola's play was on the controversial subject of a released communard who had discovered that his wife betrayed him.

Old Krauss began to have reservations, for the state-run Odéon Theatre had refused this very Zola play. If it were to be performed, the censors would certainly ban it. Moreover, Antoine's aggressively managerial behavior was too competitive for the old man with his notions of cooperation and cama-raderie. No, there would be no Zola at the Cercle Gaulois. Krauss did agree eventually that Antoine could rent his stage to perform the play. Finding a place to rehearse was another matter, however. What they found was a shabby bistro backroom with an old billiard table, and the actors had to agree to buy one drink each when they arrived to rehearse each evening.

From the time rehearsals began on March 6, 1887, Antoine spared no ef-fort in carefully planning both backstage and frontstage strategies for his new enterprise. To attract the interest of influential newspapers, he gave his firm the revolutionary name of Théâtre Libre. The troupe could not afford scenery, so following in the footsteps of Molière, he borrowed his mother's kitchen furniture, thus designing the first naturalist setting. He wrote out personal invitations to the show in the name of the famous writers of the play to be performed. To save postage, he hand-delivered them at night after rehearsals.

Work began immediately after office hours and carried on until the early morning, with a break for food on the days when eating was financially pos-sible. During one of the rehearsals, Zola himself stopped in. Impressed, he exclaimed to his court accompanying him: "C'est très bien, c'est très beau, hein."[17] With that, Antoine's troubles were over, for Zola promised to bring all of his trendsetting friends to the opening performance on March 30. Antoine had in no time short-circuited the critics and artists of the model of aesthetic play. Success was assured; the day following the opening, enthusi-astic reviews appeared in most of the Paris papers.

The authors of the plays assumed that Théâtre Libre would continue to perform their works. When this became an issue, Antoine, his confidence boosted by success, declared that he was the boss. His art firm indeed de-pended on new and fresh plays; nevertheless, it was his special management that had created surplus value out of texts supplied as raw materials. Later, when playwrights were invited to publicly read their scripts to the whole company before rehearsals began, Antoine sometimes took over if he thought the writers were bungling the job.[18] Literature was necessary, but without his art management the text of the play itself was not enough to make plays work as art.

Antoine soon established his new routine of making art work, and it was his impoverished circumstances that dictated his mode of production. A month of evening rehearsals was followed by a few performances. When Coquelin, one of the stars of the spectacles, came to Montmartre to watch a rehearsal, he suggested that Antoine add some special effects and spice up the show with a bit of technical skill. Coquelin did not even understand it was precisely by avoiding such technical tricks of the trade that the Théâtre Libre was successful in attracting both authors and critics.

The entire corps of Paris critics watched Antoine's second production on May 30, and now influential theater directors showed up to watch their new avant-garde competitor. Soon they would copy his "naturalism" by technically reproducing its authentic settings and unaffected dialogue. Got, one of Antoine's former idols from the Comédie Française, personally came to call on him. The great star began by thanking the former claque and then, with much patronizing irony, told Antoine to carry on as a jolly amateur and make do with the small contributions members of the association could afford from their low wages. Got pointed out that he knew how it was, for le Théâtre Français was also an association, albeit, of course, one with *very* professional and *technically advanced* members.

The repertoire at le Français was chosen by ballot, and roles were distributed according to a tradition dating back to the days of the monarchy. Antoine, however, had no intention of letting go of the reins of his enterprise. Soon the little avant-garde entrepreneur was standing in front of the administrator of the big Odéon Theatre, which had rejected the Zola play that made such a success at his Théâtre Libre. The man advised: "My dear sir . . . you are clearly an artist, I have seen one or two of your performances; amusing, if a little bohemian, but not really serious at all. . . . It is studio theatre for a small group of Parisians, and within six months they will have tired of you and moved on . . . you no longer know your job . . . come to me and study . . . you can make your debut in a leading role. . . ."[19] The proposal might have been tempting, but had Antoine accepted such an offer, his enterprise would have collapsed.

Antoine's *phobie des professionels* grew even stronger after such comments.[20] He genuinely disliked professional actors, thinking of them as technicians who had learned the tricks of the spectacle trade at the *conservatoire*. They had been drilled in pathetic declamation technologies and loved their public so much that their trousers were scorched by the footlights. Actresses made themselves up to look like tarts, regardless of the role they were playing.

Antoine put nature up against these techniques and was proud of having found natural acting talents for his stage. His human resource management consisted mainly in keeping his troupe far from professional technical education. Their amateur status—which paradoxically soon made many of them into stars—was a sign of their artistic integrity. Zola the Realist discovered and appreciated this purity and authenticity in Antoine's theatre, and Antoine himself later compared the stunning immediate success of his company to the joy of discovering a simple, beautiful flower growing in the backyard of an urban slum. He slowly came to realize that the spontaneity and naïveté of his theater seemed so shocking and so attractive because his company suited the Schopenhauerian philosophy of a new elite who had been criticizing the banality of the French art establishment for quite some time. Not surprisingly, many of those supporters were also eminent French Wagnerians.

The case of Antoine indicates that an art enterprise makes art work by recycling resources scattered around the cultural landscape. Certainly the scraps and fragments were already lying there idle, but they had to be activated into an aesthetic play. The Impressionists, for instance, were dismantling academic painting with their new color theories, and the Naturalist writers, armed with the theories of scientist Claude Bernard and philosopher Auguste Comte, were fighting back at Romanticism. These cultural changes conditioned the success of Antoine's project at Place des Abbesses. The visual philosophy of the Impressionists and the treatment of language by the Naturalists both contributed to the victory over the sort of spectacle theater that Zola had attacked as a dusty "box of conventions" in 1881. Antoine, the conscious art entrepreneur, became aware of the importance of luck and timing; in his memoirs he writes:

> The battle already won in the novel by the naturalists, in painting by the impressionists, and in music by the Wagnerians was going to be carried into the theatre . . . was then the field of battle, the occupiers of the place to be won, the troups ready for a

possible assault; but who would coordinate so many scattered elements? Who would give the signal? Quite simply, chance. Without being the least aware of it, I was to become the animator of forces which I did not even suspect.[21]

Antoine's theatre, as is the case with all true innovations, skipped convention. Formal codes of communication, in Schopenhauer's opinion, had nothing to do with art firms. The footlights of theatrical tradition were replaced by the "fourth wall" of the stage. Through this "wall," audience members became voyeurs secretly watching the characters in the same way that Claude Bernard observed nature through his strong microscope. Antoine hoarded genuine artifacts that replaced traditional stage scenery. Instead of being painted on a canvas, a kitchen on stage would have a steaming stove, and a shop would have real wares on the shelves. The script served as a trampoline for provoking a visual experience beyond any playwright's explicit instructions. Text turned to pictures, and all this was in order to bring art back to theatre, or as Antoine said, to bestow *"l'impression d'art."*[22]

Antoine pinched ideas wherever he found them. He admired the natural acting style of the great Irving, and when he watched a production of Sachsen-Meiningen's theater company when it came to Brussels he was impressed by their realistic crowd scenes, played by well-rehearsed actors instead of clumsy extras plucked from the street the same evening. Antoine commanded his company with boyish enthusiasm but a well-disguised iron will.

As a good entrepreneur, Antoine pictured himself a thrifty self-made man. In 1887, he himself funded the printing of two thousand brochures. He himself, he proudly pointed out, wrote the thirteen hundred personal letters of invitation to potential subscribers and wandered the streets of Paris at night alone to deliver the letters. Very soon, this effort began to pay off, as he got 650 subscriptions for eight performances per season, at a cost of one hundred francs each in advance. The queues of the theatergoers in front of his theater were matched by the backstage queues of authors and young actors eager to join the company and to "learn" how to write and act naturalistically. Antoine's art firm became an incubator for trendy playwrights and an off-academy for antistar stars.

Théâtre Libre discovered and positioned itself right in the middle of an aesthetic field of Schwung. As a private theater club, it escaped censorship by

the state and could therefore offer subscribers the banned plays of exciting "refusals." On the other hand, not being a public house had the drawback of having no casual box office ticket sale. Any extra capital had to be earned from tours in Belgium, Germany, and Italy. The enterprise was cofinanced by the amateur actors' acceptance of low wages and their willingness to help with all aspects of the business, from sewing costumes to visiting potential subscribers. Antoine himself helped buy food for the actors in the local bars and inns. Here they would sit until dawn, waiting for the media verdict—the reviews in the papers. Then they would trudge off to their daily jobs, pale but happy, as the street-traders pushed their heavily laden vegetable barrows up the streets from Les Halles to the market in the steep serpentine Rue Lepic.

## Théâtre de l'Œuvre—
## Lugné's Symbolist Undertaking

In 1893, the cashier of Antoine's tour to Rome vanished with the money, leaving nothing for the return home. This simple blow totally wiped out Antoine's financially vulnerable project. With a heavy heart, he said goodbye to his faithful actors. After seven intense years and fifty-four performances, including 111 premieres of new plays by eighty-eight playwrights—including both Ibsen and Strindberg—from eight countries, his enterprise was disbanded, bankrupt.[23]

The tiny Théâtre Libre continued to have an immense media impact anyway. Naturalist arts, mainly literature in Antoine's case, had been put to work on his stage. In its first three years, when Théâtre Libre performed off and on to little audiences packed in small rented theaters, there were no fewer than twelve thousand French newspaper articles covering Antoine's project.[24] Soon every European capital had a Théâtre Libre of its own. André Antoine, who had also proved himself a great actor and played eighty-three roles, left the avant-garde to take up a position in an established theater. The pioneering entrepreneur spent a large part of his remaining career managing the reproduction of his early creations on large boulevard and state stages. His short-lived project was thus a powerful source of innovation in the way Wagner planned for Bayreuth.

Through his aesthetic Schwung, Antoine antagonistically inspired one of his former actors to make art work in yet another new way. The avant-garde project of Lugné-Poe's Théâtre de l'Œuvre illustrates how artists' pictures are put to work. Aurelien Lugné (1869–1940) came from a family of civil servants, in contrast to Antoine, who was from a working-class family. He attended the famous Condorcet Academy at the foot of Montmartre and was accepted at the *conservatoire*. He performed as an amateur for Antoine but got sacked, probably because Antoine learned of his admission to the conservatoire. From 1888 on, Lugné studied at theater school during the day and rehearsed in Montmartre in the evenings. Every other month he was in two performances with Théâtre Libre. At the beginning, he performed under the stage names of Phillipon, Delorme, and Leroy, but eventually he settled on Lugné-Poe. The latter part of his name was borrowed from the American poet Edgar Allan Poe, then immensely popular in Paris.

Antoine and Lugné-Poe failed to see eye to eye for several reasons. Antoine was steady and realistic and believed in common sense, whereas Lugné was more of an idealistic dreamer. Antoine was a literary man, but Lugné was much more interested in the visual arts. Antoine found inspiration in texts and once worked for a bookseller; in 1891, Lugné got hooked on pictures when he moved in with his schoolfriend Maurice Denis, a painter. Lugné and Denis shared an apartment at 28 Rue Pigalle with two other young artists, Vuillard and Bonnard. Lugné, who could not afford any rent, paid his way by selling his friends' paintings to the wealthy actors he met at the conservatoire. "If you've got one of those Bonnards, call in," Coquelin would yell to him.

Antoine, who somewhat paranoically spotted competition everywhere, guessed very soon that these young men nurtured ideas at odds with his own Naturalism; he felt a counterrevolution coming. Later Antoine recalled a strange encounter in 1887 with a *chapelle symboliste* in a wooden shack that resembled a Siberian hut on the Rue Ravignan.[25] Maybe Lugné's group had already frequented the Bateau Lavoir, where Cubism was to be born twenty years later with Picasso, Braque, Gris, and the art dealer Kahnweiler. A year or so after this odd meeting, Lugné and his friends broke away to form their own avant–garde enterprise, with Paul Gauguin as their idol. They pretentiously called themselves *les Nabis* (the Prophets). In 1891,

Lugné participated in a theatrical soirée held by the Prophets for the benefit of Gauguin and the poet Verlaine. As a result, he ended up in the Théâtre d'Art, run by his contemporary, poet Paul Fort. Fort's theater resembled Antoine's only in form; it was an association funded by subscriptions that performed every other month in a hired hall. While Antoine materially constructed concrete pieces of social realism from naturalistic plays, Fort was directing ethereal formalistic performances inspired by paintings. Vuillard, Bonnard, Sérusier, and Denis prepared painted curtains that transformed the stage into a flat surface. Images were cut from gold paper and pinned to the curtains. Fort's pictorial stage poems against colorful backdrops, completed by spraying perfume, brought cries of astonishment from the audience. It was here that Lugné met the Belgian symbolist poet Maurice Maeterlinck, who suggested that it was necessary to *not* have people on stage, and that instead of embarrassing real actors, producers should go for projections, reflections, and shadows of symbolic form instead.

When Lugné-Poe embarked upon his own Théâtre de l'Œuvre in 1893, he performed Maeterlinck's symbolist drama *Pelléas et Mélisande* as a Sunday matinee at the Bouffes du Nord theater. By then, Fort was deeply in debt and had to close down his company after performing a controversial play about prostitution written by a certain Chirac, who claimed to be a true naturalist playwright in Antoine's spirit. The choice of this rough, vulgar, and almost pornographic play was Fort's actual parting shot at Antoine. Lugné must have appreciated the joke, but poor Chirac did not detect the irony and believed the scandal of his play was indicative of future triumphs. He went on to found the Théâtre Réaliste, whose productions led him to court and ultimately to prison for offending the morals of the French public. As Fort's symbolist project folded, Lugné-Poe's project moved to take up the combat with naturalism.

In direct opposition to Antoine's naturalistic positivism, Lugné-Poe's Théâtre de l'Œuvre concentrated on the negative. There was no room for pale everyday subjects. He wanted to depict symbols so brittle that they only could exist in a pure vacuum free of people. In 1890, in a typically symbolic painting, Odilon Redon depicted the face of a dreaming male, his eyes closed as he intently listens to the internal music of voiceless poetry. Just as Fort performed Maeterlinck's single-act play *Les aveugles* as a conversation among smells, colors, and sound,[26] Lugné was hoping to achieve a similarly vague weightless art, where the physical world so beloved of Antoine was minimized. It seemed as if naturalism, with its focus on what Schiller called matter, was going out of fashion. In opposition, as the aesthetic Schwung, the pendulum swayed over to the other side of form.

Stéphane Mallarmé had also conceived of an ideal formalized performance of *Hamlet* with only one actor on the stage. Another of Lugné's contemporaries, the English actor Gordon Craig, was also beginning to theorize about the future of a theater of an idealistic formalized kind in which there would be neither writers nor actors. Craig wanted to cast a supermarionette, an artificial robotic sculpture.

At the Théâtre de l'Œuvre, the physical volume of the stage was reduced to a flat surface by curtains and veils.[27] Instead of programs full of written text, Lugné-Poe printed lithographs by friends such as Toulouse-Lautrec or Edvard Munch.[28] It was Antoine who had introduced Lugné-Poe to the strange and almost mythical Scandinavians. When, as a director, he began to work with plays by Ibsen and Strindberg, he proved himself worthy of the name Poe. In contrast to the sober delivery of lines in an everyday tone of naturalistic theater, Lugné had his actors perform declamations in monotonous chant, which soon earned him the nickname *le clergyman somnambule*. The Théâtre de l'Œuvre performed for Ibsen himself, and Lugné-Poe, costumed in a romantic wolf-skin coat and riding a sled, upset Ibsen, who found it utterly strange to listen to his lines delivered as in a trance of hallucinating sleepwalkers.

If Antoine was to some extent a revolutionary communard, Lugné-Poe was a rebellious anarchist. The former liked written statements and manifestos; the latter let his direct action be inspired by enlightened and spontaneous visual flashes. In 1893, when the anarchist movement was at its height, Lugné staged a performance of Ibsen's *Enemy of the People*. As both Wagner and Antoine had done before him, he incorporated his production into the liberation philosophy of the day.

Only one year before, the terrorist Ravachol had been captured and guillotined, and now police surrounded Lugné's theatre. The hundred or so extras on stage, many of them militant anarchists handpicked by Lugné, united behind the slogan "The majority always consists of idiots."[29] With strains of "Long live anarchism!" echoing around the auditorium, arrests were made as people left. Georges Clemenceau himself described the performance as an intellectual protest against the lies and prejudice of *"l'opinion moyenne des hommes."*[30] In just one night , embedding Ibsen's text in French anarchism transformed Lugné's ethereal symbolism into a considerably more politically correct project than Antoine's workaday narratives, still rooted in somewhat dusty naturalism.

As an art entrepreneur, Lugné was nevertheless much less systematic and successful than Antoine. At most, L'Œuvre had 130 subscribers, who each paid between forty and one hundred francs for eight performances per season.[31] Lugné was forced to replenish the coffers by touring, and sometimes supporters of the private theater sold tickets illegally to a public eager for scandal.

One more legendary performance secured Lugné's reputation for notoriety. It all began in 1896, as Lugné was looking for a secretary and stage director (in French, a *regisseur*). He chanced upon a strange character, one Alfred Jarry, who was recommended to him by a famous actress and seemed rather keen to work in his company. Jarry had also written for the avant-garde periodical *l'Ymagier* (the Image Maker), a name that was bound to be popular among symbolists.[32] It was not long before this man made himself indispensable to Lugné by anarchistically infiltrating most of the aspects of his business. Jarry was instantly recognizable by his battle dress—a cycling jersey and cap—and his extremely trendy bicycle.

Before long, this avant-garde cyclist was featuring extracts from his own play *Ubu Roi,* whose main character was based upon a caricature of one of his schoolteachers. It appealed to Lugné's taste, because its imagery was more important than the text. Jarry explained to Lugné that the characters should look like puppets in the tradition of Le Grand Guignol; they should be less formal and even more grotesque. Anything ordinary and natural was verboten. The central character was to speak with a strangely affected voice. The sets should be as primitive as drawings by small children.

Jarry fancied the role of the general to be played by a small blond boy he had found playing near the theater, and Lugné agreed to this; after all, Parisian women loved small blond boys. Lugné-Poe's conviction that Jarry was creating something quite unique was strengthened by the fact that Jarry had also developed a philosophy-to-go: "pataphysics." *Ubu Roi* was a complete package and spiced with a pictorial philosophy Lugné ultimately could not refuse. In place of some banal naturalistic scenery, posters inscribed with words such as *forest* or *castle* were used on stage. Jarry also made use of symbolic imagery throughout the play, with horseback riding depicted by cardboard horses' heads hanging from the actors' necks. He was also cavalier in his approach to the unities of time and space, and Lugné-Poe often had cause to wonder how this cascade of noise and childish images could ever be staged successfully. Jarry remained adamant that there was nothing particularly strange in all of this; *Ubu Roi* was similar in many ways to the German tradition of burlesque theater. Obviously, text was nothing but pictures to Jarry. His play was really a theatrical cartoon, similar to Tristan Bernard's *Les pieds Nicklées,* which actually appeared as a comic strip after being performed by Lugné. Jarry's ability to stage a full production was proven when he acted as assistant for Ibsen's *Peer Gynt,* where he showed a particular flair for directing the scenes involving gruesome, inept trolls.

Eventually in 1896, Jarry was allowed to stage *Ubu Roi,* and the first thing he did was buy a set of expensive rattan puppets. On December 10, the date of the premiere performance, as was the avant-garde habit of the

day, an introductory mock lecture by the author preceded the show. Jarry pointed out that his play was unreal; it took place in Poland, translated as "nowhere." As soon as the Ubu's opening line, "Merde" (French for "shit"), was screamed out, the legendary scandal had legs. The play was performed only twice, which probably filled an unspoken prerequisite for it to go down in the history of avant-garde (often the case in underground enterprises). The scandalous event was widely diffused in the press, where French critic and Wagnerian Bauer took up the defense of *King Ubu* on the grounds that it was a real symbolist masterpiece. Once *Ubu Roi* was performed, Jarry threw off his secretarial disguise and fled the scene of the crime on his bike. Lugné-Poe was left with his little theater deeply in debt and the terrible feeling that he indeed had been the exploited one in this case.

As André Antoine reflected in Rome upon the collapse of the Théâtre Libre, he concluded that he had forty sous to his name, fifteen ruined colleagues, and one hundred thousand francs' worth of debt in Paris. Three years later, Lugné made a feeble thirteen hundred franc profit from the two performances of *Ubu Roi.* The cost of building the immensely successful aesthetic brands of naturalism and symbolism cannot be considered very high. André Antoine later drew on this early investment in established theaters and the French motion picture industry. Many of his actors and authors became famous, and theaters that adapted to the fashion for naturalism drew large audiences. Lugné's project also hit a dead end, but as an impresario he continued to manage great actors as well as rebels such as Antonin Artaud. His retrospective memoirs are a mixture of pride and nostalgia dashed with bitterness.

Before Antoine's avant-garde project, a number of naturalists felt unsatisfied with their singular ideas and scattered products. Antoine's enterprise accomplished their long-felt desire to capture the spirit of naturalism in concrete experiences and make their art work as an integrated whole, even though it was long after Antoine's own project was terminated. Well after Lugné's disastrous performance of *Ubu,* the event ended up becoming a key point of reference for all amateurs of modern avant-garde art. How, then, did Wagner, Antoine, and Lugné achieve success in producing surplus value out of texts and images? Lugné's own reflections on the success of *Ubu* indicate that he himself—as little as any other genius, according to what Kant said—really did not have much of a clue about how art firms produce such aesthetic surplus value: "The large Parisian audience never takes part directly in such enterprises. Thousands of scattered memories and traces are left and [when they are] subsequently collected or found they reconstruct a single whole. Thus those who never attended the show will in the future easily provide detailed accounts of the battle of Ubu and recapitulate all the invectives in the audience."[33]

## Metaphysics of Value

### Kahnweiler's Symbolic Surplus

The art firm is based on aesthetic play between cognition and perception, between knowledge formation and experience of a material world. Aesthetic entrepreneurs such as Wagner, Antoine, and Lugné were cutting a path for art in the jungle of the banal and standardized experience industry of their time. They wanted to make art work as a totality and not merely create divertissement by patching together values of existing art forms. In economic terms, "making art work" implies showing a surplus value over what the raw materials of text and image can convey either separately or combined. In the case of the art firm, this surplus value is not satisfactorily explained as either subjective consumer value or objective producer or labor value; it is of a third aesthetic kind. Such aesthetic value cannot be expected to come out of contemporary philosophy or science because these fields have in fact their Hegelian and Newtonian limits. Art entrepreneurs explore existence, but how they manage their philosophical tours into the thing-in-itself can only be understood by taking the whole aesthetic play into consideration.

Antoine's theatrical technique was remarkable. He used real furniture on stage and employed ordinary people to perform his plays. Real people would sit eating real soup, and the smell would drift out into the auditorium. The proscenium arch of his theater was the fourth wall of the stage, a window opening to matters of fact, through which the audience could watch real life without being seen. In pulling this off, Antoine did away with the theatrical representational techniques of creating three-dimensional illusions. Illusion was replaced by "real life,"[34] which also served to highlight the text of the play.

Antoine's practice of issuing invitations to subscription ticketholders in the name of the playwright[35] stressed the significance of that writer. In addition, Antoine was indirectly stressing his own unique competence as an art projecteer who eased the transition from text to life itself. Attending a performance at the private circle of Théâtre Libre was not the same as buying a ticket to some public show. Antoine was a host who enabled authors to offer, not sell, their art as a gift to a select audience. What he did with the writer's text to make it generate aesthetic value, what kind of aesthetic alchemy brought about the miracle of animating text to life, remained a mystery to the master himself. His art worked, but how did it make aesthetic value? After Théâtre Libre failed, Antoine turned into a routine manager of spectacles performed every evening. In a large number of bleak productions each year, he replicated the successes of his youth. The issue of whether or not he could have gone on making art work if he had understood, articulated, and clarified the unique art management competence that originally made his fame is a matter for speculation. In 1915, almost a generation later, the reflections of the art-dealer Daniel-Henri Kahnweiler (1884–1979) become relevant to both the Antoine case and the more general problem of aesthetic value lurking in its background.

In the first decade of the century, Kahnweiler discovered the painters he would later so successfully market as "cubists" only a stone's throw from the old Théâtre Libre. Shortly after his arrival in France, young Kahnweiler came across the unknown Spanish painters Juan Gris and Pablo Ruiz, alias

Picasso, in their Rue Ravignan studio. He also met the trendy "fine colourist"[36] van Dongen there and immediately picked up on the difference between him and the other two. The Dutchman claimed that he simply re-produced pictures he *saw* complete in his head, whereas Picasso admitted that he only had a *vague idea* when he started painting. His pictures were experiments on canvas.

The well-read art dealer Kahnweiler set out with German philosophical thoroughness to reconstruct what Wagner had already termed the "prob-lems" that the Montmartre artists were "solving" in their art.[37] Kahnweiler showed his instinctive awareness of the rules of an aesthetic play when he set up an avant-garde art firm and expanded his work as a gallerist-dealer into that of a critic contemplating art in a way impossible for artists them-selves.[38] In Kahnweiler's essays, cubism is presented as art working in the search of truth. He saw his art firm as a laboratory where the science was aesthetics. In this laboratory-art firm, Braque and Picasso worked as con-tracted researcher-artists for a dealer-critic, their gallerist Kahnweiler.[39]

Kahnweiler's essays are helpful accounts of how his art firm produced surplus value. His cubist laboratory put the artist into systematically devel-oping and realizing Cézanne's attempt to escape illusionist painting. A paint-ing is always a two-dimensional surface, and any honest artist ought to ac-cept this two-dimensional limitation of his picture. Kahnweiler, in tune with neo-Kantian thought, believed that the world is actively constructed by the mental processes in the eye of the beholder. Psychologists in both the United States and Europe were also beginning to research how observers create deep images out of flat information on a canvas. The audience in an aes-thetic play, it seemed, was able to assume a rather active part in the play, if good critics, such as Kahnweiler himself, educated them properly for their aesthetic task. In turn, this made it possible to limit the artist's part to "prob-lems of construction" of the strictly two-dimensional images that would be subsequently transformed into three dimensions by a critic-assisted audi-ence. Acknowledging the active part of the audience in the aesthetic play meant that modern artists could skip the clever use of color that had al-lowed the masters of the Renaissance to create the illusion of a third dimen-sion on a flat canvas. Kahnweiler admired Picasso and Braque for having dared to be radical and abandon color.[40] Art no longer implied lying and pretending to perform a miracle of a third dimension by means of illusion of light.

Kahnweiler had little respect for what he felt to be pretentious mysticism evident at that time in Paris. The trend was represented by the bizarre Maurice Princet, a phony metaphysician and habitué of the art cafés, who become popular for his theories about a surreal fourth dimension.[41] As a two-dimensional shadow is cast by a three-dimensional reality, this our three-dimensional world might in turn be but a projection of a higher four-dimensional reality on the walls of our Platonic cave. Duchamp, a young painter then, became so taken with Princet's speculation that he used to make objects just for the shadows they cast.[42] Kahnweiler's true cubists stayed away from such esoteric monochromatic pictures (almost in the style of architectural plans, occasionally including printed text and images). Collages and assemblages of posters, advertisements, and printed matter—authentic clipped matters of fact from the real world—replaced traditional illusion in cubist pictures, just as Antoine's mother's real furniture had replaced traditional make-believe props in Théâtre Libre.[43] The grafting of such real stuff—a concrete element such as an add-on to a Picasso canvas or the shop interior in a naturalist setting—became the task of the technician. The fourth player in the Gadamerian model at last had a role in the aesthetic play.

When Kahnweiler's art firm transformed paintings into colorless images, the works stopped being images and were made to work as texts. Under his management (and he pointed this out), painting became transformed into an "*écriture,*" into writing.[44] He then described the surplus value of cubist art work not in terms of economics but of linguistic theory. In writing, Kahnweiler says, phonetics are linked to vocal sounds. Painting is, however, ideographic, and its graphical signs resemble pictures or pictograms. The language of painting, then, is pictographic, not phonetic. Readers phonetically spell their way through texts to form spoken words that then connect to concepts in the form of images in the brain. According to Kahnweiler, however, the observer sees an image in pictograms that immediately—without using the roundabout medium of speech—gives an impression to which the individual can then apply concepts. Kahnweiler's art aims at immediately conveying information by impressing its audience without taking a detour through concepts,[45] a very Schopenhauerian aesthetic value creation indeed.

This account of the value making of art would no doubt also have pleased Kant. It fit the Aristotelian defense against Plato's accusation of humbug, illusion, and fakery of representation. Plato regarded artists as arrogant illusionists and art as a form of cosmetics engineered to seduce its audience like painted whores in an obscure brothel.[46] Aristotle replied that true art never pretended to do anything but an aid in forming ideas.[47] No intelligent audience would take a painter of still life to be in the same business as the green grocer. Kahnweiler's view of art as ideographic writing, as with the symbolizing of an apple—especially in a two-dimensional, colorless cubist drawing—is impossible to confuse with the material pleasure of eating fruit.

Kahnweiler's art was strictly a matter of researching formal ideas. In the past, artists had attempted to gain academic privileges by arguments similar to Kahnweiler's marketing discourse of cubist painting. In France during the 1600s, the Poussinists outmaneuvered the Rubenists by using a similar strategy. Artists inspired by Rubens put their faith in color; those who admired Poussin stressed the importance of form.[48] Drawing was the important thing for the Poussinists, just as Braque and Picasso praised writing in the same stroke with which they aborted color. When color does appear in the cubist's work, it is only as a loose suggestion—or color hypothesis—for the observer to freely apply to a mental picture. Honest painting should be like writing in a language of formal design. In his nominalist treatise of 1969, American philosopher Nelson Goodman focuses on the *Languages of Art*[49] that have become central to modern art since its Kahnweilian linguistic turn.

Modern art firms offer an exchange of what Goodman calls a picture theory of language for a language theory of pictures that reveals how art really is made to work. Goodman shows what happens when Kahnweiler's value theory of art is taken to its extreme. In an earlier article, Goodman spells out the argument he subsequently was to apply to the understanding of art:

> The devastating charge against the picture theory of language was that a description cannot represent or mirror forth the world as it is. But we have since observed that a picture does not do this either. I began by dropping the picture theory of language and ended by adopting the language theory of pictures. I rejected the picture theory of language on the ground that the structure of descriptions does not conform to the structure of the world. But then I concluded that there is no such thing as the structure of the world for anything to conform or not conform to. You might say that the picture theory of language is as false and as

true as the picture theory of pictures: or in other words, that
what is false is not the picture theory of language but a certain
absolutistic notion concerning both pictures and language.[50]

As aesthetic philosophy from Kant to Gadamer claims, the value of art is
truth telling, what Goodman defines as the linguistic processes of social conventions and agreements. Goodman opts for exactly the sort of philosophy
Schopenhauer violently rejected as unworthy of real philosophy. To Goodman, truth arises from the memorization and association he terms "symbolic" learning. When people read words, they learn to understand them by
association with other words, and when they see pictures—for example, a
painting in perspective—they apply similarly learned visual symbolism to
them. To Goodman, truth is strictly an *intra*linguistic relative affair. As a
radical antimetaphysician, he is against "absolutistic notions" outside the
realm of language ("there is no such thing as the structure of the world for
anything to conform to or not conform to"). Learning becomes only a matter of "relabeling," the kind of language engineering Goodman managerially termed "organization."

> Representation and description thus involve and are often in-
> volved in organization. A label associates objects as it applies to,
> and is associated with, the other marks of a kind or kinds . . . by
> virtue of how it classifies and is classified, may make or mark
> connections, analyze objects and organize the world. . . . In sum
> the effective representation and description require invention. . . .
> That nature imitates art is too timid a dictum. Nature is a prod-
> uct of art and discourse.[51]

Goodman is helpful in showing clearly the limits of contemporary analytical philosophy in making art work. His nominalism is antimetaphysical
in that it refuses any academic support to absolutistic notions as essence of
existence or being. Goodman seriously claims an image to be sad not because it conveys sadness but because it carries the label "sad."[52] When Jarry
turned Lugné's art firm into a forest by hanging up a sign bearing the word
*forest,* it was more of a desperate joke about absurd and unbearable nominalism. According to Goodman, the only tool of meaning is the linguistic
metaphor. Knowledge can never be anything deeper than *re*labeling by
metaphor, which, according to Goodman, is only "a matter of teaching an
old word new tricks—of applying an old label in a new way."[53]

To Goodman, all that can be said about art, as well as all that art itself can formulate, is cognitive knowledge like that in Kahnweiler's cubist collages. Daily ideographic language consists of frozen metaphors, labels whose glue has long since hardened. Goodman therefore claims that it is only through experience and information that people learn to distinguish a fake by Van Meegeren from a real Vermeer.[51] Art making amounts to nothing more than loosening the labeling glue and sticking the old label on something else.

On the other hand, René Magritte's famous image of the smoking pipe labeled "Ceci n'est pas une pipe" carries an irony and humor that actually pokes fun at such a limited view of art. The thing on which the label hangs,  the pipe, is seen and recognized . . . and laughed at because it does not fit! This suggests that the thing-in-itself is a pipe. In overflowing Goodman's dry linguistic limits, art reveals its surplus value as something outside linguistic cognition. Creativity in art is therefore contrary to what Goodman seems to say. It is the discovery of anything outside language. The surplus of art is negatively defined as what language cannot grasp.

The difference between Goodman and Kahnweiler is that Goodman, although also a successful art dealer and collector, is mainly in the business of cognitive philosophy while Kahnweiler really wanted to make art work. Goodman's numerous art references seem like footnotes to his analytical philosophy of language. Kahnweiler's references to philosophy, by contrast, work as links to the cubist art he puts to work in his own gallery. His essays worked as catalogues of and for the gallery Rue Vignon. Goodman applied his philosophy to the pedagogic Harvard-based Project Zero, which, in the spirit of Dewey and James, aimed at using art for enhancing cognitive analytic skills. Goodman saw art as a means for cognition. Kahnweiler refers readers to paintings in his stock while Goodman seems more inclined to attract art lovers to become logicians.

At the turn of the last century, the techniques of reproduction had improved. Now books and periodicals not only contained texts but also began putting images of art on show. Gallerists began to publish photographic images of their art. Like Walden at the famous Berlin gallery Der Sturm,

Kahnweiler also undertook publishing art books. The Munich publisher Piper printed the richly illustrated *Blaue Reiterkalender,* produced by the Russian avant-garde painter Kandinsky and his associates. Kandinsky hoped that improvements in print quality would minimize the need for art critics, whose words essentially got in the way of art and obstructed its work.[55] The main purpose of these art books, calendars, catalogues, and periodicals was to let art itself speak and limit strictly linguistic narration. By organizing exhibitions, reproducing paintings, and starting art publications, these publishers made the image work, proving that it said more than words. Malraux, who was Kahnweiler's friend and a cubist, became the aesthetic spokesman for the technologies of immediate communication through images. He collected postcards, clippings, and posters of artwork throughout his life. It is no coincidence that the most published photograph of Malraux, the first minister for culture in western Europe, shows him in his office contemplating the heap of art picture postcards scattered on the floor he used to call his "*Musée Imaginaire.*"

## Kandinsky's Rhetoric Surplus

In the 1920s, when General Charles de Gaulle's future minister for culture first made a name for himself in the art world, his battle cry was: "Out of my way, I'm a cubist!" Under Kahnweiler's cubist banner, Malraux stood up against metaphysical competitors such as the dadaists, surrealists, and other supporters of what Goodman would have banned as a picture theory of language.

On the Rue de Grenelle, André Breton opened the surrealists' avant-garde version of Sigmund Freud's Berggasse clinic in Vienna. Breton called it the Bureau for Artistic Investigation of the Subconscious. Like Kahnweiler, Malraux was probably skeptical about Breton's antagonistic activities in this bureau for surrealist investigation.[56] To Malraux and Kahnweiler, artists such as Breton and Duchamp were what Lugné had been to Antoine: pirates entering their avant-garde lagoon. Tzara's dada challenged cubism; "merz," from *Kommerz,* was the German designer Schwitters's brand against dada; and surrealism soon turned bolshevik in opposition to fascist futurists. All these avant-garde projects had their policy, strategy, and manifestos. To cubists such as Kahnweiler, these artists were either sectarian traitors to his textual view of image or simply fanatics blinded by faith in a mystical power of imagery Goodman was fighting. Anyway, avant-garde was a highly competitive and volatile market for aesthetic startup brands.

In 1934, Kahnweiler paid a visit to the studio of a newly arrived artist from eastern Europe. He was taken with this distinguished Russian, but not with his art. Vassily Kandinsky had not learned anything from impressionism, fauvism, or cubism, according to Kahnweiler.[57] Had he been aware of Kandinsky's picture philosophy, his judgment would have been even harsher. Kandinsky firmly believed that paintings could only be made to work as art if they were far removed from language. It was absurd to think of paintings as calligraphic songs to be read; real art should work as music one could listen to. Even though Picasso and Braque are mentioned in Kandinsky's treatise *Concerning the Spiritual in Art*, its heroes were musicians such as Wagner and Mussorgsky, who were more than a little offensive to Parisian cubists. To add insult to injury, Kandinsky had developed his view of spiritual surplus value of color from Madame Blavatsky's theosophical doctrine of the auras of the soul.[58]

Kandinsky's philosophical dictum came from Maeterlinck, Lugné-Poe's court poet, who said, "The words may express an inner harmony."[59] Lugné had taken the image, not texts, as raw materials for his art firm. His theater was not for author-playwrights, but for painters. He rebelled against Antoine's depictive realism and created his own language of images for abstract theatrical poetry. The spectacular technological development of the photography industry, with its monopoly on realistic depiction, made it necessary for modern art firms to develop a market for images of their very own. Two decades after Lugné, Kandinsky states: "A material object cannot be absolutely reproduced. . . . [G]enuine artists cannot be content with a mere inventory of material objects. . . . The impossibility and, in art, the uselessness of attempting to copy an object exactly, the desire to give the object full expression, are the impulses which drive the artist away from "literal" colouring to purely artistic aims. And that brings us to the question of composition.[60]

Schopenhauer claimed that music was highest of the arts and that the composer was a genius in his offering his audience a direct contemplation of will. Music was believed to work as art by generating spiritual vibration. As art, it immediately influenced the human soul in its abstract energetic way. To Kandinsky, the level of abstraction reached by music became a Schopenhauerian goal for all modern art. Earlier, painting was figurative and often had linguistic and humanistic models.[61] Within strict guidelines set by priests or religious scholars, artists used to illustrate myths, legends, biblical stories, and historical chronicles; and detailed theological handbooks instructed painters and sculptors about religious craftwork. For example, Poussin was severely reprimanded for omitting several camels mentioned in the Bible in his painting "Eliezer and Rebecca."[62] Artists, it was assumed, ought to adhere to objective textual details and not seek inspiration in the subjective style of their masters—who, like Leonardo, tended to escape from the regulated guilds to become free market art entrepreneurs.

At the beginning of the twentieth century, however, photography and other forms of reproductive technology were rapidly developing. When depictions became the matter of various cultural industries, art had to search for a market of its very own. To Kandinsky, once art is made to work in that way, "the abstract idea [creeps] into art. . . . Its gradual advance is natural enough, for in proportion as the organic form falls into the background, the abstract ideal achieves greater prominence."[63]

Making art work as a free enterprise, liberated from external models and scriptural conventions, made it as free and abstract as music. Kandinsky foresaw a boom in new art firms guided by a modern strategy he called "the principle of inner necessity." To explain the aesthetic surplus value of such art firms, Kandinsky presents a phenomenological picture theory of art with color as its main factor of production. It seems as if he is saying, Let us try to forget everything we have learned, all conventions and associations. As children we experience the world intensely and directly. But as we grow older, our impressions become more superficial. A child tastes, smells, and feels immediately with all of the senses. But the development of intellect alters the nature of our contact with the world as we increasingly use our memories to build up a history of past experiences. Fire is red and is hot; therefore we associate to the sensation of heat when we see anything that has the same fiery red color. Yellow lemons are sour, so we associate yellow with sourness. Our associative memories link together the signifier (red or yellow color) and the signified (sourness or heat). But if we want remain playful children, we should not let color turn to such signs.

According to Kandinsky, there is another, more direct way of seeing color. He claimed that research showed that adults demonstrate a direct sensation and taste of color that indicates a different perception of color, one which is not learned. Certain foods, for example, might be experienced as colors: a sauce might taste "blue," for instance. In the same way, the sight of a certain color might trigger a sensation of sound. On this basis, claimed Kandinsky, color therapy, or *chromotherapy*, has been successfully used as a medical technique. Kandinsky claimed that cognitive association and learned responses could not adequately explain the good effects of chromotherapy. "Generally speaking, colour is a power which directly influences the soul," concluded Kandinsky in shaping his value theory for art firms. "Colour is the keyboard, the eyes are the hammers, the soul is the piano with many strings. The artist is the hand which plays, touching one key or another, to cause vibrations in the soul."[64]

For children, this sort of soulful impact of art is always obvious. Now, according to Kandinsky, the development of modern art will work at maintaining the link between sight with sound in grownups. Making art work, then, implies keeping man's mind alert and open to color. A century before Kandinsky, Goethe had exhorted artists to abandon representational, languagelike art and adopt color as the basis for their painting. In this Goethean tradition that Kandinsky now sought to revive, black and white were the traditional colors for designing scriptural signs that have only denotative value as signifiers. A denotation—a sign drawn in black and white—cannot make surplus value, since it only parasitizes the preexisting value to which it refers, relates, or associates. The actual domination of the language theory of pictures has chased away color and made black and white as popular as the noncolor color of intellectual designer products. A century after Kahnweiler, trendy people therefore dress up as calligraphic signs to be read as minimalist messages. Kandinsky already had attacked designer formalism. He wanted color to counterbalance this intellectualization and liberate people from the cognitive imprisonment of false black-and-white symbolism.

According to Kandinsky, real symbols used in art, the forms of objects produced by designers, should not be linguistic. Meaning should come from within, like the divine geometry Schopenhauer thought proven through presentation and not formal discourse. The main purpose of such inner-oriented forms would be to condition and help the immediate impact of color. For example, a triangle might sharpen a color, or a circle deepen it. Future form would become dutifully subservient to color, which would hit the strings of the human soul, its vibration facilitating the materialization of art.

This can be seen as Kandinsky's minor contribution to the long-running artistic dispute between color and form, which was the reason for the row between the Poussinists and the Rubenists in seventeenth-century France. Using Plato's philosophy as a defense, the Poussinists claimed to represent a form of art worthy of academic status. They were proud to have moved on from the primitive craft of color blenders and now to represent an intellectual industry of ideas and thoughts. In French, one word for idea, *dessein*, is remarkably similar to the word for drawing, *dessin*. *Avoir un dessein* is to have both a plan and a sketch. *Dessiner* means to draw, whereas the verb *designer* is to point out, to indicate. The word *design* possesses a platonic depth far removed from its mere technical accomplishment. It signifies thoughts and ideas that were regarded as *Segno di Dio*, signs from God.[65]

The Poussinists demanded to be respected as intellectual academicians by virtue of the fact that they were such designers. Depiction was the discursive language of artists; it gave them the status to issue official historical paintings in their capacity as court academicians long before the reports of historical chroniclers were printed. Depiction was the link between image and writing, and this was the justification for the presence of artists in the salons of Versailles. Kahnweiler was evidently attempting to elevate his cubists to a similar status in the French Republic. Even in the 1600s, however, men who held beliefs similar to those of Kandinsky threatened designers. These were the adherents of Rubens, artists who put their faith in color in their quest for academic value, for truth. The Rubenists constructed defensive arguments that were sufficiently intellectual to prevent the established Poussinists from devastating them in an academic conflict.

Just as Kandinsky referred to Goethe, the Poussinists referred to Aristotle. Their principal spokesman at court, Roger de Piles, agreed that images were perfectly capable of revealing absolute truths, to which the Rubenist claimed that this surplus value did not depend on design or depiction. The role of an artist's image is to make ideas concrete; its real aesthetic surplus value lies, so to speak, in the incarnation of ideals.[66] De Piles made his point by creating a rhetoric value theory for art firms.

As an orator must have a good command of grammar, so too an artist must have the necessary technical abilities. Just as grammar itself has no voice, the technical skills of drawing have no eyes. Would not a blind sculptor, he asked, through touch with bare hands be able to model a true bust? The painting gets special rhetorical value since, de Piles claimed:

> The painter is like the orator, the sculptor like the grammarian.
> . . . A painter must persuade the eyes, just as an eloquent man

must touch the heart. One need not point out the evidence that an orator must have a good command of grammar and speak intelligently and with precision in order to be persuasive. It is equally superfluous to point out that a painter must be able to draw as well as possible in order to impose the eyes.[67]

Form—and the Greek theories which legitimize it—is therefore necessary but insufficient for the art firm enterprise to succeed. Drawing must be mastered, but color is what really adds art's aesthetic surplus value. Those still doubting the value of the colorists found strong theoretical support for them in Rome. The Italian philosopher Giambattista Vico defended poets against grammarians who regarded poetry as inferior to their own intellectual rules.[68] Just as Kandinsky later claimed that children approach art with an open mind, Vico claimed that poetry best survived among simple people whose vibrant language had escaped the dictatorship of the textual scholars. For Vico, true poetry had nothing to do with grammar but instead was inspired by gestures, emblems, and popular images from bountiful folktales.

A similar approach is found today in the work of Ludwig Wittgenstein. If Nelson Goodman's American nominalism took Kahnweiler's linguistic theory of pictures to its extreme, Wittgenstein's philosophy can be seen as indirectly advocating an extension of Kandinsky's picture theory of language. When Wittgenstein spoke of linguistic pictures, he was referring to sentences, propositions constructed with words.[69] Wittgenstein, who grew up in a milieu imbued with Goethe and Schopenhauer, suggested that one did not *know* if an image was true or false; one rather immediately *saw* if something was art.[70] For Wittgenstein, real truths could not be proven mathematically or logically. Like Schopenhauer, he did not think that the criteria of truth could be tested cognitively. Mathematical equations and logical formulas were only closed, self-referential relational tautologies, for which the word *truth* was actually much too large. Wittgenstein was, without ever saying so, most certainly applying Schopenhauer's interpretation of truth. He claimed that modern philosophizing, whether it be written, spoken, or thought, was hopelessly limited by language. If a linguistic image suggested ideas beyond language, they could never be proven by means of a philosophy of language. Language was not an instrument or mirror that could be used to reconstruct real life outside its limited jurisdiction. Provided certain knowledge belongs to the realm of philosophy, language nevertheless sets the limit of all facts that can ever be known, according to

Wittgenstein. "Knowledge" in this perspective becomes a relative concept, however, while truth concerns the absolute.

What separates Wittgenstein from Goodman is that the Austrian's writings are imbued with poetic nostalgia for absolutes beyond what he felt were the narrow boundaries of language. For Wittgenstein, who was actually a subversive Schopenhauerian working hard at discouraging all his best Cambridge philosophy students from becoming academic philosophers, a serious search for truth had to take place outside modern language philosophy. Academia, he believed, is locked up in language systems, while the most interesting existential questions of philosophy are situated in a speechless territory.

To Professor Wittgenstein, real truth seekers should flee the universities, those analytical asylums of a mad modern civilization, and escape to the Soviet Union, which was then the trendiest place for radical Cambridge materialists. Schopenhauer kept his faith in art, but Wittgenstein was 100 percent pessimist. To him, modern art was no solution. He even preferred movies with tough cowboys to avant-garde events. Further, he thought little of music after Brahms (although Ravel had composed a special one-hand concerto in honor of Ludwig's own pianist brother, who had lost an arm in World War I).

For life's blessed incarnations of absolute truth, Wittgenstein uses the word *zeigt*, "to be shown," in the revelatory meaning of the word. Truth shows itself as the experience of a sudden revelation of an image. Further, he shared Schopenhauer's opinion that university philosophers are bad art critics, because they close out the possibility of such ephemeral truth.

Wittgenstein's theory of images is often referred to as "immanence theory." Philosophers of reason, such as Goodman, have criticized the proponents of image theory as primitive shamans or magicians, since they imply that their images *possess* an essence. The Christian church attempted to tone down the magic when it commissioned artists to produce images of saints; the idea was that the images should not themselves be sacred but should venerate the saints of whom they were only representational "shadows." Symbolists such as Saussure and Goodman see themselves in the same way that Hume—who invented "causality" to fight religious superstition—did: as modern inquisitors, methodically hunting down reminiscent immanence theorists. In his early article already quoted in this chapter, Goodman attacks the immanence "obscurantists" as followers of the dangerous French metaphysician Bergson. Like a sheriff from the Wild West, Goodman issues a warrant for "the mystic," whose transparently European portrait perfectly fits poor Wittgenstein:

> The mystic holds that there is some way the world is and that this way is not captured by any description. . . . Since the mystic is concerned with the way the world is and that that way cannot be expressed, his ultimate response to the question of the way the world is must, as he recognises, be silence.[71]

Obviously Sheriff Goodman will roundly reward whoever captures mystics, dead or alive, be it Henri Bergson, Arthur Schopenhauer, or Ludwig Wittgenstein. Wittgenstein and his group were European killjoys, who called philosophical games in universities meaningless, tautological nonsense. Knowing Wittgenstein's bolshevik sympathies, one cannot escape seeing an element of intellectual McCarthyism in Goodman's fear of obscurantist threats to democracy. Better to make truth banal language than to fall into the aesthetic totalization trap. Better to stop the metaphysicians before they have turned their truth surplus-value theory into an aesthetic Marxism legitimizing the dictatorship of artist-proletarians. Better to stop them by legislating that only scientifically proven theories are allowed.

Fortunately for those still fearing metaphysicians, more than fifty years after Kandinsky referred to psychophysiological research, the American philosopher of art Arthur Danto has suggested that even the pictures theory actually might have a sound scientific basis.[72] Psychologists, although asserting that animals cannot understand drawings, have found that they do seem to recognize color photographs. Small children recognize both drawings and color photographs. This idea is relevant to the question of whether or not perception alone accounts for how images are understood—that truth might be revealed without any cognitive learning behind it. Danto suggests it is an innate sense of perception, much like Kandinsky's inner necessity. Alongside these theoretical reasons for taking image theory seriously, ancient Roman rhetoricians, some of whom inspired Vico, put forth a wealth of arguments supporting a nonmystical acceptance of color as the basis for truth of a more pragmatic kind.

The Romans Cicero and Quintilian directly applied Greek theories of rhetoric to management.[73] In Rome, courses in rhetoric resembled human resource management schools. Cicero stated that rhetoric was a practical tool for political discussion in the forum; it was not a nice game like passing time in Palestra.[74] As with marketing or management today, rhetoric was performance oriented to making profit. Rhetoric as management would succeed only if the marketer was passionately convinced of his argument. He had to physically believe in what he mentally advocated. A calm and collected symbolist would never make it on the market, since it was possible to influence others only if he himself were both mentally and physically possessed by what he was saying.

According to Cicero, it is impossible to cheat in rhetoric. An orator's body must submit itself to the passions he seeks to transmit to his audience. Rhetoric is therefore the basis of the art firm, and its performance, a physical display of the orator's bodily being as a *Ding an Sich,* in Schopenhauer's Kantian terms. An orator must be what he says. Quintilian claims that it is possible to falsify philosophical arguments, but such false rhetoric will never have the desired effect. A philosophical discursive argument may well have shallow, although logically correct, foundations, but successful oration must always be based upon sound skills.

A talented speaker has no need of external linguistic ornamentation. Using his voice as his tool, he paints a picture where his words turn, in effect, into poetic colors. Discursive truth means only that the signifier indicates something signified, which, however, is hopelessly absent. Both painters and orators instead bring color to torrid language and imbue their images with a fascinating rhetorical presence. This is probably how Kandinsky wanted to make art work.

## Genette's Immanent Object

Wagner, Antoine, and Lugné-Poe all worked at changing conventional banal show biz into Schopenhauerian art enterprises. Kahnweiler and Kandinsky reflected aesthetic surplus value as a symbolic or rhetoric product. Goodman and Wittgenstein, each in his own way and probably unintentionally, helped demonstrate Schopenhauer's conviction that the paramount philosophical problems of being today can never completely find a solution within the realms of symbolism or rhetoric. Aesthetic values emerge in between, so when art firms take images and texts and make them work as art, the surplus value exceeds their value as single depictions, as illustrations of texts or descriptions, and as information of images. When art works, its aesthetic surplus value adds something that is missing, what lacks or falls short of individual images and texts.

To paraphrase Jean-Paul Sartre, to make art work is perhaps to perform a metaphysics that presents being out of nothingness. Indeed, French Bergsonian philosopher Gilles Deleuze once suggested that avant-garde art carries out the Schopenhauerian legacy by practicing negative metaphysics. He claimed that the first modern art firm was invented at Lugné's Théâtre de l'Œuvre by no less than Jarry's *Ubu Roi* project. Jarry introduced the play as the fruit of his new mock philosophy, pataphysics. With Nietzschean arrogance, Jarry declared pataphysics to be the modern successor of outmoded metaphysics. Although metaphysics was searching for eternal, transcendental, and universal one-and-only Truth, its modern heir wanted to document the unique, special, and ephemeral. Jarry's *canulard*, his bizarre French pun about pataphysics, shares the pragmatist James's view of truth as something situational and case-specific, not having universal and eternal relevance. In the opinion of Deleuze, *Ubu Roi* was pioneering a new form of philosophical truth that balanced on the Nietzschean borderline between modern and postmodern metaphysics. To be sure, pataphysics is an anarchistic revolt instead of metaphysical revolution. This is direct action liberated of its claims to Schopenhauerian transcendental universality. The art firm to both Sartre and Deleuze is an "art brut" business à la Bakunin, booming after the death of both God and the state.[75]

The contemporary cradle of this sort of philosophical business was modern theater. Art history confirms how theaters became the natural incubators of new art firms. Upon joining the Bauhaus school of design, Kandinsky immediately helped set up a theatrical laboratory in which design students were able to experiment with rhetoric and symbolism of design. In practice, much of their education consisted of making performances and parties. It was not sufficient to make smart drawings on paper or even manufacture prototypes; design had to be presented as Antoine staged texts and Lugné preformed images to make it really work.

Not surprisingly, Bauhaus veteran Joseph Albers introduced such experimental performances in the United States. When an individual's eyes meet the constructed forms of a picture, the result is a fusion of what Albers calls, in a rather Goethean fashion, "factual facts" of form and the "actual facts" of the colors.[76] Such encounters have to be staged as aesthetic plays, however, which Albers did as an art teacher at Black Mountain College. Albers became the mentor of Robert Rauschenberg, John Cage, and Merce Cunningham. Together with artist friends in the New York art world, they developed Albers's Goethean happenings into what today is called "performance art."[77] American director Richard Schechner then theorized how performances produced units of aesthetic surplus value he chose to call "actuals,"[78] overlooking the fact that what constitutes contemporary demand for this modern Dionysian art is European aesthetic philosophy. Schechner instead focused on superficial similarities between performance art and primitive rituals, since "actualizing is plain among rural, tribal people, and it is becoming plainer among our own young and in their avant-garde art."[79]

Karl Marx once talked about management in terms of making surplus value by blending work and capital as chemical substances in the modern alchemist's retort of the industrial factory. In a performance, the raw materials of image and text are tossed into the melting pot of the art firm. The product is an incarnation of the indissoluble union of two value-making processes: symbolism and rhetoric. Kahnweiler insisted art had a symbolic meaning, that it worked as rhetoric. Schopenhauerian management cases from avant-garde history, such as that of Lugné's competition with Antoine, illustrate how art firms evolve by balancing antagonistic methods.[80]

With too much emphasis on rhetoric, it all ends up in a materialistic star system. At this point in theater history, managers such as Gordon Craig and Bertolt Brecht emerged. They innovated by dampening the noise of empty declamatory virtuosity. Brecht made himself known for radically cutting out the pathos of color and presenting form alone in flat, dispassionate readings of text.[81] Cool formalism was to chill down an overheated rhetorical production. Craig wanted to get rid of the stars altogether and give sole responsibility to the director, but when the pendulum schwung too much toward form, Kandinskylike innovation emphasizing materiality, such as the reintroduction of color, again came into fashion. Such Schillerian Schwung is not only relative, however; there has to be an absolute equilibrium point for the pendulum.

In considering absolute value, the French philosopher Gerard Genette's theory of art, which refers to "immanent objects," is helpful. He claims that the value of a work of art is never equal to either its physical images or textual notation, since image and text—in Genette's terms, "manifestations" and "notations"—are only factors producing aesthetic value. For Goodman, by contrast, image and text are two distinct and mutually exclusive forms of art. To him, there is *autographic* original art directly manifested by the artist's work, and art that could be technologically replicated by means of some notation, which he calls *allographic*. The *Mona Lisa* is a typical autographic picture, while a copy of Don Quixote is an allographic book. Art-dealing nominalist Goodman, who cannot accept any "obscurantist" inner values, commodifies art as original signed pieces or certified perfect copies one could easily trade for art on the market.

Genette, however, notes that art, in reality, is far fuzzier than Goodman would wish.[82] For example, a work of art might consist of several objects. Without being allographically mass-produced, an image might exist in

different forms or versions. Several pictures could thus belong to one and the same work of art, just as a single sculpture can legally exist in many versions, each of which is considered an original. Further, the same musical work might exist in choral, orchestral, and piano editions. Although Mahler might have scribbled in Schumann's score, for example, the symphony is still regarded as Schumann's own. Although a doodle or blueprint might not form part of a single work, art critics might reckon that a sketch does. Despite damage, and occasionally even destruction, a work might be regarded as surviving thanks to reconstruction and conservation. To make art work therefore implies discarding the marketing idea of art as a unique product.

In their crusade against metaphysics, nominalists condemn any practice that acknowledges art of any kind besides original and copy. It is precisely in a third, in-between, position that Genette situates what he sees as the aesthetic surplus value of an art work. This he calls the immanent object. Art in a piece of music such as *Tannhäuser*, for example, is an immanent object that might be interpolated between Wagner's original score and concrete *Tannhäuser* experiences one might have had in opera performances. In architecture, the surplus value of work is a similar intermediary mix of both the architect's abstract design and the experience of dwelling in the concrete building. The immanent object of ballet is the hybrid of the dance on the stage and the choreographer's notation; a gastronome grasps the aesthetic value of a dish as the fusion of the notations in a richly illustrated recipe book and the direct eating experience of the plate of steaming food on the table or stage in front of her.

From an art firm perspective, Genette's definition is indeed more problematic than Goodman's simpler idea that art is merely the unique product or the certified copy for sale. No wonder Anglo-Saxon legal practices in search of an unambiguous concept of art fit for a market economy have opted for the latter nominalist definition. In this tradition, art could be considered a marketable property only if either formally written down, registered, and notified in accordance with legal copyright protection or fixed in matter, as with a painting or sculpture.

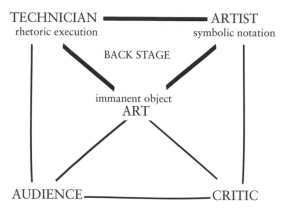

*Backstage Management of Images*
*and Language to Project Immanent Objects*

In continental Europe, however, a third legal position exists that is much more in tune with aesthetic philosophy. In 1880, Josef Kohler, a German jurist, published *Das Authorenrecht,* in an attempt to define immaterial property rights for immanent objects of Genette's kind.[83] Kohler, who admits to being inspired by the Kantian-Schopenhauerian view of art, recognizes that art has both inner and outer form. Outer form to Kohler is what Genette calls manifestations, the bodily gestures of a dance, the bricks of a building, or the words of a novel. Inner form has to do with the feelings a person gets out of a work. Kohler ultimately concludes that something else, a third Schillerian phenomenon in between inner form and outer matter, constitutes the essential aesthetic value of art. In modernity, Kohler believes, creators of this essence—Genette's immanent object or Kant's thing-in-itself—are to be entitled to proper legal state protection, because they contribute highly to the aesthetic wealth of nations. In Kohler's view, the state should acknowledge an *Urheberecht* founded on a competence for making art work by unlifting—in German, *Heben,* something from a profound hidden origin, *Ur.* It takes some acquaintance with continental aesthetic philosophy to fully appreciate Kohler's doctrine. This explains the limited impact on an international legal practice under the domination of Anglo-Saxon property law. Nevertheless, Kohler indicates what juridical conclusions this model of aesthetic play gives rise to. In terms of the art firm, the aesthetic surplus value of aesthetic play should be considered as hybridizing into an immanent object of, on the one hand, form, the symbolic value of a notational text, and on the other matter, as rhetoric colorful images.

# 6

## Artistic Companies

### Cases of Aesthetic Management

#### David's Festival Firm

In the East Prussian port of Königsberg, the aging Immanuel Kant, founding father of the enlightened "business of being," toasted the universal significance of the seizing and sacking of the Bastille on July 14, 1789. His first enlightened enthusiasm occurred, however, before the guillotine began working and official art was called in to extend the metaphysical politics of the Parisian rebellion.

In 1792, Robespierre, the leader of the party of radical Jacobins and himself a management scientist of the Revolution, sought a new metaphysics to fill the void left by the monarchy and the church. He turned to the painter Jacques-Louis David (1748–1825). During the Reign of Terror between 1792 and 1794, the industrious David staged numerous propaganda events in the public spaces of Paris. As master of ceremonies for the Jacobins, he managed their event marketing by *La fête de la Liberté*, *La fête de la Réunion Republicaine*, and finally, *La fête de l'Être Suprême*, which occurred just before the fall and "liquidation" of Robespierre.

David started out as a maker of images, a craftsman expecting to receive tenure in the French court. He trained in the Royal Academy of Art and in 1774, on his fourth attempt, was finally awarded a prestigious scholarship to study at the Royal French Institute in Rome.[1] Competition for the Prix de Rome was intense. Six candidates were required to spend ten weeks in isolation and produce an image which would illustrate the text of whichever classical myth was the year's chosen subject. In Rome, David joined the ranks of the other artists being trained by an élite corps of court masters in the Palazzo Mancini.

On his return to Paris in the early 1780s, he worked at painting pictures for the biennial exhibition in the Louvre. The commissars, a group of academicians, selected art for the exhibition from artists' submissions, and then the chosen pieces were put on display in the Salon Carrée, the public gallery of the Louvre.

At that time, academic art concentrated on just putting images to texts. David chose to illustrate Corneille's play *Horace,* which he had seen in the theatre the previous year. He certainly picked this Roman story, which had recently been the subject of a controversial pamphlet by Jean-François Marmontel, for its actuality.

When David returned to Rome early in 1785, rumors began to spread that he was working on a fantastic painting in his private studio. After this word-of-mouth advertising campaign, he opened the doors to his workplace, and queues of people lined up to witness the unveiling of the freshly varnished painting. To this vernissage came foreign artists, then Italian artists, followed by nobility, cardinals from the Vatican, and all the others curious to see the picture before it was dispatched to Paris. The knowledgeable audience immediately recognized the painting as indeed being from the play *Horace,* but at the same time they realized that the chosen scene was nowhere to be found in Corneille's text. The artist, perhaps anxious that his static style would never be able to render the famed rhetoric of the author, had created a new image to avoid disappointing an audience so familiar with the text.[2]

Four years later, in 1789, the year of the Revolution, David achieved greater success when he found the courage to paint, *verbatim,* a well-known text by Voltaire. The Brutus for his subject was not the Brutus who murdered Julius Caesar, however, but Roman consul Lucius Janius Brutus, who went down in Roman history for opposing King Tarquinius. David's picture, *Lictors Bringing to Brutus the Bodies of His Sons*, was to be hung in the Louvre.

Voltaire's play was first performed in the theater in 1730; in 1786 it was revived by the Comédie Française. Then only one performance was given because of the inflammatory nature of the plot. Although the Parisian press expressed concern that David's picture would also be censored, the opposite happened. As is often the case, the rumor, together with the notoriety of the Voltaire play, proved to be good publicity for David's painting. He was praised for the daring innovation of placing the central figure of Brutus in shadow on one side of the picture. In the background, the bodies of his two executed sons were being carried in on stretchers. As the story goes, Brutus himself had condemned them to death for betraying the public by taking part in Tarquinius' monarchist conspiracy.

In the months following the storming of the Bastille, many people wondered what else was concealed in the shadows around Brutus. Was this a painting about duty versus freedom? Or a father's terrible fanaticism? Progressive critics claimed that the artist was a modern genius, while conservatives expressed concern at this "morgue républicaine" that seemed to forebode a terrific "férocité."[3] The discussion and controversy about the painting paid off for Voltaire, just as the furor over his play had paid off for David. The text marketed the image, and now the image promoted the text. By public request, Voltaire's play was once again performed in 1790.

What happened at the theater shows how David's painting provoked a desire for direct physical action, not just for visualizing the text. At the doors of the playhouse, the audience had to be disarmed of sticks, swords, and pikes. Some, however, managed to smuggle pistols in beneath their clothing. The republican rhetoric on stage was met with whistles from the boxes. Cries of "À bas les aristocrates" ("Down with the aristocracy") rose from the pit. When it came to the line "Vivre libre et sans roi," cries of "Long live the King" erupted from the boxes of the nobility, while the populistic pit shouted back "Vive la Nation!"[4] Even Voltaire, whose name also made a tumultuous dadaist cabaret fashionable in Zürich in 1916, would have been envious of such audience participation!

*Brutus* was performed against meticulous Roman scenery. The actor Talma, sporting short hair and bare legs and wearing a toga, was not only acclaimed for his performance; his appearance launched a new Parisian fashion on the spot. When someone shouted "Vive Voltaire!" at the end of the play, the actors rushed out to the foyer and returned to the stage carrying the marble bust of the dead writer. A piece of art was performing on stage! In the furor that ensued, members of the audience began scribbling impromptu poems in praise of Voltaire. Pieces of paper bearing their paeans were thrown onto the stage to be recited by the actors.

When *Brutus* was performed again two days later, the actors added a faithful enactment of David's renowned painting. Under the watchful gaze of Houdon's bust of a supercilious Voltaire (and a considerably grimmer old Italian painting of Brutus), David's image hybridized with Voltaire's text as an improvised tableau vivant on the stage of the Comédie Française. Art was made to work better than books or paintings ever had.

One year later, David himself experimented with another innovative hybridization of his image with Voltaire's texts. Voltaire was to be laid to rest as the first occupant of the new Pantheon. His remains were drawn on a huge catafalque through pouring rain. At various points along the route, dancing, singing, and readings took place in honor of the great philosopher of the Revolution.[5] Alongside the catafalque, city worthies and sundry notables carried a vellum edition of his complete works. David's own painting of Brutus was also carried in the procession.

When David became master of ceremonies for the Jacobin party in 1792, the catafalque that had carried Voltaire reappeared, almost like a relic, at his first political event. As David now excelled in technical special effects, he built various stages of celebration along the route, using trees, fountains, hills, statues, doves, teams of oxen, and of course soldiers with drums and horns , flags, and torches. This revolutionary feast was performed with all the old trappings of veneration, however, and in a rhythm of the deliberate slow movement of visitors to a place of pilgrimage or of noblemen in courtly ceremony. Though after new content, participants still clung to the old format of churches and castles.

At the time he directed these festivities, David was already a famous art entrepreneur among the revolutionaries; he undertook projects far bigger than traditional paintings. One of these projects was an immense picture of the Oath of the Tennis Court (Jeu de Paume), commemorating the event which took place on June 20, 1789, when the members of the National Assembly swore not to dissolve until the kingdom had a new constitution. In 1791, people stood in line at David's Paris studio to take a look at the sketches. The purpose of this picture show was to raise funds for the final painting, since the old royal incorporation of art had been crushed and a new state was not yet in place.

To this end, David decided to waive the usual entrance fee, which at the time in a majority of cases produced greater income than the sale of the paintings themselves. Now the multiples were for sale to finance the cost of the main production. Two centuries later, Christo Javacheff systematically employed the same method for financing his artistic company. For David, though, the sale of these engravings was disappointing, and when the state finally gave him the money to work on the Oath painting, alas the subject was no longer pressing. It was never completed. In this journalistic age, painting was far too slow a medium of documentation, so art had to be made to do other sorts of work.

Although the Jacobin festivities arranged by David did feature technicians, artist, and critics, there is no doubt that the most important player was the audience.

David organized the Parisian revolutionary street mob as a modern audience, renaming it "the people." In 1793, he declared the importance of the audience to his art work: "Before the eyes of the Almighty, I wish to put on show nothing but you; great and generous people, you; French people, only people truly worthy of liberty . . . May love of humanity, liberty and equality bring life to my brush of my painting."[6]

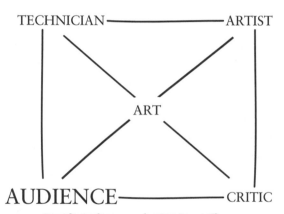

*David's Audience as the Dominant Player*

David was no longer just a craftsman using brushes to paint on canvas. He innovated as today's French luxury industry turns art from aristocratic haute couture crafts into catwalk spectacles for mass promotion of prêt-à-porter products to the people. When the French luxury goods corporation LVMH appointed John Galliano, a fan of French Revolution fashion and a graduate of St. Martin's School of Art, to Christian Dior in 1997, French journalists instinctively thought of David, calling the polytechnician-capitalist and CEO of LVMH, Bernard Arnault, the new Robespierre.[7]

David undoubtedly was the father of both political parades and private event techniques. He became an elaborate technician who constructed magnificent live performances out of a series of tableaux. One of his famous scenes featured eighty-six commissioners from all the departments of France, who drank toasts to the revolution with water from a "Well of Eternity." At just the right moment, thousands of pigeons were released from their cages to carry messages of freedom to the whole world. At the other extreme, the final tableau in the festival for *L'Être Suprème* was silent, creating a metaphysical vacuum. This sublime silence was eventually filled by a male choir that urged the people to obey their oath and not lay down their arms until all the enemies of the republic had been defeated. In 1783, under *l'ancien regime,* David had painted the antique oath of the worthies from Corneille's play *Horace.* Now, in the modern era of 1791, he exhibited his drawings for the painting of the modern oath at the Jeu de Paume, thereby manifesting a social contract the participants in his performances solemnly swore allegiance to. David's artist workshop developed into a designer studio where he conceptualized organizational symbols for oaths, promises, and contracts. He invented new emblems and armorials necessary and fitting for the new nation.

David called for the Royal Art Academy to close, since it produced narrow-minded craftsmen able only to copy old conventional truth. They had outlived their usefulness. Modernity, David declared, was now in need of enterprising artist-philosophers.[8] Royal academicians or guilded craftsmen were unfit to make art work for the modern nation, because they lacked links to philosophy. Real artistic companies were the business of practical philosophers managing an aesthetic play of sublime Schwung that would inspire the virtues of freedom, brotherhood, and equality. David's fellow Jacobins appointed Friedrich Schiller honorary citizen of the Republic, and in David's Kantian spirit his artistic company attempted to achieve more than just painting pictures or writing text. His events were so successful that it's almost a miracle he himself escaped the guillotine after Robespierre's execution.

Because his artistic public company had been banned, David discreetly returned to his easel and was later appointed Napoleon's court painter. When the Emperor visited David's studio some fourteen years after the Terror, Napoleon was disappointed. The former Jacobin wanted to show him his latest masterpiece, *Leonidas.* Unfortunately, Napoleon could find no trace of aesthetic energy in this dull military picture, which stood all alone in the artist's studio. Perhaps the emperor thought David terribly outmoded. Instead of allowing more natural poses, David had relapsed into following Winckelmann's imitation of classical statuary. He had been as innovative as an aesthetic manager as he was outmoded and passé as a painter.

When Daniel-Henri Kahnweiler examined David's paintings to investigate the dilemma of political art, he concluded that

> It is strange that the French Revolution made an artistic dictator out of a classical painter like David. . . . But was this style really suitable for the Revolution or the Empire? One might well doubt it. Is it not strange that this style became predominant despite this? How could the enthusiasm and energy of the time be expressed in such a rigid style of art? . . . It seems that the bureaucrats, without the least idea about visual art, simply forced the intelligentsia to accept this classical, moribund style, despite many of them being opposed to it. A style of art without the slightest relevance to this vibrant and intensive age was kept alive artificially.[9]

Napoleon and Kahnweiler were both probably right; David was never a great painter, and his repeated failures in the earlier scholarship competition probably made him sense that his paintings by themselves lacked vitality. David's real talent was to found an artistic company that made both books and paintings work as props in aesthetic plays. David's case, as well as other theatrical cases, contributes to an understanding of this managerial competence.

## Stanislavski's Backstage Studio

Coquelin the elder, admired by André Antoine and one of Aurelien Lugné-Poe's best art buyers, describes the role of the actor in this way: "The actor sees the costume on an imagined person and puts it on; he sees his walk, movements, gestures, hears his voice and copies them; he takes note of his physiognomy and borrows it. In short, the actor grasps each trait in his imagination and transfers it not on to a piece of canvas, but on to himself."[10]

Not everyone who admired Coquelin's art agreed with his views on how to make art work. Constantin Alexeyev, better known as Stanislavski (1863–1937), was one of those who were at once critical and complimentary. According to Stanislavski, painting and performing were not identical. He cautions that

> [i]t is no little task to carry over to the stage those principles which were created in painting, music, and the other arts so far ahead of us. Will the speaking voice ever be able to express those

delicate nuances of emotion which are heard in the orchestra and its instruments? Will our material and definite body be able to take on the unexpected contours and lines we see in modern painting?[11]

Stanislavski's family was deeply interested in the theater and had even installed a miniature theater, complete with scenery, curtains, and wings, for their own performances in their home. Here Constantin and his siblings staged plays and tableaux vivants, and soon Stanislavski was receiving private tuition in dance, acting, singing, and directing.[12] The Alexeyev family was also committed to interesting and amusing performances. One time, they collected Japanese costumes for a whole year and invited a traveling troupe of Japanese acrobats to help them prepare their own performance of *The Mikado*.[13]

Constantin's father was a rich textile manufacturer specializing in the manufacture of heavy gold and silver brocade. When Constantin entered the family business, he began to live a double life; he was textile manager Alexeyev during the daytime and the acclaimed actor Stanislavski in the evening. Even though in tsarist Moscow it could be damaging to a bourgeois young man's reputation to be seen spending too much time backstage and harboring professional acting ambitions, theater was accepted when it existed within the bounds of the private home. The unspoken understanding was that only a "decent" repertoire would be performed to "decent" friends, far removed from the hoi polloi.

Stanislavski had the necessary entrepreneurial drive to work "determinedly and almost blindly" for what he was most interested in, regardless of what common sense might advise. He was not content with aesthetic play as a hobby; his goal was to run his own artistic company and manage it as professionally as his family's industrial firm was managed.

In 1888, Constantin spent thirty thousand rubles of his own money to set up a private Society for Art and Literature, an action that for one thing enabled him to continue his double life. In addition, Moscow's cultural elite became members of this private society, as famous directors and scenery designers found they could earn a little extra money by helping out with the amateur performances of the group.

Soon the group had its own premises, with a studio, ballroom, stage, and spacious foyer, all decorated by artist friends of the society. The money raised by selling their works paid for a spectacular inauguration party.

Stanislavski became the society's "demon director," using Chronegk, the legendary managing tyrant of the Meiningen German court theatre, as his inspiration. Still Stanislavski continued his double life.[14] In fact, this was perhaps his salvation when tsarist values were turned upside down by Lenin's Soviet Union; then it became prudent for the art manager to tone down his capitalist background in industrial management.

Stanislavski's private art enterprise resembled Antoine's and Lugné's avant-garde projects until shortly after the beginning of 1897, when a certain Nemirovic-Danchenko contacted the young amateur director and the operation went from a temporal project into a durable company. Nemirovic was a theater critic and board member of the imperial Mali Theatre. The theater was bureaucratic, and Nemirovic tired of trying in vain to institute reform from within. He wanted to establish a private company and immediately perform the texts of Chekhov and other Russian writers he felt were promising.

Stanislavski was enthusiastic. He too dreamed of an artistic company with broadly didactic aims, so that what began as a friendly lunch for two gentlemen ended early the next day with breakfast for business partners. Instead of providing the sponsorship for the new theater which Nemirovic had originally hoped for, however, Stanislavski successfully persuaded him to form a public joint-stock company. The ruling classes, on which serious private theaters had to rely for audiences, would never take a private enterprise backed by only one capitalist like him seriously![15] A joint stock company, on the other hand, with the explicit aim of bringing aesthetic education to poor intellectuals, might garner

the support of rich Russian sponsors in quest of social respectability. Nemirovic and Stanislavski agreed to name their new company the Artistic Theatre, with the two partners as the principal (but not the only) shareholders.

From the very beginning, Nemirovic concentrated on business matters. In fact, it was not until May 1898, when actors and repertory had already been decided, that shareholders gathered for a general assembly. To avoid shareholder discussion, they received just a cursory recap of the planned

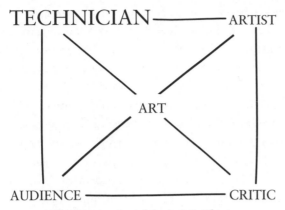

*The Construction of the Artistic Theatre*

budget. One third of the total budget of one hundred thousand rubles went to artists, 20 percent to costumes and settings, and 15 percent to a new budgetary post in the theater, as well as administrators and directors.[16]

The architecture for the new theater, which they moved into in 1902, gave additional proof of the position of art in this company. Regular theaters generally devoted three quarters of their space to the audience. Actors were crowded into backstage corners, and scenery—since there was no space left—was brought in from outbuildings. Meanwhile, the audience relaxed in gilded salons and bars, elegant restaurants, smoking rooms, and foyers. At the Artistic Theatre, however, the audience had to make do with 25 percent of the available space, and it was spartanly decorated. During the performance, attendees were asked to skip all the noisy applause that would threaten the spell of the play. Most of the building was in fact devoted to backstage technicians handing both physical production and production discipline.

The artists were subject to hard company rules of conduct, including exact working schedules and stipulations for attendance at all rehearsals, even if they were not cast in the play under preparation. There were also fines for breaking the rules. The theater had a revolving stage, a modern electric lighting system, and powerful hand-lacquered spotlights. Responsible for all the high technology and the financing of the new house was Savva Morozov, an eccentric industrial magnate and radical avant-garde patron. He joined the management tandem of Nemirovic and Stanislavski in 1899, thereby creating a managerial *troika*.

During the first season, nine plays were performed, seven directed by Stanislavski and four with him in the starring role. In December 1898, Chekhov's *The Seagull*, a play chosen by Nemirovic and staged by Stanislavski, represented a major breakthrough. From the beginning of their company, the two had tried to split up top management responsibility. Nemirovic, the literary critic, held an administrative veto over the choice of repertoire, while Stanislavski, the famous actor, decided how plays chosen by Nemirovic were to be performed on stage. Clearly the success of the Artistic Theatre was less the result of any specific literary style than of its innovations in backstage management. When staging historical plays, whole expeditions were conducted to the distant parts of Russia where the plays were set. Inspired by Antoine's naturalism, Stanislavski collected authentic costumes, bought second-hand furniture, and even brought back "natives" to give the performances in the capital a little local color. The clever technique of such detailed naturalism displayed Stanislavski's skill in industrial management. Modern methods for efficient industrial management applied in his family factory inspired his analytic approach to art work. He later wrote: "To fathom the play to its gold-bearing vein, we had to break it up into fragments."[17]

Despite the first year's artistic success, the theater was in the red, and signs of conflict between art manager Stanislavski and theater administrator Nemirovic began to surface. Shareholders refused to cover the loss, and ticket prices were pushed far over the pain limit of the poor intellectuals originally intended as the audience. The artistic company was facing the traditional dilemma of finding funds with a minimum of strings attached. Stanislavski, himself a part of the moneyed class, was less afraid than Nemirovic, who felt his power waning in the shadow of his partner's great aesthetic success. Only when municipal subsidies were refused did Nemirovic finally agree to accept the financial help of one their richest patrons. Millionaire Morozov, who roundly supported both Gorky and Lenin, saved them from early failure but at the same time put one of his clerks in control of everyday payments.[18]

The original harmony of the Nemirovic-Stanislavski division of management in repertoire choice and execution of performance soon turned to discord, however. Nemirovic took up directing, pushing Stanislavski's naturalism to the extreme with more method than talent. His production of Shakespeare's *Julius Caesar* was preceded by a trip to Rome with the scenographer Simov. Backstage production planning for the play led to formal organization of factorylike departments bearing responsibility for text, Roman ethnography and archaeology, coloring of décor and costumes, weapons and other requisites, modeling of décor and scenery, acquisition and purchases, as well as direction and rehearsal of the crowd scenes. Contrary to Stanislavski and Morozov, Nemirovic lacked practical industrial experience and therefore had a mechanistic way of conceiving technique. Stanislavski and Morozov were familiar with modern methods of production and tended to look for its philosophy, while the Nemirovic individual formalized matters of technique in an almost rigid spirit of "the principles of scientific management," which were later globally marketed by the American engineer and consultant Frederick Winslow Taylor in his 1911 management handbook. For Stanislavski, technique was something complex and concrete; Nemirovic saw it as a technology, a set of rules to get the job done.

Cooperation and balance between art and administration broke down when Stanislavski and Morozov dared air their skepticism about Nemirovic's technological naturalism, and when Nemirovic claimed full credit for the success of a Gorky play they had team directed. On one side stood Nemirovic, Chekhov, and most of the actors, who felt the naturalistic production routine for producing performances with standardized preparation was a good cash cow. On the other side, Stanislavski, Gorky, and Morozov wanted experiments to make art work. Although finances were still a problem, Nemirovic was probably slightly relieved by the shift in the power balance when Morozov committed suicide. As Nemirovic suspected, Morozov had tried to get his friend Gorky connected to the theater company. In addition, he and Stanislavski secretly planned to launch another company in Petersburg that would have strangled the Artistic Theatre in Moscow.

Nemirovic also accused Stanislavski of making their company into an irresponsible playground for his antiliterary ideas on performance. Again, the disagreement seems rooted in contrasting views of technique in an aesthetic play. Nemirovic thought directing was the practical managerial technology for executing plans for shows, while Stanislavski was on the lookout for new processes for making art work.[19] Directing frequently technical teamwork was changing into a soloist art under Stanislavski's influence. *Real* art, to Nemirovic, was equal to literature, and a director was nothing more than a good literary critic; the main task of directing was helping the audience read the text.

Stanislavski was driven by another point of view. He was in the process of turning directing into a university for actors, and this simply reinforced Nemirovic's belief that Stanislavski was a good actor with a twisted ambition to subvert theater into a backstage business for the sake of its own. Unfortunately, thought Nemirovic, Stanislavski's fixed idea of a long-term artistic company only confused the professional actors and upset their craft.

Stanislavski soon noted that this negative attitude turned off most of his actors. They did not seem as excited about making art work as they had been. They poked fun at his ideas and rejected his instructions, and this developed into a significant problem when Stanislavski, in search of new forms of expression, shifted over from Antoine-inspired naturalism to symbolism. After initial concentration upon naturalistic historical plays, Stanislavski wanted the Artistic Theatre to develop Lugné's way of making art work. To him, the whole point of having a regular company, instead of doing only one-shot, avant-garde projects, was to gain leeway for technical research and development by experimenting with several styles in one organization. He wanted to invest in works more in the mood of Lugné, with both Chekhov and Maeterlinck appearing in the new repertoire. Could the analytical method, which had worked so well for naturalism that it actually became standardized, really manage a symbolist line of production?[20]

> After all, if you examine each separate stone of which a cathedral is built you will never picture the edifice rising high into the sky. And if we smash Venus of Milo into little bits and make a separate study of her nose, her ears and toes, we'll hardly see the loveliness of this masterpiece of sculpture, the beauty and harmony of the divine statue. And that is exactly what happened in our case: we had cut up the play into so many bits that we could no longer see it as a whole and live it.[21]

Stanislavski concluded that to continue working in the spirit of this style would kill new art, and the murder could not be concealed by any magnificent scenery and costumes. The simplistic routine had to be scrapped; new techniques of work would have to be adapted to make art work anew. Although this was Stanislavski's managerial conviction, Nemirovic was happy with established working methods and doubtful about the symbolist test run Stanislavski and young radical actor Vsevolod Emilievich Meyerhold had undertaken together in 1905.

The two had set up a laboratory where actors from the outside joined the few from the Artistic Theatre still interested in making art work. The studio lab was marginalized by the "main operations," which were dominated by Nemirovic, who gradually slid back into straight traditional factory management. Surely, he argued forcefully, a private little Moscow theater could not afford to develop its own production methods, or entertain such frivolous fantasy as that of an art beyond literature. At most, Stanislavski's experiment was to be regarded as on-the-job training for young talent, hardly as art in its own right! Nemirovic grew more and more irritated with

Stanislavski and his research colleagues, especially Sulerzhitsky (a follower of Tolstoy) and Meyerhold, who may have poked fun at Nemirovic's pedantic love of methods for making art work more efficiently. In perhaps a retaliatory move against Nemirovic, Meyerhold launched an ironic slogan: "Taylorism of the theatre will make it possible to perform in one hour that which requires four at present."[22]

Meyerhold persuaded Stanislavski to invest his own money to start up the studio, and soon this work began to influence and intrude upon the regular business of the Artistic Theatre. Meyerhold himself was busy developing what was to become his biophysical method to make art work contrary to the literary theater Nemirovic clung to. Instead of starting out with the text of a play, Meyerhold thought that spontaneous bodily movement was the source of an actor's creativity. The Schopenhauerian body-in-itself should speak up in the theater. When Stanislavski adapted Meyerhold's approach, Nemirovic protested that Constantin ought to get a grip on his senses and be wary of throwing out good old methods that had been so useful in finalizing numerous productions, even those which would otherwise have remained stuck in the swamps of long, expensive rehearsals. Meyerhold ought to be imprisoned in his lab so that the chaos did not contaminate the rest of the theater. Even though Nemirovic continued to patronize Stanislavski, Stanislavski gave Meyerhold full freedom. It is not at all clear if, as Nemirovic claimed, their first attempt to stage a play in this new way really failed aesthetically. The lack of public success was due mostly to the revolution of 1905, which scared away the audience and put most theater workers on strike. The failure was instrumental in justifying Nemirovic's fears about Meyerhold's methods, though it did not deter Stanislavski, who still hoped to realize his artistic company by reforming the ways to make art work and converting Nemirovic. Stanislavski regarded the first flop as the initial down payment for a necessary long-term investment. His reflections, similar to those of Wagner after the Tannhäuser flop, led him to think that in traditional theatre

> there was not even enough to show the stage director's [Meyerhold's] technique, ingenuity, and planning, for the actors were too young in their art. The stage director could only demonstrate his ideas, principles, researches, ingenuities, but there was nothing that could give life to them. And without that, all the interesting plans of the stage director turned into dry theory, into a

scientific formula that caused no inner reaction in the spectator. I was convinced again that between the dreams of the stage director and their realization there is a tremendous distance, and that the theatre is first of all intended for the actor and cannot exist without him. For the new art new actors were necessary, actors of a new sort with an altogether new technique.[23]

After the 1905 upheaval, the Artistic Theatre once again had to be saved from bankruptcy by touring. The 1906 tour to Poland and Germany made Stanislavski an international star, and undoubtedly this irritated Nemirovic even further. When Morozov committed suicide, Nemirovic took advantage of the situation and threatened to leave for a supposed position at an imperial theater if the business was not reorganized with managerial power centralized with him.

Stanislavski refused to openly confront Nemirovic and assume the position of owner-manager. In 1908, he was made to resign as a main shareholder, and the dual art and administration team of Stanislavski and Nemirovic was definitely dissolved. Now Nemirovic alone assumed the position of CEO. He was thoroughly fed up with Stanislavski. After a dispute at a meeting of the board of the Artistic Theatre, Stanislavski was humiliated with the offer of a simple employment contract: each season he would be allowed to perform one experimental production in exchange for which he had to direct two traditional productions and perform on stage when called upon. Finally in 1911, Nemirovic took complete control by marginalizing Stanislavski, who was graciously given a few rubles to carry on his private experiment, now officially called the Studio.

Although Nemirovic had effectively killed off Stanislavski's hope of running his own company, the Artistic Theatre continued producing with Stanislavski as an incorporated brand name. He stayed on, no longer in the capacity of general art manager but as an employed actor and house director. He was occasionally allowed to bring in some novelty to add a truffle to Nemirovic's pretty conventional repertoire. A hard little paragraph was carefully written into Stanislavski's contract, which stopped him from doing any outside acting or directing that might in any way compete with the Artistic Theatre.[24] From that day forward, Nemirovic forced Stanislavski to engage in constant diplomatic negotiations to obtain any resources for making art work. His position resembled a feudal serfdom in a golden cage. Backstage, Stanislavski maintained a tiny haute couture company in the prêt-à-porter corporation. At the very least, however, Nemirovic provided Stanislavski with good training so that he hardly suffered during the Bolshevik dictatorship later on.

In 1911, Stanislavski brought in the theatrical theorist Gordon Craig to direct *Hamlet*. Craig had also wanted to move away from the traditional theater of illusion and décor. The stage was to become an architectural space by the use of screens, which would be moved into different positions while the curtain remained open. Through skillful use of electric lighting, Craig finally introduced what Stanislavski in despair described as "spotlighting [which] creates miracles everywhere other than in the theatre."[25] As in the case of Meyerhold, he also gave total freedom to Craig, who was introduced to him by no less than the eccentric dancer Isadora Duncan. Since Craig was trained as an architect and had no theatrical experience, Stanislavski was obliged to take care of the actors while Craig focused only on stage techniques. Just before the premiere performance, the heavy iron screens collapsed on the stage like a deck of cards. Had Stanislavski been able to control and reorient the whole theater, it might have turned out otherwise. At any rate, Nemirovic was more surprised than satisfied when *Hamlet* was a success in spite of its technical shortcomings. With growing irritation, Nemirovic realized the consequence of his control; Stanislavski's artistic company had turned into an interesting laboratory embedded in an otherwise fairly normal theater.

Because this creative cocoon was never allowed to develop, however, Stanislavski turned to writing. From 1906 on, Stanislavski took notes for new methods of art work that would replace the mannerisms of traditional ways of acting. He needed longer rehearsals, and this, of course, caused unceasing clashes with Nemirovic's rational administration. A major tilt occurred when the schedule finally collapsed in a production of Maeterlinck's *L'Oiseau Bleu,* which exceeded its budget because of innovative light and sound effects.

Stanislavski nevertheless felt it necessary to improve art work by a time-consuming, two-stage process of art work. First, the ensemble would help the director with ideas, and the payoff would come in the next phase through the director's inspiration for the finished production. In 1912, he put the process to work in the studio. Members of the ensemble were invited to register as students, with their studies being done in their spare time. The audience for studio productions was made up of colleagues from within the theater industry. Since the first performance was a success, Nemirovic, in his usual management style, commanded that the Stanislavski system become a compulsory method of work for the entire theater. By now Stanislavski had resigned from his managerial and administrative work at the theater. He no longer was running an entire artistic company but just heading a small product development studio within Nemirovic's corporation. In 1916, a new group of students founded the second studio, followed by a third in 1920, and a fourth the following year. When the Bolshoi contacted Stanislavski, he also founded their opera studio in 1918.

Marginalized, Stanislavski became primarily a backstage pedagogue in his studios. After a triumphal tour to the United States in 1922, he was encouraged to publish in English, and he became internationally known as the philosopher behind new actor training. Strasberg's Actors Studio used his model as a method. A Tolstoyan sense of ethics permeated his first experimental unit; in that spirit, he generously donated land for the studio's self-sufficient farm and egalitarian commune by the Black Sea. This retreat, so far away from Nemirovic and the everyday Moscow production stress, has inspired several similar utopian communes in the history of theater. Copeau in France, Grotowski in Poland, Barba in Denmark, Wilson in the United States, and Pistoletto in Biella have all isolated their studios from established cultural centers and corporations. For Stanislavski, who learned a hard lesson from daily conflict with Nemirovic, the motivation was obvious: "This experimental work . . . cannot be carried out in the theatre itself, where there must be performances every day, in the midst of financial concerns, the heavy work of artistry and all the practical difficulties of a large company."[26]

The studio became Stanislavski's metaphysical lab for managing art work. Nemirovic was satisfied with theatrical Taylorism as a method of arts management, but of course it could not solve the fundamental problems of the business of being. When it came to creating life on stage, Nemirovic relied on the soft and fuzzy factors of "inspiration" and "talent." Stanislavski, however, wanted to tackle head on the core question of how to make art work. Because he believed in aesthetic philosophy, he refused to let art depend upon chance or coincidence. He attempted therefore to articulate a "soft" management philosophy that could help achieve high Schopenhauerian ambitions for an artistic company.

When Stanislavski wrote his soft methods on paper, he did so not in the form of principles but in the form of a drama. He had a young man, appropriately enough a former stenographer, write a long, detailed diary of his two years at a certain Professor Tortsov's theatrical school. When it was time for exams, the attentive student wrote down his professor's final words, with which the true identity and convictions of its author are revealed:

> The method we have been studying over the past years is usually called "Stanislavski's system." But this is wrong. The strength of this method is that it was not thought out or discovered by anyone. Both the psychic and physical parts of the system are found within our own organic nature. The laws of art rest upon the laws of nature. A newborn child, a growing tree, and a nascent work of art are closely related phenomena. My life's task has been to get as close as I could to the laws of nature. It is impossible to discover a system. We are born with the gift of creation, and our creations must be realised one way or another. It is this *way* that we call *system*.[27]

Thanks to natural laws, the Kantian *Ding an Sich* can be grasped in art directly and without mediation. Stanislavski was equally inspired by the contemporary French psychiatrist Ribot and the Russian psychologist Secenov. They made him abandon the hard technology of tyrannous directors instrumentally using actors as media; instead, he favored his new soft technique, which turned him into a sort of Schopenhauerian guru, who reminded his actor that "it is not he who is creative, it is his nature; he is merely an instrument, a violin in its hands."[28]

Stanislavski's soft art management was irreducible to rules of method. It was a Tolstoyan philosophizing system for actors, not a factory system for actors delivering text. Stanislavski stresses the differences between literature and the work manifested by art on stage, because "we must not forget that a written play is not a complete work of art. It can only become so when it is brought to life by the vibrant human emotions of actors on a stage, in the same way that a musical score is not a symphony until it is performed by an orchestra and is heard by an audience."[29]

An educated audience is perfectly able to read scripts aloud and play scores at home. They do not go to the theater to experience the book, just as they do not go to a concert to experience a score. The task of the artistic company is to supply what Genette called an immanent object, where surplus value hides between the lines of a script and the manifest play on stage.

Theater that made art work should not be, as Nemirovic wished, a humble servant of literature. Stanislavski situates the immanent object in what he terms the "subtext."[30] When an actor has dug out the subtext and found the right pitch in which to sing its Schopenhauerian song, he can "create a real life for the human soul which exists in the role and the play, and transfer this life to the stage in a gracious artistic form."[31]

When art works, the audience believes it. This credibility signals the aesthetic surplus value called truth. As Kandinsky had, so too Stanislavski traced trustworthiness to something spiritual, unattainable by trickery, masks, gestures, or other superficial methods. Nor should aesthetic truth be mistaken for scientific truth, however. Science looks for the universal truth, but humanity on stage is not a matter of exposing "general human traits." Stanislavski's metaphysics is, in this respect, like the pataphysics of Jarry-Deleuze, distancing itself from classical universal Kantian transcendence.

Stanislavski finds that everyday life abounds with uninteresting repetitions, averages, and clichés. Firms in craft and industry glut modern markets with uniform and standard mass-produced wares. The modern role of art then becomes that of helping retrace a human individuality of the unique and exceptional. Art should be made to work by revealing things of singular interest, life in its specific and individual nuances. When Stanislavski directed crowds in mass scenes, he never regarded them as collectives. Instead he always prepared detailed individual instructions, often including a minibiography of the character, for each and every actor playing an individual member of the crowd. Art returns dignity to the individual in everyday life and reenergizes poor, burnt-out existence. If Lenin's engineers could electrify the Soviet Union by extracting external energy from wind and waves, Stanislavski wished to produce aesthetic energy out of human nature, the great power plant of life. Stanislavski's artistic company turns its actors into generators of energy by "allowing the conscious to work upon the unconscious, not directly, but indirectly. Because there are certain sides to our souls which respond to consciousness and will. These sides can in turn influence the workings of the soul which cannot otherwise be directed."[32]

Schopenhauer believed in finding the essence, the thing in itself, in the bodily mix of mind and matter. Stanislavski's system aims at helping each artist create essence-energy by fusing mind and matter. Mind is found in the subtext of the script. Of course, a subtext is not just another text, not other words and more phrases. To find the subtext is not to write new speeches, or adapt a book to a play.[33] Stanislavski, an adherent of Schopenhauer's philosophy, must not be mistaken for a theatrical Freudian therapist, asking his actors to verbalize their subconsciousness in words of their own. His artistic company was no Berggasse clinic for actors and its stage no analyst's couch for individual therapy. Finding the subtext implies generating "the enterprise, the activity . . . that the actor's craft is based upon . . . A drama on the stage is an action that is performed in front of our eyes, and the moment an actor steps onto the stage he becomes an active person."[34]

The subtext must be brought home in action on a bridge between mind and matter. Stanislavski devised mental techniques to help actors deliver subtexts in physical activity. He asked them to try to imagine the play as a physical image, to try to feel the role of the character's intentions while speaking the lines, and to try to reconstruct the character's life as an inner motion picture on the individual's mental screen. Further, he cautioned them to avoid pure fantasy and reminded them that the inner picture should remain reasonable and trustworthy; above all, acting should be natural.

Stanislavski's techniques set out to train his pupils to use their imagination. To help them avoid using routine gestures, he had them act while they sat on their hands. He had them learn yoga and Dalcroze's rhythmic dance therapy. He asked them to think about the characters' lives before the play. What had their character done off stage? Where did they come from and where were they going?

Combining what was said, the noted text, with what was acted out, a bodily manifestation, Stanislavski had his actors make art work out a third immanent surplus value on stage. Only through total preparation and effort could an actor hope to create such life on stage, a creation devoid of cheap rhetorical effects calculated to reap a coveted audience reaction. The player must remain "a monk in a monastery"—an epithet Meyerhold had once used on him. Actors must forget about the front stage and ignore the gaping hole of the proscenium arch. Only by taking Antoine's fourth wall seriously can the performer hope to realize Stanislavski's "system." If the vanity market in the auditorium puts its claws in the actor, all the performer can do is "leave the theatre. Otherwise he ends up in the clutches of the director who imagines that he can replace the actor's lack of ingenuity with his own ideas. This is an abdication from independent creation in favour of becoming part of the scenery."[35]

## Diaghilev's Frontstage Ballet

The Artistic Theatre played Chekhov to packed houses in St. Petersburg in 1902. The company was in its naturalistic period, so some journalists complained that these Muscovites were hopeless prisoners of dull reality and boring truthtelling.[36] One sophisticated Petersburg critic of the Artistic Theatre declared that when Stanislavski replaced traditional stars with his more artistic ensemble, he ended up with gray, everyday provincial realism. Further, maintained this critic, it is not a given that art will automatically follow the abandonment of show-biz convention or rejection of the demands of an audience. In chic St. Petersburg none would deliberately try to make art reflect a miserable reality that everyone is sadly aware of anyway. Convention is worth skipping only for seducing audiences to dream "beyond good and evil."

This was at least the opinion of a group of St. Petersburg artists who published the periodical *Mir Iskusstva,* "The World of Art." The group included Benois, with whom Stanislavski would later cooperate and whom he already admired for his encyclopedic knowledge of "everything relating to decoration and costume."[37] The circle of people surrounding Benois made Wagner pilgrimages to Bayreuth, were regulars at the opera and concerts at the conservatoire, and fervent fans of the Marinsky Theatre Imperial ballet. In the early 1890s, Sergei Pavlovich Diaghilev (1872–1929), a petty aristocrat from the provinces, joined this party. Diaghilev was a law student from Perm with musical pretensions who would soon become St. Petersburg's foremost art critic and eventually the innovative director of an artistic company known as the Russian Ballet.

Diaghilev traded law for lessons in composition from Rimsky-Korsakov, and he became a full-fledged habitué of the theaters and salons. However, the young snob could never hope to become a genuine Petersburg dandy. Although from a noble family, his coat of arms was not ranked high enough to warrant a permanent place in the tsar's court. Stanislavski worked his way from the cultivated salon to backstage research into human nature; Diaghilev's art firm was driven by the opposite motivation, to escape the shadows backstage and become a celebrity in the glittering gala of the frontstage salon.

Diaghilev immediately started to engineer his way into crème de la crème society. Equipped with a monocle and a remarkably shiny *chapeau-claque,* he set off on a trip around Europe. Nicknamed "the Chinchilla," he conducted his own Grand Tour of all the best palaces and museums. He studied what was to become the capital of his artistic company. Back home in Petersburg, he wrote articles about art and curated art shows that combined pictures with music and flower arrangements to perfume the exhibition rooms. His fortune already appeared to be made when the tsar himself and some of his court attended his second show of paintings. Once again, for genealogical reasons, there appeared no invitations to court balls. Still Diaghilev was firm in his ultimate goal, which was court incorporation.

Then Princess Tenishev invited him to her apartment to discuss the hot paintings she had collected with the help of Benois as her private curator.[38] Diaghilev arrived, accompanied by the trendy Swedish portraitist Anders Zorn and the railway magnate and opera patron Mamontov. In the end, the princess and the magnate became his first patrons. With 12,500 rubles he set up the *Mir Iskusstva* art magazine, devoted to pure aesthetics under the motto of "L'art pour l'art." Whereas Stanislavski used text as raw material, Diaghilev always took images as a point of departure for his projects. The idea of a journal appealed to Diaghilev because recent advances in print technology enabled accurate reproduction of works of art.

The art magazine became Diaghilev's printed gallery; it was often illustrated by unknown foreign artists but featured primarily the pictures of progressive Russian collectors. Under Diaghilev's clever management, the publication also became his sure *passepartout* to wealthy salons.[39] The doors soon opened on the first exhibition of impressionist painting in St. Petersburg.

 Clad as a clown in a ridiculously small borrowed morning coat, the plumpish Diaghilev rushed to welcome the tsar when he learned of his surprise visit to the gallery. Things had indeed worked well for the Chinchilla! Shortly afterward, his mentor Prince Volkonsky was appointed director of the imperial theaters. Diaghilev had his feet firmly planted in the waiting room of the courtly corporation.

Thanks to his magazine, an amazingly productive team of painters and musicians surrounded Diaghilev. They all met every Tuesday and were served tea and cakes by their old servant, Sergei, under the supervision of Diaghilev's former amah. This creative team undertook to infuse the operation of court stages with visual art. With a combination of taste and brilliance, they began by editing a dull annual report of the imperial theaters into an impressive and ostentatious art book. Little did it matter that it cost the prince ten thousand rubles more than was expected! In 1901, Diaghilev was picked to produce a new play at the Marinsky. It seemed as if his strategy to publish and curate himself into the official art world would bear fruit. From now on, he innovated the art firm into an artistic company from the frontstage position of a critic.

Back in his headquarters around the steaming silver samovar, his jubilant group of art lovers threw

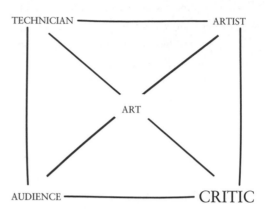

*Diaghilev's Critic as the Dominant Player*

themselves into the Marinsky assignment. Alexandre Benois was to have responsibility for the sets of the first act, and two other painter friends were to decorate the rest. Léon Bakst designed all the costumes except one for which the artist Valentin Serov already had some good ideas. Nuvel assisted with the scenery. Finally, the chosen choreographer was called in to look at the drawings and listen to the music. Although traditional ballet was conventional dance under the direction of a ballet master, their ballet was going to be a manifestation of art, a *Gesamtkunstwerk* in the true Wagnerian sense.[40] Painting would inspire music into dance.

Unfortunately, court intrigue threw a monkey wrench into the plans, and Diaghilev was dismissed. Soon afterward, Prince Volkonsky was transferred to duller duties at court—perhaps a moralistic reprimand for the somewhat extravagant behavior at Diaghilev's party. The team did not give up, however. They gleefully carried on with the magazine, working into the night to present a cascade of new images, both foreign and Russian. When princesses and magnates tired or ran out of money, new benefactors were found and charmed, and eventually even the tsar himself became a patron. In 1904, Diaghilev withdrew from publishing to curate a huge exhibition of historical Russian portraits. At last, castles and estates throughout the empire, even the estate of old Tolstoy, opened their doors to the charming Diaghilev. A tide of noble and royal portraits washed up in Petersburg.

It was 1905. Russia was at war with Japan, a grand duke was murdered, and Diaghilev's opening speech for this grand exhibition of genealogical icons assumed a prophetically nostalgic tone. Diaghilev claimed that the portraits constituted a grand testimony to a glorious but passing period in history. He raised his glass to toast the hope that they all at least might die in the aesthetic spirit of beauty that his show aspired to commemorate.[41]

While workers were demonstrating for freedom in the streets of Petersburg, the most radical members of the establishment were applauding Isadora Duncan's free-dance revolution. Her Hellenistic veiled dance was not crafted in the stock music commissioned in the orders of choreographers for the classical ballets. Duncan seemed to simply improvise on extracts of works ready-made by contemporary composers. Both Benois and the young choreographer Michel Fokine were a part of the audience at one of her performances, and when the pair went on to work together at the Marinsky in 1907 Duncan's way of recycling ready-made pieces of art into her own work was clearly a source of inspiration. Benois drew some sketches for the benefit of a friend who was a composer. The music and images were then presented to Fokine, who, like Duncan, allowed himself to be inspired by scores and drawings. The result was *Le Pavillon d'Armide*. The ballet was also notable for casting one of Madame Pavlova's young pupils in the role of a slave; it was the debut of Diaghilev's future dream boy, Vaslav Nijinsky.

Diaghilev's success with the exhibition of historical portraits led to Grand Duke Vladimir's offer to become responsible for marketing the tsardom to French investors by means of Russian art. Having already conquered Petersburg's salons, Diaghilev now had to repeat the achievement in Paris. The music publisher and theater manager Gabriel Astruc became his local agent. Astruc introduced Diaghilev to the Duchess of Greffuhles (the model for Proust's Princesse de Guermantes). Diaghilev's gallant comments about the Duchess's art collection made her suspicious. Her distrust waned, however, as soon as he sat at her piano and played pieces of exotic Russian music. She decided on the spot to support this cultivated man, concluding that he was worthy of her influential patronage.

The first foreign festival of Russian music, to which Diaghilev's former teacher Rimsky-Korsakov was invited, was a great success. Grand Duke

Vladimir then supported Diaghilev's proposal that Mussorgsky's opera *Boris Godunov* be presented in Paris by the Russian Imperial Theatre. This most Russian of operas, regarded as too parochial in Moscow where imported French and Italian operas were more popular, was to prove a great success with Parisian audiences.

The curtain went up on the first performance at the Grand Opera in Paris on the tsar's birthday. Standing in the middle of a luxuriously decorated stage was the principal singer, the great Fyodor Chaliapin, surrounded by the cast wearing embroidered textiles gathered on a special expedition to the Russian provinces. This was historicism combined with fairy tale naturalism, for Stanislavski already had considerable influence on the staging of Russian opera.

The carefully managed audience included the French president and three Russian grand dukes. Through the performance, the tsar was expressing his gratitude to the French Republic for its financial support. This spectacular gift, produced by Sergei Diaghilev, featured the tsar's best orchestra, conductor, singers, dancers, and technicians. The fact that Diaghilev had agreed to leave behind as collateral for the use of the Opera the costumes and scenery that proved so enchanting to the audience indicates the budgetary limitations of this imperial publicity campaign. Russia was now firmly on the aesthetic map for Parisian salon society. After appropriate awarding of medals and honors, the gay intelligentsia of Paris—from Marcel Proust to the young Jean Cocteau—flocked to Diaghilev, just as the ladies gathered around the virile Chaliapin.

Everything was ready for the next phase of the great Russian marketing campaign, with Diaghilev as official master of ceremonies. Just before midsummer in 1909, however, Grand Duke Vladimir suddenly died, and with his death Diaghilev lost his key contact at court. This would certainly be the end of his courtly incorporation. First, he lacked money. A manufacturer of galoshes in Riga promised to put up funds, on condition that Diaghilev make use of the influence the man thought he had at court to ennoble him. Second, the tsar reneged on his promise to provide costumes and scenery, and Diaghilev was no longer allowed to rehearse at the Hermitage. In Paris, Astruc managed to put together a loss guarantee package totaling fifty thousand francs in case revenue fell below twenty-five thousand. All the Russian court had to come up with was passage for the orchestra, singers, and dancers to go to Paris during their contracted summer break in Russia.

Against his better judgment, Diaghilev was pushed to set up an independent artistic company. Despite a desperate lack of resources, he took the risk of allowing the summer 1909 performance in Paris to proceed. As a bold entrepreneur, he hired the Châtelet Theatre and invested all he had in front-stage marketing.

The contrast between the two Russian entrepreneurs is obvious. Stanislavski gradually became embedded in matters of managing production, while Diaghilev's enterprise thrived on the basis of complex and innovative art marketing. A good show was necessary but not sufficient, since it was imperative that the auditorium meet the expectations of the art market. The celebrities of the private salons, a marketing channel Diaghilev mastered, made their way to the renovated auditorium of the theater by the Seine.

Astruc assisted as the talented director of the front stage. He undertook to decorate the balcony with a garland of beautiful women, which included actresses from the best theaters in Paris. In their midst was the queen of glamour and avant-garde, Isadora Duncan herself. The premiere gained even more kudos because of the presence of such stars as Chaliapin, Ravel, Saint-Saëns, Fauré, and even the popular music hall star Yvette Guilbert. The production was daring but successful. The stars of the ballet, Nijinsky and Karsavina, soon received lucrative offers to perform in the private salons of Paris: "La gala Russe, quelle soirée, quelle salle, quelle assistance."[42]

Despite the fact that the performance was a theatrical success, the company's finances remained a problem. Income exceeded twenty-five thousand, but they were still seventy thousand short of the costs. Astruc declared Diaghilev bankrupt. With twelve sets of scenery and 670 costumes as security, Diaghilev raised a loan from the theater of Monte Carlo. With the death of Grand Duke Vladimir, all hopes of financial support from the tsar were gone for good. Diaghilev either had to sink or swim on the rough market for ballet. Three initial contracts with the Met in New York; another with Thomas Beecham, heir of the pharmaceutical industry; and one with the Opera Company in London and Teatro Colón in Buenos Aires were the bread and butter for what was to be known as Diaghilev's Ballets Russes company.[43] When Diaghilev returned to Paris once more, he could afford to bring with him only the stars of the Imperial Ballet.

After Russian art, Russian concerts, and Russian opera, Paris now had to be content with Russian ballet alone on stage for a whole night. As usual,

tours were carefully planned in Moscow. The informal St. Petersburg samovar board of Diaghilev's artistic company felt it important to go on offering the Parisian audience a pure Russian-brand product. They found the
subject matter for the new ballet *The Firebird* in Afanasiev's old book of
folktales. When the commissioned composer procrastinated over the project,
it was quickly handed to one of Rimsky-Korsakov's alert young pupils,
Stravinsky. This was followed by ballets such as *Cleopatra* and *Sheherazade*,
whose barbaric pomp served to reinforce Diaghilev's reputation as a despotic
producer. Soon colorful Russian exoticism became Parisian fashion. Interi-
ors were decorated in Bakst blue, and the first modern fashion designer, Paul
Poiret, made Sheherazade dresses.[44]

Despite the fact that the Metropolitan Opera was on French tour with
Caruso and Diaghilev had no Chaliapins on the program, the 1910 season
was a resounding success financially as well. The following year, the tour included the Casino Theatre in Monte Carlo, and the company also performed
at King George V's coronation gala at Covent Garden in London. Russian
ballerinas were popular in London, where Pavlova was to settle and perform regularly (also in the music halls alongside acrobats and trapeze
artists).

As a good art manager, Diaghilev kept his distance from such show biz.
Entertainment ballerinas meant nothing to his artistic company, for the attraction of Diaghilev's ballet was its male dancers, the likes of which had
never before been seen in European ballet. This was something quite different for balletic performances on a variety stage. One contemporary critic
pointed out that although Diaghilev might have saved dance from becoming
mere spectacle, he had also designed it in a nonnaturalistic way after the latest innovations in visual art: "This is an aristocratic tradition, with something of Boucher and Beaumarchais clinging to it . . . it is immensely serious
as Art, but never for a moment serious as Life."[45]

Having reproduced *The World of Art* in his magazine, Diaghilev's next
task was to paint tableaux vivants in his company. People in Moscow may
have been trying to get closer to nature, but Diaghilev turned his back on
organic life. He wanted modern artists about him in order to create a *mouvement artistique* comparable to the technical artificiality of the modern
*mouvement mécanique* that had provoked such scandals when presented in
dada and futurist art.[46] Diaghilev was now the industrious chairman of an

artistic company whose board consisted of his old Russian friends and whose managing director was the choreographer (usually, his current lover). Following the tsar's lead, George V of England, King Alfonso of Spain, and Prince Louis of Monaco offered Diaghilev sporadic protection. Although he was never a radical or revolutionary, his strategy was to blend aristocracy with avant-garde and create an irresistibly modern market mix. He avoided any association with mass entertainment while producing sarcastic criticism of conservative cultural life. After Nijinsky was dismissed from the Marinsky Theatre for having danced in too scanty a costume, he performed *L'Après-midi d'un Faune* for Diaghilev in a *succès de scandal*. In sharp contrast to Debussy's music, Nijinsky created an almost concrete criticism of traditional ballet culture. When traditional critics protested, sculptors and painters including Rodin and Redon wrote in defense of Nijinsky. The scandal surrounding *The Rite of Spring* is equally legendary.

In the ballet *Jeux,* Nijinsky demonstrated choreography inspired by sport, with the help of a consultant from Dalcroze's German institute of dance. Diaghilev devoured modern art and used it as the basis for a cascade of innovative productions. He was an avid museumgoer and found most of his business ideas in artist studios, private galleries, or public collections.

Diaghilev had planned for the choreography of *Faune* to be inspired by ancient Greek art. Nijinsky, however, whom he had sent off to the Louvre, ended up in the wrong collection, so that when dancers performed sideways to the audience, it was because Nijinsky had visited the Egyptian and not the Greek section of the museum. Diaghilev assumed that his dancers would be technically proficient and kept in physical trim by balletmaster Cecchetti. He himself saw to the more important part of human resource development in the form of gallery visits and longer trips to look at art and museums. When the unfaithful Nijinsky, who had married a rich girl, was dismissed and Massine employed to replace him, Diaghilev's first act was to organize a trip to Italy. Massine recalled their visit to the Uffizi gallery in Florence:

> We stopped at the medieval paintings . . . and then he asked me during that visit whether I though I could do a ballet. I sharply answered, "No." Then a moment later I looked at Simone Martini's *The Annunciation*, a most remarkable painting, with the archangel and Maria in a very dramatic pose. I thought for a second, and something came to me which I could not explain even

now. I turned round to him and I said "Yes, I think I can do not one, but a hundred ballets for you." That was the beginning.[47]

This was how Diaghilev made art work. He aesthetically educated his company in the quality of having images, not choreographic notation or convention, inspire dance. First Fokine, then Nijinsky and Massine, and finally Serge Lifar, a young dancer from Kiev, all went through the same art training. They were fed with books about art, were taken on trips, and managed to dance under the spell of the brightest avant-garde images or famous classical paintings. Young artists queued up for Diaghilev's attention, in the hope of being presented to his famous acquaintances in the salons that were sometimes a better marketplace for modern art than an art dealer's gallery. There they were stimulated to make modern art work as motion pictures.

In 1917, the young Jean Cocteau, who played the part of a gallant outgoing Nietzsche in Diaghilev's Wagnerian aesthetic play, introduced Picasso, who—thanks to this—found himself a Russian ballerina wife while producing sketches for the set of Cocteau's ballet *Parade*. In this production, the dancers were to be dressed as skyscrapers and equipped with megaphones to imitate the noise of modern traffic.

Stravinsky introduced Diaghilev to Marinetti and his friends, the futurists Balla and Depero, who provided Diaghilev with scenery and flashing electrical sculptures. To the great irritation of André Breton and his puritan surrealists, Joan Miró and Max Ernst were also employed to embellish stage scenery. It is not surprising that during their Diaghilev periods, both Massine and Lifar managed to amass substantial collections of avant-garde art. Diaghilev used to decorate his programs with original artwork, exhibited new pictures during the intermission, and on occasion commissioned artists to paint an enormous picture as a curtain backdrop. When short of money in the late 1920s, Diaghilev sold Picasso's curtain for *Quadro flamenco* for 175,000 francs.

Further, Naum Gabo, Kandinsky's colleague at the Bauhaus, was permitted to experiment with metal robots. In the early 1920s, when the whole company was fortuitously incorporated by the Societé de Bains de Mer, which ran the Casino Opera of Monte Carlo, Cocteau, on an opium high, planned a grand project for the ultimate avant-garde theme park. It was futuristically branded "Plastic Hall."

The Monte Carlo engagement was one of the rare long-term contracts for the Russian Ballet. It came right after a serious financial flop in London that made Diaghilev consider stabilization of his undertaking as a registered public company. In 1916, he had tried touring, the usual trick when in need of cash. Two American tours were organized, the last planned for a reduced company of dancers who were supposed to bring in the money for the core company remaining in Europe. The tour idea failed, so he then considered setting up a limited liability company to get some peace. Stockholders were going to get, if not sizeable dividends, their marketing share in the company's "continuing accomplishments and unique publicity."[48] About this time, Princess de Polignac proposed the Monaco contract. Before the conservative elite in Monte Carlo pushed Gunsbourg, the director of the opera house, to terminate the cooperation, most of the world's avant-garde artists had already paid a visit to the duchy as Diaghilev's guests. Fashion queen Coco Chanel not only designed dresses but also underwrote the production of the ballet *Le train bleu,* an homage to the legendary Pullman train shipping habitués from Paris to the roulette tables and gala dinners. Outside the Café de Paris, the cubist Braque, in his beloved bowler, arrogantly whistled Maurice Chevalier's latest tune, and in a letter home to his art dealer (Kahnweiler), Juan Gris complained about the boring millionaires and gambling gold diggers.

Diaghilev's art company was successful in luring Gris to Monte Carlo. Kahnweiler, who was well aware of Diaghilev's powers of seducing young painters by hyping his rich art-loving audience, was extremely jealous. Instead of marketing cubist painting as products, Diaghilev had the painters help him make art work by creating settings, program illustrations, costume design, and backdrops. For a Picasso design, he paid one-fifth of the wages of an experienced scenographer like Benois. In addition, he acquired the accoutrements of art, or as Matisse once summed it up, "What Diaghilev wants is my name."[49]

It was crystal clear to Kahnweiler that Diaghilev wanted colorful stage rhetoric, and that he did not give a damn that all the pure cubists aimed for was for their pictures to become intellectual texts. Kahnweiler as an art dealer wanted to retain his hold on his artists and not share them with some marketer eager for cut-rate advertising. Although Kahnweiler remained on good terms with Diaghilev, he tried to persuade his cubists to go on making modern art for his gallery and not bother with a stage that clung to what he considered an old-fashioned form of painting. "The modern stage," according to Kahnweiler, "is not a bit ashamed of admitting to be nothing but a picture. This you understand by the great golden frame that surrounds it. Theatre also uses both linear and aerial perspective to create the illusion of depth . . . Theatre is, quite simply, painting."[50]

Shamefacedly, Gris admitted to his dealer that he had been seduced by the pitch about the large audience of art-loving luminaries. Kahnweiler responded that Diaghilev had turned both Gris and Braque into simple decorators. Gris returned home, never realizing that Diaghilev had already passed on the order to Picasso, who was quicker to respond by cable. A year or so later, Kahnweiler breathed a huge sigh of relief, for Gris no longer obeyed Diaghilev's every whim. He returned to the craft and no longer helped in making art work.

As Lugné had done earlier, Diaghilev made painting perform on stage. As Antoine himself admitted, this meant a time lag between the production of images and their use for art work. When cubism or fauvism was in the bud, Diaghilev and his court of young dandies preferred Baudelaire or Beardsley.[51] For this reason, cubists never got a job when they needed it most.

Diaghilev's formula for skimming the cream of visual art was soon imitated. La Cigale, a theatre in Montmartre, produced dadaist performances in the same spirit under the management of a certain de Maré. In the 1920s, the Swedish art patron Rolf de Maré was urged by Fokine, the choreographer who was working in Stockholm after he was dismissed so that Diaghilev could make room for Nijinsky, to set up a competing art firm. Following Diaghilev's strategy, he headhunted his protégé Jean Börlin from a position with the Swedish Royal Theatre.

It was not only the fact that it was Fokine who gave de Maré the idea that upset Diaghilev. Like the Russians, Maré began by presenting folklore pastiches and—in Diaghilev's style—invited artists such as Leger, Duchamp, and René Clair to the Swedish ballet. After only five years, de Maré naïvely lost control of his company and was cheated out of a significant amount of income by the administration of the Paris theater on which he had taken a long-term lease.[52]

Despite the constant financial pressure of finding public support, underwriters, sponsors, and patrons, Diaghilev managed to keep his art firm going for about two decades. During this time, Western culture witnessed a transition from court incorporation to making art work in a modern market system.[53] Diaghilev began as a protégé of a grand duke; toward the end, Lord

Rothermere, a newspaper tycoon, sponsored his art firm for public relations and the love of one of its ballerinas.

From beginning to end, Diaghilev not only handpicked and trained choreographers but in his role as a producing critic also maintained the right to the final cut, dictated the length of the costumes, made amendments to the music, and even rejected sketches by Picasso. When there was a shortage of Russians, he employed Polish or British dancers and gave them Russian names to support his brand! When the Bolsheviks changed the name of the Marinsky to the Kirov Ballet, he performed for émigrés and Parisian avant-garde in Monte Carlo. He was appreciated by futurists, cubists, and dadaists as well as by the Bloomsbury group of intellectuals. Diaghilev even provided Lord Keynes with his lady, the Russian ballerina Lydia Lopokova. He miraculously escaped bankruptcy, strikes, and a number of lawsuits on the basis of his failure to pay wages to dancers, musicians, composers, and painters.

Diaghilev started as the patron of loyal dancers drilled in feudal etiquette and ended as a manager in a tough labor market where dancers gained in professional respect what they lost in job security and wages. Under the Soviet regime Stanislavski spent more and more time backstage in longer and longer rehearsals; Diaghilev kowtowed to his audiences with a frontstage frenzy of just the right marketing mix of avant-garde novelty and bleak reruns of glorious galas. He began in an era when dance was a bodily decoration, like the infamous absent second-act ballet in Wagner's *Tannhäuser*. By the time Diaghilev died of diabetes in 1929, dance was a fashionable hobby for upper-class and middle-class children. Their instruction was managed not only by stars but also by poor retired or jobless dancers turned ballet instructor. Diaghilev the critic, himself neither dancer nor choreographer, neither worker nor capitalist, became a most unlikely art entrepreneur. When King Alfonso of Spain asked him what secret power it took to run his enterprise, he replied good-naturedly, "I just make myself indispensable."

On Christmas Eve 1928, Nijinsky was scheduled to make his final public appearance at the Paris Opera. It was a Stravinsky evening at the Palais Garnier, with both *The Firebird* and *Petrushka* on the program. Nijinsky was not on stage, however. He sat motionless beside Diaghilev in one of the boxes; after the performance, he was wrapped in his coat and led out to the waiting car. For some reason, then, perhaps due to a premonition of Diaghilev's death nine months later or a reluctance to leave the gilded auditorium, Nijinsky put up a struggle. In the Parisian night, in the last minute of the Diaghilevian era, the empty shell of the great Nijinsky, once Diaghilev's incarnator of art, cried out in agony, "Je ne veux pas."[54] It was a death sigh of metaphysical essence Lady Ottoline Morrell had sensed in Nijinsky's art fifteen years earlier: "When dancing you are not human," she had said. "You are an idea. And isn't that what Art really is? You have read Plato, I am sure?"[55]

## Metaphysics of Politics

### Discovering the State of Nature

Jacques-Louis David abandoned the traditional idea of art as picture painting or book printing and made art work for aesthetic play. To be sure, it was not only a shrinking market for paintings that made David leave his studio and direct processions of people carrying books and paintings through the streets and squares of Paris. Nor was it really the demand for documentation that made people frequently wonder whether David ever finished his revolutionary painting of the oath in the Jeu de Paume.[56] Strangely enough, the contemporary *Journal de Paris* does not even mention the oath he set out to paint. One might even ask whether or not it had ever taken place. David was not supposed to write history; he was expected to make it an event! When barely 10 percent of the estimated cost of the painting was raised by subscription (and those donations came mainly from David's own group of Jacobins), the French state stepped in to subsidize it. It is no wonder that David now moved to a better studio situated next to the siege of the legislative body of which his artistic company became a branch in the business of being.

That the picture was never finished signals what the Jacobins were really after. Texts and images, documents and paintings performed the public service of consecrating the hall where the oath was sworn. The revolution badly needed new faith but had neither time nor money to physically replace ancien-regime cathedrals or castles.[57] Books and pictures, engravings and pamphlets all became ready-made materials for aesthetic production, props for performances infusing old monuments with the right revolutionary spirit. David modernized old context as one of the first content entrepreneurs.

According to both Napoleon and Kahnweiler, David was obsolete as a picture painter. Not that he was particularly obsolete in the craft of painting, for he had never been a really great painter. He simply lost the magical touch for the metaphysical business of making his own art work. After the revolution, plenty of artifacts were confiscated from chateaus and churches, and the more confiscations, the more questions. What should be done with it all? Ought confiscated art to be sold for its gold and silver value to raise money? Was its old aesthetic surplus value produced under l'ancien regime completely corrupt and compromised? Or might it still contain something of natural genius with a universal value even after 1789? Should revolutionaries perhaps ban exportation and incorporate the trappings of the old kingdom in the new state?

It was not long before the bonfires of coats of arms and royal portraits died out. State museums were established, and the newly nationalized property was inventoried and stored by the curators of the Republic. Its main purpose was no longer to be accessible to connoisseurs as something to be imitated. It was, in the process of being moved from chateaux and churches, cleansed of its premodern despotic poison in the archives of the Republic's museums.

Now the old artifacts had to serve new causes. They received, as it were, modern artifictions that made them again work as art and serve as public utility. For that end, some art was better material than other art. Old artifacts such as painting and literature became less important than three-dimensional, monumental architectonic sculpture. Two-dimensional paintings were considered as dull as school posters or information billboards, while architectural monuments were much more efficient.[58] Perhaps it was for similar reasons that Kant's aesthetic philosophy never spoke of individual paintings, only of walls of galleries decorated with an interesting mosaic of collections of pictures. Kant, as well as others, was mainly interested in the aesthetic power of art for mobilizing scattered individuals into one public body. Sculpture and architecture provided the space embracing an audience. They were the skeleton, the contextual form, of the revolutionary public flesh and blood. For Diderot, the city was an architectural theater for festivals and allowed the audience to "occupy its most sumptuous buildings, and see them surrounded by a countless mass."[59]

The public was to become the audience of modernity, the democratic people. David the festival director was a hands-on predecessor of Stanislavski or Diaghilev, who later so convincingly directed and choreographed common folk on stage. During the time of the revolution, as happened later during the command of Chronegk of the Meiningen Company, people were staged as disciplined mass. The old static and pyramidal arrangements were dropped, and directors of revolutionary feasts were instead inspired by snaking processions of ancient friezes and Roman victory columns. Jean-Jacques Rousseau had already formulated the strategy of modern art in public service.

> What then is the purpose of these performances? What is on show? Nothing at all really. For wherever liberty reigns, affluence and welfare reign as well. . . . Gather people together and you will have a feast. Or, even better, make a performance of the audience. Make it into the actors so that each and every one become visible and loves himself as others reflect him, so that they are all more strongly united.[60]

New public art was designed to produce democratic people out of the chaotic crowd and the uncontrolled mob. The festivals of the revolution claimed to offer a natural spectacle but were scarcely spontaneous Dionysian riots. They were carefully planned and managed well within the bounds of the law. Even though half a million Parisians took part in the processions, they were rather like Apollonian festivals that only occasionally descended into feverish Dionysian festivities.

The festivals had to be different from the old hierarchical parades because costumes of the old guilds and corporations were banned. One had to invent an immanent object of something previously unseen: the natural, ordinary and universal people. Processions were directed along more "natural" lines, according to gender or age. The players were no longer formed as hierarchies, parading their rank in society; they instead represented immanent philosophical virtues such as motherly love, faith, or courage. If symbols of the old guilds were carried in the processions, they would only be burned at the end on a large bonfire. David, of course, had studied classical art in Rome and copied modern symbols from even older emblems. Occasionally the solemn and serious atmosphere was interrupted by recent inventions such as aerostats, the colorful balloons that were uplifted into the universe by a natural force of the same sort that made the audience transcendentally incarnate "the people."

This force, the immanent object of modern public performance, was the will of the people, rather than the will of the world, as Schopenhauer had it.

Jacques-Louis David presented himself as being directly employed in the service of that people's will. He considered his talent to be a genial ability to express their will from the metaphysical depths of their collective soul. He claimed, for instance, that people's will, like an art angel from the sky, commanded him to paint Marat's death: "David, take your brushes . . . revenge our friend, exact revenge for Marat so that his enemies pale when they see his twisted features . . . I heard the voice of the people, and I obeyed."[61]

The will demanded art, but the art firm also had a responsibility to nourish the idea of this people that were to become the raison d'être, the real being, of modern democracy. David began to donate paintings as offerings on the altar. His own rhetoric in the National Committee appears to have been well in line with these artistic homages with which he decorated the chamber. He presented his art firm as a pedagogical affair intended for the aesthetic education of a mob into a moral mass. When he proposed a huge sculpture to be situated next to the Pont Neuf in its honor, he wanted the details of the statue to be publicly explained on signs and posters hanging from it.[62] His pictures celebrating the heroes of the Revolution were also explicitly didactic. David's martyrs were often depicted at the moment of their death in order to illustrate most clearly "the sublime traits of heroism and virtue."[63]

The painting of the dead Jacobin Marat in his bloodstained bath was intended as an instrument for aesthetic education. With reference to a painting of another republican, Lepelletier, David gave detailed instructions on how a father ought to use his picture to instruct his son about the immortality bestowed upon heroes by the nation.[64] The revolutionaries even wanted to establish a popular university as a French equivalent to Oxford in the midst of the Palace of Versailles (the most monarchic monument of the old era).

It was as the organizer of an artistic company that David was elected to the National Committee of General Security at the behest of Dr. Marat himself. Everything was to follow the material order of nature. David suggested that the royal school of art with its artificial regulations be abolished; from 1791 on, anyone was free to exhibit—and even train artists. Art as free enterprise was to be made to work by natural philosophers instead of conventional craftsmen.

David himself became responsible for state education, *instruction public*, before becoming a member of the totalitarian Security Committee that sent innumerable members of the nobility and clergy to the guillotine. The carnage of Madame Guillotine working at full capacity in the Place de la

Concorde accompanied Monsieur David's festivities promoting the democratic idea of a universal people on the nearby Champs-Élysées.[65] The artistic firm made history to the extent that it was not the very storming of the
Bastille in 1789 that was celebrated at the first national ceremony, July 14,
1791. The real cause was a celebration of the grand July Feast of the Federation held on the Champ de Mars one year earlier under the leadership of
the Marquis de Lafayette.[66]

## Designing Cultures for Nations

By the middle of the 1790s, the Republic explicitly encouraged every French
artist to "establish an enterprise which will immortalise the glory of the nation."[67] The early revolutionaries regarded themselves as natural philosophers with a mission to ensure human rights for the oppressed of the world.
This enlightened quest for liberty was doubtless the reason Immanuel Kant
proposed a toast to the Revolution in Königsberg. A few years later, the
peaceful planting of trees of natural freedom, the centerpiece of early revolutionary feasts, was being replaced by military processions with banners
and cannons. When the idea of a special differentiated nation developed
counter to that of a general state of human nature, something named "culture" was about to emerge. Regional differences and folklore began to attract the interest of artists; maybe nature alone was not enough as a source
of inspiration. According to Quatremere de Quincy, one of David's contemporaries and another festival organizer, art was not only next to science but
really belonged between science and literature. Perhaps something could be
learned from the old masters as well as through the attentive study of nature. Art gradually swung over to be viewed as a "materializing encyclopae-
dia" of nature's opposite, culture.[68]

Jacques-Louis David shifted from state content-provider to national for-
malist. In an ironic twist—having escaped the guillotine himself—he became
Napoleon's incorporated court artist, with academic privileges of the kind
he had abolished as a Jacobin. General, Consul, and eventually Emperor
Napoleon was quick to use art to forge new social forms. He began by com-
manding campaigns and expeditions to the pyramids of Egypt, which Kant
once regarded as the manifestation of sublime aesthetics. Instead of letting
the Vatican bless his reign, Napoleon directed his own coronation, with the
Pope held hostage in a humiliating subordinate role. The show was documented by David, the dutiful photographer ready to touch up his paintings

at the Emperor's command. Art seemed no longer to have a content value in and of itself but was only functioning as protocol for the constitution of the nation. On the one hand, Napoleon imposed censorship upon the small theaters that were havens for revolutionary agitators. On the other, the nation increasingly relied on theatrical forms when a natural state was to be disciplined into a national culture. Napoleon regulated the theater business into a formal network of state theaters, each with its own company and a repertoire overseen by censors who carefully inspected its content. In addition to painters and writers, inventors and engineers gradually came to be regarded as aesthetic geniuses.

France was also swept by the wave of rationalism against which Schopenhauer later would react in Hegelian Berlin. The state really moved into the category of nation when it became industrialized, and by the middle of the nineteenth century Europeans appeared increasingly convinced that the wealth of nations came out of the rational factory organization which had tamed the nature of people both as producers and consumers.

Despite this, industry was still regarded an aesthetic affair run by artistic companies. After the theatrical district of Paris, the Boulevard du Crime, was demolished, the show went on in the shopping arcades of the nascent bourgeois economy. Goods from factories were put on show in a theatrical manner that management professors today refer to as event marketing. New factories pushed their output into the market through modern stores that actively seduced their audience by theatrical means. The forms of marketing were new, but the content of the goods and services provided was not. When new hotels were built on the Italian and French Riviera, for instance, they were careful imitations of the palace homes of their wealthy guests, though adapted to the logic of rational management by means of almost military standardization. The shops and department stores also offered new forms of purchasing familiar objects. Furniture, fabrics, glassware, and ceramics from modern industry were often reproductions of earlier crafted goods. Today tourists admire design classics in the Museum für angewandte Kunst in Vienna or in London's Victoria and Albert Museum. Originally, old items were collected so that manufacturers would have an archive of contents to replicate with the new technologies of reproduction.

Not only were historical objects popular in the marketplace; in addition, historical painting borrowed its motif from classical works. Even politics became dramatized by means of old motifs, as happened when Napoleon's nephew made his entrance on the French political stage masquerading as his famous Corsican uncle.[69] Theatrical form furnished ideas for new technologies trying to recycle old content into new market forms. Marketers launched cultural products organized in repertories of styles, fashions, collections, and product lines for cultivating the natural people in the mass audience in the national market.

By the middle of the nineteenth century, the grandchildren of the Revolution were slowly but surely turning into a middle-class audience that constituted what the French sociologist Bourdieu calls "the field of cultural production." To this new middle class, culture became an efficient instrument of differentiation. Balzacian bourgeois bureaucrats would walk from their cultivated homes to their offices under commercial shopping arcades. For their wives, department stores became mundane meeting places offering commercial entertainment while their husbands were working. Early marketers had theater architects design huge stores where industrial artifacts were staged to attract sales.

The revolutionary program of enlightenment was based on contemplation of nature. Now, only a few years later, urbane aesthetes strolled by goods staged in the windows of shopping arcades. Tourists knew how to appreciate the busy commercial streets that romantic philosophers had fled in search of roaring seas and fields of swaying corn. Both types of bourgeois, native *flâneurs* as well as visiting tourists, were after a culture that could grant them status in a world where their own class searched for a social foothold between workers and nobility.[70] Taste and consumption became tools of a third class category, one positioned between posing as a bohemian fake laborer or turning to snobs and humbug aristocrats.

Nouveaux riches Americans were especially good at constructing social status by means of European culture.[71] The United States was certainly responsible for a part of the initiative driving cultural consumption of artifacts from the archives of Europe. Art became a symbolic commodity for private use, something one bought and used, instead of its existing as a public good of the state. Tourists from America, enchanted by European heritage, spent fortunes on collections to cultivate their identity.

This cultural consumerism eventually led to aesthetic preoccupation with the outer form termed "product design." Earlier, the aesthetic field of the European middle classes was cultivated by social forms in manners of conduct and methods of cognition.[72] The difference between a civilized person and a cultivated person was only visible in a subject's behavior. Product design now attempted to materialize form and freeze culture in concrete, manufactured artifacts of consumption. Toward the end of the nineteenth century, this led to new markets for luxuries that the cultural-economic pioneer Thorstein Veblen identified as "conspicuous consumption." Now products became rhetorical means for bragging about the status of consumers formerly respected only as the subtle and tacit symbolism resulting from good breeding and aesthetic education.

Perhaps the European bourgeois bureaucrats were procedural Schillerian educators acting as Deweyan critics in the aesthetic play of modern middle-class civilization. The bureaucrats became experts in form and symbolism, tracing precise meaning back through time and ascribing attributions and hidden signification. Those critics came to base their modernist expertise on systems of logic that subtly regulated the social into socio-logy, technique into techno-logy, and psyche into psycho-logy.

The formal scientific interpretation of art, aside from its practical execution in fine arts salons, became an integral part of national education. One century later, this led universities to provide young students with their aesthetic education in film, music, art, or literature.

American capitalists, on the other hand, looked upon art as Adam Smith would have; it was a charming and pleasurable means of communicating social status through wealth. With the Americanization of European manufacturing, industrial world fairs and exhibitions became the place where whole nations boosted their status by means of products loudly signaling what critics interpreted as "technological development." The market for European art that developed at the end of the nineteenth century was probably a result of aesthetic marketing carried out by large American department stores. The marketers of Marshall Field and Co. in Chicago or John Wanamaker's in Philadelphia, the precursors of Bonwit Teller or Barney's, featuring Salvador Dali and designer clothes, played their parts as critics of good taste by offering customers both concert halls and art galleries, supplied by the most respectable art houses in Paris.[73] Some private dealers opened public galleries and put art on show as luxury goods. Those pretending to be civilized need only book a tour to Paris to convey that invisible and elusive *je ne sais quoi* of *la civilisation française*.

## Legendre's Mirror of Modernity

Art became ensconced in modern society by following both public and private avenues. When it turned into materialization of democracy, however, as in David's feasts, or into formal methods for designing goods and technologies in the modern nation, it deviated from the narrow path of aesthetics. The art firm lost its unique aesthetic competence and became contorted into either a totalitarian bureau of political propaganda or banal design management. The totalitarian aberration mobilized and mastered the masses on the political markets of democracy. Banality, on the other hand, excelled in new technologies, which organized business according to forms, manners, and methods.

In the artistic company of Jacques-Louis David, the double threat of the total and the banal was always present as a mix of a coolly cognitive Apollo and the emotional and flamboyant rhetorical Dionysus. David's information

signs on the sculpture celebrating the Revolution were precise notations about the meaning of the symbols used. At the same time, he was polishing his rhetoric until it was as sharp as the edge of a guillotine blade. Later, Stanislavski ended up in the company of Gorky, the serious senex of Soviet totalitarianism. On the other hand, Diaghilev pathetically fought against old age by surrounding himself with immature, beautiful, and banal puers. As Stanislavski withdrew into writing methodology  and brooding backstage, Diaghilev became a snobbish frontstage superficiality. Their respective artistic companies became easy prey of matter and form.

After 1789, Schillerian polarization made its appearance in a multitude of dualistic guises. Modernity seemed to be divided into two split identities and social schizophrenia, with nature versus culture, public versus private, and national versus universal. The French psychoanalyst Pierre Legendre has suggested that art firms such as Wagner's, Antoine's, Lugné's, Stanislavski's, and Diaghilev's have a uniquely modern mission to cope with that madness of modernity. It is even imperative for the constitution of a functioning modernity that artistic companies be incorporated in society.[74] The death of traditional metaphysics has turned art into the sole remaining therapy.

Modernity meant giving up the hope for absolute religious foundations. When Louis XVI was guillotined in Paris, the umbilical cord to an archaic metaphysical society was severed. This separation was reinforced when Napoleon crowned himself emperor in Nôtre Dame. Bonaparte wanted to be a modern Justinian, a legislator.[75] Unlike his Roman and canonical predecessor, however, this modern emperor was not satisfied to rule in God's name. Napoleon was a modern, legislating superego who grabbed the crown from the pope's hands and anointed himself. This act of arrogation rationalized the pontiff out of modern existence and burned the bridge back to the absolute, guarded by the pope in Rome, once and for all. Napoleon, the self-made entrepreneur, placed himself at the top of the pyramidal throne of the Trinity, thereby making the claim to incarnate the immanent subject of existence. He constructed his own set of laws, the *Lex Napoleonis*, which destroyed the religious objective basis of canonical law.

Bourgeois social sciences next took a stab at legitimating law, and their early attempts showed distinct signs of imitating religion. The development of secular marriage ceremonies is one example of a profane imitation of a religious procedure.[76] Comte, the French father of modern sociology, developed a full-fledged rational religion from nineteenth-century positivism; its positivist chapel on the Rue Payenne in Paris was decorated with icons of rational saints such as Galileo, Newton, and Copernicus. Instead of a monarchy presided over by the grace of God, there was now a secularized state, rooted in human, Hegelian intellect.

When absolutist values were dispensed with, relativistic social sciences, particularly modern economic theory, became the only raison d'être for society. Social forms such as contracts and exchange were backed up by scientific doctrines from social theories of relativity after this death of God. In the absence of a third option, modern phenomena such as democracy or technology lacked any kind of absolute footing beyond itself. This idealistic vacuum attracted a number of political systems of belief; modernity became the age of ideologies. As the religious impact of positivism faded, the lack of faith again became such a dominant feature of society that some social scientists, inspired by George Bataille, explicitly embarked on a sociological search for "the sacred" in the first half of the twentieth century. They missed the holy thing-in-itself. There was an urgent need for modern metaphysics.

On the whole, however, any hope that social science might replace "the absolute" religion no longer found support in modernist thought. Wittgenstein's skeptical and sharp analysis is a good Schopenhauerian example of this. He showed convincingly how social science, with all its theories of balance and relativism, its mathematical equations and economic accounts, can easily be exposed as logical tautologies void of absolute truth. Wittgenstein saw no acceptable way to replace such self-referential emptiness with some new philosophic metaphysics. At the same time, he also noted that modernity seemed to work without a religion or science of the absolute. Even in a world after God's death, man does not appear to be lost or paralyzed. Although humans are torn between incompatible dualism and incommensurable polar forces, they still miraculously manage to find energy enough to undertake their enterprises. Being and essence, the absolute sources of creative energy, are obviously still at work. Modernists still find the spontaneity springboard for their self-confident actions.

Wittgenstein, himself an antiphilosophical philosopher with a modern engineering education, explains this phenomenon in a mode reminiscent of Schopenhauer's aesthetic play. Modern action can be understood as game. In other words, a modern enterprise is equal to an art firm with a foothold in the aesthetic realm between the dualisms of work and capital, commerce and culture, democracy and technology, or plan and market for stereoscopic images.[77] Further, such spectacles are supported by the nose. Apart from an individual's two eyes, this third organ plays the role somewhat like the line between signifier and signified, or the equal sign between the two sides of an equation, or the vertical line that balances the business account in double-entry bookkeeping. Again, it all has to do with the third position so crucial to classical aesthetics as well as to Genette's contemporary theory of the immanent object hovering between notation and execution. In still another attempt to pinpoint how art is made to work, the geographer Gunnar Olsson talks about a "limiting penumbra through which signifier and signified are kept together and apart . . . [a] bar of categorical meanings."[78]

Signs of fraction, equality, or identity are, however, only logical operators patching together parts into a single unit. Pierre Legendre, like the European aesthetic philosophers who denied intellectual world making, points out that viewing the "third" as some fine dividing line in a game of logic must be avoided. Using Freudian terminology, Legendre instead suggests that the third is the totem, the ritual object or concrete taboo, the unutterable but still present and extant, that must be taken seriously when an individual is shaping a stable constitution of modernity.[79] The third is reducible neither to a meaningful cognitive symbolic design nor to a colorful rhetorical gesture. It needs concrete territory all its own. In his own way, Legendre tries to explain the inexplicable: "This is why this place of distance can be defined as that of this third which controls the play of binary opposition. This place is both a home of contents—science and general skills—and also the centre of the power to divide and command—we may call the dogmatism—that constitutes every culture."[80]

Legendre refers to "the place," but Rousseau describes a modern art work as being simply *rien si l'on veut*. Instead of despairing, the individual now realizes that a perfect definition is unattainable by argument. The third unknown is, to use the terms of an American Wittgensteinian, Susanne Langer, not reachable by discourse but by presentation only.[81] Since the proof of the pudding lies in its eating, art consumers, those receptive audiences instructed by art critics, can grasp what it is all about. They experience, in a sense, the Kantian argument that aesthetic judgment is about conceiving without concepts.

All in all, this confirms the central position of art and art firms in modernity. Legendre explicitly relates the legal constitution of modern society to art. The nation state is an aesthetic phenomenon for which neither politicians nor managers have the final responsibility. The need for the absolute can now be met only by art. Therefore, Legendre expresses his gratitude to Ingmar Bergman, Cocteau, Magritte, and the Japanese film director Ozu for their inspired interpretations of the third. They make art work as an immanent object of nothingness, *not* to be confused with void and empty nihilism. Like Schopenhauer, Legendre urges individuals to decline the proposals of rationalist philosophers who today appear as political experts or management consultants. Basically, they cannot handle nothingness; they are a poor fit for the business of being and only fill up the void or empty with nonsense. Personal, social, or corporate identities, marketed in a multitude of products and services, are nothing but the vulgar stuffing Legendre calls *le plein industrialiste*.[82] Instead of providing people with art, they profiteer as quacks, curing what they pretend to be the modern neurosis of horror vacuii.

In sharp opposition to Freud, Legendre rejects all talk of neurosis as a diagnosis for modern madness. To him, the problem of dualism can never be remedied by patching together new identities. In addition, the philosopher Deleuze has, in company with the psychiatrist Felix Guattari, accused therapists of neuroticizing the *schizos* and addicting them to profitable, interminable psychoanalytical treatment. Their way out is similar to Legendre's. People have to face the fact of a fundamental and irreparable duality and, instead of nourishing false hopes of "identity," go for what they provocatively call schizoanalysis. "The task of schizoanalysis is that of tirelessly taking apart egos and their presuppositions, liberating the prepersonal singularities they enclose and repress, and mobilizing the flows they would be capable of transmitting, receiving or intercepting."[83]

The flows that schizoanalysis sets in motion resemble the Schillerian Schwung provoked by art firms. To Legendre, the Shinto mirror in the Ise Temple in Japan, for instance, serves this purpose and initiates a Schopenhauerian contemplation.[84] The Shinto mirror is the mythological dwelling place of the dynastic mother of the Japanese imperial family. Only the emperor himself is allowed to look in it. Every twenty years, a new mirror replaces every old one. All the old mirrors can be seen in the museum beside the temple, but they are face down, their reflecting planes forever hidden from glance. To the audience, art firms should, in Legendre's terms, make art work like such a mirror. The critics should be like Ise priests protecting the negative by keeping them pure and clean. This negative is the elusive third aesthetic field, an absolute point of reference for both rhetorical speech and cognitive thought. No one but the emperor is permitted to see the front of the mirror. This fixed point works as an absolute only as long as it remains metaphysically negative.

In modernity, Freud had insight into the mirroring process that transformed man from a collective being into a complete individual. Like the priest of the temple at Ise, Freud knew that mirrors were powerful and had to be carefully guarded. The mirroring process of modernization can go terribly wrong, just as the act of reflection did for the handsome Narcissus.

Freud, however, developed his psychoanalytic theories at his clinic on Berggasse in Vienna in somewhat the opposite direction from contemporary avant-garde entrepreneurs such as Breton in Paris.[85] Legendre deplores the fact that Freudians have come to focus only on the problem of individuation instead of exploring socialization by means of art. The patient in real need is not some single Narcissus but modernity in general. Perhaps this was why surrealists, the Freudian avant-garde entrepreneurs par excellence, tried to remain on the societal level by constantly flirting with modern politics. Some, like Louis Aragon, became victims of Stalinism; others of fascism, like Salvador Dali; while their philosopher-king Breton seems to have remained in the aesthetic in-between limbo by allying himself with Trotsky. The following narrative reveals that Freud himself actually might have had an intuition that reduced a discovery of societal implications to merely a matter of individual cure.

On June 16, 1922, Freud summoned up the courage to meet an author whom he had long suspected of being a rival in the search for the mirrored constitution of modern society. Freud, who himself took inspiration from Greek tragedy and Elizabethan drama, scheduled a time to dine with Arthur Schnitzler. Using his plays, Schnitzler had turned the seats of the Burgtheater into an artistic company, into a collective equivalent of Freud's individual couch on Berggasse. In the darkened auditorium of the theater, well-heeled customers could, like some Narcissus under treatment, watch their own neuroses being reflected on stage. The theatrical production of *Hamlet* turned the conflicts of the Prince of Denmark into a collective session of autoanalysis along Freudian lines. Art thus incorporated in the Viennese society helped loosen a resistance that psychoanalysts would have had to break down with years of therapy. To Freud, Schnitzler's success and the popularity of the theater was perhaps a sign that modern man had recognized his need for therapy. Schnitzler's artistic company offered an effective method for Narcissus to distinguish between the body in the mirror and his own subjective self.

Freud was competitive, and now he seemed to spot a dangerous opponent in Schnitzler's artistic company. He had struggled to make his own method achieve legitimacy as a modern business of being. To give therapy a position on the medical market, he subscribed to both scientific argument and market protection by providing credentials for all therapists.

Freud had long discerned in Schnitzler's work hypotheses and ideas that drove his own research.[86] In addition, Schnitzler and Freud shared a May 6 birthday, and each was a doctor of psychiatry. Their dinner conversation on June 16, 1922, might have been romantically staged as a surreal encounter of doppelgängers.

There were differences too, however. Freud would rent out small individual pocket mirrors in his clinic, while Schnitzler's artistic company mass-marketed a giant mirror incarnating its audience in the incorporation of a red velvet salon and gold-gilded proscenium frame. Legendre criticized Freud for abandoning his original conception of dualism, which would have led to an approach of Schnitzler's kind. In an early essay on the interpretation of dreams, Freud compared individuals to an empty theater where the caretaker—the controlling rational self—has fallen asleep. In the darkness of the night, the caretaker of consciousness no longer upholds the fuzzy border between stage and backstage. All manner of bizarre extras and odd characters from the depth of the back stage are now free to step forward. Dreaming is like an abandoned theater. Sleep is like Antoine's fourth wall between stage and front stage that screens off dreams from wakeful consciousness. Dreaming, according to Dr. Freud's theory, was the free performance of the unconscious. Under the art management of Doctor Schnitzler, however, theory turned into a practice of collective daydreaming for an awake audience.

In his reinterpretation of Freudian tradition, Legendre finds support for art firms—serving both the private and public—that do not deviate into either the banality of the market or totalitarian political propaganda. Legendre considers theatricality as essential for restoring social order and making law again work as art. What happens in a courtroom seems an aesthetic play of judgment between the formality of positive law and the materiality of natural law. The courtroom is the location of a third place of performative justice. The art firms bears the responsibility of being a good model. To Legendre, theater is the last locus for contemplating the *négativité à l'échelle de la culture* equal to modern metaphysics.[87] Stanislavski retreated backstage to connect the conscious and the subconscious in his pre-Freudian form of production, whereas Diaghilev connected the consciousness of the glamorous extrovert au-

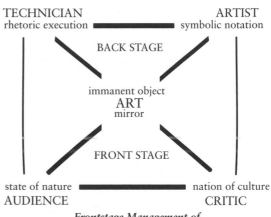

*Frontstage Management of*
*Reflections of Nature and Culture*

ditorium with the subconsciousness of the stage in the frenzy of front-of-stage marketing. If backstage management of immanent objects and frontstage marketing are written into the Gadamerian model of the aesthetic play, it might take on the features seen in the figure.

What sort of metaphysical mirror does an artistic company provide? To single individuals, it might still be as treacherous as Narcissus' pond. Nijinsky himself struggled against his aides in the Paris Opera when they wanted to bring him back to the asylum. Lost in madness, addicted to Diaghilev's mirror, he was imprisoned with no escape route. His last letter to Diaghilev is a poor victim's grotesquely sad hallucinations about the complete perversion of the idea of the third thing in itself:

> I am a man with feeling and reason. You are a man with intelligence and without feeling. Your feeling is evil. My feeling is good. You want to destroy me. I want to save you. I like you. You don't like me. I wish you well. You wish me ill . . . I am God within yourself. You are a beast, but I am love . . . I am not yours. You are not mine . . . I am yours. I am my own. You are mine. . . .

I am a prick, but not yours
You are mine, but I am not yours
Mine is a prick because the Prick
I am the Prick, I am the Prick.
I am God in my prick.
I am God in my prick.
Yours is a prick, not mine not mine
I am a prick in His prick.
I prick, prick, prick
You are a prick, but not the Prick[88]

# 7

## Art Corporations

### Metaphysics of Industry

#### Culture for Workers

Wagner, Antoine, and Lugné—all early pioneers of the avant-garde enterprise—ushered in the idea that entertainment differs from art, and groundbreaking entrepreneurs such as Stanislavski and Diaghilev negotiated their artistic companies into big theatrical businesses of their times. One interesting aspect of the development of art firms is how they got on the public payroll during times when the primary national concern appeared to be industrial production. To be sure, countries did depend on full industrial employment, but art firm politicians somehow managed to negotiate aesthetics into a central position in the educational and cultural policies just the same. As politicians, art managers navigated into public policy shores on Schopenhauerian art ships, rocking from side to side in a Schillerian Schwung. This incorporation of art as a socioeconomic institution could be written into the Gadamerian art firm as connections between the aesthetic players.

In Europe today, this institutionalization has resulted in vital state-financed networks of public theaters and art space; indeed, art seems central to the constitution of European industrial socioeconomies. Signs of such institutionalization are already evident in avant-garde enterprises.

202

A trip to Wagner's Bayreuth was no entertainment for empty minds; it demanded all of the attention of the audience. At the outset, even its appearance was far from routine, since the spartan exterior of the Schopenhauerian sanatorium stood in sharp contrast to the usual decoration of feudal opera houses. A visitor's first glance at the setting clearly set the tone that the point of the visit was neither pleasure nor leisure.

Distractions were prohibited; in fact, they were prevented. There was no opportunity to eat or drink oneself out of concentration on the real task. There was no more posing, flirting, gossiping, or even leafing through the score during a performance. Wagner, the efficient manager, switched off the lights, locked up the auditorium, and hid the conductor and orchestra out of the reach of the audience. Wagner, the industrial engineer, designed a perfect ergonomic workplace where everyone could collectively experience the staged vision and share its acoustics.

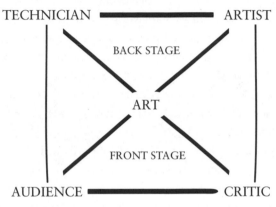

*Art's Incorporation into the Socioeconomy*

His opera became a university for aesthetically educating citizens in audiovisual value making fundamental to modern metaphysics. The art firm as a dual workplace for undisturbed aesthetic production and contemplative consumption, as a Schopenhauerian manifestation of modernity, overshadowed the material and ethical shortcomings of its industrial reality.

By the time Pauline Brunius, director of the Royal Dramatic Theatre in Stockholm, returned from a visit to Stanislavski in Moscow in the 1930s, she was thoroughly indoctrinated with the idea of judging an art firm from an industrial perspective. She declared that a "collective notion of work had replaced ambition" in backstage production at Stanislavski's art firm,[1] and the same modern aesthetic spirit of work also influenced frontstage consumption as well. If an audience cracked nuts or slurped drinks, Stanislavski would ask them to quiet down and be considerate of the Schopenhauerian contemplative consumers in the group. Theatergoers were taught respect for their comrades.

Soviet actors, now involved in the aesthetic education of their audience, elevated work to art. What Stanislavski, the skilled manager and industrial engineer, called "my life in art" in his autobiography was actually an account of his *working* life in art. Aesthetic education in his studio followed a pedagogy of worker self-management.

This artistic company later provided such spiritual support to Soviet political economy that Stalin had the state pay the rent on the Artistic Theatre and exempted the organization from tax liability as well. In addition, the Bolsheviks paradoxically allowed Stanislavski to charge an entrance fee and keep the gate receipts! The Artistic Theatre was one of the few self-supporting entities remaining after the Revolution; Stanislavski, whose family textile factory was confiscated by the Communists, was still free to manage his business of being. In her optimistic account of modern Russian theatre, Madame Brunius adds that the Soviet Union was an ideal industrial state, because there were no unemployed actors. Art firms symbolized full employment in the industrial postrevolutionary Soviet Union. Theater became a workshop for Marxian labor value propaganda.

Works of art locked up in private collections were liberated to full employment on public markets.[2] After the French Revolution, the Louvre reopened its doors to make the collection serve as aesthetic education for the citizens' *bonheur social,* and individual property rights converted single texts and pictures into marketed merchandise. Since theaters lost their royal monopoly on all newly written plays, the head of the state-run Comédie Française began regarding himself as an administrator of *"une société des talents."*[3] When just anyone could buy good texts, the incorporation of talented human resources became a strategic factor for theaters. As a result, managers devoted much care and consideration to the recruitment of actors and allocation of roles; the organization of sabbaticals was manipulated so that the theater's own stars did not force competition when earning extra money on other stages.

The business of avant-garde enterprises depended directly on innovative labor management. Théâtre Libre, which might well have been called Theatre Liberal, was actually operating as a producer cooperative, mobilizing penniless amateurs in hard competition with the regulated guilds of big established show biz. Entrepreneur Antoine marketed his theater as an incubator for natural working-class talent and sometimes even intentionally hid from the press the professional backgrounds of his middle-class actors.

Diaghilev once replaced an established star with a naturally talented flamenco folk dancer and frequently made new talents perform under false
Russian names to uphold the media image of a company that naturally expressed an authentic folk spirit. Populist heroes replaced the traditionally
drilled stars on the art firm stage. Art was presented as the aesthetic surplus
value of the industrial political economy.

When the French Minister for Education Aristide Briand appointed André
Antoine head of l'Odéon, France's second national theater, it was on the express condition that he relinquish management of his private theater to his
actor Firmin Gémier.[4] Gémier certainly did not get the job as a result of having first played King Ubu with Lugné and Jarry. Gémier was a working-class
hero, a poor orphan known as a noisy hooligan of the Ambigu claque, and
thrice rejected by the Conservatoire. Gémier was a hardworking actor who
played so many roles concurrently that his cues were scribbled in hat lin-
ings, on shirtsleeves, or on the back of actresses' fans.

Gémier was a man of the people who honored his class, especially when
staging superb crowd scenes. He was an educator of the masses who in 1911
championed a people's theater. He was an industrial genius who set off on
tour with thirty-seven trailers of equipment drawn by eight steam engines.
In two circus tents that took six hours to erect, he was a mass marketer to
an audience of 1,650 at a time.

In 1920, a third state theater opened in the shadow of the Eiffel Tower, the
Parisian monument to modern communication technology. By then, Gémier's
traveling theatre had found a permanent home in the Théâtre National Populaire, a democratic art corporation where workers made art for other workers. French Socialist leader Leon Blum pointed out that theaters were an important way of providing education for as many people as possible.

Modern French theater was not far from Schiller's ethically inclined court
theater, where the monarch in his box was aesthetically inspired to fulfill his
moral responsibilities. Stanislavski's French friend Copeau argued for a theater of regeneration which would reform the class struggle between labor
and capital by a Schwung of aesthetic energy.[5] By means of concrete and en-
ergizing recreation, the art corporation could and should provide popular
education to the worker exhausted from laboring on the treadmills of capitalist reproduction.

In the early twentieth century, French theatrical entrepreneurs such as
Dullin, Jouvet, Copeau, and Pitoeff argued in favor of the incorporation of

their art firms into the public service of the state.[6] In 1951, Jean Vilar, who created a theatrical festival in the courtyard of the Palais des Papes in Avignon and attracted a large audience of young students and schoolchildren, was appointed manager of the new Théâtre Nationale Populaire. The state also began granting financial support to technical-administrative incubators for art firms geared to public markets. The fact that French artists became eligible for national unemployment benefits was one sign of their state incorporation.

Art remained incorporated in the educational policy of the French state until 1959, when President Charles de Gaulle appointed Kahnweiler's friend, the Cubist poet, publisher, and art critic André Malraux, as the first French minister for culture. The Houses of Culture introduced by Malraux became monuments for art, extending subtle aesthetic support to the national industrial economy.

With public backing, European art corporations undertook the Schillerian task of providing the aesthetic education of producers as consumers of culture. In Europe, the move toward modern art corporations began long before Malraux. In 1890, for instance, the Social Democratic paper *Berliner Volksblatt* published this caution: "That part of the people which has been won over to good taste does not merely need to read plays of its choice; it needs to see them performed. But capitalism does not allow performance of plays of a revolutionary spirit. Unless they have become box-office successes police censure will ban them for open public performances. But for a closed private society such limitations do not exist."[7]

Two thousand persons paid attention to this advice and founded the Freie Volksbühne society, with the aim of producing theatrical art for workers. The founders of the society were critical of the entertainment spectacles offered by Kolportageroman, Witzblätter, and Zirkus. They wanted to present real art. They were also critical of regular theatrical enterprises that performed good plays with subscriptions far too costly for ordinary workers. Bruno Wille, a writer and one of the leaders of the movement, wanted the Freie Volksbühne to put on three new plays a season for only 1.50 marks. Two thousand members immediately subscribed, which meant that actors could be paid in advance and affordable premises rented for Sunday matinee performances.

In Berlin, the idea of a club for cultural consumers had come by way of Freie Bühne, a theatrical society inspired by Antoine's Parisian art firm. His

French naturalism, with its touch of social determinism, was hardly the ticket for German Socialists, however, who wanted to mobilize workers into active cultural consumers. The goal of this club was to foster revolutionary confidence and courage through aesthetic education. Members believed that traditional, optimistic plays were often better than naturalistic dramas, which blamed the wretched position of proletarians on imponderables such as the natural environment and genetic inheritance. It was therefore more the form than the content of Antoine's avant-garde enterprise that the Germans found attractive.

Wille persuaded the Prussian police that the Volksbühne was a private club and not a Social Democratic hotbed of public revolutionary propaganda. If he had not been successful, he would not even have been able to provide his poor audience with plays allowed only for performance in the old and expensive courtlike Deutsches Theater. The progress of Wille's society was stormy; some wanted to stage plays with revolutionary content, while others were happy just having an organizational form which would unite as many workers as possible into a single political audience. Before long, Wille abandoned his first project to start the New Free Folk Stage. Under the new management of Social Democrat Franz Mehring, the old Freie Volksbühne grew to ten thousand members, who subscribed to an increasingly conventional repertoire.

The directors of the sixteen commercial theaters in Berlin were of course impressed by the market for this new enterprise.[8] A huge organized popular audience was putting on its own shows in hired theaters. As a result, established theaters charged their new competitor high rents for access to their theaters and expensive technical equipment, and the Volksbühne society was increasingly forced to contract theaters on expensive long leases to gain access to stages. After the Prussian police abolished theatrical censorship in 1896, the immediate political utility of the Freie Volksbühne decreased, since radical plays could now be performed in public. At this point, the direct support of the Social Democratic Party declined, and the society was disbanded.

As a legacy, however, Freie Volksbühne educated an audience in genuine aesthetic play. Its members desired something other than materialistic entertainment and founded a market for art. When the Party, wanting to find forms to diffuse political moralistic messages, abandoned the theater, its audience, still hungry for aesthetics, reorganized their Freie Volksbühne in 1897.

The rejuvenated society became a truly aesthetic movement, and a while later it merged with Wille's breakaway group, which had also expanded considerably in the meantime. The two societies formed a cartel best regarded as a cultural consumer co-op. Before long, a total of fifty thousand subscribers ensured the financial stability of this art firm. Just before the outbreak of the First World War, the foundation stone of Berlin's most modern theater was laid, and with the construction of the Volksbühne's theatre on Bülowplatz the audience at last had its own house for aesthetic play.

The market pull for this new playhouse developed over a long time. The society's performances on Sundays and holidays were regularly sold out, and since Max Reinhardt had made his breakthrough in Berlin there was also great demand for evening performances as well. Reinhardt's public success came about in 1903 with Gorky's *The Lower Depths,* the very play that had earlier made Stanislavski a reputation. Upon learning that Reinhardt was about to rehearse the Gorky piece at the Deutsches Theater, the Volksbühne invested in seats for its Sunday matinees.

The Volksbühne also began underwriting new productions. In 1909, a donation to its building fund from the Berlin city council was negotiated, and the foundation stone was laid in 1914. Reinhardt had already agreed to take responsibility for future productions as well as for operating costs. In return, he obtained a guarantee to fill half the auditorium with Volksbühne subscribers.

The Volksbühne developed a contextual form for which Reinhardt supplied the contents. As an art manager, he cleverly blended culture with entertainment. In fact, stern critics such as Alfred Kerr, who preferred the symbolical over the rhetorical, thought him much too colorful. Reinhardt was also a smooth operator who even succeeded in staging another production of Gorky's play despite the fact that war was raging between Germany and Russia. In addition, he soon developed his own artistic company to subcontract dramatic productions to a number of stages. As top executive, he moved among the various theaters, where members of his staff were concurrently producing plays signed by the master.

As operations expanded, Max Reinhardt soon became a well-known brand. He was constantly on the lookout for interesting new spaces suitable as contexts to fill with contents. He played in sport arenas, amphitheaters, and scenic open-air locations. He laid the founding stone for the Salzburg festival. While Reinhardt was very busy discovering larger and more spectacular packages for his branded mass production, consumers back in Berlin decided to self-manage the operations for their Volksbühne. They hired actors and directors for their new theater house and finally inaugurated their own art corporation with a spectacular staging of Immermann's popular fantasy *Merlin*. A frontstage consumer co-op had turned into a corporation managing backstage production of its own.

Reinhardt became too much of a backstage capitalist for the Volksbühne. In 1924, they hired Erwin Piscator as their managing art director. The fact that Piscator, born Erwin Fischer, made a name for himself as a sharp critic of the Volksbühne is not as ironic as it sounds. He had no problem with what happened on stage; his criticism, and subsequent management strategy, centered around the passivity of the audience.

In 1919, Piscator participated in political street fights when Communists and Social Democrats, led by Wilhelm Liebknecht and Rosa Luxemburg, marched through the streets of Berlin. He socialized with art "actionists" such as Grosz, Huelsenbeck, Haussmann, and the Hertzfelde brothers, the politicized Berlin phalanx of the dadaist movement. Piscator applauded when Russian actors abandoned Stanislavski's backstage studios for frontstage agitprop actions in Soviet factories.

Soon Berlin's Bolsheviks had their own street theater, and Piscator was its Jacques-Louis David. They performed in pubs, beer halls, and factories. Hertzfelde, who created photo collages under the assumed name of Heartfield, put up political posters in place of scenery. Actors were recruited among Syndicalist and Communist unionists. Piscator in fact pushed art frontstage so violently that even the theater critic in the Communist periodical *The Red Flag* wondered if such undeniably efficient political propaganda could still be considered art. No wonder Piscator, after his group disbanded in 1921, prided himself on having proven scientifically that a Communist could be as good at advertising as any capitalist.

Piscator made ample use of modern communication technology. Photographic realism held more impact than painted illusions, and his idea of having actors perform in front of motion picture projections was new and effective. He became the main event-marketing consultant at Communist Party conferences. Bertolt Brecht, the German dramatist, found that Piscator regarded theatre as

> a parliament, and its audience a legislative committee. The important matters of general concern on which this parliament was to judge were presented visually. Instead of listening to M.P.

speeches about certain intolerable social situations, an artistic copy of the situation was performed in the theatre. The ambition of the stage was to facilitate for the audience, its parliament, to make political decisions based on presentations of depictions, statistics and quotes. Piscator's theatre was not after applause, but rather wanted to stimulate a discussion.[9]

Brecht believed that art, acting in the service of workers in industrial society, was returning to its original Kantian role of aesthetic judgment. Instead of having people express their taste in buying decisions, as capitalist advertising intended, Piscator wanted theater to offer aesthetic support for the audience's involved participation. He started his assignment for the Volksbühne with a play about some executed strike leaders in Chicago and was ecstatic when the pressure in the auditorium rose dramatically and culminated in an almost revolutionary outburst of applause at the end of the performance.[10]

Art consumption was empowering its audience to schwung from a role of passive cultural consumer to that of an involved political activist; workers had taken over the means of cultural production. The Volksbühne was transformed into a democratic self-managed art firm that united its audience under a roof of its own. It was "[a] theatrical company which could begin performing safe in the knowledge that it already had an audience which not only liked theatre, not only liked the stage, but which had itself built the building in which they were sitting and in which the performance was taking place."[11]

Four years and nine productions later, Piscator's time at the Volksbühne ended as dramatically as it started. When he pushed the edges of the dramatic envelope too far in the production of an historic play featuring Lenin against a backdrop of documentary footage from the Russian and Chinese Revolutions, the board of the Volksbühne pulled the plug on his film projector. They had had enough of this rabble rouser's teaching art consumers to be engineers of revolution. Tired of the confusion between back stage and front stage, the board longed for the quiet days of good old Max Reinhardt and coveted a clear distinction between labor and capital.

Although Piscator received support from a small group of young radicals, the matter was closed as far as he was concerned. This consumers' cooperative had become an art corporation manipulated by corrupt board members lining their pockets from subscriptions. Consequently, "[p]oliti-cally insecure elements in a stable time created a movement that in a time of turbulence became a nice and secure Sunday tea party. Inspired political agi-tation had turned into a consumer co-op."[12]

Piscator concluded that the artist-critic cell of the avant-garde was regress-ing into the fusion of technique and audience that had been the hallmark of Reinhardt's mass marketing. At the same time, the board of the corporation maintained that Piscator's subversive program was too much for the Volks-bühne, which was trying to provide cultural consumption for workers in times when they lacked the money to enjoy the fruits of the industry they themselves had produced. This was an audience with little energy left for po-litical activities. What this market occasioned, claimed the board, was nice performances like *A Midsummer Night's Dream*!

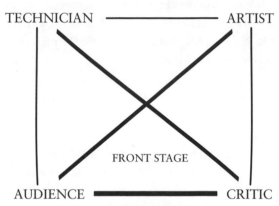

*The Volksbühne Board's Incorporation of the Front Stage*

Piscator's provoca-tion disorganized an audience that needed to unite. The Volks-bühne wanted to re-place avant-garde ac-tivism with attractive art, since the role of an art corporation was to organize the front stage of the aesthetic play. By sacking Pis-cator, the board hoped to regain market control in a way that might be expressed in terms of Gadamer's model as seen in the figure.

As might be expected, Piscator was less interested in audience building than in political mobilization. With the rising tide of graphic, phono-graphic, and motion picture technology, theater had to increase its produc-tivity to stay afloat in constant competition with capitalist media that were also struggling for survival through rationalization and mechanization. Armed with film projectors and a smidgen of mechanical engineering, Pis-cator and Bauhaus architect Walter Gropius set out to capture their vision of an industrialized version of baroque opera that would operate like a well-oiled machine, a total theater moved forward by efficiently meshing cogs. They imagined an aesthetic factory where audiovisual technology would present social facts and figures as art. In a Germany where capitalistic marketing and advertising were now taught under the heading "propaganda," Piscator boasted about the media effectiveness of his revolutionary artistic company. Stepping out of the Volksbühne into the rough and raw urban neighborhood of the *Scheunenmarkt* would be shocking to someone having spent an evening in Reinhardt's nostalgic fantasy. On the other hand, Piscator administered doses at Marxist-Nietzschean speed that made Berlin's decadent modernity and hectic industrial chaos appear more sublime than frightening. Piscator's art made one feel good and "purified. One felt energy flow! It felt good to swim and row along the traffic stream. Traffic and lights, noise and technique had all acquired meaning."[13]

By the time Piscator was thrown out of the Berlin Volksbühne, a whole movement of societies for cultural consumers had institutionalized their theaters as art corporations in cities throughout Germany. Following Hitler's 1933 victory, Piscator fled to New York. There, with other German emigrants, he founded the legendary theatrical studio at the New School for Social Research.

Back in Germany, meanwhile, the whole Volksbühne movement was struck by economic depression and became easy prey for the Nazis. Bülowplatz, the square outside the Volksbühne, was renamed Horst Wesselplatz, and aesthetics schwung between the two Schillerian poles, communist to the left and fascist to the right. While Berlin subsided into a nationalist right-wing culture, Piscator mixed with leftist international film and theatrical producers in his exile in the United States.

When Goebbels, who had dabbled in the expressionist avant-garde, claimed that true art was the natural expression of national folk art, Piscator maintained that Marxist art was international culture.[14] Goebbels used art as a nationalistic instrument for ethnic differentiation, while Piscator believed in its transcendence into a universal humanism. In Germany, the idea of art as culture for working-class people toppled over into the totalitarian claim to manifest the superior biological nature of the working German people as an Aryan race.

Later on, in 1963, Willy Brandt gave Piscator a theater in a Berlin polarized by the Berlin Wall. Modern industrial corporations were hailed in the West as the vanguard of democratic consumption, while the Eastern combines symbolized rational technology for socialist production. On one side of the Berlin wall, surplus value was looked upon as the fruit of material objective work; on the other, as resulting from subjective judgments of buyers. In this split Berlin art scene, polarization fostered aesthetic play. Two Volksbühnes existed, one on each side of the wall. In the west, Piscator headed the new "free" Volksbühne. On Horst Wesselplatz, formerly Bülowplatz and now renamed Rosa Luxemburg Platz by the German Democratic Republic, the ruins of the grand 1914 building were rebuilt. Workers were bussed to performances from the industrial combines of the GDR, since this art corporation was part and parcel of East German industry and its central planning.

Theater was the explicit concern of the East German trade union. As the communist states put all their efforts into the production of industrial and defense goods, consumer products grew scarce. Members of GDR trade unions had to satisfy their need for consumption in a way similar to that of their parents, who had founded the Volksbühne half a century before. An official text from 1950 postulates the public interest of art corporations for the working life in the socialist planned economy: "The German Volksbühne expresses its gratitude to the trades unions for supporting its establishment and development. The theatre anticipates that the cooperation with trades unions, particularly in the single factories, will encourage the working masses to attend it in the future. The grass roots of the Volksbühne are the industrial factories."[15]

Almost half a century later, the former rebel agitator Piscator was more at home as a theatrical entrepreneur on the liberal western side of the wall. In the east, Brecht was given a playhouse of his own at Schiffbauerdamm, with the explicit mission of motivating members of the East German trade union in their socialist struggle to increase state wealth. The trade union agreed to fill Brecht's auditorium in exchange for an aesthetic mobilization of the GDR planned economy that resulted in an almost Kantian "organisation of its parts into a rationally and optimally functional whole."[16]

Trade union takeover of East German art firms sometimes met with resistance. When Brecht threatened to create problems, the trade union called upon young and ambitious playwrights such as Heiner Müller and commissioned them to develop plays around scenes from factory production. The party counterbalanced Brecht's aesthetic idiosyncrasies by having its art firms perform down-to-earth dramas intended to motivate workers. Art easily conformed to union requirements when backed by a Communist Party command that "theatre performances for factory personnel should only be arranged to those plays that have a thematic or special interest to union members."[17]

## Nature of Work

In 1910, a young journalist named Walter Stenström returned to his home in Sweden, his head full of the ideas he had picked up in Germany. Taking the Volksbühne movement as his model, he founded the *Skådebanan* (a Swedification of the German word *Schaubühne,* meaning "show stage") art corporation with the assistance of Prince Eugen, also a successful painter, and of Count Carl Carlsson Bonde, the last royal censor of the Dramatic Theatre in Stockholm. The main aim of this Swedish art corporation, like its German model, was to increase mass consumption of art by promoting the availability of cheap theater tickets. Skådebanan acted as an independent producer of plays sent on tour around the country. Lectures were organized as sideshows, and they published a popular theatrical periodical where actors and playwrights, as well as plays, were featured. In 1917, they rented premises in the Stockholm *Folkets hus.* This "people's house" sheltered the cultural activities for workers organized by the Social Democrat labor movement. Skådebanan ran the theater for only two years until 1919, when the rent went up exponentially.[18]

The Skådebanan grew as rapidly as its German model did. By the end of the 1920s, a typical year's schedule would include seven hundred performances and one hundred lectures and realize the sale of approximately 250,000 tickets.[19] The mass market for art remained volatile, however; when the post–World War I crisis arrived, unemployment rose and the number of cinemas increased. With the advent of talkies, cultural consumers in both Germany and Sweden shifted their entertainment interests from the stage to the screen. In Sweden in 1932, only 344 performances were staged, and ticket sales dropped to 142,000. In Germany, the crisis was even worse; membership in the Volksbühne fell by 90 percent. Since the Berlin branch needed forty thousand members to cover its costs and it had only nineteen thousand, a subsidy of 450,000 marks from the Nazi government arrived at a particularly good time. While Goebbels was busy incorporating the Volksbühne for his Nazi propaganda ministry, Skådebanan in Sweden was being incorporated as a subscription network to a new nationwide touring state theater, the Riksteatern. Swedish Minister of Education and Ecclesiastical

Affairs Arthur Engberg, a Social Democrat with strong Nazi sympathies, bought the private Skådebanan and incorporated it with his public Riksteatern. He granted Skådebanan 25,000 kronor in exchange for its nine thousand enlisted members neatly organized into fifty-two local groups. Skådebanan thus gave the new Riksteatern an instant market of subscribers. After the merger, their representatives met at the national congress that inaugurated Riksteatern in 1934.[20]

Dramaten, the national dramatic theater, still dominated the theatrical life of Stockholm. Its new house on Nybroplan was occupied in 1908 and in part privately sponsored by state lotteries. This artistic company was to operate as a joint stock company with thirty-five shareholders, whose dividends were free tickets to performances when things were good.[21]

Swedish private theaters, dominated by Albert Ranft's theatrical corporation, now faced stiff competition.[22] Real estate companies and building contractors had started to finance the young Swedish movie industry, which produced attractive films to keep up the rent of the theaters by filling them with audiences. In the provinces, the state-subventioned Riksteatern would soon put most of the private theatrical touring companies out of business. The remaining private theaters were driven into banality, and only cabaret producers of comedies survived by continuing to offer populist folk entertainment.

Ragnar Klange's touring company was the last to survive as a private populist *folkteater* into the 1960s. From 1936 on, Klange produced an annual show that always incorporated *Folket* in its title. The word comes from the German *Volk,* and the Swedish people were the only heroes of the avalanche of burlesque banalities that allowed Klange to stay in business so long. The playbill included *Heja Folket* (Hello People!), *På kryss med Folket* (Cruising with the People), *Folket av idag* (Today's People), *Folket de ä vi* (The People—That's Us), *Hatten av för Folket* (Hats off to the People), *Leve Folket* (Long Live the People), *Folkets hushåll* (Household of the People), *Folket i spegeln* (The People Reflected), *Folkets husarer* (The People's Hussars), *Se Folket* (See the People!), *Opp med Folket* (Up the People!), *På extrakryss med Folket* (More Cruising with the People), *På Folkets begäran* (At the Request of the People), *Folkets kavalkad* (The People's Cavalcade), *Folkets speldosa* (The People's Musical Box), *Folkets rundtur* (The People's Round-Trip), *Folkets parkering* (Parking with the People), *Folkets pussel* (The People's Puzzle), *Folkets underbara resa* (The People's Wonderful Journey), and finally, in 1963, *Här kommer Folket* (Here Come the People).

Klange marketed the message that the Swedish national identity is its eth-
nicity, the people, the folk.[23] He survived as a private content provider for
the Swedish Social Democrat Party metaphysics, which promoted the idea
of Sweden as a safe and cozy home for its folk. In addition, a somewhat
more sophisticated metaphysics was also provided by art corporations such
as public theaters.

In 1919, Sweden's first civic theater, the Lorensbergsteater, was founded
in Gothenburg. Much later, when Stadsteatern, the Stockholm civic theater,
was set up in 1960, it was of a different character than the nine that already
existed. In 1954, Gothenburg was given a second stage, the Folkteatern,
which was supported by the national trade union. Now it was Stockholm's
turn to have a union stage. The relationship between Stockholm's Stadsteatern and the Dramatiska Teatern was similar to that between the Volksbühne and the Deutsches Theater in Berlin. On the one hand sat a bourgeois
playhouse founded and funded by private capital, and on the other a trade
union house for the worker's culture.

The art firm histories of the Volksbühne and Stockholm Stadsteatern dif-
fer to a degree on some points. It took the Volksbühne twenty-five years to
afford a roof over the heads of its subscribers on Bülowplatz. Stockholm's
folk theater, the Stadsteatern, was started in an empty building by the national trade union LO, which rented out an empty theater in its new Stockholm center. In the 1960s, the brand new Folkets hus, originally planned as
a picture theater, was forced to contend with the advent of television, which
drew the audience away from the movies. The trade union simply had no
tenant for its expensive new theater in a building designed by the famous
Swedish architect Sven Gottfried Markelius. At least a theater would bring
in some rent.

The Swedish trade union had already begun incorporating theater. Skådebanan, still operating as an organization supported by subscription, was run
with additional support of both the national union movement, LO, and the
Swedish employers' federation, SAF, whose CEO was an ex–trade union
man. In the spirit of the GDR practice of incorporating the art firm with the
back stage of the national economy, Skådebanan's number of subscriptions
was swelled from 5,900 to 28,000 by union members. Thanks to the alliance with the trade union partner, turnover jumped to five million kronor
from a mere 250,000.[24]

Stockholm got its Volksbühne, the Stadsteatern, when the union needed a tenant in its new house. Now, long and fruitless discussions about building a new theater in Stockholm had materialized; the Swedish director Per Lindberg originally got the idea after observing Max Reinhardt. As happened in Germany, other suggestions came from communists and anarchists. In the middle of the Second World War, a new civic theater was proposed to the city council by communist Gustav Johansson, who described it as a theater symbolizing the egalitarian *Folkhem,* with an architecture far removed from "the old court theatres like the Opera and the Dramatic Theatre, where the wealthy and powerful sit in the stalls and the society of classes is hierarchically represented all the way up to the third circle, from where the proletariat, admittedly, may catch a glimpse of the Devil in *Everyman* but never see the Lord in that famous play."[25]

The *new* Dramatic Theatre was still very much an old-fashioned court theater. A private consortium and money from the state lottery paid for a building that looked more like a classical museum than a modern art firm in the Schopenhauer or Wagner sense. Its wealthy bourgeois donors revealed their meager understanding of a modern art firm when they extolled their new building for adding "the other two visual arts: monumental painting and sculpture"[26] to the theater.

The city worthies, who did not want a socialist civic theater, thought that one theater was more than enough for Stockholm. In the 1950s, however, with the support of liberals, tours of the Dramatic Theatre's productions were scheduled in the city's expanding suburbs. At the same time, the retired functionalist architect Markelius set to work on a design for a new house inspired by Gropius and Piscator's dream of modern theater. Markelius was not only familiar with the work of the Bauhaus architects but had also taken part in contests in theater design in the Soviet Union. In the absence of financial subsidy or the backing of a private consortium, the Markelius plans for the theater never materialized. Instead his Folkets hus, which he had been thinking about since the 1930s, became a reality. In 1959, despite the protests of right-wing councilors, the Social Democrat majority on the city council voted in favor of renting out the large cinema to a new theater projected on the orders of Olof Palme by Harry Schein, an Austrian-born engineer who was later to become the Malraux of Swedish social democracy. Schein was successful in negotiating credit for the new theater, thanks to a convincing calculus, "perfect and imaginative at the same time, perfect in the sense that they come to such a low total as to be politically acceptable; imaginative if you compare them to the real costs the theatre would later incur."[27]

The German Volksbühne, built on Bülowplatz with capital of its own, was a home for theater consumers. The Stockholm Stadsteatern was to be a house for theater producers. Schein's calculations offered three alternatives to the funding authorities: first, a house with a contracted company of about thirty actors; second, venues of externally produced content; and third, housing for a media consortium of radio, television, and other partners. Schein wanted the first alternative and therefore made it look the most economical on paper; a quarter of its income would come from the state, a quarter from the city, and the rest from ticket sales. In reality, the percentage of income from ticket sales followed the norm for most public theatrical art firms—closer to 20 percent than the 50 percent in the sales pitch. Apart from block bookings by the unions, it was the educated middle class rather than workers who made up most of the audience. By the time all this became obvious, the union and party had already committed themselves politically to the new house and its fixed company of players.

The Berlin and Stockholm theaters both interfaced with industry. The Volksbühne was a house for workers' culture, and by the early 1970s the Stadsteatern was the house of cultural workers. After the student revolt of 1968, the Social Democrat Party faced heavy attacks from the left. The trade union that had guaranteed working stability in Sweden for the first time during the postwar era was shaken by wild strikes. Schein also found it as hard to maintain artist loyalty to Social Democrat values as trade union leaders did

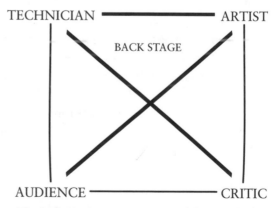

*The Stadtsteatern's Incorporation of the Back Stage*

to keep workers voting for the party. As cultural workers moved to the left, audiences of the public art firms grew smaller.

Finally, the board of the Stadsteatern appointed a new manager, Vivica Bandler, to work on improving frontstage marketing. Her unwritten—though very important—instructions were not to look askance at revolutionary theatrical workers.[28] Bandler managed to fill the theater by staging musicals and offering progressively marketed subscriptions to schools and workplaces. At the same time, subsidies from the state and the city council rocketed from two million kronor in 1960 to ninety million in 1990.[29] This partly reflected the fact that the number of stages increased to four under Bandler's management.

The cultural workers backstage pushed for more participation and more productions, but most of the cost increase could be attributed to stricter union regulation of working time. After Bandler came Per Edström, a backstage-oriented director, who got the job on merit from actor trade union work. To the front stage, Edström projected a bleak image, but he was beloved by the back stage. "Why build a new auditorium? We crave more stages," shouted his cultural workers. The new director opportunistically paraphrased Stanislavski by advocating a "theatre of actors," and no doubt about it, Stadsteatern's main mission was to provide full employment for cultural producers. In terms of the aesthetic play model, this Swedish art corporation saw the smooth running of the backstage workplace as its main managerial mission.

## Cases of Aesthetic Management

### Father Alf in Democratic Industry

#### Visionary Leadership

It takes special skills to make incorporated art work, whether it involves laying out design in an engineering company, creating fashion in a textile factory, conceiving architectural shape and form in a building firm, or directing plays in a public theater bureaucracy. The Swede Alf Sjöberg (1903–1980), internationally known as the aesthetic mentor of Ingmar Bergman, is an appropriate case study of a manager operating in an art bureaucracy. His career developed during the time when theater in an increasingly industrialized Sweden was incorporated into the country's socioeconomy. First it became firmly embedded in Social Democrat educational policy; Sjöberg himself was operational in this political incorporation of art. After his early education, Sjöberg was admitted to the Royal Dramatic Theatre drama school in the same class with Greta Garbo (who as a drama student was still named Greta Gustafsson). During his seven years as an actor, he played about fifty roles, which gave him theatrical credibility. He spent his entire life fighting politically for his beloved Royal Dramatic Theatre, all the time masking his Schopenhauerian ambition under a thick layer of political rhetoric, since modern incorporation rests on metaphysics but of a less explicit kind than in the times of Wagner or Stanislavski.

Sjöberg often referred to the Moscow Art Theatre as the management model of a good art firm. As if inspired by Stanislavski, he ran the theater informally, not as a CEO-Nemirovic but as a stubborn gray eminence putting his practical aesthetics to hard work as he systematically directed 138 plays in fifty years. After World War II, when Cold-War American analytical pragmatics and Marxian Soviet political economy discredited aesthetic education in a Sweden eager to distance itself from its strong German roots, Sjöberg managed to maintain an intellectual connection to Europe and its continental philosophy by modernizing metaphysics. In fact, his Royal Dramatic Theatre was one of the few Swedish institutions practicing aesthetic philosophy after 1945. The patriarchal aesthetic manager "Father Alf" operated as an undercover Schopenhauerian professor.

As an art manager, Sjöberg made himself extremely visible frontstage. He presented his views on theater in articulate lectures, interviews, and essays in Swedish publications as diverse as the staff newsletter at Dramaten, *Biografbladet* (The Cinematic Journal), and *Konstrevyn* (The Art Review). Backstage, he was an art alchemist in the public laboratory of the royal theater. He blended the raw materials of national heritage—-texts from the national library with pictures hung in the national museum. Sjöberg discovered the best interpretations of Strindberg's theatrical texts in images of El Greco and Wöfli. A painting by Le Nain perfectly matched the meaning of a drama by Paul Claudel. Reading Shakespeare evoked in

Sjöberg Piranesi's engravings, Michelangelo's frescoes, and works from Picasso's blue period.[30] When the playwright Arthur Miller mixed flashbacks from the past with events in the present, it was to Sjöberg a poetic application of cubist painting, as "when Picasso paints a profile and an en-face in the same portrait."[31] Pictures by such masters as Hieronymus Bosch, Breughel, and Dali were revived (by theatrical aesthetic education) as painted performances of contemporary poetry by Eliot and Ekelöf.[32] With an open curiosity reminiscent of Diaghilev, Sjöberg cooperated with contemporary image makers such as Swedish artists Grate, Sköld, Claes Oldenburg, Stellan Mörner, and "the X" Erixon. In the early 1970s, he urged painter Roy Friberg to render a text into colorful rhetoric that would visualize the symbolic signs and materialize "concrete movements of our secret desires, our fear and intuition . . . Dead forms threatening to bind us and control us . . . A symbolic system of significations extending its strange scope far out into nature-universe."[33]

Sjöberg not only mixed text and image. His own biography reveals how he slowly hybridized an aesthetic third way of management from that of two older colleagues, the extroverted popular metteur en scène Per Lindberg, a Swedish follower of Max Reinhardt; and the introverted Freudian dramaturge Olof Molander. By anchoring texts in images, he turned theater into something durable and concrete. He wanted to combat "all that nonsense about theatre being an art of the ephemeral."[34]

Father Alf worked hard frontstage to stimulate an art market's visual desire; undoubtedly he saw other media as popular prep schools for his theatrical audience. In addition to his work on the stage, he directed eighteen films, the first of them produced during the silent movie era. Before the advent of television crushed the Swedish motion picture industry, stage directors used to shoot many Swedish films by hiring actors on summer holiday. In that way, work performed in Sjöberg's theatrical art corporation sometimes ended up being widely diffused as a motion picture. Staged work served as a prototype for screen production. *Miss Julie,* a movie that earned Sjöberg the Golden Palm in Cannes in the early 1950s, was one such technical spinoff of a stage production. Not so *Hets* (Frenzy), whose script was written by a young wannabe novelist who would reluctantly skip his literary ambitions to become another prodigious summer filmmaker and later Sjöberg's colleague at the Royal Dramatical Theatre: Ingmar Bergman.[35]

Sjöberg's last film, *Fadren* (The Father), was produced in 1968 by actors performing a Strindberg play at the Dramatic Theatre in the evening and then spending the day filming it. Shortly after, the Stockholm studios were closing down, bringing the good old Swedish tradition of summer filming to an end. Sjöberg's art worked in radio also. At that time, the Swedish state capitalized on tax-financed public art by regularly broadcasting plays as popular education. From the 1930s to the mid-1960s, 160 Sjöberg performances were documented and distributed by Swedish state radio.

Whether he was facing a mass market or tutoring a theatrical audience, Sjöberg worked as a carefully prepared professor of philosophy. After modern art's Schopenhauerian turn, artists took on the habit of attaching ideas to their work. Some, like Salvador Dali, did so superficially. For more than fifty years, Dali managed to hook Freudian surrealism, fascism, nuclear physics, DNA research, Catholicism, and finally chaos theory to paintings that all the time looked more or less the same! Others, like Sjöberg, made more scholarly connections. He was so meticulous that each staged play seemed as if it were documented with academic footnotes. He marketed Brecht as a lesson in Sartre's existentialism and Gombrowicz as an exercise in Foucault's poststructuralism.

In the early 1960s at the Venice Festival, Sjöberg encountered the French structuralist Lucien Goldmann and immediately incorporated his discourse into performances of Witkiewicz's and Gombrowicz's plays. Later Sjöberg soaked up Levi-Strauss's anthropology and Laing's radical psychiatry. Long before any Swedish scholars had read him, Sjöberg lectured backstage technicians and actors as well as equally puzzled frontstage audiences and critics about a new philosophy of a stranger named Michel Foucault, who "discovered a universe of beauty, strictness and necessity within a Swedish reality where man was made redundant."[36]

Listening to Goldmann's lecture in Venice, Sjöberg cursed narrow-minded Swedish authorities who refused him funds to tour with his production of Gombrowicz. In Sjöberg's estimation, officials had failed to grasp that theater was their real university, where new philosophies could be tested and exposed for the benefit of a democratic state. They did not have a clue about what art work meant. Postwar politicians saw little reason to consider art as anything other than mere decoration, or at most expression of individual feelings. They thought theater was about playing plays, while it was all about philosophizing.

Sjöberg, the metaphysical art manager, was even more disappointed when the Nobel Prize for literature was refused his favorite playwright, Gombrowicz, a declared Schopenhauerian. It seemed futile to present metaphysical dilemmas if no one was interested in philosophy any more. Instead of resigning, however, Sjöberg carefully repackaged philosophy in the much more politically correct guise of research. In intensive frontstage campaigns aimed at incorporating his kind of art into the public sphere, he felt he must single-handedly assume the role of the critic: "Unfortunately there is a great gap between creative artistry and critique. Let us hope that a semiotic perspective can overbridge the gap. Researchers, with their greater consciousness of such matters, may remedy the situation. Today critics distance themselves from both artistic creation and the audience; it operates in a void."[37]

One century after Schopenhauer and in a time of philosophical *baisse,* Sjöberg opportunistically replaced *philosophy* with the scientific-sounding term *research.* Sjöberg frequently quoted scientists he hoped would politically legitimize a metaphysical art corporation. Research would restore to theatre the role of making art work in the service of transcendental human universalism. Art would be respected as a way of world making in service of modern democracy![38] This strategy of incorporation seemed to work pretty well until 1968.

The Swedish Social Democracy neglected to further humanistic values in a time of economic expansion of the Swedish mixed economy, and Sjöberg felt that art corporations had much to contribute in a situation that lacked human values. He actively solicited political support for the arts from the parliament; he had high hopes for the new cultural policies of the Swedish Social Democrats. He particularly respected Prime Minister Tage Erlander for acknowledging that "there was so much left to be done" once material consumption needs were satisfied. It seemed as if Erlander's party comrades were also slowly realizing "the efforts needed in cultural matters."[39] At the same time, in the aftermath of the 1968 European cultural revolution, the revolutionary neo-agitprop shelled him with their heavy, vulgar Marxian artillery, targeting him as an old idealist clinging to an obsolete and dusty royal theater.

To Sjöberg, who in 1935 visited Stanislavski and Meyerhold in the Soviet Union, the 1968 radicalization was a soft flashback of Stalinist terror. In one final attempt to counterattack leftist groups, the art manager set out to celebrate his art corporation. As a good German metaphysician, Father Alf poetically declared that his Royal Dramatic Theatre in fact incarnated the Social Democratic vision of a real Folkhem based on industrial work. It was a transcendental home for all people, a miniature model for the democratic state:

> [During] special hours the theatre is illuminated as a beacon in a surrounding ocean of darkness full of invisible life. In order to repeatedly perform one needs stable unchangeable structures.

Not merely material constancy, but firmness in all the fists that carry, hands that signal, the whole system of will and power, complementary, in opposition, but ordered nonetheless into a single whole. . . . Even the craftsmen and labourers, the whole technical apparatus, the cashiers and caretakers, all belong to a single language community, all share common codes of action that incorporate them into the image projected on stage. All are uplifted into a system, which during the violent political struggle of opposing forces, is in constant search for something tacit but essential not just for themselves but for the generic system in which they fuse with all mankind.[40]

The new cultural policy, launched in 1974 in the Swedish aftermath of the 1968 student revolt, gradually incorporated theaters into plans for industrial democratization under the heading of "cultural work." Art was to be managed as any work ought to be managed: democratically. It was to be legally planned by index-linked wages and regulations regarding working time. The work of American cultural economist William Baumol was cited as the theoretical justification for using state subsidies to keep pace with the wages of employees within more easily rationalized branches of industry.[41] A public theater was now considered a "model" factory where "culture work" was regulated in participation with unions, as it should be in any other industrial job. Considering art to be industrial work led to the singling out of aesthetics, however. There was no difference between making art work and manufacturing a plastic bucket, but in the process of establishing solidarity with regular workers art work constantly ran the risk of being diverted from its philosophical aim.

Once upon a time, before aesthetic philosophy redefined art as the business of being, theater was a routine craft. During the reign of Gustav III, who founded the first Swedish national theater, actors were supposed to work individually at a standardized pace of one day for every forty lines in the script. Halfway through their learning period, the first common rehearsal took place, with the second just before the premiere performance. The company would meet in the theater foyer for the readings. The actors read their parts in turn, from extracts copied by a clerk or prompter from the script. Each individual part was called a role simply for being separately copied on a paper roll. Work was split up since individual actors were seldom given the complete script.[42]

Previous to the Schopenhauerian turn, the performance of a play was a highly standardized and easily decentralized work process. The characters were common types, like those of the *commedia dell'arte,* each with its distinctive costume (often kept by the actor himself or herself). The scenery was assembled out of a set number of locations kept in the theater's stock. Entrances and exits would be decided at common rehearsals, as well as some nice special effects worked out and backdrops ordered from the stored stock. The old theater was an assembly line for outsourced components delivered just in time according to conventional design. An eighteen-century playhouse was a place for bringing together the audiovisual frontstage consumption of acting services with the direct satisfaction of bodily needs (hunger, thirst, and fornication). The theater was a material shopping mall with bars, kitchens, and brothels. A century later, Wagner, Antoine, Lugné, and others introduced aesthetic philosophy and metaphysical business ideas that led to a growing emphasis on backstage preparation.

By the end of the 1960s, a director at a Swedish theatrical institution could count on about eleven weeks of preparation for each of two annual productions. The making of a play was a protected research-and-development process, a creative cocoon incorporated inside a theatrical factory so that Stanislavskis and Nemirovics could do their jobs together. Rehearsals followed a set weekly timetable. The hours between 10:30 A.M. and 3:00 P.M. were divided into morning and afternoon sessions. Sjöberg's art was well managed and focused on human resources. Actors waited their turn to be worked on in the room behind the thickly padded doors protecting the rehearsal area. Loudspeakers would summon them to the creative cocoon, where, in its own surgical suite, art was made to work. Here Sjöberg operated like a master surgeon, assisted by his technical and administrative staff. He was in control of such perfect performance machinery that neither a post as CEO of the Dramatic Theatre nor a Hollywood contract offered by David Selznick (on the initiative of Ingrid Bergman) seemed attractive to Sjöberg. Backstage, the art manager controlled his art corporation, his huge power plant for the fusion energy of images and texts that Wagner would have envied. As a young art manager Sjöberg, exclaimed:

> How glorious the director's calling! See the heavy columns move
> on reluctant wheels of stage machinery, the backdrop rise and
> disappear, the footlights flash. . . . Listen to the silence that fell
> when one single man in the stalls gave the signal, take note of

the lithe material in these well-trained bodies and voices which
respond to the slightest command, see the empty stage and how
it is miraculously animated by the hand of the director. Experience the power of one single man as a creator—finally man himself is acting God.[43]

Later, in the middle of his career, Sjöberg was fascinated by Swedish
sculptor Bror Marklund's method for working with clay in his studio: "Suddenly, after all the discussions, sketches, leafing through books, he stands in
front of the clay and lends his hands to the shapes, the clay begins to bubble
and grow while his restless fingers try to keep up. He is like a magician; half
absorbed in this organic growth, in the material itself, he drums forth his
characters like a Lapp shaman on a magical drum."[44]

Indeed, there was much similarity between this method and the way he
himself made art work.

### Dramaturgical Products

By September 18, 1973, when Sjöberg began rehearsing his 127th production at the Dramatic Theatre, he had been doing his homework for *Enemies*
by Maxim Gorky for several years.[45] He personally rediscovered the play in
Paris and translated the text from French. Twice he traveled to the home of
the painter Roy Friberg on the west coast of Sweden to discuss in detail the
images for the scenery. On September 3 of that year, he gave a well-rehearsed
presentation of Friberg's set models to twenty craftsmen in the workshops
of the Dramatic Theatre. The lights were turned off, and one remaining
spotlight illuminated a small model of the stage, executed by the painter according to Sjöberg's instructions. Sjöberg was not content with picking the
play only. In the 1940s, the Russian sculptor Tatlin as well as Gropius, the
Bauhaus architect, inspired him to design "scenic spirals to break with traditional central perspective."[46] Actors were given texts and stage artists a
sketch by Sjöberg, who designed the scenery of his plays. In an early article
in *Konst Revy,* Sjöberg stressed the art manager's duty to give his artists the
overall general idea, which

> then becomes the job of the visual artist to express through his
> own temperament. An artist works under strict discipline . . .
> and must still be able to make a personal contribution . . . Of
> course the scenery painter looks in to see what has happened to
> his work when the director's is lighting the final scenery . . . in

this remarkable job, craving ceaseless devotion from all participants, and unconditional willingness to be subservient to the
overall idea—a plan of much greater importance than the single
participants of the project.[47]

The briefing to the craftsmen took the form of a political speech, with
Sjöberg lecturing the workers on Gorky, the play, and its politics, and concluding with a word of encouragement to "try even harder," especially if the
Social Democrats lost the election that autumn. The workers' enthusiastic
applause signaled that Sjöberg's leadership had transmitted the feeling that
the world was their theater, where together they must struggle for democracy and justice.

Here, in the beginning of the work process, Sjöberg used rhetoric to secretly continue the aesthetic tradition that a century before had named art
the successor to metaphysics. In the early 1970s, political activists who
demonstrated for democracy and justice on the streets of Stockholm thought
they knew Marx and Mao, but they had no clue about who Schopenhauer
was. They did not care for the pictures or texts Father Alf constantly referred to. They found it hopelessly conservative to go to the National Library, the National Museum, or the Royal Dramatic Theatre; nevertheless,
those who heard him talk could hardly avoid being taken on his rhetorical
ride. In the words of Vilgot Sjöman,

> Alf Sjöberg speaks eloquently and intensively. And his rhetoric
> has an emotional curve. He starts haltingly, subdued: the first ten-
> tative rotations of the propeller blade! Then the plane suddenly
> takes off with its cargo of actual ideas, actual readings: and all at
> once, the heavy weight seems easily born. Two or three trains of
> thought are interwoven to an evenly climbing perspective, a
> broad, intensely radiant arc standing out against the clear sky.
> Until the arc suddenly curves back to its point of origin, and the
> plane lands again with a few concluding remarks, a summary.[48]

The *Enemy* rehearsals in 1973 showed how Sjöberg combined art with
the routines of industrial production. After showing the stage design to the
craftsmen, the script was presented to the actors. Then Sjöberg worked as a
text-focused dramaturge. The first few days of rehearsal were devoted to
positioning on the stage. In the rehearsal room, within lines on the floor
marking the dimensions of the stage, the actors read aloud from copies of

the script. The routine followed by Sjöberg began by putting the actors in their tracks and providing them all with a set of "fixed boundaries, a solid point from which other complex problems can then be tackled." The actors jotted down notes of their bodily movements and positions, according to Sjöberg's naturalistic stage choreography. The art manager's assistant, the production manager, kept careful records of the movements in a book where the actors could later check spatial details without disturbing Father Alf, who frowned upon any flippant playfulness: "My mother never came to terms with the fact that I became an actor and not an architect. . . . I developed a guilt-complex—many young artists did in those days—the reaction was that you couldn't sacrifice enough for the theatre and art . . . over the course of the years I have been horribly strict on people who haven't pulled their weight and shirked their responsibilities."[49]

Sjöberg's aesthetic play hardly emerged out of a work climate of playfulness. Instructions were short and precise in order not to drown actors in interpretation. Sjöberg now sculpted his play in actors' clay as fast as possible. At this stage, there was friction in his machinery when some actors had problems matching his commands with their own feelings. "Alf knows everything, of course. I don't think he sees the actors as individuals, but as what he can get out of them as a group. His instructions come thick and fast, and you have to find something to say, not for the sake of saying something, but to stop you feeling like a puppet."

Sjöberg saw his role as an architect of systems on stage, and he legitimized this position with what the audience expected to get: "The audience does not value individual actors but combinations of actors. The actors are part of a system and the interaction between them is what the audience perceives. When casting roles it is important to notice which individuals interact interestingly."

Swedish public theater then operated with fixed companies of actors whose jobs were secured by lifelong union contracts. This situation contributed to the establishment of close, long-term, postproduction frontstage relations between artists on stage and "their" auditorium. Some actors that Sjöberg neglected individually backstage were later compensated by the frontstage attention of their audience.[50] Sjöberg hints at this complicity when maintaining that "it is the prerogative of a cultivated audience to share the act of creation with a famous actor so that together they might experience a new reality."[51]

By September 27, 1973, positioning was complete, and the next stage of art work could begin. Sjöberg got back to a dramaturgical style of management and proceeded with the process of textual interpretation. Although he gave a brilliant forty-five-minute lecture on the historical background of the play in the attempted Russian revolution of 1905, Sjöberg was not talking about the past. He explicitly used history to forge a feeling of presence. As a result, the whole cast was deeply convinced that Gorky's *Enemies* was as much about Swedish theater during the economic boom of the 1970s as it had been about Russia in 1905.

That done, Sjöberg's work now began pushing the actors into the third aesthetic realm, beyond analysis of text and physical materialization of stage images in between form and matter:

> To work on this play we have to enter Gorky's level of understanding, to push our analysis as far as possible, to that tacit and indefinable point which we will only recognise once we get there. Gorky's idea was not that economic structures were unimportant, or that Marxism was wrong and that an intuitive understanding of life was the only right way. Gorky was saying that both theoretical explanation and empathic understanding of human life ought to be able to be combined. . . . In the same way, explanation and understanding have to co-operate in the theatre.

When Sjöberg talks about explanation and understanding—terms borrowed from a scientific epistemological discourse—it echoes Schiller's form and matter. *Explanation* refers to the scientific analysis of material facts; *understanding* stands for the attempt to grasp how man forms intentions for action. Of course, both paths to knowledge are necessary for aesthetic Schwung.

Sjöberg himself managed by Schwung; the pendulum movement between material images and formal text went on until dress rehearsal on November 27, when the cast left the attic rehearsal room for the main stage of the Dramatic Theatre. There, surrounded by Friberg's scenery, they worked two two-hour sessions every day. During the normal working day, there were usually one or two "situations" that intensified rehearsal. When this happened, work would grind to a halt, and the art manager would step in to rescue the interpretation with either a long lecture or a few more personal instructions to actors who had "lost the plot." The longer the rehearsals progressed, the more the work strangely began focusing upon "pauses" that were like in-between spaces for aesthetic Schwung. This had little to do with hermeneutical interpretation; Sjöberg himself stressed the difference between making a text work as art or as a study of literature. "I believe," he said, in a rather Stanislavskian remark,

> that literary scholars are misled because they cannot visualize the text in front of them—as theatre. All . . . plays are full of silent scenes waiting to be delivered by the actors . . . if you carefully listen to these mute scenes the play will lose its flatness and vagueness in the depiction of its characters! For it is precisely in acting out such silences that you will track down the true human dimensions of characters.[52]

The challenge then lay in how to handle the in-betweens, how to reach the right Schwung in acting; this was the creative dilemma each player faced individually. At this point, Sjöberg's art management consisted of abandoning each actor to the audience. Father Alf had done his philosophical homework on the play. Now he expected his actors to be just as diligent. Sjöberg claimed, with reference to Walter Benjamin, a philosopher of the Frankfurt school who wrote on art work in the age of reproduction, that art management ought not to prescribe rhetorical effects, tricks, or methods, a fact that was frustrating to an actor looking for clear intellectual instruction: "Sjöberg might tell us to 'Take a step forward.' Most of his instructions are about physical movement on stage, not about the development of characters. By saying something like that he only signals a deeper problem, which he never attempts to explicitly analyze. Like not wanting to utter God's name. But of course verbal communication isn't the only way of communicating. . . ."

To put individual artists in Schwung, Sjöberg sometimes pushed them violently into the void. In his interpretation of Gorky's *Enemies,* the central character Tatyana gives meaning to the play when she turns away from her own class and voices her support for the revolutionary workers at the end of the drama. The actress playing Tatyana seemed skeptical of Sjöberg's description of the character during rehearsals. On October 27, as she was standing on stage thinking out her own interpretation of the play and thoughtfully chewing gum to gain time for reflection, Sjöberg interrupted her: "Spit out that chewing-gum," he attacked. "You don't chew gum on the stage of the Dramatic Theatre!" Later Sjöberg justified his brusque command:

> Why do you think I told her to spit out that chewing-gum? So that she might show her face at last. Her colleagues on stage have a right to confront a human face, not just a set of masticating jaws. Chewing is aggressive. Chewing is a flight from embodiment, an attack on the process of co-operation. It is so typical of that actress who I know arrives late, out of laziness, lethargy and obstinacy—because she is problematical, her own existence is as problematical as this rich land-owner she plays, who has to be converted here to her line of wild protest "Thank God for not being rich." I can say no more for I have no right to . . . expose their private and work situations, which explain such resistance to my instructions. But with secret signals, attacks and ambushes I can attack their phobias and internal barriers. How do you think a surgeon feels before setting to work? You need stamina. But even so, most of the director's work takes place away from the stage. What you see in rehearsals is merely a fraction. It is the same as with all work, the informal part matters the most. It is in the private relaxed fearless conversations in confidence, when no-one overhears, on street-corners, in the canteen, on the way home, in a thousand chance locations, that you make contacts, and utter the words no-one else can hear—but that matter most.

To some actors, Sjöberg's pedantic lecturing and precise instruction were destructive. It was patronizing and resulted, they felt, in totalization, which left no empty space for aesthetic players. In the beginning of the 1970s, a young radical actor felt himself to be a student revolting against an authoritarian professor; the actor portrayed Father Alf as

> a director of the old school. His relations with the actors can be pretty dangerous sometimes. Just look at people who have worked with him for a while; they can't offer any resistance. You end up with a father-child relationship. If you see him as a director from a historical perspective, it's easier to explain his method of work. In the good old days the theatre was full of divas, and

directing stars must have been tough. If he didn't stand up for himself, the director ended up little more than a prompter.

Others found ways to handle his sort of patriarchy by carving out a third, free realm of their own. One older actor even thought that "it's perfectly possible to influence Alf if you're patient. You can sow the seed by suggesting something new or an alternative reading. He never fails to bring it up two or three days later, by which time it has had time to mature. The remarkable thing is his enormous desire to communicate. Sometimes he rushes in to you to tell about some newly published book he just read.

Father Alf himself hoped to be doing aesthetic education both backstage and frontstage. In the spirit of Schopenhauer, he wanted to influence Swedish educational policy and see theater teaching existential philosophy. Since he himself was political, he thought it clever to hide his philosophical message under a thick layer of academic "theory" and "science." Both Schopenhauer and Kant would, of course, have objected to such smartness. Kant might have been intrigued by Father Alf's lack of faith in art's aesthetic quality being clearly conceived without any explicit use of theoretical concepts. The Swedish establishment showed the aging Alf Sjöberg due respect, but only as a theatrical craftsman, not as an aesthetic philosopher. To the bitter end, however, he went on preaching his deep faith in the philosophical role of art:

> I want to prove that we at the theatre understand what's going on in society. Have you read my latest article in the staff magazine? I tried to write about these things there, to talk about my inspiration from social anthropologists and sociologists. But the critics are uneducated. Why should they be forced to think and read Barthes?! They attacked me when I introduced actual theoretical terms. Not only was I criticised by the critics, but by the audience too. They didn't understand me so I must be careful with terms like empathy and sympathy. . . . They think theory is strange although many concepts clarify perfectly what we do in the theatre. I also have to remind myself constantly that few actors are academically educated. . . . Naturally it would be madness to show this sort of pandemonium to the actors. They would be paralysed by such definite results.

## Mother Osten and Industrial Democracy

### Storytellers' Coach

Textbooks in management in the early 1970s told only stories of industrial management. Bosses then were attracted to becoming rational "scientific" managers. Science meant social status, and scientists were expert authorities. Now, in the next millennium, managers want to be respected as creative artists; management books boast that "every business is a stage," and the new economy firms believe their businesses can learn from what makes art work in theaters and museums. If this is to be taken seriously, the lessons the theater really can teach cannot be ignored.

A long time ago, I wanted to figure out how management might be connected to aesthetics. A fellow doctoral student told me that Sjöberg at the Royal Dramatic Theatre might show me what the link was. I had been invited by Sjöberg to attend rehearsals of Gorky's *Enemies* as an academic doctor. The famous old master wanted to be respected as a scientist and longed for scientific authority in order to win political victories for art.

I felt pity for the great artist, mentor to Bergman, friend of Meyerhold, and comrade to Garbo, lip-synching the jargon of "system theory" and posing as a "poststructuralist." It was even sadder to note actors poking fun of the old man in the same way Stanislavski had once been made a laughing stock by Nemirovic's conservative actors. How they pulled the old man's leg. Actors who wanted to leave early were in the habit of asking Father Alf a "philosophical question" in rehearsal. While the master concentrated on delivering a long, serious answer, they would simply sneak out of the back door to some lucrative gig in town. In a coffee break during rehearsal for Gorky's *Enemies* in 1973, a popular Swedish actor, Ernst Günter, aired his Maoist criticism of Sjöberg's mise en scène to me:

> He's sculpting the scenery. Just observe how he has us move chairs to different positions. . . . On the theoretical level he's very thorough, but it's like he can't be bothered to lower himself to the practical level. . . . He's even trained the prompter not to give whole sentences, so that the actors don't get a chance to feel their way into their parts. I'm the sort of actor who has to find at least a bit of himself in the role he's playing. The only way round these problems is to say something at once. If no one dares say anything, then nothing will change.

I eagerly documented everything in a detailed rehearsal report that not only contained Sjöberg's own ideas but unfortunately also the criticism of his crew and the gossip behind his back. When reading about Günther's attack, Sjöberg immediately expressed his bitter disappointment at this pretentious "rebellion against the old authoritarian style of directing."[53] The play had by then opened, and admittedly the critique of *Enemies* left a lot to be desired, but as Sjöberg emphasized to me in a long letter, everyone working with him remembered rehearsals as a wonderful, happy time. Sjöberg pointed out that the criticism came from an actor who had himself produced his own version of *Enemies* for radio, using the same cast as the production at the Dramatic Theatre. Günther, the disloyal actor, had faced Sjöberg, so wrote the master, with such "indiscreet crimes against solidarity and camaraderie" that he felt deeply "embarrassed on the behalf of the culprit."[54] Besides, Sjöberg wrote, one could not take seriously a self-taught actor such as Günther who lacked "vocal techniques," which caused lots of problems for a professional art firm. Professional actors should be able to spit out their chewing gum and quickly jump on the Dionysian wagon without losing Nietzschean speed and the momentum of Schillerian Schwung. Diaghilev always looked for artists who could grasp his tacit intentions from a minute aesthetic hint. That was the kind of aesthetic professionalism Father Alf found lacking in Günther. In Sweden in 1973, however, such an attitude was interpreted as sheer authoritarian elitism, because this was the era of participative workplace democracy.

Later, while writing his memoirs, Ingmar Bergman described the political situation during the 1970s as a provincial cultural revolution against professional directing. The drama school at the Dramatic Theatre, which Günther of course had not attended, was closed. In the political spirit of 1968, actors were cultural brothers and sisters incorporated in the revolutionary fraternity of the international proletariat. Art was industry, not a guilded craft in dusty court theaters! When Bergman claimed that good acting required tacit knowledge and technical skills, radical students threw him out of the new state-run drama school. Among these students was even his own son, who "waved the little red book and whistled, ingratiatingly cheered on by Niklas Brunius, the principal of the school at the time."[55]

In 1939, Bergman (still to become a world-famous director) and Olof Palme (appointed head of the Dramatic Theatre) were refused an apprenticeship at the drama school by Dean Brunius's Aunt Pauline. Bergman went into self-imposed exile in 1976 after being unjustly accused of tax irregularities by Swedish authorities. It was symptomatic of that time for Marxist moralists to accuse an apolitical artist of crimes against the state. Perhaps it was equally symptomatic that Bergman, who in his memoirs accounts for his youthful, almost Heideggerian, aesthetic fascination with Nazism, found refuge in the Munich *Residenz Theatre*. Bergman had great respect for old Father Alf, who had, with equal passion, lined up with the allies during the war, because Sjöberg "was politically committed and spoke passionately about Theatre as a weapon. When the movement blew in over Dramaten, he wanted to man the barricades together with the young. His bitterness was great when he found himself reading that the Dramaten should be burnt to the ground and Sjöberg and Bergman should be hanged from the Tornberg clock outside in Nybroplan."[56]

The year 1968 saw no worker or peasant revolution like the one in Gorky's play; it was the scattered revolt of young people in the rapidly expanding middle class. The self-appointed proletarians were university dropout "students" who liked to be called "intellectuals." The number of students at Stockholm College, for instance, grew from five thousand to twenty-five thousand during the 1960s. In the West, students were staging mass demonstrations, acting out the part of the proletariat on the new mediatic stages of streets and campuses. This was more publicly visible than the fifteen underground avant-garde stages for playwrights and amateur actors hoping to be discovered by the established theaters that already existed in the Stockholm of the 1950s.

This old art scene was generally too conventional for young rebels. Acting careers in the traditional theatrical trade really did not appeal to the growing number of intellectual youth, although many had begun acting in one of the country's six active student theaters.[57] An actor, later turned director, recalls the attitude in the 1970s theater establishment: "The directors were the only ones with the right to be intellectual. Actors not. I suppose I must have been fairly intellectual, because I was more or less told to quit acting. I only took up acting when actors were allowed to think."

In traditional, well-oiled theater organizations, Marxist students were confronted with a theatrical management they would immediately classify as capitalist Taylorism. A theater was like any factory ready to become occupied by its worker-actors:

> We actors began to ask ourselves what we were there for. We
> began asking ourselves about being informed about what we

should play by being simply named on some cast list posted on the information board. If you weren't on that list, you could do nothing about it. Other people decided our job for us. We were just supposed to be instruments. They just asked us to be talented and gifted. There was incredible pressure on actors to be geniuses. No one helped you out; you had to be the best and compete. That was great for the real talents, but hard for average guys like me. Then came the '60s, when there was more emphasis on the collective, more concern about frontstage communication with the audience, the narrative competence. What became important was the story you told, not your talent. This epic turn was terribly important. The pressure dropped and you felt more liberated. Later on all turned political, became ideological and dogmatic, but these were the reasons why it all started.

Cultural revolutionaries soon presented themselves as cultural workers. Creativity was collective, and one had to destroy false prophets claiming to be individual geniuses. Fight the monopoly of bosses who force upon the people their idea of the world as a capitalistic will! Unite against totalitarian art in cells, brigades, or other free groups! A leader of one free group attacked Sjöberg, Bergman, and all other theatrical tyrants, accusing these art managers of believing that they rightly had the mission of

> God the creator, ruler of the universe, decision-makers, visionary strategists. As if launching a play and its actors were like constructing a rocket base for American astronauts. . . . In this sense Sjöberg as boss is not far from the Inquisitors who step forth in place of the Saviour and say: "Only chaos holds mankind back, coercion can set her free." This thought has led Sjöberg into a cult of the individual, a hymn of praise to the thesis: "In art there can be only one will."[58]

What was wrong with the old art firm was that a single manager ruled its entire production. At the start of the 1970s, individual will was anew, as once in David's and Robespierre's revolution, to be replaced with the "people's" will. In 1968, no one even worried about what Kant, Schiller, or Schopenhauer might have to contribute to such a quest. Aesthetics was mega-out; Marxist Hegelianism had taken over and made sociology and anthropology fashionable for all those eagerly searching for the legitimate will of the people. It was sociology that replaced philosophy for the new class of cultural workers. The Swedish sociologist Harald Swedner quickly produced hard survey evidence that bourgeois culture hardly supplied what the people really needed. Old art could not mirror new society. The fact that he published his findings in the Social Democratic periodical *Tiden* indicates that the party was leaving the aesthetic education defended by Sjöberg and supporting art as "folk culture."[59]

The rapid expansion of television during this time brought about the collapse of the Swedish film industry. New media such as TV lured away the audience for old media types such as film and radio, which traditionally mass-diffused theater productions. In addition, audiences in theaters, identified by Swedner as the evil supporters of obsolete "bourgeois high-culture," were becoming more meager. While markets shrunk for the performing arts, a growing number of theater students graduating from university and the new national drama schools wanted to work in the old houses. Theater became a hot job market while theater managements all over Sweden wondered how to fill their houses. Fewer and fewer enjoyed the shows, while there was a booming demand for theater courses at the university level. Sociologists and anthropologists studied carnivals, rites, and fairground attractions, as well as avant-garde happenings, in order to empirically reconstruct the true nature of the "people's will." Such popular forms of culture were supposed to voice the popular culture that became the immanent Ding an sich young politicized intellectuals so much desired. It became a tricky task to maintain the position of incorporated art in such a political climate.

In 1969, Social Democratic politician Carl Albert Andersson headhunted the Finnish theatre manager Vivica Bandler for the CEO position at Stockholm's Volksbühne, the Stadsteater founded in 1960. As in Berlin, with its Deutsches Theatre and the Volksbühne, the Stockholm theater landscape was increasingly polarized. To the right was the Royal Dramaten; to the left, Stadsteatern was both physically and mentally embedded in the house of the Social Democrat national labor union.

Bandler had a good record of radical directing and successful art management of a small private Swedish-speaking stage in Helsinki. In Stockholm, the situation was critical. Stadsteatern lacked an audience, and Bandler was ordered to increase its frontstage attraction.[60] Today one would talk about marketing and management, but then, such capitalist terms would have caused riots both frontstage and backstage. Bandler had to maneuver her art corporation carefully and opted for a double system of soft and hard art management, whereby she herself could "cherish" her staff in a "warm Mummy," soft, participative mood, while the hard decisions were made by her financial manager, who agreed to play the nasty part of the "bad guy." The latter explained Bandler's marketing success as depending on the fact that she never "sneered at the artists" but just picked box office hits such as *Fiddler on the Roof* without ever debating the issue in the industrial democratic manner of the day.[61] Going for light entertainment in the short run was just a part of Bandler's politics for saving Stadsteatern as an art firm in the long run.

Bandler segmented her art market in a Schillerian way. In addition to the large and small stage in place when she arrived, she smuggled in a third stage, disguised by the description "a simple rehearsal space" in the theater's budget. Between the large stage for musicals and spectacular entertainment and the small one for traditional bourgeois culture, betwixt matter and form, she designed the third space with the following innovation strategy à la Nemirovic in the back of her mind: "Something I often wondered about during my twelve years running and directing a poor little Swedish-language theatre in Helsinki was: why do the big theatres always have the resources and the little ones the ideas? Couldn't you bring the groups with ideas under the budgetary roofs of well-funded theatres? Give them support without stifling and subduing them? Rather like a sow suckling her little piglets?"[62]

Soon frontstage manager Bandler, the Nemirovic sow, found her Stanislavski piglet for backstage experiments. In 1971, she hired a guest director, Suzanne Osten, who was operating somewhat like an art consultant to Bandler's theater. With the subtle support of Bandler, Osten would incorporate art in Stadsteatern.

Osten's biography was typical of the new generation of corporate art managers. A nineteen-year-old student of art and literature with little theatrical experience, Osten had promoted herself to demon director of her little student theater in Lund. A feminist Antoine of the Swedish welfare state, she founded her own "Pocket Theatre." Like most middle-class radicals, Osten grew curious about the scattered debris left from an avant-garde tradition two generations earlier. It would not be until one decade later that the music industry would seriously introduce dada or surrealism into an international teenager cult, but Suzanne got the avant-garde spinoff of German idealism. Her German mother was a Freudian film critic, acquainted with both Brecht and Sjöberg.

Osten was soon unhappy staging small fringe events; she had the ambition to reach large audiences. Like young Diaghilev dreaming outside the Marinsky or Antoine outside Le Français, she was an outsider longing for a managerial career inside an art corporation. After attending the university, she tried to sneak into Dramaten backstage by becoming the assistant of her great idol: "I was determined to learn from Alf Sjöberg. He was the best in Sweden. . . . What I wanted from him was his fantastic analytical ability, his unique knowledge of theatre. . . . But I never got near him. . . . I was pretty aggressive and easily got arrogant in that manner young people believe appropriate. I wasn't humble. I could not afford to be."[63]

Rejected by Father Alf, she (who might be termed Swedish theater's Mother Suzanne) ended up as apprentice to Ernst Günter. To capture her audience outside the regular theaters, she founded a street theater. Political trends soon helped her find a much more certain captive audience: "Eventually we built an audience of schoolchildren and prisoners. That was great, for they were stuck with little chance of escaping. They were happy to welcome us once we managed to break down their initial resistance."[64]

At a distance, Mother Suzanne seemed to market her art by the same frontstage methods as Father Alf used. To reach out to school classes, she wrote an article, "Children's Theatre Is a Class Issue," that brought her much publicity. Her next step, quite typical of her generation of art firm politicians, was to organize an action group for Socialist theater workers. Its moralistic members were so full of their Marxist message that, Mother Suzanne later admitted, their own children were completely disgusted about their politicized parents.

By 1971, Osten had knit her own tight network of young feminists with high public visibility. With the support of young leftist journalism school graduates who were now taking control over the Swedish media, including the influential daily paper *Dagens Nyheter,* the network—called Osten's "girls' mafia"—stirred the 1970s up into a cultural "decade for middle-class women." Osten worked to incorporate art in the calm eye of the political hurricane that twisted Sweden from a disciplined democratic industry state into a wild workshop for industrial democracy.

Sweden in the 1970s debated social change in managerial terms. Wildcat strikes, unheard of during almost thirty years of efficient social democratic state-capital corporatism, shook the country to its roots. Unions demanded more direct say in the management of corporations, and the popular issue of "decentralization" for an "industrial democracy" was even the topic of an in-house investigation of Stockholm's Stadsteater. When the only result was tens of thousands of words and "four thick folders but no decisions," Bandler asked Osten to go to work on it. Bandler, who had paid lip service to "the creative forces" inside her own company, preferred in this case to bring in Osten as an external consultant. This decision aroused protest backstage, but Bandler persisted and earmarked a small budget for a new touring project for children and young people to be managed by Osten. Bandler declared that she wanted to offer children a happy, fairy-tale world and include a subliminal political message for parents.

Osten, Stadteatern's new Stanislavski, immediately seized this opportunity to found her own studio, a well-protected cocoon inside Bandler's house. Although Osten swallowed Bandler's bait, she was spurred on by her underground ambition and cleverly channeled more and more of the theater's resources into a budget under her control. Her studio, of course, needed actors of its very own because

> the actors couldn't play children's and adults' theatre at the same time. Children's theatre happens in the morning, adults' in the evening. That was a simple administrative reason for demanding actors who could perform in the mornings. They couldn't play on the Large Stage in the evening as well. I had to add: "Look at what a managerial muddle it would be. We'd never put on a good production."[65]

The fact that she was originally assigned a children's theater helped her argue the need for a special stage. She manned her children's theater and then undertook an intricate rhetorical operation to transform her group into a regular, full-fledged art firm. In times when personnel—rather than customer—satisfaction was politically correct, she began by noting that her in-house company had problems performing for children because the

> children we encounter, their needs and reactions, wake differing feelings in us. When we're confronted with them we feel drawn into the children's world, a world one would rather leave be-

hind. All teachers, actors and nursery staff feel the same because they don't really want to be imprisoned in the kids' world. They want to be visible in the world of adults, a world they feel excluded from. They feel alone since they meet too few other adults in their job.[66]

No doubt she wanted to perform to grown-ups, to teachers rather than their pupils. Astonishingly, she succeeded in this desire by cleverly playing on the popular socialist myth of conservative forces stifling the innate playfulness of grown-ups. She succeeded in convincing politicians, who had given her money to play for youngsters, that adults were more childish at heart than the youngsters themselves. So it was her brilliant rhetoric, vaguely rooted in the avant-garde fascination with childish banality, that finally rendered her the desired position inside the art corporation. She maintained that children are much more mature than adults. There had been enough patronizing condescension toward children from old-fashioned conservatives, who were intellectually lazy folks wanting children's theater to be "easy." Therefore, Osten concluded, as she played on this sensitive string of morality, children had the "democratic" right to be treated as adults, and adults had an equal right to conquer their stolen childishness. This would provide, as Mother Suzanne put it, "a space where you're still allowed feeling emotions."[67] In 1975, she founded *Unga Klara* (Young Klara), her studio theater in the theater. Incorporation accomplished!

In this way, Suzanne Osten resigned as mother to schoolchildren in her frontstage audience. To her backstage artists, however, she was truly loved as Mother Suzanne. This emotional relationship was as important to Osten as to Stanislavski, since neither of them actually paid their ensemble themselves. Osten used the Stadsteater ensemble as an internal labor pool from which she attracted talent for productions in her art firm. Young Klara, like the studios of the Moscow Art Theatre, became in-house training centers for the staff. Both incorporated art firms developed human resources in a work environment, kept reasonably free from corporate control, and were also protected from the critical audience of the frightening black hole Stanislavski wrote about.[68] Osten still performed primarily for prepaid school classes, and Stanislavski's studio performed primarily to other theater workers. Under Osten's management, Young Klara became an important star incubator during the 1970s, much as the Moscow studios had earlier.

## Mise en Scène Processes

This was the era of soft management, and Young Klara was managed more as a friendly family firm than as a factory. Osten's autobiographical writings confirm that she saw herself as the founder of a theatrical family. Her art corporation compensated for her having been neglected by her own mentally ill mother, and the neglect she visited upon her own daughter. Rehearsals in Osten's Stanislavski studio turned into workshops that reminded her of her own Waldorf schooling. In preparatory seminars, actors met art critics invited by Mother Suzanne to lecture as storyteller/experts to inspire her children's creativity. She co-opted audiences from the position of cool consumer to the position of critic in "reference groups," early integrated in the production process. Her incorporated aesthetic play was a skillfully spun cocoon of internal support and dependence.

In the midst of her special space, where both rehearsals and performance took place, Mother Suzanne ran something resembling a kindergarten where artists, technicians, invited audience, and cooperating critics happily played aesthetics together. Anna Roll's admiring feminist portrait of Mother Suzanne is quite interesting (and in contrast to Vilgot Sjöman's account of Father Alf the powerful patriarch):

> For several months I have watched Suzanne's own creativity. I have seen her sit on the floor, legs crossed, explaining Alice Miller's psychoanalytical theories to her group of actors. I have seen her lead improvisations in schools and chat with school children. I have seen her discuss scenography, discuss the objectives of the enterprise, refer to recent literature, and present art books as a source of inspiration and association. She has interviewed guest lecturers, led countless practices and yoga sessions, and made her actors turn into parents, children, even babies.[69]

Sjöberg had transcendental aspirations. He made it politically credible that art could be made to work as a representation of a democratic society. Sjöberg's theater mirrored a world worthy of humanity. That was what he wanted the audience to see front stage.

Osten, on the other hand, put her own backstage matriarchy on public show as a concrete incarnation of her democratic utopia. Sjöberg was product-oriented—what counted was the performance—but Osten wanted attention focused on the process of rehearsals. To use the terms of the philosopher Arthur Danto, Osten was also transfigurative, whereas Sjöberg was transcendental in a Kantian sense. Sjöberg used to paint his own stage and convey its pictorial effect by his own colorful rhetoric, although his theoretical lectures were perhaps more aimed at frontstage critics and intellectual audiences than at the cast backstage. Osten actually was primarily pedagogically oriented backstage. Her rehearsals contain lectures by academics speaking to her creative "family," with a special dramaturge usually included in this family group. According to Osten, a dramaturge was her spokesperson, someone who would formulate her practices in words.[70] Stanislavski built the Moscow studio into a managerial prototype for creative art firms all over Russia. Osten had a similar ambition; mirroring a good society was not as satisfying to her as it was to Sjöberg. She wanted to aesthetically engineer a prototype to be reproduced out there in real life. She delivered the mise en scène of a new society while her dramaturges assisted her in the process of designing her utopia.

> You won't notice them [the dramaturges] at performances, but they've meant a lot to me. They're another essential element. Because we see ourselves as a model institution we want our work to be expressed in theory. Not that our method of work should be copied exactly, but simply because we have the lucky situation of having resources to conduct experiments that can inspire other groups . . . we may for instance explain our ideology to school teachers.[71]

Osten believed art firms could improve the quality of working life in general. Paraphrasing Stanislavski, she wished everyone to have "lives in art" and was much more influential in Sweden than Stanislavski ever was in Russia. In Sweden, art firms like hers became firmly and politically incorporated into the mixed-economy model of the welfare state. Her art firm flourished symbiotically with a social democratic policy for planned economic growth under conditions of an industrial democracy. In Swedish cultural policy, Stadsteatern in general and Osten's art firm in particular actually came to play a role rather similar to that claimed by theaters such as the Volksbühne in the German Democratic Republic. Making art work meant developing democratic management models useful for regular industry. In a way perhaps similar to the incorporation of Flemish art in Dutch commerce, Osten's theater during the 1970s was given a specific function in the industrial economy of the Swedish welfare state.

The nation at that time was a planned economy run according to the so-called Swedish model, which rested on long-term wage agreements negotiated on the national level by the employers' federation, SAF, and the national trade union, LO. Once all the wages had been contracted for the next period, Swedish industry set to work. The whole point was to avoid using extra money as incentive for productive work. Within the frame of given wages, productivity had to be strictly managed by nonmonetary incentives. MBA graduates, who were growing in number and soon managed most Swedish public and private enterprises, were trained to perform two tasks only: cut costs by rationalization, or improve output by creating nonmonetary incentives. During periods of falling productivity, such as occurred during the mid-1970s, the model began to crack. Managers attempting to improve worker results resorted to pay raises and threatened the Swedish model's corporativist planning. To save their model, Social Democrats and their central union supported a vast number of experiments that promised to find new nonmonetary ways for stimulating productivity. This was the context in which Mother Suzanne's theatrical studio provided content by nourishing the metaphysics of the Swedish model.

Instead of truffling her political discourse with terms from aesthetic philosophy or scientific jargon as Sjöberg did, Osten systematically used politically correct managerial terms (collective decision making, decentralization, work democratization, participation, team work, self-managed groups). The high media visibility of art firms made her especially interesting for politics. In France—a nation characterized by union strikes—theaters, concert-halls, and opera houses are visible arenas used for labor market conflicts. In Sweden, the stages were instrumental for conjuring up a climate of harmony in the planned labor market between capital and labor. Perhaps, Osten seemed to say, aesthetic democracy could save the harmony of the endangered Swedish model.

> We believe in the utopia of a motivated company trusting its "research project" and united in this faith. The concept "process" was a signal to engage a long struggle against institutional factory production, with actors on cast-list collecting their scripts from the office . . . an unbelievably turgid repertoire . . . haphazard productions, a struggle for tenure work contracts, a jungle of union agreements regulating theatre working, an audience who

bought subscriptions to plays of which they had no idea . . .
against this vast, amoeba-like organisation . . .[72]

Just replace "actors" with "workers," "audience" with "consumers,"
"theater" with "factory," or "company" with "teamwork" and Osten's political point is clear. She designed a management style to make art work as
the incorporated democratic heart of industrial society.

From October 1983 to April 1984, Osten worked on the project "Hitler's
Childhood."[73] Like Stanislavski, she extended production time considerably
and moved far from Sjöberg's Taylorized mise en scène. Sjöberg had gone to
the library and read a text that reminded him of a painting he once saw in a
museum. Osten started work the other way round, with no ready text. The
actors worked full-time on improvisations interspersed with lectures and
Suzanne Osten's seminars on ideas she felt important to the project. The
text developed during rehearsals, and it was only at the beginning of January 1984 that the playwright Niklas Rådström (the acting family dramaturge) delivered the first complete script. Rehearsals began with the study
of four books by psychoanalysts Alice Miller and Morton Schatzman, mixed
with documents on Nazi concentration camps. The cognitive assumption
was that an audience would never grasp a story of which each individual
actor did not have a personal knowledge. Sjöberg believed in intuition and
temperament, while Osten was already toying with concepts belonging to
the "knowledge society." Sjöberg believed in the actor's tacit talent, while
Osten offered them the possibility to simply tell a story for which they had
to store up and digest epic elements. Sjöberg commissioned scenography
and had assistants take over simpler instructions to actors. With Osten,
everything was done in common; the entire family included technical and
administrative staff. Sjöberg lectured, while Osten's family met at least once
a week to debate the work in progress.

By the middle of December 1983, the group went off to a retreat and
heard lectures by philosophers; psychologists; historians; and Keith John-
stone, a Canadian expert in improvisation. Approximately seventy experts
acted as hired consultants on Osten's Hitler project. Its overall theme of
"antifascism" was developed using psychoanalyst Miller's theories of how
children tend to reenact the humiliations of their childhood. The story was
anchored in actors by asking them to summon up their childhood memories
playfully in improvisation. The outcome was carefully documented and

archived by Osten. The scenographer present during improvisations drew
sketches for scenery. When Rådström turned the imagery into text and
brought the first script, Suzanne Osten brought loads of reproductions of
pictures by Magritte, photos of Kienholz sculptures, and portraits of Marc
Chagall. Diaghilev had to bring his dancers to the museum, and now pictures were accessible in art books. A collage of notes, sketches, newspaper
cuttings, and reproductions soon covered the storyboard in the rehearsal
space. Mother Suzanne called it all "eclectic journalism." Once this creative
phase of the scenery was finished, everything went on as a Sjöberg production. Nevertheless, numerous media accounts always focused not on the
final show but on Osten's creative phase. Art work meant little; working on
art was paramount. Although articles about Mother Suzanne were very similar to those about the self-governing groups in Volvo's new "democratic"
car plants, they were most certainly much more efficient in spreading the
gospel of industrial democracy.[74]

Osten, of course, made the link to industry by never missing a chance to
accuse her Nemirovic-boss Bandler of running her theater as an inhuman
conveyor belt. Her factory had no cold rehearsal rooms, no frightening
anonymous auditorium; good Mother Suzanne obtained a permanent cozy
space for her own family. Both media and politicians bought her nice saga
about industrial democracy. In the Nietzschean spirit of Palme's political autobiography, *Politics as the Will*, Osten reflects on how the Swedish model
taught her the kind of managerial storytelling that proved so successful in
incorporating her kind of art into Swedish socioeconomics:

> My chaotic childhood taught me to clearly state what I wanted,
> and why I wanted it. . . . If you needed something you had to mo-
> tivate the costs. In school I learned to act rationally; I had to
> rewrite passionate essays according to an academic dry structure;
> point by point, 1, 2, 3. . . . Cultural politics during the boom of
> the 1960s taught me that reasonably organised people with struc-
> tured projects always eventually got what they wanted. Creativ-
> ity was rewarded, provided its utility could be accounted for, and
> that it had been realistically budgeted. Theatre meant Will. . . .
> The welfare state protected it from outside attacks.[75]

# 8

Flux Firms

## Beuys's Aesthetic Management of Social Sculpture

### Extending Art as Capital

While he was serving as a Stuka combat pilot during World War II, Joseph Beuys (1921–1986) was shot down behind enemy lines in the Caucasus Mountains in the depth of winter. He was rescued by nomadic Tartars, who wrapped him in quilted tent cloths and fed him fat drippings. To be sure, this experience was a physical one of life or death for the pilot, but it was also to have significance in, and mark, his art as well. Swaddled in this way, he was not only rescued but also reborn to nature by the warmth of the felt and the energy of the fat that put his life-flux in motion.

Beuys reveals to his audience through autobiographical anecdote how he made art work. He wished to expand a static concept of art to accommodate the miracle of generating life-giving aesthetic energy. The work of art had to become a concrete model for aesthetic power plants. In a lecture from the mid-1970s, he further supports his position:

> Only the expanded concept of art is fit to become a useful instrument, an appropriate tool, for a revolutionary-evolutionary process of system change. . . . The point of expanding the concept is to provide room for the human being. . . . The expanded

concept is thus not limited to the actions of those we today use
to call artists: the painter, the sculptor, the dancer, the actor, the
poet and so forth. Provided one turns the concept of art into an
anthropological concept it will work as the tool or the vehicle
for changing the organisation of society.[1]

In 1921, Beuys was born to stern and solemn Catholic parents, who lived
in northern Germany on the Dutch border. His father managed a small dairy
in the town of Kleve. The boy Joseph was shy and dreamy and had a romantic passion about nature. He got his training as a sculptor at the Düsseldorf Art Academy between 1947 and 1951. To Beuys, sculpture was the experimental outcome of what he called "plastic transformations," when
movement brings chaotic hot energy into cold static order, as when fat
heated by the hands of an artist is left to chill into a given form.

In the early 1970s, the *fat* and the *felt* of the defining moment in the Tartar camp again surfaced in Beuys's work. On the floor of the stage of the
Stockholm Museum for Modern Art, wooden sleds, each carrying a roll of
gray felt, seemed about to be pulled not by stuffed dogs but by chunks of
something completely out of place in a museum where special materials are
traditionally used to mediate the message of the artist. Although Beuys had
solid academic training as a sculptor, he avoided using traditional media for
representing what was supposed to pull the wooden vehicles. To Beuys, the
use of professional media such as marble, brass, canvas, or oils brought clo-
sure to the art he struggled to expand into an existential experience. In the
1960s, after the postwar popularity of abstract expressionist painting, the
time had come for a new generation to redefine art and have it work for
society.

Instead of using an inorganic, durable, and distinctly shaped material,
Beuys sculpted what was to represent the sled-pulling energy in organic and
amorphous matter. Chunks of greenish grease emitted a bizarre organic
smell, as if they were living beings sweating on the hot museum floor. Beuys's
art worked enigmatically indeed and puzzled even the most thoughtful museum visitors. The fat, the felt, the wax, and the copper he used were materials carefully selected for their immediate physical, almost primitive, impact. A tiny, intense injection of this art provoked a Schillerian Schwung.
Like a mighty Dionysian stream—or to use the term closely connected to
Beuys's art, like a *flux*—it worked to transcend the audience into new and

uncharted territory. The fact that Beuys referred to himself as a *fluxus* artist emphasized his feeling that art should be the source of such conveyance. He explains how a material such as fat could put the individual into flux Schwung: "The flexibility of the material appealed to me particularly in its reaction to temperature changes. This flexibility is psychologically effective—people instinctively feel it relates to inner processes and feelings . . . [without this] . . . none of my activities would have had such an effect. It started with an almost chemical process among people that would have been impossible if I had only spoken theoretically."[2]

In choosing his medium, Beuys injected the concept of creativity, which had been so banalized by barren psychological formalizations, with a fresh content anchored in concrete substance. He wanted the Schillerian pendulum to swing back to matter, which to him was something natural, something living and fragile, and thus capable of decay and death. He explained, "Yes, I would like to be a better materialist or find a materialism that really takes matter seriously by establishing a dialogue with matter replacing the monologue focusing on its exploitation only."[3]

In 1974, Beuys made a lecture tour to the United States with an "energy plan for Western man" that came off as pretty strange to the contemporary art world. Those who expected a piece of performance art found an artist with a compulsion to combine art shows with philosophy. Although Beuys lectured like an old German professor, his inspiration was Paracelsus' alchemy rather than the formalisms of Newtonian science generally used in scientific allusions.

In 1979, the wooden sleds experienced in Stockholm were exhibited in the theater of the Guggenheim Museum, accompanied by a pile of copies of the *Wall Street Journal* and some other odd objects that had been part of a New York action piece "I Like America and America Likes Me." For this piece, Beuys was carried, rolled up in thick Tartar felt, from Kennedy Airport to a cage in the new Soho Gallery of the German art exhibitor René Block. The gallery floor was covered with hay and the pile of papers. There Beuys spent three days communicating with a live coyote, just as he had previously communicated with nature in the form of a dead hare in the Düsseldorf Gallery Schmela in 1965, or with a white horse during a performance of *Iphigenie* at a Frankfurt theater festival in 1969. He wanted his redefined art to reach out to nature.

To highlight their role as makers of aesthetic energy, Beuys called his objects *generators, introspectors, accumulators, filters,* or *infiltrations.* He drew with chalk on rough blackboards or on scrap paper using blood, rust, or oxidized minerals; he documented traces of matter rather than painted images. He believed in such traces of the absolute almost to the extent that the Catholic faithful view their relics. Beuys conceived of rot, rust, oxidation, and other forms of material decomposition as aesthetic outcomes of art work.[4] To forcefully fetter matter in form, he believed, would destroy the tension between living matter and the pure form generating aesthetic energy.

Beuys was not the first to work this way, of course. Marcel Duchamp, for instance, produced a picture with sperm,[5] which certainly added to the concerns of museum curators who then had to seriously contend with the problem of decomposition when conserving time-bound works of art no longer pretending to eternal life.

To clarify his view on matter, Beuys reversed Marxian jargon, proudly calling his artwork "fetishes." For those unacquainted with the metaphysical aesthetics of art work, there was always a dash of religion and esoterism in his actions. The first widely circulated media picture of the artist shows a bloodstained Beuys in a 1964 performance; he is holding up a cross as if he were exorcising some evil vampire.

Despite all of this evidence, it would nevertheless be unjust to call Beuys's art symbolism. The flux he searched for aimed at restoring immediate contact with nature; therefore, neither mediating methods nor symbols were really what he was about. His preoccupation with nature was no "naturalism." His focus on matter was distant from an ideological "material-ism."

"Yes, I believe that all questions central to the world, man, and mind have their answers in matter," he explained. "I am however not a materialist in the sense of materialism. For materialism has abused matter, wounded it, made it sick and brought it to extinction. I am a materialist in a different sense. I would like to live with matter, think together with it and so forth. Such a materialism has a moral dimension absent in the old type of materialism."[6]

Like the pile of *Wall Street Journals* in the Guggenheim in 1979, most of his objects of art not only played a part in his actions but were also made to work as art by plastic transformations during the same action. Instead of using painters' or poets' ready-made material, as Lugné and Antoine did, Beuys activated neutral objects with flux energy, as if they were charged batteries. When he incidentally used others' artwork in his performances, he justified his action by explaining his motivation as wanting to transcend the art work, as he had done in performance by adding a chapter to *Ulysses* on "Joyce's own request" in 1962, proposing to elevate the Berlin Wall by five centimeters purely for "reason of proportions" in 1964, or when he termed a performance "Marcel Duchamp's overestimated silence," also in 1964.

Beuys looked upon art as a vehicle for social change. He stored and preserved his old work like victorious racing vehicles brought to rest in a garage. His exhibitions were case libraries for metaphysical management models with the explicit aim to "show people something they can identify with, i.e. to demonstrate, develop, construct something in the spirit of a business firm. So that people can look at this firm, this vehicle and discover and study something they can connect with and get inspired by. That is, to my mind, the crucial point of it all."[7]

Beuys has the tone of a management guru when explaining how he wants art to work for organizational change:

> We seem to forget the fundamental issue . . . that only that which reaches the heart of our contemporary culture and can transform it is worth calling art. But contemporary culture has nothing to do with what cultural institutions are doing. Our contemporary culture is totally determined by what one may call the "nature of economy." In other words, we live today totally in an economic culture. We should not fool ourselves believing we live in any other form of culture.[8]

At a lecture for new business faculty at Witten-Herdecke, a private German university, one year after Beuys's death in 1986, the keynote speaker, a terribly thin, energetic man, talked a lot and with much passion. While he was speaking, he constantly drew graphs on a blackboard. The keynote he struck was that management and economy were activities of value creation, exactly as art was. Old industry had developed ways of extracting values out of nature, but new economy needed to learn from art how to make knowledge-value, competence-value, and other sorts of immaterial value.

The lecturer then went on to sketch a history of art on the blackboard. Art had, he claimed, once symbolized religious forces controlled by the chieftains, the priests, and the kings managing society in the past. At the time of the Middle Ages, powerful states were founded on Roman law. The Industrial

Revolution was characterized by its impressive development of external
sources of power, and now the new economic order is distinguished by a
radical shift to different sources of energy. External scientific power (steam,
electricity, nuclear energy) no longer dominates the scene; now aesthetic energy propels the era.

People are about to discover their inner aesthetic energy, continued the
lecturer. A distinct difference can be seen between force and power on the
one hand and this new aesthetic energy on the other. Aesthetic energy, contrary to mechanical force and political power, cannot be tapped by science
or tamed by politics. This inner energy is of a third aesthetic kind. The new
economy, he concluded, runs on aesthetic energy generated when art is made
to work.

What this speaker was referring to was a new art that was making its impact on socioeconomic reality. For a while, avant-garde art was hovering
above reality; now it was time for it to land. Once art descended upon it,
economic reality would also change and require fresh definitions of art and
of business and economy. For one, the economy would have to be managed
differently. In the post–World War II world, said the lecturer, metaphysical
foundations are close to breakdown. Ideas of liberalism and socialism have
lost their energy and have frozen into stiff ideologies completely deadlocked
by the Marxist-capitalist dualism. The keynote speaker finally typified the
Berlin Wall as the sad monument of this crisis of totalitarian terrorism versus the banality of colonial commercialism. Only aesthetic energy generated
by art could defrost the Cold War dualism.

The keynote speaker that day in 1987 was Johannes Stüttgen, filling in
for his deceased master, Joseph Beuys. The physical and philosophical similarities between the master and his student were amazing. Stüttgen replaced
Beuys, who had been suggested for an appointment as an adjunct management professor of art at the new Witten-Herdecke University just before he
died. Artists were frequently appointed professors in art schools and design
departments, but at that time, a position for an artist on a business school
faculty was still out of the ordinary. A great number of artists were preoccupied with the business world in a critical or ironical way; pop artist Andy
Warhol is probably the best known.

This new set-up was much more concrete and explicit, however. After
Warhol's biting irony, Beuys focused on social constructivism. Had Beuys

himself been the speaker that day, he probably would also have argued for the aesthetic overlap of art and economic value creation, since he clearly believed that an art inapt to design a society and unable to cope with central issues of its society, in final resort the problem of capital, is unworthy of being called art.[9] Further, he held that his expanded concept of art is actually identical to the extended concept of economy.[10] The positive response that day in 1987 testified to the fact that Beuys's expanded view of art worked amazingly well for managers as well as business teachers.

## Human Capital When Everyone Is an Artist

Beuys thus envisioned his expanded art as a dynamo of human energy that could transform the environment. If art became the content of a new economy, the business context would in turn be reshaped by its energy. In the 1990s, Ken Friedman, another fluxus artist-turned-management professor, observed that Joseph Beuys was then rethinking art along social lines.[11] To Beuys, many artists had already vaguely sensed this new managerial task for art, but unfortunately they were primarily like "Marcel Duchamp . . . that lazy bugger who made nice and interesting experiments to shock the bourgeois. . . . He however completely lacked systematic categories of thought . . . , [and] he had no methodological consciousness for his own work."[12]

Tired of jokes and banal humor, and driven by social engagement, Beuys began to build and develop, without which, as Friedman later noted, "Much of the art that emerged from fluxus would have been less interesting."[13] To found his socially engaged flux firm a century and a half after Schopenhauer, Beuys took up the thread of aesthetic philosophy reconnecting art and economy. Soon he began puzzling the art world by holding such people as Schiller, Novalis, and Nietzsche far above the elegant joker of the day, Marcel Duchamp.[14] To those familiar with German aesthetic philosophy, Beuys's strange lectures are easily decoded as a showcase of Schiller's aesthetics repackaged as his expanded flux art management. Beuys actually set out to reformulate the entire classical political economy in aesthetic terms.

When in the early sixties Beuys offered an aesthetic redefinition of capital and labor rooted in art, he also became a pioneer of human capital management. It did not matter whether an individual was a doctor, forester, financial banker, teacher, or simple laborer; Beuys's democratic proposition was

that "everyone is an artist." Art is the main source for human creativity in
work. By the vehicle of art, the artist offers an escape route from the me-
chanical-inorganic world.[15]

Beuys aesthetically formulated an identity between art and human capital
in his famous dictum *Kunst = Kapital*. His flux firm became the model for
the flux moving toward a new society of a third aesthetic kind in between
formal political planning and materialistic profit orientation. Beuys took his
job as professor of monumental sculpture seriously, redefining it as a modeling of better societies that he called "social sculpture." Sculptures in clay or
bronze were only minor means for
the real artistic contemporary challenge: the big, invisible sculpting of a
great social *Gesamtkunstwerk*.

At the Düsseldorf Art Academy,
Professor Beuys began teaching social sculpture. He was inspired by
German aesthetic philosophy sprin-
kled with old shamanic wisdom. In
his biography, the Tartars stand for wisdom far removed from the mechanical, Newtonian, or Cartesian kind of scientism. The Tartars gave him a life-
saving experience of true matter and then invited him to stay on with them,
to become one of their tribe, to return to nature. Beuys decided to return
with the German soldiers who finally found him, however. When the mad
materialistic bloodbath was over, central Europe woke up a binary world
decapitated by an Iron Curtain. To Beuys, the post–World War II world was
a sad remake of Schiller's bipolar darkness of barbaric banality and totalitarian terror. Europe was squeezed hard between backstage Moscow and
frontstage Washington, between the economic doctrines of producer dictatorship and the market hegemony of the consumer king. Europe, felt Joseph
Beuys, could regain its dignity only as a free in-between zone.

Young Beuys had instinctively withdrawn into art after the intensive war
experiences of steppes, plants, and sunsets over expanses of snow. Natural
science had always attracted him, and after the war he even helped a
moviemaking comrade shoot nature documentaries. He took lonely, long,
meandering hikes and lived an isolated and reserved existence, searching
for his own free position in between the Eastern and Western propagandas.
This was the cold era of Marxism versus McCarthyism, an era when a Ger-

man talking about Kant, Schelling, Schopenhauer, Nietzsche, or a third aesthetic realm ran a serious risk of being banned as some nostalgic Third Reich fanatic.

Sheltered by the Düsseldorf Art Academy, which appointed him professor of monumental sculpture in 1961, Beuys quietly began constructing his vehicle, his own art firm for social sculpture. Encounters with American happening and performance artists from the fluxus movement turned the academic professor into an action-oriented entrepreneur. He not only began having shows in galleries but also frequently participated in performances and happenings. After the picture with the crucifix in 1964, he also became the pet of German news media, a standing that irritated some of his academic colleagues. Just as fluxus artist Yoko Ono became world-famous by teaming up with the Beatles, Beuys turned into a German media star by rubbing elbows with celebrities such as Andy Warhol and Willy Brandt. Ultimately, Beuys cast himself into a living brand.

A typical portrait of Joseph Beuys reveals a strangely uniformed civilian. He always wore gray felt hats, which became exponentially more expensive as his international reputation as an artist took off. His wife, the daughter of a professor of zoology, always tailored his standard angler's waistcoats, and the blue jeans completing his outfit were American. His thin face appropriately seemed as ascetic as Christ's; for Beuys, Jesus incarnated ethic energy. Christ was the "mighty steam engine" of humanity.[16]

In Düsseldorf, Beuys studied sculpture under Ewald Mataré, an artist who often worked with religious motifs. Mataré immediately spotted Beuys's talent. Perhaps Beuys carried the same aura that Novalis once sensed around Schelling and Schiller. In the sculpture studio, in an atmosphere akin to that of a medieval guild, Joseph Beuys, the anarchistic rebel, applied himself with surprising ease to the strict monastic discipline of his craft. In 1950, however, when Beuys was proposed as a candidate to a departmental chair, Mataré opposed his appointment on the grounds that he thought his genial disciple too self-centered to teach.

A well-known photograph of Beuys shows him in his felt hat, proudly posing in front of a gigantic skeleton of an elephant in the little German town of Kassel. It is signed with his slogan Kunst = Kapital and sold as a postcard. The elephant may be the one whose skeleton, carefully packed in wooden boxes, Goethe had delivered to him. Goethe, who used the bones to test a missing link to a hypothesis, kept them hidden in the back of one of his closets so that no one would call him mad. Beuys did the same thing with his philosophical evidence; bit by bit he took it out of his aesthetic archive and exposed it in the daylight of his performance. This was guerrilla warfare on dualism that would culminate in a spectacular unifying *mega-event*. According to his friends, had Beuys been alive at the time of the fall of the Berlin Wall in 1989, he would have greeted the event as a marvelous confirmation of his ideas.

Beuys made a careful study of Rudolf Steiner, whose ideas he introduced to the art students in Düsseldorf. Around 1900, Steiner modernized much of German aesthetic philosophy under the label of *anthroposophy*. The blackboard notes Beuys used in his performances show symbols strikingly similar to those designed by Steiner and preserved on his teaching blackboards in Goetheanum, the headquarters of anthroposophists in Dornach, Switzerland. Steiner was a Goethe scholar, who was also inspired by the same Madame Blavatsky who exerted her influence on Kandinsky, Diaghilev, Stanislavski, and other avant-gardists. The fact that Beuys, like Steiner, also demonstrates influence from the esoteric Wagnerian sect of Rosicrucians and from Tantric Buddhism, took part in anthroposophist circles indirectly qualifies him as an heir of both Goethe and Schiller! By the turn of the century, Steiner had organized his own Schillerian Schwung Waldorf schools to reform public education against materialism and positivism. In this same spirit, Beuys wanted his flux firm to reshape society.

Inspired by Steiner's practical anthroposophy, Joseph Beuys now launched a number of associations, parties, and groups to get his audience to move in the third direction. Together with Nobel laureate Heinrich Böll, he established a Free International University in Düsseldorf in 1972. Earlier, he had attempted to admit all students to his class even though he was ignoring the formal rules of his state academy. When this led to dismissal from his professorship, he started a meta-party for nonvoters, a student party, and a party for animals. In 1979, he actually invented the German Green party, founded as a direct result of his expansion of the concept of art into the domain of ecology. The popular appeal of its eco-aesthetic program indicated that natural philosophy, of which aesthetics was once an important element, had perhaps not been completely wiped out by the politicized scientific ideology that then dominated thinking in Western Europe. To an increasing number, the message of the strange professor Beuys (who started out by masquerading in the media as modern magician and shaman) seemed to make plain old common sense.

The mainstream Western political and academic establishment had little understanding of Beuys's aesthetics, however, because they still regarded science in its Newtonian and narrow Cartesian sense as the unified body of meta-knowledge perfectly suited for managing all human affairs. But small cracks were beginning to show in the rationalistic armor. When scientific management failed, especially after the 1968 student movements, the court-philosopher to the dominant Social Democratic, Jürgen Habermas, blamed it on a rationalistic scientism he labeled *Verwissenschaftlichung*.

Paradoxically, Habermas and other Marxian thinkers of the Frankfurt school of social science wanted to cure democracy of inhuman technocracy by means of logical reasoning rooted in the very rationalism they themselves identified as the source of the social sickness. Instead of democratizing technocracies, their sociology actually tended toward technocratizing democracy.

Academic philosophy really had little interest in aesthetics either. Social philosophers debated only Kant's first and second Critiques and considered the third one irrelevant for society outside theaters, museums, and concert halls. Not until the mid-1980s did French postmodern philosophy reinterpret Kant's aesthetics as socially relevant. Until then, the natural philosophy of Goethe, the old elephant in Kassel, and all that did not fit the scientific logical paradigm was filed in archival dustbins as outmoded and superstitious garbage. On this barren frontier, Beuys was really a pioneer. His art brought back to daylight a philosophical heritage repressed in the German underground since 1933. In his 1973 manifesto for the Free International University, Heinrich Böll explains it this way: "The Nazis' blood and soil doctrine, which ravaged the land and spilled the blood, has disturbed our relation to tradition and environment. Now, however, it is no longer regarded as romantic but exceedingly realistic to fight for every tree, every plot of undeveloped land, every stream as yet unpoisoned, every old town centre, and against every thoughtless reconstruction scheme."[17]

From 1972 through 1977, the period during which Beuys remained suspended from his teaching post in Düsseldorf, he traveled like one of the Tartar nomads, lecturing about his art management theories of "social invisible sculpture," "Art = Capital," and "Everyone = Artists." Documentation of his extensive travels shows both an amazing strategic consistency of his content as well as tactical smoothness in grafting his message to the actual political and artistic context.

When Beuys got sacked from the Düsseldorf Art Academy, it was, of course, after one of the student occupations, which happened frequently in the aftermath of 1968. The death of Benny Ohnesorg, the impulse for the 1968 revolt in Berlin, triggered formation of the student party, and later the violent terror of Baader-Meinhof was a sharp contrast to Beuys's own peaceful anarchism. Beuys systematically transformed museums and galleries into theaters for lectures and installations. During a seminar in the Institute of Contemporary Art in London in 1974, he produced a great number of charts on blackboards, called *Richtkräfte,* "forces of direction," later exhibited in New York, Venice, Bonn, and Berlin.

It was in Kassel, though, in the shadow of Goethe's elephant, that Beuys established his most efficient theater during the Documenta art shows that took place for one hundred days every fifth year. There he systematically combined the presentation of material object with idea. In 1972, he installed the office of the free university in the Documenta. In 1977, he presented his installation *Honey Pump in the Work Site,* where honey was pumped in circular flux through a closed loop of transparent plastic pipes inside the main exhibition building. Parallel to this Documenta installation, Beuys spent his hundred days debating his concept of Art = Capital with people such as Marxist Rudi Dutschke.[18] Beuys felt that an expanded concept of art would fuse with an extended concept of business economy to constitute a new umbrella for both capital and labor in what he called social sculpture. Objects he had earlier given away after showings were now assembled in installations and traded to art collectors for rapidly rising prices.

Beuys's main concern, however, was to find more human and natural ways of management under the inspiration of art. Contrary to the Marxists, Beuys saw no reason to abandon the powerful business tools developed by capitalistic firms. Although Andy Warhol claimed to be a master of "business art," Beuys in 1977 declared to the press that if advertisers were gangsters, he meant to become "the gangster of gangsters."[19]

Beuys was certainly qualified as both a brand manager and a concept developer. His dictum Kunst = Kapital caught on as quickly as any soft-drink slogan, and he appeared costumed in his trademark bizarre outfit long before marketers minted the term "branding." He saw nothing wrong in fueling the media with scandals and eye-catching press releases. In 1981, he was accused of using commercial advertising and marketing techniques; he quipped, "My entire life is advertising, but one should perhaps try to understand what I have been marketing."[20]

Beuys's lecture on art to a woodenlike dead hare and his residence with a living coyote during a New York performance were not the sum of his shock value. In 1985, he shocked leftists by promoting a Japanese whiskey, and shortly before his death he entered into an advertising deal with Coca Cola. This contract would have brought 100,000 DM to fund his last grand installation, *Seven Thousand Oaks for Kassel,* initiated during Documenta 7 in 1982. Beuys wanted seven thousand oaks to be planted in the Kassel region. For this final project, he expanded art in time and space. The last of the oaks was planted during Documenta 8 in 1987, one year after Beuys's death.

Trees could soon be found far away from the Documenta exhibition spaces; the project implied an extension of traditional city economy. Beuys established a team of workers and surrounded the project with several events that gave birth to art products for sale to finance the entire project. In June 1982, for instance, Beuys and his assistants publicly melted down a gold copy of an old tsarist crown. During the performance, they cast the material of this empty power symbol into a mold of a hare, the Celtic votive animal for peace. The golden "hare of peace" was subsequently sold to a collector to pay for planting some of the seven thousand trees.

Beuys's art work demonstrated that his Kunst = Kapital carried little glorification of the market for art. In the direct presence of the artist, no one could ignore that art had its origin not in financial capital or political power but in the existence of a living human being. All forms of capital are rooted in human concrete and real creativity. Beuysian capital is anthropological in the sense that its art is the "being human," his interpretation of the managerial term "human capital."

Those who had the privilege of directly communicating with the eloquent and patient Beuys do not remember some lonely star or isolated genius. They encountered a lively and engaged man eager to cooperate and communicate with his fellow human beings. By finding social forms for such encounters, Beuys wanted to prove his second principle: every human being, like himself, could be an artist in his own way. Most visitors to Documenta easily drew the practical conclusion that humanism ought to be at the core of a new economy from his lessons. Monetary capitalism might be the traditional

model for Western Europe, but as Beuys put it, it was time for a new economy for Central Europe, a new economy based on the human side of business. In the early seventies, he debated these issues with socialist reformers
such as Ota Sik.

The Documenta in Kassel, the Institute of Contemporary Art in London,
and the Guggenheim in New York became stages for the performance of
what may be called Beuys's Gesamtkunstwerk. Kassel was to Joseph Beuys
what Bayreuth was to Richard Wagner, a place radiating the aura of a new
era. From 1963 until his death, Beuys attended all the Documentas. In Kassel, which also became an aesthetic meeting point for artists from the East
and the West, Beuys presented shows he hoped would provoke a development in a third direction alternative to the two ruling world ideologies. The
flux toward this future social sculpture was the point of all his efforts; in
European modern art Beuys marks a renaissance for philosophical aesthetics
by making art work as a vehicle for the exploration of new social forms.

The contact with the fluxus movement undoubtedly "outed" Beuys and
turned him into a mass marketer of expanded art. At the same time, he consciously smuggled something very Central European into Western avant-
garde. In 1963, Professor Beuys invited his new fluxus friends to a big Fes-
tum Fluxorum Fluxus at the Düsseldorf Academy. The Swedish ethnologist
and fluxus artist Bengt Klintberg took part in this riotous party, as did the
father of American fluxus, John Cage; along with Nam June Paik, George
Maciunas, Alison Knowles, and Dick Higgins. When Beuys began performing, Klintberg recalls that the cool American fluxus following immediately
changed into a sort of shaman, magical cult. Klintberg, with his ethnologi-
cal sensibility, intuitively deduced that Joseph Beuys was driving his art firm
vehicle in a direction his American friends little suspected:

> The contribution by Joseph Beuys, Siberian Symphony, First
> Movement, was very different from the other ones. The compo-
> nents of his piece, mathematic formulas on a blackboard, a
> piano prepared with piles of earth and a dead hare all seemed to
> be parts of an alchemic experiment, and Beuys himself radiated
> an intense personal involvement during his performance. He
> could not be related to a Dada tradition. He was an innovator
> of archaic rituals, explaining eternal questions about life and
> death.[21]

What Klintberg undoubtedly uncovered was Beuys's first public attempt to bring back European metaphysics via the Trojan horse of a flux firm. Beuys was already consciously fueling his art vehicle with a secret mix of aesthetic philosophies from Novalis, Hölderlin, Schelling, and Schiller that he had tanked up from Steiner's anthroposophic station.[22] His fluxus art left the domain of dada play and had entered the field of aesthetic play. In search of the philosophical roots of Beuys's artwork, his American friend Caroline Tisdall recognized his fascination with the third in-between aesthetic field as she constantly stumbled on the "[t]hreefold structure . . . that fascinated Beuys. He had pursued triads, trinities and triangles through his studies of western philosophy, early Christianity and natural sciences from the Holy Trinity through alchemy and on to Rudolf Steiner. . . . He saw threefold form as governing natural structure and human nature, and it recurs throughout his sculpture, drawing and actions."[23]

In this tradition of European aesthetics, Beuys positioned his flux firm right in the business of being. He was forty years old when he entered the arena of public art, so he already had his personal archives filled with most of the ideas and objects he later presented as content to his audience. By his early sixties, he was therefore free to concentrate on reforming the context of art into aesthetic play. Failing to reform his own teaching institution, he embarked on a number of mediatic activities all geared to one overall goal: a new aesthetic economy with the human being in its center as the real piece of art.

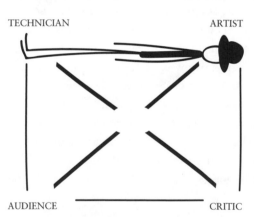

*Beuys and the Flux Firm's
Incorporation of the Human*

After his death, a number of publications and retrospective shows indicated that the man the media had once taken for a mad activist was rather a stubborn, strategic art manager. Beuys respected both dada and happening but could accept neither the former's empty nihilism nor the latter's wild activism; art was to reassume its classical aesthetic mission and generate an energy flux reforming society. His awareness of the subtle balance between form and

matter as well as his fear of both totalitarianism and banality led him to develop a special art management that would have made Schiller proud. Only
two years after his master's death, the faithful disciple Johannes Stüttgen
published an analysis of Beuys's flux firm, one strikingly akin to the
Gadamerian model of aesthetic play.[24]

Beuys emphasizes the flux of aesthetic energy transforming chaotic material energy via movement into form. His conception of the process of aesthetic production was inspired by both Paracelsus' alchemic transformation
model of *Sulphur-Mercurius-Sal* and Steiner's model of human creativity as
a flux between "willing," "feeling," and "thinking." Beuys did, however,
prefer to speak of the flux in more earthy terms such as flows of energy from
"the legs," "the heart," and "the head."

Two flows, the flux of ideas and the flux of matter, actually stream from
a creative person such as Beuys in his gray-hatted head, heart protected by
the angler's waistcoat, and blue jean leggings. Works such as *Honey Pump*
from 1977 or the *Seven Thousand Oaks* from 1982 through 1989 were
Beuys's attempt to put such double-sourced flux to work. The artworks,
flux-firm models for aesthetic powerplants, both consist of hardware such
as a circular pump, stones, and trees, and software ideas diffused by Beuys's
teaching in lectures and seminars. The software flies into the cognition of
the audience and gives rise to concrete action or reactions. Hardware, the
heat of felt and fat, for instance, perceptively flows in the opposite direction
and inspires ideas and thoughts of the critics. Stüttgen labels the effects of
such mixed fluxes "incarnation" and "transubstantiation," religious terms
much in the spirit of Beuys. The fluxes of aesthetic energy make an audience
and the critics act and reflect. The result of it all is the social sculpture. In
Stüttgen's rendering of Beuys's flux firm, the social sculpture consists of a
foundation, the incarnated *Sockel,* and transubstantiated ideas for which he
uses Schelling's term *Substanz.*

## Simmel's Metaphysics of Organization

To Beuys, making art work as social sculpture meant creation of new social
forms. The real art work was social and took its starting point in the people
going to the museum or theater. The audience was his art workers. Rhea
Thönges, a member of Beuys's seven-thousand-oak team, says that this is

why "the interest for Beuys among his contemporaries is comparatively different from that arisen around Picasso. How could anyone, or all of us together, be expected to carry on a work by Picasso? But Beuys meant that we should carry on his art work. He claims that art is a work we all together have to accomplish."[25]

Beuys's intention of expanding the old concept of art anthropologically therefore put human beings in the center of the aesthetic play, and fluxus itself began to acquire a social dimension.

Joseph Beuys's main achievement was to forcefully focus public attention on the importance of art and aesthetics for reorganizing modern society. He made it clear that he rejected traditional leftist as well as liberal worldviews outmoded and unfit for the times. Ideas of a similar nature had actually inspired investigations into the aesthetics of social form by German sociologist Georg Simmel (1858–1918) a century earlier. In his essay "How Is Society Possible?" Simmel refers to Kant as the philosopher who defined modernity as an era when individuals themselves would form reality. In 1800, Kant was preoccupied with how nature gets its unity, while Simmel, who posed his question around 1900, wanted to understand social reality.

Sociologists then began wondering how a coherent cultural unity might be acquired, given an enlightened Kantian modernity with no faith in God-given absolutes. Modernity is unstable and rocks in its relativity; existence must get its security by simple temporary stabilities. Social scientists, such as Simmel's friend Max Weber in the newly organized German Reich, now concocted a German national science called "sociology." In the learned *Verein für Sozial Politik,* they engaged in a number of detailed empirical investigations of the "social question," which resulted in the Reich's stabilizing policies to resist ideas subversive to social order such as Bakunin's anarchism and Marx's revolutionary religion of a new absolute. Simmel's attitude toward such mainstream sociology echoes Schopenhauer's toward Hegelian philosophy. He remained skeptical, thinking that neither science nor social science could offer an escape from the constitutional relativism of a modernity where a society is "directly realized by its own elements because these elements are themselves conscious and synthesizing units."[26]

In a way that would make him as popular with postmodernists as he had been misunderstood by mainstream sociology, Simmel states that society is a self-organized aesthetic unit. Social order is a temporary synthesis achieved by individuals exerting what he calls *synthesizing.* At this very point, Simmel introduces his concept of "social form," which coincides with Kant's aesthetics and Beuys's idea of society as an invisible social sculpture. To Simmel, modern men shape social form as lifeboats on the stormy sea of relativity. For a little while, in short, intensive experiences of pragmatic truth, as James might have put it, social art forms offer ad hoc security and order. Simmel insisted that the stabilizing effect was a social work of art.

Simmel was himself an art-loving sociologist. He collected art and counted Rodin, Rilke, and Georg among his friends. He devoted his youth to the study of Raphael and Michelangelo; his student Georg Lukacs, who later became a totalitarian Marxian art commissar, regarded him a sociological Monet. Instead of focusing on dry methodology, as Weber had, Simmel developed a poetic impressionistic style of writing that, to the anger and envy of his sociological colleagues, made many of his books into bestsellers. He wrote in such a way that the reader immediately grasped how social forms become reality through an aesthetic process brought about[27] "when a spontaneous and subjective abstraction of reality is performed, much in the same way as an artist works. . . ."[28]

To Beuys and Simmel, the capital and labor of future social sculpture was art and artists. Simmel also echoes Schiller when he states that social forms of modernity emerge in the aesthetic play of *Schwingen zwischen Gegensätzen,*[29] swinging between contradicting positions. He identifies modern form and matter, in between which this takes place as "the very dualism that split up humanity as well as each individual soul known today under contemporary denominations of the socialistic and the individualistic tendency."[30]

The latter tendency of liberalism—a democratic ideal as charming as a wild English garden—leans toward matter of fact and nature, while socialists prefer form and discipline planned as a symmetrical jardin of a Cartesian French chateau Simmel notes that: "The rational organisation of society is aesthetically very attractive, regardless of the effects it has on individuals in this society. Such an organisation aims at turning life as a whole into a work of art."[31] Socialism is attractive as a formal work of art, and Simmel cites the English liberal Macaulay, who suggests that those advocating a competing liberal organization care little for "symmetry, but for practicality. We forbid nothing merely because it is alien and aberrant. And we never set up rules which have a wider application than for the specific cases we wish to regulate."[32]

Not only in politics do human beings rock between form and matter. The societal competition between the opposites of socialism and liberalism has a legal parallel in the conflict between the continental, formal, top-down Roman law and the English common law, the latter being rooted in a more material bottom-up tradition. Roman law is based upon logical deduction and judgment by subsumption. A judge matches the case at hand with the relevant rule out of a list of general written principles. Roman law reminds the individual of what Schiller named form. Common law, on the other hand, is less concerned with formal principles. Common law is "judge made" and consists of an historical collection of material cases and their concrete verdicts in court. A wide array of singular cases makes up the tradition of "remedies," or proven historical cases. A good common law judge is therefore little preoccupied with logical deduction by means of universal form. The competence of this jurist resides in a Socratic capacity to become submerged in the very case to be judged in court. Therefore common law is sometimes also called *case law*. The judge decides by focusing on the specificity of the case rather than using universal principles. This is why it is deemed inappropriate for a common law judge or lawyer to preempt a judgment; how could some cunning calculus ever predict a verdict depending on the situational wisdom of the court?

In Roman law, such speculation and forecasts are quite acceptable. Application of law in the Roman tradition strives to be formally programmed by universal theory. Georg Simmel's contribution stressed that the active element in such social programming is aesthetic. He observed how scholarly

Roman law debates were so imbued with aesthetics that one could mistake the old Italian universities, the renaissance cradles of this formal rationalism, for classical academies of art.

To the political and legal dualisms might be added another important managerial dichotomy of social order. It is no doubt the formal spirit of Roman law that underpins the scientific management of modern industry. Common law, on the other hand, has inspired a human relations management practice more like a craft, like growing a kitchen garden. The techniques of such a craft are best taught on the job, and the tacit knowledge of its practical skills is often used as an argument against formal theory-based management education. In the case of legal education, it was only at the end of the eighteenth century, under the growing spell of rationalism, that English universities reluctantly followed the continental tradition and began to offer legal tuition. The Harvard Business School, a pioneer of management education, developed its method of management teaching by copying the Harvard Law School's pedagogy, rooted in common law. Instead of examining passed verdicts in court, it focused on making new managerial decisions. This Harvard Business School case method is therefore indirectly an example of common law management opposing the Roman rationalism of scientific management. Most other MBA programs now lean toward scientism. As Simmel observed in the political-legal domains, form seems to win over matter because aesthetically case law and its liberal art only offers "[o]ur spirit an uncomfortably unstable picture that we can neither perceive without exposing ourselves to new tensions nor understand without repeated effort, while the socialist egalitarian society with its organic whole and symmetrical design offers us a grasp of its social picture with a minimum of spiritual exertion."[33]

Georg Simmel's sociological aesthetics accounts for preferences and choices between rationalism and empiricism in any of their political, legal, and managerial guises, as a Schillerian Schwung of social forms between form and matter. In modernity, where Kunst = Kapital and Everyone = Artist, according to Joseph Beuys, individuals can control the rocking of the boat by sculpting social form right in the middle of the third realm. According to Simmel's sociological aesthetics, such stabilization is the grand business of modern artists and their art work. Simmel's deep-rooted belief in art and the way this makes him different from other social scientists has a lot in common with Schopenhauer's relation to academic philosophy.

Simmel's contemporary, Max Weber, also names three social forms of power: rationalism, traditionalism, and in between them the charismatic form.[34] For Weber, rationalism is also based upon formal logical concept ideals, while traditionalism reflects the idea of natural law. These two belong to the utopia of possibility and the empirical everyday normality, but the third—what Weber calls the charismatic—is, as he puts it, *ausseralltäglich,* beyond the normality of the everyday. Weber speaks of charismatic personalities. He names holy prophets, shamans, and leaders of genius such as Napoleon. Simmel, however, explicitly speaks of art and artists.

Weber finds examples of charismatic leaders in history, while Simmel's artists belong to the avant-garde of the future. Simmel's sociological aesthetics declares that art and artists will have a central role in designing modern society. Weber, somewhat like Hegel and according to Schopenhauer, expects the methodological social scientist to be tomorrow's philosopher-king. When Weber discovered the "ideal types," for instance, he felt that he had come up with a sociological methodology for social scientists to pinpoint something in between a law of nature and a concept of reason; science, not art, was to socially construct the third realm.

Simmel never believed in such social engineering. Instead, he talked about the new era of a "qualitative individualism" by which modern moderns will express their inner universe. In this new era, only the artist—not the social scientist—can avoid conforming to given traditional roles or rational plans in order to allow Schwung and metaphysics to permeate her social sculpture. To Simmel, this was how Goethe and Rodin sought to express the dynamics of life between matter and spirit. Simmel's firm belief in the artist's ability to break out of the conventional prisons of dualism is increasingly shared by social scientists who realize the social impact of art and aesthetics.

French sociologist Pierre Bourdieu explains why social scientists aiming to change society ought to learn from the work of socially engaged artists such as Hans Haacke:

> I think your work [that is, Haacke's] represents a kind of avant-garde of that which could be the action of intellectuals. It could serve as a critical analyser of the moment of transmission of knowledge in relation to the moment of the conception and of the research itself. Everything makes me think that intellectuals are not at all concerned about the moment of the performance, and that they do not make it an object of research. And it is to a large extent for this reason that they are so little effective. I think they should take inspiration from research like yours . . . to give full symbolic effectiveness to their unveiling of social mechanism, particularly of those who rule the world of culture.[35]

In this way artists like Haacke or Beuys today continue Schiller's aesthetic education of man. Simmel has explained the need of their art firms in his *Soziologische Ästhetik,* and Joseph Beuys has shown how his flux firm makes art work as capital, urging everyone to become an artist. Flux firms of Beuys and others manufacture concrete social models while adding this essential aesthetic surplus value, which artist and management professor Ken Friedman catches:

> [Nam June] Paik isn't a TV executive, though his work requires engagement in broadcasting. Beuys wasn't a politician, though social sculpture is political art. Christo isn't a construction engineer, Kirkeby isn't a model maker, Andersen isn't a landscape architect and Knizak isn't a furniture maker even though they do many of the things engineers, model makers, landscape architects and furniture makers do.[36]

# 9

## Postmod Performances

### Big Bang Berlin: Rephilosophizing the Third

In 1979, French philosopher Jean-François Lyotard (1924–1998) claimed that the world seemed stuck in a *postmodern* condition. Lyotard coined this term in a report on the future role of the university, which was commissioned by the Ministry of Higher Education in Quebec, Canada.[1] Lyotard further argued that in postmodernity, philosophers can no longer uphold the grand meta-narratives that once legitimized the modern Western university. Ludwig Wittgenstein and Kurt Gödel had convincingly shown that systems of knowledge can neither be self sufficient nor traced back to some universal meta-language from which the truth of all scattered sciences can then be deduced. Therefore, the university and its philosophers—the scholarly experts and degreed decision makers—could no longer ground their authority on the safe bedrock of unified science.

Lyotard speaks explicitly of two crumbling rocks that represent the grand narratives in crisis. His first concern is the Hegelian dialectics of mind, with its hardcore offspring in scientific materialism and soft prolongation in Jürgen Habermas's hope for rational universal consensus. The second concern is the grand narrative of human emancipation, fertile soil for Newtonian liberalism from Adam Smith to John Stuart Mill, by way of Talcott Parsons as well as Niklas Luhmann's formal theory for social systems. Like the polarities of matter and form in Schiller's aesthetic play, Lyotard's two grand narratives threaten to suffocate innovation and creativity. On the one hand is "la terreur"[2] of closed totalitarian formalism; on the other, materialistic degenerate banality.

Lyotard's criticism of the modern university once instituted by Humboldt in Berlin also echoes Schopenhauer's attack on Hegel's barren state philosophy in the very same city university. In this postmodern condition, concludes Lyotard, mankind has lost faith in global universal scientific truth. Justice and knowledge can now be rescued only on small local "islands" where creative projects generate new ideas for temporary social forms.

Fifteen years after the fall of the Berlin Wall, at the mausoleum of binary modernism at Brandenburger Tor, markets for postmodern performances supplying aesthetic play are indeed booming. In the 1970s, university dropouts ended up in political sects; now they perform art start-ups in museums, art space, theaters, media corporations, and creative industries in the cultural economy. Lyotard's postmodern condition has since petered out, supplanted by a late modernism where unified general science has lost its former appeal. Those making art work now cope continuously with a chronic postmodern condition, which raises the question of how aesthetic energy can be generated by such postmodern performances.

By 1993, most of the traces of the Berlin Wall existed only in memory. Although only four years had passed since the wall came down, FRG shops and cars swiftly invaded GDR territory, and visitors were really forced to speculate about where the wall once separated the dialectics of the spirit and emancipatory humanism. The Berliner Luft was empty of its brown coal; the acrid fragrance of GDR chemicals lingered in nostalgic minds rather than in the nostrils. Now, on the steps beneath the tattered and torn red flag that flew over the Volksbühne building, the audience enjoyed a smoke during intermission at a postmod performance.

Berlin was an open city. Mile-long convoys of lorries bound for Poland, Belarus, Ukraine, and Chechnya jammed the autobahn on their journey eastward. With Nietzschean speed, videos, CDs, and computers assaulted the man on the street as the products of the day chased him from his sheltered collectivity down the slippery slope of wild capitalism. A year earlier, a visitor to St. Petersburg told me how the whole town was mesmerized by television and watched entranced as sloppy amateur Siberian kick-boxers slaughtered each other to the tune of techno pirate music. An American think-tank consultant named Francis Fukuyama paraphrased Hegel, declaring history to be stone-dead, and management expert Tom Peters predicted that business from now on would thrive on chaos. The show-biz banalities from Kurfürstendamm and Kaufhaus des Westens flooded into East Berlin and soon diluted what remained of the broth of totalitarian propaganda. Clearcut bipolar distinctions between commerce and culture were swept away. This was a scene beyond Lyotard's wildest dreams.

Europe was slowly recovering from the shock of the perfectly timed big bang that detonated its binary power blocks. Precisely two hundred years after the French Revolution, the wall came down; Berlin followed Paris. Liberalism and socialism, the modern twin political manifestations of Schiller's form and matter, were destabilized and balanced in aesthetic limbo. The term *postmodern condition,* first elaborated for diagnosing science, seemed to fit the entire society perfectly, and once again questions emerged. Could capitalism be a global winner without the countervailing power of socialism? What about new social sculpture proposing different local stabilities? These questions in themselves made a market for postmodern performances.

During this period, Stockholm's Stadsteatern was trying to attract a younger audience and find a way to persuade politicians to continue subsidizing its operation. Monica Ohlsson, a dramaturgist at the theater, revealed that she had heard of a theater in Berlin whose auditorium was always filled to the limit with students and the unemployed. Rumors circulated that subscriptions were abolished to bring in a younger crowd and that ticket prices were drastically reduced, even in the face of neoliberal demands that they be raised to cover skyrocketing costs.

Ohlsson worked for Peter Wahlqvist, the new CEO of the theater and the man in charge of its seven stages. State subsidies for Swedish art had risen in line with the wage-increase index and employment legislation coming into force in the 1970s. Even though costs were escalating with inflation, attendance figures remained static. Interest in the backstage working conditions that marked the art corporations of Sjöberg and Osten was waning and would soon be replaced by a concern for the frontstage marketing of art. No longer did the Swedish media report about factory work and industrial production. What currently fascinated the audience was the popular investment game of the financial markets.

Following a series of CEOs with strong union backgrounds, Wahlqvist, the sixty-eight-year-old rebel, presented himself more as an art marketer than a cultural worker. His choice was a wise one. Even public investigations into the social role of public culture going on during the same time admitted the importance of marketing and advertising for art.[3] It was obvious that the invisible wall between commercial management and culture was cracking.

Sweden was in the process of switching from Stanislavski to Diaghilev, and Wahlqvist adapted smoothly to the change. Once a leftist rebel, he shocked his old comrades by declaring that he had grown tired of the moralistic, "interminable Brecht" and that he now rather enjoyed the glamorous and gay part of art consumption when "[t]he stage was full of flowers and . . . people showered the actors with champagne. And my opinion, and I don't care what anyone thinks, is this is what we really long for."[4]

What Stockholm experienced was a minor repercussion of a Western postmodern shock wave with Berlin as its epicenter. I spent the beginning of the 1980s immured in its Western capitalistic enclave during the time that I was working in a research institute funded by Bonn and the United States to preserve intellectual life in a walled-up West Berlin. I recall—a little shamefully—the cool feeling when I crossed Checkpoint Charlie on my weekend tours or strolled on the old cobbled streets between the dilapidated gunholed facades of World War II, or watched the Brecht Ensemble on Schiffbauerdamm, or got drunk on cheap vodka, or gulped Solianka soup, or picked up girls in outmoded discos. All this was not only cheap but also chic for a Westerner with intellectual pretensions. For me, a visa to East Berlin was like a free pass to a thrillingly sublime Marxian theme park. Westerners, especially those fostering a hope of an egalitarian welfare state, were easily bribed with vodka-laced cultural communism. Who cared about Stasi or Gulag as long as there was a CIA and Vietnam!

In the mid-1980s, a Swedish translation of *The Aesthetics of Resistance*, the trilogy of German Communist poet Peter Weiss, marked a final artistic attempt to aesthetically rescue the ethos of the once so successful Swedish welfare state designed cooperatively by the Social Democratic Party, the national labor union, and the Swedish employers' confederation. Weiss, who had collaborated with both Sjöberg and Osten, wanted to reanimate faith in the communist ideal through aesthetic reflection. Members of the national labor union, which was then still formally incorporated into the Social Democratic Party, even formed a committee that set off to East Berlin on a study tour, headed by the former Communist leader C. H. Hermansson. Inspired by Weiss's book, this study party was to search for Eastern aesthetic support for saving the Swedish social dream of a mixed economy, even though the postmodern condition already dominated the situation. Time had run out for bipolar modernity.

In the early 1980s, the Social Democrat strategy for incorporating the economy in the labor union met with fierce resistance, and populist capitalism struck back. Widespread direct union investment in companies underwritten by the pension-fund—a clever scheme concocted by the Swedish Social Democrat strategist and ex-Berlin economist Rudolf Meidner—was stopped by violent mass protests orchestrated by the Swedish employers' confederation. Pension fund investment, argued the opposition, should be carried out over the stock exchange. Instead of cementing the power of unions by making them into collective industrial owners, the capital markets should be deregulated and opened up to individual ownership.

The frieze of Pergamon, which plays a central role in Weiss's argument, was on display in East Berlin. Since the city was a guarded island offering a suitably stable Socialist environment, the location was judged ideal for planning the last desperate cultural resistance against the neoliberal attack on the Swedish model. The move, however, came too late, because European consumer capitalism and its financial markets were now as popular as unions had been when a majority still identified themselves as workers. During a short period in the early 1980s when the Social Democrats lost government power, the opposition cleverly rushed the deregulation of capital markets and sped up tax reforms so that individual stock investment became very attractive. To counter union power, corporations were encouraged to pay their employees with currency they could mint themselves: shares and stock options. As the shareholder perspective spread, the overall idea of what economy and management were about also changed dramatically.[5] Marketing replaced work organization in the common conception of how the wealth of the nation was made. Production was something managers outsourced abroad while they made money by pleasing shareholders in financial markets. In retrospect, Swedish conservatives pride themselves on being far more effective than their political model, Margaret Thatcher. Swedish Social Democrats were lost in political space until Tony Blair proposed his third way as a social sculpture alternative to that of the iron lady.

A sign presaging this new era of consumers and markets manifested in Stockholm when its Stadsteatern moved from the home of union-led economics, the People's House, to the former house of the Swedish Parliament on Sergels Torg, right in the financial center of downtown Stockholm. In the mid-1980s, Swedish Prime Minister Olof Palme was assassinated on a Stockholm street as he was leaving a theater showing a Suzanne Osten movie. By the end of the 1980s, Osten, the cultural *pasionara* of old workers' Sweden, found herself in Palme's office, commenting with bitterness about the world after the fall of the Berlin Wall: "Today only efficiency and performance count in the public sector. Humanism is enfeebled."[6]

In the midst of this east and west turmoil, I was assigned to find out how a playhouse called the Volksbühne was coping with this confusing postmodern condition. On the recommendation of dramaturge Ohlsson in Stockholm, I arrived full of curiosity and anxious to explore a Schillerian Schwung in a contemporary Berlin version. What a physical feeling to bike through Brandenburger Tor up the Unter den Linden Avenue and pass by Hegel's old Berlin University, where Schopenhauer and Schelling once tried to popularize aesthetics, presaging the breakdown of the grand narratives.

How exciting as well to discover that the media success of the Volksbühne originated in their staging of *Die Räuber,* written by Freddy Schiller himself. Directed by Frank Castorf, the Schillerian robbers were cast as homeless tramps and squatters. It was a steaming Dionysian performance, a sweaty intercourse between the tattered bandits coming from the back stage and the front stage, a volk audience made up mostly of equally ragged youngsters spending their few marks on theater instead of beer, the Tresor, or some other techno club. The Schiller show was an organic experience with material qualities similar to a social sculpture by Beuys. This theatrical postmodern performance could have been inspired by flux firm shows in art spaces.

Castorf's production was packaged in Bert Neumann's expressionistic set design. He sculpted the set as if it were an aquarium or terrarium, or maybe even a subsidiary of Fish Labor, the coolest Berlin bar of that time. On stage sat an open cubist box with a sloping floor from which actors, props, and various fluids dribbled down on the audience during the show. The steep, soapy proscenium actually slid actors down to the audience. No division existed between back stage and front stage; in postmod performance, Antoine's fourth wall had indeed fallen. The frontstage audience, abused by Diaghilev as a narcissistic mirror, had dissolved, and backstage offered little shelter for a Stanislavskian cocooning company. Back and front seemed as blurred as east and west.

The Berlin Volksbühne was a place where art balanced on the thin edge of the in between; Nietzsche would have christened this art firm Dionysus Inc., with the *Räuber* performance stirring up Schillerian sludge from the very bottom of the German aesthetic pond. Not only metaphysics but also scattered elements of local art history were cleverly recycled in Castorf's postmod performances. In 1926, Erwin Piscator directed his avant-garde production of *Die Räuber* on the very same stage. Across the square from the Volksbühne, redesigned by Neumann in expressionist style, lay the Babylon Cinema, where Fritz Lang's masterpiece *Metropolis* once had its premiere.

In the archives of the theater, I later stumbled on an old picture of Traugott Müller's 1926 scenery for Piscator and immediately recognized Neumann's box. Now it was Castorf who scandalized the cultivated critics with his antiliterary theater. Critics in 1993 asked him, as their grandparents had asked Piscator in 1926, "Wo bleibt . . . das Wort?"[7] Piscator had already directed Schiller's text as a polyphonic piece sung by actors dressed in modern driving coats and long trousers. Now young people in Berlin applauded Castorf's rocked-up performance as Berlin leftist dadaists once appreciated Piscator's show. They all stamped their feet to the Rythmus and its Tempo an sich.[8]

Postmodern performance does not use art in a traditional academic fashion. Castorf's success hardly depended on historical footnoting, since nobody in his audience had the slightest clue who Schiller, Piscator, or Traugott Müller were. What made this performance cool was not its relation to something old and dated. For an intensive moment of magic, Castorf made it schwung toward an absolute summoning of streams of immanent objects and metaphysical mirrors. Castorf's aesthetic management developed the Schopenhauerian business of being into a Beuysian of becoming, updating the old Schwung of Antoine, Lugné, Stanislavski, and Diaghilev to after-the-wall performance.

Shortly after the wall fell, Castorf, then only a guest director at the Volksbühne, produced Paul Zech's play about Rimbaud, *Das truckene Schiff*. His staging of the play, typically placed in the same location by Piscator in 1926, was derived from Chabrol's films and the silent classic *Dr. Jekyll and Mr. Hyde*.[9] Although Castorf hides his references to theatrical art, he is overtly informative when it come to the contemporary sources for raw materials.

Instead of sampling from texts as Antoine did, or paintings as Lugné did, Castorf fishes from multimedia reservoirs of movies and music. Diaghilev would visit the museum, but Castorf switches on his television set or goes to the movies. Stanislavski would read plays; Castorf plays records or attends rock concerts. His interviews—and he confesses to spending more than half of his working time being interviewed by the media—are full of film references from the 1970s, from Stallone's *Rocky* to Kubrick's *A Clockwork Orange*. Before 1989, he was a typical East German film club freak, fed up with all the politically correct films imported to the DDR from the Soviet Union and Sweden. Although he preferred forbidden movies, he still admits that the 1970s movie *Picasso's Adventures* by Swedish comics Hasse and Tage is one of his favorites.

Antoine successfully launched forbidden plays in his private theater club. Castorf samples from once-forbidden cinematic imagery matched with equally censored music once smuggled back to Germany from Hungary by young GDR rebels dressed in parkas and Wrangler jeans. The young people were good at spotting Western decadent consumer banality amid Eastern totalitarianism, and that is how Castorf cultivated his taste for trash.

After 1789, David's paintings and books were carried in the processions of Parisian street performances. The early modern avant-garde used texts and images to cook up art that worked. After 1989, Castorf concocted his Berlin homebrew from the second-hand avant-garde of Nietzsche, Magritte, Ernst, Luis Buñuel, Kurt Schwitters, the Animals, the Rolling Stones, Jimi Hendrix, Federico Fellini, Andriej Tarkowski, Steppenwolf, and Samuel Beckett, but instead of putting static texts and images in motion as avant-garde entrepreneurs did, he arrested the mediatic flow in immediate images. Movies are frozen into stills, stereo albums deconstructed into singles and loops. He explains his postmodern performance: "I am looking for a certain type of continuity and discontinuity in people's behavior. . . . Every situation is like a single-song 45rpm record, isolated in itself, and yet still just an extract of the whole LP. . . . I would like to see the development of an apparatus of theatrical performance with linguistic sensuality and power analogous to the cinematic techniques of editing and cutting motion pictures."[10]

When I was part of Castorf's audience, I felt Joseph Beuys had put it right; this was really art extended to the atmosphere of a rock concert. Thrash techno kids and grunge guys poured out from the old shabby paneled Stalinist auditorium into the foyer once restored with marble recycled from

Hitler's Reich Chancellery. The house smells of beer and salami. In the ticket hall, a flickering screen shows a nonstop cycle of the Volksbühne's latest rock video, a black-and-white clip in between Jackson Pollock's splatter and Eisenstein's *Potemkin*. In the darkness outside, the fires are still burning in the shantytown oil drums of the homeless who are demonstrating against the evictions taking place in Prenzlauer Berg, Volksbühne's gentrified neighborhood. We are far from the black box avant-garde stage and the whitewashed museum cube of the abstract art space. Extended art, sucking aesthetic energy from roots buried deeply in old avant-garde, is embedded in a concrete material context.

The evolution of such postmodern performance makes an interesting story. According to sources, it all began in 1990 when Castorf was asked to direct *Die Räuber*. A scant two years later, he was famous as Germany's most accomplished aesthetic energizer; his performances extended not only into the frontstage auditorium but into Rosa Luxemburg square, the Scheunenviertel block, and all of unified Berlin outside his playhouse. Art merchandising was formulated using carefully selected materials and design. In the small pubs in Prenzlauer Berg, people were lighting their cigarettes with old-fashioned Volksbühne matches that were made of uniform brown DDR cardboard and lead-printed in old-fashioned fonts. Creating this packaging was a challenge, since printers were then scrapping old machinery and materials and rapidly replacing them with Western design and technology.

*Rothwelsh*, the underground, subversive argot of outlaws in medieval Germany, inspired the logos and posters for Castorf's marketing campaign of *Die Räuber*. Neumann designed it all on his orders and helped enlarge art far beyond stage scenography. As real business does, Neumann actually redefined art marketing as the "extension of what theater is all about, namely, art work."[11] With art in the center, aesthetic energy of the postmodern performance beamed from the inside out.

Although such a development was unheard of, Neumann soon took over the entire advertising budget of the theater. Theatrical periodicals hummed with the news that the Volksbühne, a public, tax-financed institution, was investing the incredible sum of 300,000 marks in marketing. Neumann even established his own advertising agency, LSD, short for Last Second Design. This inside-outside shift, where the atmosphere of the stage was influencing overall communication strategies, met with resistance from some Berlin politicians out of touch with commercial marketing budgets, who thought

Neumann far too expensive. For a brief time, advertising was handled by a regular agency using modern low-cost technology and a style of communication completely out of touch with what Castorf was performing on stage. Luckily, LSD soon regained its Volksbühne contract so that old Honecker flags and red Mayday banners could fly above the house again. By 1993, the Volksbühne was a model of art management, a space of pilgrimage for people eager to experience the postmodern Berlin performance of Beuys's flux vision. Despite its outward appearance of anarchic spontaneity, this making art work all rested on Castorf's conscious managerial strategy.

In March 1991, Castorf declared that he wanted to expand Neumann's *Räuber* scenography to a complete *Konzeptalbum*, a full-blown, site-specific strategy plan, for this old theater on Rosa Luxemburg Platz: "This theatre's only chance is to become engaged and offer underdogs a public space. My strategy can work only if it incarnates itself in this house. Only then could it take on a public key position by embodying a shift in critical thinking. That is the only possible strategy I can envisage for the time being.[12]

Castorf took over a Volksbühne in deep crisis. After the fall of the wall on November 9, 1989, there were fourteen public theaters in united Berlin, not counting private theaters and independent theatrical groups. In April 1991, the well-known critic Ivan Nagel quickly commissioned a report for the Berlin Senate, in which he recommended in plain language that state finances be made available to save all Berlin theaters, an impressive aesthetic investment in theatrical performances for the future capital of the German Federation. Nagel the critic, who had the full support of the local government, thus turned into a strategy consultant and curator for the cultural landscape of Berlin theaters. He suggested that each stage be differentiated so that it might make art work by a division of specialized aesthetic services offered to reshape a new Berlin. West German politicians were postmodern enough to assign to art the Kantian duty of reunifying the public space of European democracy.

At that time, Mayor Momper indeed needed help from all corners in unifying "Ossies" and "Wessies" in his enlarged city, which was soon to become the metropolis of the FRG. Overnight Berlin became a life-sized studio for socially sculpting a new world. Beuys, who had his last grand installation right next to the wall, would have recognized the situation as a giant social sculpture. Christo Javacheff's twenty-five-year-old project for wrapping the Berlin Reichstag was suddenly put on top of the postmodern political agenda. Overnight Berlin became the world's hottest building site. Not only architects were in demand. The Berlin Senate realized that art was crucial in a Schnitzlerian way as a therapy mirror for East-West schizos just liberated from their political straitjackets. In his new function as a consultant-curator, critic Nagel therefore assigned a site-specific therapeutic task to the art performed at the Volksbühne. The architectural presence of its old Berlin building made it ideal for serving as a sociocultural clinic: "The building is strikingly horrible. This is the place where one ought to found a young theater with a desire for aesthetic innovation and political courage. . . . In this monument, one has a unique chance to really make things happen."[13]

Frank Castorf was consciously coached by the city of Berlin into becoming the most suitable candidate for managing this mission. Soon journalists of the new capital would greet "Frankie boy" in mock-Nietzschean terms as a postmodern trash Dionysus:

> At that very moment the ruthless and diabolical Dr. Frankentorf in his Volksbühne laboratory let loose the ghosts of Jünger, Nietzsche, Wagner, and Lenin, uncut by censure and unprotected by safety nets. His mighty show of thunder and lightning caused terror and fear throughout Berlin. Gone was our spleen and depression. Quaking and trembling we fled in terror from the frightening eruption in the midst of our German capital.[14]

Just one year after the birth of Nagel's strategic plan and under the protection of the cultural senator Rollof-Momin, "Dr. Frankentorf" (aka Frank Castorf) became the captain-in-command over what he—in Eisensteinian jargon—marketed to the media as his *Panzerkreuzer vor dem Prenzlauer Berg*.[15] Just as Beuys marketed with the felt hat, Castorf now began marketing his art firm in scandalous interviews to the media and in biographical books, the first of which was already out by 1992.

Not unlike Joseph Beuys, Frank Castorf cast himself as a child of a totalitarian regime. He was born in 1951 to the east of Ulbricht's wall, and his parents still run their little electrical shop a few streets behind his theater. A member of the middle class (described as *petit bourgeois* in the GDR), he enrolled as a theater student at Humboldt University. There in 1976, he produced a thesis on Eugene Ionesco's absurd aesthetics. His first theatrical productions in West Germany appeared late in the spring of 1989.

Castorf would probably have liked to remain in Hegel's old temple as a privileged socialistic scholar with the keys to the aesthetic "poison-cupboard" where all the good books were locked up deep within the library. In Moscow, however, Andropov was applying the thumb screws of censorship. Even researchers found it difficult to acquire the texts of Bakunin or Ernst Jünger, whom Castorf still holds as far more subversive than Lenin.[16] When academic freedom was inhibited, Castorf, in accordance with good old GDR tradition, found refuge backstage in theater. He continued in the German tradition and started out as a dramaturge in distant GDR provinces. He scribbled long Hegelian essays so full of philosophical content that they both bored and confused his poor actors. The Schopenhauer in him had not yet overthrown his Hegelian indoctrination.

Before long, however, he was to discover the market for metaphysics. Matters came to a head one day when young Castorf rushed up onto the stage to show his actors what he really meant. Direct action turned the dramaturge into director, and the action provoked two reactions: he achieved a reputation for wanting to make art work, not just writing about it; and he got sacked. Cocky, smart, and well-versed in the legal system of the GDR, Castorf won a lawsuit against his former state employers.

Although they could not fire him, they instead deported him to the tiny theater in a godforsaken place called Anklam, a place where nobody from Berlin wanted to work. Without any explanation, fourteen days before the premiere of Brecht's juvenile work *Trommeln in der Nacht,* the police arrested one of Castorf's male actors who had been listening to the politically correct Marx. Castorf carried on calmly and used one of his favorite actresses, Silvia Rieger, in the role instead.

Then, without warning, the director of the Anklam theatre, in conjunction with the local commissars of the Communist Party, decided that the dress rehearsal would be closed to the public. The order came too late, however; the theater was already packed with Frank's friends and colleagues. In addition, this was a group of seasoned theatergoers who habitually made journeys from Berlin to dress rehearsals throughout the province. In East Germany, a dress rehearsal was the only chance to see an uncensored production, to get a glimpse of art at work, because if censors deemed the performance not to be *Werktrau* (if the staged version deviated from the approved written text) they would immediately stop further performances. The atmosphere in GDR dress rehearsals was like that in Antoine's and Lugné's private theater clubs. They were loopholes for escape from the political control of art.

Now, in Anklam, all of Frank's Berlin friends had arrived, eager to watch what this clever fellow would add between the written lines. Refused entrance, they enthusiastically provided Frank's biography with its first good scandal, loudly shouting: "Out with artists and Jews—in Germany we've heard this before."[17]

Scandal is Castorf's favorite kind of art extension; it is art provoking public reaction in a way similar to how young Piscator made art work. That night in little Anklam, however, the auditorium was cleared, party bosses settled down in their seats, and the play was ordered to begin. The actors wanted to quit, but Castorf, again perfectly aware of the legal restrictions for managerial action, persuaded them not to give the bureaucrats an obvious reason to sack them all.

The traditional disciplinary hearing followed the next day. "But dear Herr Castorf, you must realize that a common audience never will grasp your ingenious production," said the local GDR bosses. They were using the socialist version of a classic argument that so frequently blocks Western corporate innovators wishing to launch a product for which the market is deemed unripe by conservative CEOs. In theory, the GDR management flattered Castorf's art but postponed indefinitely its working in practice. Once again, Castorf prided himself on his grasp of the law in this worker's state; in return, he negotiated carte blanche for staging a final production in Anklam. It was Ibsen's *A Doll's House,* one of his favorites.

After 1989, Castorf never again prided himself on being a heroic, resistant type, since he believed that dissidents or martyrs never get a chance to make art work. Castorf still seems proud of how he made art work in the Communist state by being pragmatic, smart, and even clever. His cool cynicism about Communism's dull banality is clear in a reflection: "It wasn't that rotten, the time in Anklam and after. I felt sort of alive, I was putting on my fight and that was perfectly OK. To get the same feeling today, we have to put up straw men. . . ."[18]

The GDR, like most communities under totalitarian regimes, had its private clubs, associations, and underground coteries conscious and proud of their undertaking and of the fact that these efforts left a trail in the Stasi files often thicker than they would have earned in regular free-world art critique. Young people had ample time to play avant-garde games, thanks to the state nurseries that liberated from bad conscience Frank Castorf in East Germany and Suzanne Osten in Socialist Sweden and enabled them to turn the theater into their real home. Nor was the wall any real problem to Castorf. Dr. Frankentorf believed that totalitarian states become a banal experience from the inside. The pale city of Berlin, stinking of brown coal, was a neorealistic scene, an expressionistic reptile terrarium for his youthful aesthetic day-dreaming. After the wall fell and the commercial culture flooded through the Brandenburg Gate, Castorf flipped from being a Hegelian hippie to assuming the practice of an aesthetic psychoanalyst.

Frank Castorf felt his performances put the new Germany on his couch, with theater as therapy for the postmodern condition:

> East Germany became a state for farmers and workers. In the Federal Republic, the individual was king, incarnated as a cultural consumer. No longer did happiness imply a lifetime of steady employment—bliss came through shopping! Before the Wall came down, if things went wrong, there was an overall industrial organization to blame. Now people were supposed to self-manage. If things went wrong in the Federal Republic, the only one to blame was you yourself. Now after 1989 there were no stupid bureaucrats or ridiculous state officials to use as scapegoats. The Ossies found themselves in a postmodern vacuum, and that was the root of their desperate condition. They were unprepared for any of this. From the inside, the totalitarian GDR had only been a banal, boring drag, with a dash of repressive thrill now and then. Only laziness and alcoholism remained as therapies for individual failure.[19]

The Wessies did not expect the Ossies to shift overnight from Hegelian Marxism to liberal capitalism, however. The condition was more complex than that, since it was postmodern. Now no one could build an existence on ideology, and life had to find stability in between. This was a situation that Ossies were completely unprepared to face. At the most, says Castorf, the GDR was good at awakening a raw aggression that had been building up muscles for the real fight when the wall came down and hard market competition took off. Talking of the Communist bureaucrats, Castorf asserts with a sleepy yawn what Heidegger might have asserted about the Nazis had he wanted to: "No, I really can't be made to hate those petit-bourgeois. They were like our garden gnomes. I laughed at them, actually in a warm friendly way. They certainly weren't the super monsters who pretend they were much more heroic than they really ever needed to be."[20]

Castorf concluded that there was a desperate need for helping people cope with their postmodern condition. Young Castorf learned the tricks of how to make art do social work from a pack of shaggy lone wolves hunting the cultural sewers of old Berlin. They had helped citizens survive the boredom of dictatorship; now it was art that should help them maintain their sanity in postmodernity. To make art work, Castorf applied the aesthetic education he got from the grand master who had roamed down the banal totalitarian dirt of East Berlin. He still looks up to that pioneer of postmodern art, "Heiner Müller, who was my friend but whom I never asked for help. He was a fuse, a safety valve against censorship. His undoubtedly great literary talent, carefully designed and self-made, his competence and privilege to transgress boundaries, his cynical attitude toward both systems—this was a grandiose attitude under the decline of that Roman Empire and its petit-bourgeois saga of GDR."[21]

## Cases of Aesthetic Management

### Müller Performing Matter

For all those in the West after 1968 who bartered Schopenhauerian philosophy for political ideology, the Hegelian hangover after 1989 was often painful. As one of my West Berlin friends commented, "On the other side of the wall, they knew everything about us while fooling us completely by their Stasi propaganda."

At the same time, the Ossies felt let down by Western market democracy. Overnight it had reduced them from proud workers to poor unemployed consumers. To avoid this, Heiner Müller (1929–1995) recommended vaccination with a dose of cynicism. He snickered at the naïveté of blue-eyed Communist idealists such as Peter Weiss, who paid obeisance to the GDR from cozy exile in Sweden without even getting paid off by Stasi for his system support. To him, postmodernity was an old condition; he never believed in grand ideological narratives.

Müller knew what he was talking about. As a youth, he was an obedient journalist well remunerated by the state he served to keep telling its Marxist story. A GDR poet always had to put up with a bit of prostitution. When later accused (not entirely unjustifiably) of collaboration, corruption, and informing, Müller responded, "Who am I to have the right of remaining clean in a dirty world?"[22]

No artist born under totalitarianism ignored the unholy alliance between art and consultancy. Making art had its price, and completely uncompromising artists could never survive. Unlike the wealthy Schopenhauer or the tenured state professor Beuys, art managers such as Castorf and Müller could not afford to be complete idealists. What made them into artists was not so much their ideals, however, as their taste for anarchistic, sublime adventure, perhaps the same type of desire for good green grazing that attracted clever fat rabbits to gambol by the Berlin Wall and risk their lives in the no-man's land between the shadow of watchtowers. Some claimed Müller belonged to a subversive sect of murderers.[23] Others remember him as a Dracula-like predator ready to hunt down anything that might feed his hunger for new art materials. Regardless of these impressions, Müller did have some concrete insights. First, he knew how to break out of the grand Eastern narrative and then how to manage postmodernity, an age when innocence and pure art were forever gone.

Müller's career began in the 1950s, a time when the art of the GDR was firmly incorporated in the economic apparatus of the East German state. Art at the Volksbühne and at the Stockholm Stadsteatern was mainly legitimized as labor union culture distantly derived from the grand Hegelian narrative. As a good social realist, Müller knew his job was to make art work to labor union order. His early plays told stories based on documentation from Berlin building sites or the production lines of the Siemens factory. Although Müller's journalist wife did fieldwork and quasi-sociological research, her husband wrapped up the grand narrative in poetical packaging.

Later, Western theater, such as Osten's Stockholm firm, was going to copy this Stalinist dramaturgy. Today, after the fall of the wall, management consultants are purchasing similar custom-made plays that serve as instruments of organizational change in capitalist corporations. One could call Müller a Communist playwright-consultant for the management of human resources in GDR's state industry. The difference between his job and that of the capitalist management consultant is slight, a fact Müller admitted after 1989. Consultants cement their authority by quasi-scientific method. Müller used the same tricks and arranged "seminars for workers" and set up "reference groups" to guarantee the authenticity of the epic.

So far, so good, one might conclude, but Heiner Müller did have a serious problem. Although he worked hard to do the same professional storytelling job for the Communist regime that any advertiser or consultant would do for capitalist clients, his texts always turned into poetry. It was as if the texts themselves turned to art, no matter what. Müller sensed how plays by themselves broke out of the Stalinist templates. They burst the limits of social realism and ended up as poetical documentaries about the windswept lumpenproletariat inhabiting the chaotic workplaces of an economic tragedy.

His first success, the play *Lohndrucker,* was to be followed in 1961 by *Die Umsiedlerin,* but the censors stopped it after the dress rehearsal. Müller soberly concluded that the first play was probably allowed as a secret weapon in some unfathomable political-economic power struggle. Had it been a book, it would never have been printed. For Müller, like Antoine, theater afforded a freedom that literature hardly ever enjoyed; in the GDR, as is seen in the case of Castorf, a dramaturge had the possibility of publicizing his texts on stage without having to pass the strict censorship of books and articles. In addition, Müller had enough protection and boyish charm to sneak through the controls imposed by formal evaluations.

After the success of *Lohndrucker,* Müller spent two years developing the performance of *Die Umsiedlerin,* which was actually prepared in a Communist management college. The theme was mismanagement in a planned economy. When Müller's black humor appealed to the laughing audience during the dress rehearsal, it was immediately banned. His satirical portrait of life on a collective farm was so funny that it was socialistically unsafe. His unintentional play about East German industrial misery got him in real trouble, because it ridiculed the image of the heroic GDR worker he was commissioned to promote. Intuitively, Müller felt that economic reality was already marked by what German sociologist Dirk Baecker in 1994 would term—to the delight of Müller—postheroic management.[24] Thus did something beyond his rotten, corrupt, and opportunistic character simply compel young Heiner to turn his back on totalitarian heroic propaganda narration. At least, this is how he himself explained the awkward situation that Kant or Schelling would have immediately identified as his stroke of genius.

Because the regime invested in him, they could not let him go easily. His good Communist comrades encouraged him to change his style. They had had enough trouble with old Brecht, they said, not to need another "eastern Beckett."[25] During the ensuing Kafkaesque process, Hans Eisler, a composer who had collaborated with Brecht, suggested paternally that Müller "ought to be happy to live in a state where art is taken so seriously."

Müller was then asked to deliver a standard, self-critical, apologetic confession. As a special privilege, Helene Weigel, Brecht's widow, sat him down at her husband's old desk in the Schiffbauerdamm theater and proceeded to dictate his letter of apology to the Party in the very room where actresses had prostrated themselves before their beloved Brecht. Weigel knew the required rhetoric, and in the service of the Party she soon stripped another author bare. No explanations, no excuses. The corporation demanded flesh. Pull your trousers down and shit out your confession. That's the price for making art work, Müller seems to think in his unsentimental conclusion, making a hidden reference to Brecht: "To me creative writing was more important than moral. . . . I never considered prison nor exile an alternative. My life was that of an author, more precisely as a playwright, and plays only exist in performance . . . then I didn't feel the least ashamed."[26]

How quickly it was over and done with! Once the apology was accepted, the Party pushed Müller into a corner as a dramaturge in the Volksbühne, Castorf's future house. Müller knuckled down, wrote, and then plotted and negotiated to get his work performed.

Totalitarianism taught Müller a good lesson, one that made him work in a new way. He knew that he was weak, easily corrupted, and eager to please as an artist. He also realized that his art, if protected from the all-too-human artist, had a purity and poetry untouchable and incorruptible by cognition. The man Müller might be a cigar-smoking drunkard, but Müller art had a strange aesthetic eroticism elevated beyond reach of bodily lust and low sexuality. In his memoirs he writes that "as soon as I begin to take notes they turn into artifacts. Speaking and writing are definitely two different things. When you write, the text takes over management. . . . Then you come to the point where you are forced to accept the split between art and life."[27]

In a nutshell, this is Müller's definition of how to make art perform in a postmodern condition. Art, not the artist, has to provide its own self-management; in order to discern the right management, Müller started to write in a duetlike way, where voice and body perform a liberating dialectic. This dualism between decoupled body and soul would wash off the ugly stamp of political intentionality that could easily infect art with totalitarianism. It was as if Müller wished to reestablish a Schillerian matter-form polarity in between which he would find the creative flux of what he called textual art. Müller brought poetry back to the stage by writing texts so lyrical that they seemed to defy practical performance. They were texts without roles; the actors' sounding bodies were lobotomized, eliminating clever cognitive communication. Even in stage directions, Müller avoids instrumental instructions and instead offers poetic images, such as "the university of the dead" or "limitless space," to indicate what atmospheres he wants his audience to share in the performance.

In this strange postmodern way, Müller skillfully balanced on the wall, aesthetically playing out form and matter to find a free space for art. In 1968, the year of student revolt, Müller's work was performed in Munich; when the old Stalinists attacked him, he was defended in headlines in the West German press. When he was forbidden to print a portrait of the Stasi-sponsored terrorist Ulrike Meinhof on his book cover, he retaliated by declining the publication offer by Brecht's West German publisher Suhrkamp. After accepting literary prizes in the West, he made icy comments that helped to thaw his colleagues in the East, and his views on self-writing texts became steadily better suited to the theater in the West. He also attracted new critics far better than Party censors such as Eisler. Philosophers began throwing light on his strategy of writing. Lyotard's essay, Derrida's deconstructionism, Foucault's poststructuralism, as well as his own friend Paul Virilio's Nietzscheanism became new intellectual trends that in the 1980s indexed Müller intellectually to a postmodern audience sick and tired of the ready-made Marxian epic. In the East, art was struggling to escape totalitarianism at the same time that Western artists were busy saving the aesthetic play by tricking capitalist commercial banality.

## Wilson Performing Form

To escape the carnage of World War I, Marcel Duchamp immigrated to the United States, exporting with him his *fin-de-siècle* pun, dada, which—almost three generations later—resurfaced in Europe as an avant-garde cult. In the United States, the term was recycled and repackaged philosophically to better suit a postmodern market for Beuysian extended art. Composer John Cage, one of the flux artists who inspired Beuys and whose wife had been Duchamp's assistant, contended that American Zen improved Duchamp's art into a metaphysical business of being: "Nowadays Dada has a space, an emptiness that it previously lacked."[28]

A space, however, needs places to happen, and in search of these concrete sites the American version of dada turned to performing. Theatricalization of art was not a new way to make it work, however. Art in books or paintings had long used performance to work; since David, artists have used theater as much as theater uses art. In 1909, for instance, Oskar Kokoschka got tired of painting pictures, and in his play *Mörder, Hoffnung der Frauen* he painted the actors to look like the natives in the Vienna Museum für Völkerkunde, so that the audience could see the nerves on their skin.[29] In collaboration with dancers, actors, and the composer Paul Hindemith, Kokoschka wanted performance to create an immediate and absolute experience that he missed in traditional painting.

The painter and graphic designer Schwitters resorted to theater to present the constructivist version of dada that he rebranded as *Merz*. Under the banner *los vom Dichterwort*,[30] Schwitters wanted to create a theater of direct experiences. Merz was life, and life was immediate and could never be mediated through books or pictures.

Theater was, of course, the only way for Vassily Kandinsky to make his art work as acoustics of color and optics of sound. Kandinsky even tried hard to persuade Stanislavski to stage a production at the Artistic Theatre. In the 1920s, Parisian surrealists shocked their audience by putting new content in conventional context; they simply staged crazy soirées in such respectable concert halls as the Salle Berlioz or the Salle Gaveau.

Using the same recipe, the rich futurist Marinetti paid well for a fine theater that had once been the stage for Lugné and Jarry. The latter cycled off happily after he persuaded Lugné to stage *Ubu Roi* in 1896, and Tristan Tzara returned to his writing after only a ten-week-long happening at the Café Voltaire in Zürich in 1916. Some artists merely sought out the gilded frame of theater to mount a short-lived attack against the bourgeoisie. Others—the true pioneers of what today is called performance art—saw it as a more basic method for making art work.

Historians of performance art show its development as a form of aesthetic education, a modern way to realize Schiller's pedagogy. In the United States, performance developed in education rather than in entertainment, since theater professionals were hardly prepared to try aesthetic experiments as risky as those of Antoine and Lugné. In Europe, performance also had a hard time getting staged; Wagner's *Tannhäuser* fiasco is a case in point. Later, Gropius was but partially able to realize his theatrical architecture, and then only in his own college, Staatliche Bauhaus. By sacking Piscator, the Volksbühne also put an end to performance art and blocked cooperation with Gropius. It was in the Bauhaus school that Kandinsky was able to make his performances, not at the Artistic Theatre in Moscow. Oscar Schlemmer constructed his architectural installation, the House of Pi, and organized mechanical ballets, thanks to the Bauhaus school stage as well. As has so often been the case with modern art, however, it was only when the new world enthusiastically picked up, refined, and repackaged old-world ideas as performance art that it really got going in Europe.

Before reaching theaters, performance art developed as teaching. Josef and Annie Albers started up the performance business as an outgrowth of their employment at Black Mountain College in the United States in 1933. Out of aesthetic pragmatism of the John Dewey kind sprang an American practice of education that turned teachers into art critics and opened the minds of students to aesthetic experience. The American liberal arts tradition of education in rhetoric meant that democracy rested upon the ability of the citizens to express themselves by putting their fellow citizens into enthusiastic, playful Schwung. This made the average American college student and the American university fertile incubators of performance art.

Along with another ex-Bauhäusler, Roger Schawinsky, the Albers conducted their legendary summer course in 1948; it marked the birth of modern performance art. Among the students was John Cage, Beuys's future friend and the gifted young pupil of Kandinsky's old comrade, Arnold Schönberg. The roster also included the painter Willem de Koonig, the architect Buckminster Fuller, the director Arthur Penn, and the dancer Merce Cunningham. Out of after-supper concerts grew what was to become famous as "performances." It was a free way to make art work. Cunningham might, for instance, perform his interpretation of Indian choreography. Cage played a prepared piano full of rubbish in connection with lectures about Erik Satie, whose work *Le Piège de Méduse* was then recreated in another "concert" performance.

At Black Mountain, the content of Satie and Duchamp was made to work in new contexts. To the European sources, Cage and his friends also added an oriental touch by throwing Zen into the performative melting pot. In 1956, it was Cage's turn to run a course on his own at the same New School in New York where Piscator had spent the war teaching with other refugees from Nazi Germany. Among Cage's students were the future fluxus artists George Brecht, Dick Higgins, and Al Hansen, as well as the man who was to diffuse performance under the brand name "happening," Allan Kaprow. Robert Rauschenberg, Claes Oldenburg, Jim Dine, and Jackson Pollock also joined in. They constructed combines, collages, and action paintings and began performing their art as theater to astonished gallery audiences. In remakes of the mechanical ballets of the 1920s created by Fernand Leger, the

Swede Otto G. Carlsund, and Oscar Schlemmer, machines put objects in Schwung in galleries turned into theaters. The painters developed merry and messy Sturm und Drang séances, where the process was everything and the end result was meant more for the garbage can than greedy collectors. The point was to make instant and ephemeral art full of intensity and at the same time escape all conventions of the commercial art trade.

In addition, such transitory performances shared the advantage of abstract art in being incomprehensible for CIA censors tracking down Communism in the arts.[31] In 1959, according to a performance legend, Kaprow sent out his famous invitation to an opening at the Reuben Gallery in New York. The invited audience was given written instructions, turning art consumers into real creators in this original happening, which, according to Kaprow's invitation, "means nothing clearly formulable so far as the artist is concerned."[32]

Just as Beuys would later want to theoretically transcend Duchamp, Cage aspired to more philosophical sophistication than Kaprow. To him, the Zen master Suzuki was what Steiner became to Beuys. Suzuki inspired Cage in a very Eastern Schopenhauerian way to make art work as contemplation of "the nature of Mind and the nature of divine influences."[33] Cage's example inspired the French artist Yves Klein, a judo teacher in Nice and an esoteric Rosicrucian, to expose emptiness by meditating in a Parisian gallery before the opening. Schopenhauerian Schwung survived and grew into flux during its American exile. At the same time in Europe, the leftist Hegelianism in its gray Brechtian guise of Marxist orthodoxy was still blocking a philosophical understanding of aesthetic Schwung. Kaprow was booed in Paris when he wanted to show the Europeans a "happening" in their own dada tradition. European art critics thought Kaprow's performance a romantic, confused, badly organized fiasco that had nothing to do with "theatrical activity or any other kind of creative activity."[34] The critics of performing arts still ignored performance art. The next important European reencounter with its own romantic roots came in 1963, when Beuys invited the fluxians to Düsseldorf. Twenty years later, the process of East-West fusion prepared by Beuys, Cage, and company took a concrete turn, however, when the condition turned postmodern.

In the early 1980s, two gentlemen introduced to each other by no less than Ivan Nagel had a serious talk in a hotel room in Rotterdam. One was American Robert Wilson; the other, Heiner Müller, came from the Soviet

GDR. From that time forward, Wilson from the West began making art work with Müller from the East. Fascinated by his new friend, Wilson exclaimed: "How different we are!" The fact that they were really Schillerian antipodes created Schwung between Wilson, the Texan mise en scène star; and Müller, the East German dramaturgist. Wilson is pragmatic and interested in effect; Müller was more philosophically preoccupied with causes. The German was obsessed with text, but his hermetically cleansed writings gave the American, so passionate about images, a sensation of freedom and empty Zen space. Müller finally found in Wilson someone in theater who did not get bogged down trying to interpret texts and killing them by projecting individual intentions. Wilson never wanted to pin down content in art; he merely tried to "find room for" it by putting it in context.[35]

At one point, Wilson told Müller—the child of totalitarianism—about Wilson's childhood nightmares in which giant toys, market monsters from the shopping malls of banality, attacked him in horrible supermarkets. Wilson was born in a Western commercial world so obtrusive that it forced many sensitive people into autistic inner exile. This banal Disney World of consumption seemed a totalitarian nightmare from the inside out. Since the 1960s, Wilson had used performance as a kind of aesthetic therapy to resuscitate freedom and win back mental space from commercial colonization. In so doing, he was as successful as any good manager. A beautiful fish in the New York avant-garde bowl, Wilson was canonized as a true surrealist by the poet Louis Aragon, André Breton's friend. When the serious wordsmith from the East found the gay imagist from the West, he discovered more than a great postmodern performer. In Wilson, Müller also encountered a highly professional aesthetic energizer. Wilson, in addition to university degrees in design and architecture, also held an MBA, though his art management has little in common with the storytelling for corporate culture that is termed the "management of meaning."

In 1969, Wilson made his breakthrough at New York's Brooklyn Academy of Music with a performance entitled *The Life and Times of Sigmund Freud.* Following this was a long series of strangely beautiful performances unfit for either Broadway commercialism or off-Broadway avant-garde; they were neither the stuff for long-running immediate success nor especially politically engaged. *Deafman Glance* in 1970 was based on his almost therapeutic friendship with a deaf mute he had adopted. A performance of *Ka Mountain and GUARDenia Terrace* was on the playbill of an

Iranian avant-garde festival in Shiraz; the performance lasted 268 hours. This was followed in 1974 by *A Letter from Queen Victoria*, and in 1976 by *Einstein on the Beach*. Wilson's description of his art echoes both Lugné's symbolism and Kandinsky's rhetoric of optical acoustic: "You don't have to think about the story, because there isn't any. You don't have to listen to the words, because the words don't mean anything. You just enjoy the scenery, the architectural arrangements in time and space, the music, the feelings they all evoke. Listen to the pictures."[36]

Heiner Müller fought for life space for art squeezed by the good intentions that paved the way of the totalitarian GDR. In an industrial society where the slogan "time is money" was a commonality, Robert Wilson became a marketing expert of aesthetic timing. Whereas the entire media world sped up the flux of sound and image, Wilson slowed action down to arrest existence in Zenlike contemplation. Performances such as *Deafman Glance* were not only a strange product of this temporal Zen alchemy; Wilson also sensed the right moment to market art at home and for export. The premiere was at the Brooklyn Academy of Music in 1970, but it was in Espace Pierre Cardin in Paris a year later that New York art critic Susan Sontag discovered Wilson.[37] For her it was a long-expected gift, similar to when André Antoine finally made naturalistic texts and impressionist pictures work in his Montmartre theater.

In an open letter to his long-deceased colleague Breton, Louis Aragon, the doyen of the avant-garde, canonized Wilson alongside Father Breton in his hyped heaven of surrealism. To Aragon, who was completely out of fashion with politicized Parisian students of 1968, Wilson incarnated a prodigal son returning to aesthetics from the anaesthetic chill of social realism. Things thereafter seemed to move fast for Wilson. He received an invitation from Farah Diba Pahlavi to perform at the Shah of Iran's avant-garde festival at Shiraz, and today Wilson is a global expert in postmodern performance.

After initially performing in his Manhattan loft, Wilson now presents his projects in European theater festivals, houses of culture, state opera houses, and civic theaters. Every performance makes art work as the source of a manifold cascade of media images and designed objects. Long before art became recycled by commercial advertising and industrial product design, Wilson practiced his kind of art merchandising. An average Wilson year would see about ten art exhibitions, a number of video productions, and several design exhibitions derived from stage performances. Wilson manages installations for museums, exhibits scenery sketches in galleries, puts props and settings on show in design museums, and produces videos for television channels such as *Arte* and Channel 7 in France. He teams up with rock stars such as Tom Waits and Lou Reed and produces interior design for Armani shops (as well as a documentary on Giorgio Armani's life). He also designed the Armani show for the Guggenheim Museum. He designed the event opening Mitterand's new Bastille opera on the day of the bicentenary of the French Revolution. While European technicians and scientists were brain-drained to the United States, Wilson found a financial foothold on the European market at a time when American national endowment money for the arts was growing scarce. The postmodern condition prepared the metaphysical market for his performances.

The fact that Wilson is a frequent guest director on the established stages of Salzburg, Vienna, Berlin, Hamburg, Venice, and Paris makes him more an heir to Diaghilev than a son to Breton. He replaced Coco Chanel with Giorgio Armani and is as close to modern dance as Diaghilev was to avant-garde choreography. Waits and Reed are his Picasso and Braque, with Philip Glass playing the part of Stravinsky. Fine art, fashion, media material, popular music, television commercials—nothing escapes his voracious postmodern appetite for new performance materials.

When we once met in the south of France, Wilson asked me to drive him to some friends who were collecting beautiful Danish design. On the way, we stopped at the Matisse Chapel in Vence, where he fell into a trance, focusing especially on its simple chairs. I almost physically felt the intensity with which he observed those objects. Had Massine felt the same way when Diaghilev put him in front of a Renaissance painting in Florence? A friend of mine later spent an afternoon with Wilson in September 2000 in Berlin. They met in a commercial gallery for oriental art, where Wilson carefully scrutinized Chinese sculptures as if he wanted to physically experience the delicate poses and gestures of the statues. After dropping the names of some of the collectors he was personally acquainted with, he kindly asked the dealer to fax illustrated quotations for some of the objects to his Long Island office. His assistant then drove him to the Berlin Guggenheim, where a special private visit was hastily improvised. The next stop was the Vitra Design museum and finally a chat with a dealer in Bauhaus ceramics. During this tour, which took less than two hours, Wilson studied not only artwork but also the layout and architecture of all the art spaces with an impressive accuracy and expertise. Not a detail seemed to escape him. This man was completely clear about what he wanted and how he was going to perform postmodern compilations of items from his private collections—items as heterogeneous as Chinese sculptures, Bauhaus ceramics, or Danish designer chairs. When I went to see his magnificent staging of Wagner's *Rheingold* in Zürich, the influence from his collected statues was not hard to recognize. Wilson had managed his old art work anew.

Wilson's equally Diaghilevian talent for quickly integrating brand new art into his postmodern performances impressed Heiner Müller. In strict managerial terms, Wilson actually reduced the lead time between art and its postmodern performance in a theatrical business where usually "innovations in the visual arts arrive only after extremely lengthy delays. He has reduced this process considerably. In a normal theatrical enterprise, innovations arrive only after they have become wallpaper patterns."[38]

No wonder Müller became fascinated with Wilson, who seemed as talented as he himself was in negotiating advantages for art out of a hostile context. Müller noted that Wilson made art work as a true risk-taking entrepreneur would. During theater rehearsals, Wilson was anxious to find expressions to balance his performances in very Schillerian fashion: neither too sweet nor too obvious. As a child of market capitalism, he respected the art customer. Watching Wilson at work, Müller found someone as afraid of failure and as obsessed with market success as any manager.

Müller the Marxist also admired Wilson's innovative use of audiovisual techniques originally developed for show biz or commercial event marketing. Wilson uses extremely advanced and sophisticated lighting effects for painting his scenery. He has his client/theater pay for an entire technical crew of some fifteen people, whom he can pick for his project according to contract. As part of the agreement, setting and stage props crafted in the theater workshops following Wilson's design belong to him after the stipulated run in the theater. In addition, his deals include costs for special workshops at his Long Island Watermill Center. It is indeed hard to find loopholes in a typical Robert Wilson contract.

Heiner Müller discovered a Texan cowboy-manager as obsessed with the freedom of art as he himself was. Individual intentions were like inalienable human rights to Wilson, who refused ready-made interpretations of his work with his mantra "no one, no one, no one can direct our feelings." The art of Müller and of Wilson remains empty spaces, mirrors free from what Pierre

Legendre called *le plein industriel*. In Müller's case, the industrial GDR was full of moralistic Marxism aimed at making people produce. Wilson's American industrialism constantly targeted consumers with media messages to trigger buying decisions. "Keeping the mirror clean" made both opt for a hard art management of a formal and normative kind, one which would leave no doubt about its arbitrary artificiality. They wanted to stall the soft psychological discipline legitimized by fuzzy allusions to a natural order that made individuals easy prey for both totalitarianism and banality.

In his global headquarters on Long Island, Robert Wilson manages to run several parallel performance projects by sampling videotaped rehearsals from all over the world. His performances are prepared in two periods. During the first five weeks, he gives only physical choreographic instructions to actors (move to the left, right, go slow, fast, relax the tension, come straight toward me, to the left, to the right, around tree two, to the porch, stop). All this is mute, and only in the second period are sound and light added and adjusted. Between the first and second round of rehearsals, the actors are left to practice individually with the videotaped documentation of the mute version. The same tapes are used as materials in Wilson's Watermill workshop, where the performance, like the prototype of a new car model, gets its final design. Wilson really manages his art as a high-tech Max Reinhardt would, flying in only for the final cut of what his assistants have prepared on location.

Such rational management enables several parallel productions. For instance, Wilson scheduled diverse projects for 2001: Bilbao Guggenheim, Aïda, Aventis, Barbican, Dior, Frosch, Galigo, St. Francis, Copenhagen, and Vox Humana. From the legendary Thursday evenings at Wilson's Soho loft in the early 1970s grew a postmodern performance studio, not only marketing each performance but also handling finance by raising funds from some one hundred world sponsors from the United States, France, and Germany.

Like clients in private banks and main shareholders of corporations, each donor must be given special care, be it someone who "gives millions to the homeless," is "a husband of a big corporation," "son of a multimillionaire art patron," "married to a media conglomerate," "girlfriend of a big-shot art lover," "cousin of a millionaire," "black friend of a famous singer," "danced with Balanchine for years," or close to "big-money X foundation." In this respect, R. Wilson does even better than R. Wagner, because his contracts include special clauses for mention in the program and free seats on opening night for main donors contributing an average of $100,000 each. In addition, Wilson also holds onto about 250 minor donors, each of whom contributes around $10,000 for student scholarships to Watermill Center workshops. It is easy to understand how Müller, who made his art work under harsh totalitarian conditions, suggested that Wilson was able to subversively protect art from the overwhelming forces of banality through managing professionally in an industrial style. The only chance for art to survive is to become allied to and make use of the forces of industrialization while preserving its shoots of fantasy, creativity, and intuition. This is the real challenge. In that respect, Wilson is extremely important, since he has introduced a wholly new method of production.[39]

With the second millennium upon us, widespread consciousness of the breakdown of the legitimacy of modern discourse made the markets for Müller and Wilson, who were preparing the ground for postmodern performance. Frank Castorf at the Volksbühne serves as an ideal management case.

## Castorf's Media-Consumption Metaphysics

### Berliner Boxer

Once Frank Castorf became the director of the Volksbühne, he began a fierce fight to conquer his own in-between aesthetic territory. He was boxing his way in the rubble between crumbling modern dualisms: commerce and culture, East and West, capitalism and communism, even Müller and Wilson. In gratitude to Müller, Castorf declared he could not imagine any burnt-out, sixty-year-old father figure having anything to say to a young after-the-wall audience's *Daseinsgefühl*.[40] Castorf then turned in the opposite direction and threw an equally hard blow at "the rarefied aesthetics of Robert Wilson."[41]

Castorf obviously wanted to conquer and defend a position in between the two old champions. When Senator Rolof-Momin sounded the financial gong, Castorf had two Volksbühne directing victories to his record in preparation for this title match; Eastern totalitarianism had taught him that "theater is like boxing; you must never let them know where you're going to hit."[42] Castorf now rephrased his Nietzschean will to postmodern power in the Western jargon of heavyweight contenders: "I had just seen *Rocky I*," he relates, "and totally identified with the Italian kid from the slaughterhouse who struggled to get his first match—I felt it was the same for me."[43]

Postmodernity is about sampling and fusing high and low, old and new, so Castorf began his career by recycling an old German avant-garde tradition. More than fifty years earlier, Erwin Piscator, a champion of the self-defense of noble art, snarled at the press in the same Volksbühne theater: "At the moment we care as little about creating 'art' as a boxer cares about adopting an aesthetic pose when he lands an uppercut on his opponent's chin."[44] We will either be renowned or dead. In neither case will we have any problems with subsidies,"[45] Nagel stated.

The bell rang. After the first year, following a stormy debate, the Volksbühne won the German critics' prize. They were not rewarded for making perfect art. In fact, Rocky/Frank was rather infamous for sloppiness and carelessness. In the periodical *Theater der Zeit,* an article about Castorf sketched him not as an artist but as an aggressive risk-taking fighter.[46] Reducing costs and raising ticket prices was nothing for him. After the old subscription system collapsed with the wall, Castorf drastically reduced prices to attract the poor to his postmodern playhouse. How like the time in 1914 this was, when the Volksbühne consumer co-op lowered ticket prices. Now nice doormen, who looked like one of them, welcomed the unemployed and students. The German media and its theater critics did not reward the perfection of the plays, but rather *das Werbekonzept der Volksbühne*—the total marketing concept of the Volksbühne.

When Castorf received the reward for the best theater, it was also a prize for scenographer Bert Neumann, whom he had turned into a history-conscious, innovative designer and marketing manager. The graininess of Neumann's cool Volksbühne video certainly rang a note of familiarity for those who had seen historical photos of Piscator's avant-garde back projec-

tions. In Castorf's Volksbühne remake of the film *A Clockwork Orange* from Anthony Burgess's novel, Alex hangs ten meters above the stage and slowly moves a match toward his petrol-soaked body. Oranges rain down; people piss in beer cans; and actors throw paint, blood, milk, and water over each other in the best traditions of the 1960s. It sprinkles like a Pollock painting and steams like a Paul McCarthy performance. Finally everything is dusted in chalk against a backdrop of the Theresienstadt concentration camp. From the workshops next to the stage, Castorf's technicians exclaimed, "[t]his is a new style. Brutal, brutal, brutal and a whole mass of piss routines. Never before has there been such a mess on stage."

In a radio broadcast on February 28, 1993, one reviewer claimed that Castorf's spitting, vomiting production was receiving standing ovations. Volksbühne was a boxing ring at the center of media interest. On the first of March, fifteen skinheads, dressed like Alex and his Droogs, called for more violence from the stalls. The actors left the stage and threw out the skinheads, who in turn smashed several windows. Despite the episode, the Volksbühne's press officer reported that everyone was still welcome at the theatre! Castorf's postmodern performances presaged television reality shows such as "Big Brother," which would soon fill the European media. Castorf's own comments on this new realism were clearly intended to shock journalists:

> Reality, fiction and art are all blended in a mixture where you cannot tell them apart. . . . What I find interesting is the way a text grows into a context . . . because I work by provoking coincidental encounters between people. This I like insofar as it cannot be planned. . . . Take the riots in Rostock-Lichterhagen as an example. That was Reality TV, perfect open-air theater. Young people thumping each other for a whole week. And a confused police force that had no idea what to do. And all the people standing around just applauding this enflamed scenery.[47]

When the bell rang for his second year, Rocky/Frankentorf had his own private pirate flag flying from the roof of his house, with its *schlagender Hässlichkeit,* its terrifying ugliness. Of course, it looked like the red flag raised by Soviet troops above the Reichstag in 1945.

Only three years had passed since the fall of the wall, and young Ossies and Wessies on ecstasy pills were still mixing at rave parties. At the Volksbühne, they now also merged with more traditional Western spectaclegoers and created an audience similar perhaps to that of French revolutionary festivals inspired by Rousseau. The middle classes in the balcony looked down on the heaving masses in the stalls in the same way that trembling aristocrats watched David's processions on the streets of Paris.

Castorf's next round made his postmodern performance work as a fullcontact marketing hit, and he won it at Nietzschean speed. His whole team knew that the trade of becoming takes fast company, a kind of business where you never take the time to settle down, find yourself, explore being. A stage technician recalls how Frank was fighting in a frenzy of flux:

> During the first year Castorf directed five productions himself. He's hyperactive, and we were working flat out. I don't know if it's just a matter of time before a lot of us collapse. But a lot of us have energy left. We've got to get it right, because Castorf is the theatre's last chance. Castorf is a locomotive who pulls a whole load of strange people into the theatre. People come in from the street to paint scenery. Half the crowd he brings with him are useless. They only show up once or twice. Sometimes they go into the workshops to paint and ruin a whole backdrop with a few minutes' carelessness.

Many were surprised at how older actors seemed to cope better with the stress than younger people did. Some old GDR actors had an insatiable desire to work with Castorf. They were high on his aesthetic energy after many quiet years. Suzanne Osten created a Stanislavski studio in Sweden in the 1970s with longer backstage rehearsals. Postmodern performance seemed to be exactly the opposite of such cocooning. Castorf sped up the pace of life in the Volksbühne's old body. Müller once commented upon time and the East German bankruptcy in 1989: "The GDR was a gift to a generation of the defeated, Communists, emigrants, prisoners, and concentration camp victims who could now live out their lives in peace and quiet. That really was the point of it all. There was such a lot of time in GDR. That made it into a slow-down state."[48]

GDR had been *extensity*; Castorf now provided what was the secret desire of his generation: *intensity*. Complaints of weak hearts and sleepless nights were common; something previously unheard of, market stress, was sweeping away the good old production routines of the old GDR workhouse. An elderly carpenter commented about the transition from GDR extensity to FGR intensity:

> Everything happens so bloody fast today. We get a sketch or a simple model, and ten days later we get designs from the scenographer's assistant. Then we have five weeks at most before the stage rehearsals, a week before the premiere. And then they make changes, they might tear down a whole set of scenery the

day before and perform the premiere among the pieces. I remember the old GDR days. God, how nice and slow they were! We had six productions a year. Now we have at least one a month. And in those days there were loads of people working here. A lot have been fired, but to tell the truth they were the ones who didn't do much. But everyone was supposed to have a job in those days. Full employment meant that most of them drank coffee and got in the way. And then there were the political administrators, who would never lend a hand when you needed it. There's more space for work in the workshops now.

The tempo and intensity that built up when the Volksbühne entered the market was physically exhausting for the old house too. The architecture of the building was in poor condition, even though the Soviets had made some repairs to what was once a bombed-out skeleton. Representations of the hammer and sickle were everywhere; the acoustics were appalling. During comedies, the audience would laugh in the wrong places because the lines reached them too late. In the 1960s, stage workers stole materials and rebuilt the stalls themselves to get better acoustics.

Like the wall, however, everything was starting to collapse. As Ivan Nagel recommended, Castorf took a competitive advantage out of all the confusion. He directed his house into a technical state of decay that he cleverly integrated into the performances. In the words of a workman:

This was the most modern theatre when it was built in 1918. The technical side of things was great. Now the stage turntable is stuck and the electricity cables can be deadly. Our sound equipment is old, not to mention the heating system. The building is appallingly badly isolated. As soon as you touch the cables and pipes, they start to smell and spark. But places like this do have a certain charm. You can change things, saw away and carve without worrying too much. The place changes, and you get a feeling of work in progress. And we daren't close for refurbishment, because then we'd lose momentum, and possibly the audience as well.

Frank Castorf entered the third round. Now he was fighting for the life of his old house by expanding his crew in new postmodern directions. Just a year after Castorf became the boss, there appeared a great influx of actors from all over Germany, all wanting to play on the new Berlin scene. Frau Becker, Castorf's secretary, wrote nice replies while the press department scarcely had time to sort the piles of media stuff about the theater and about the boss himself. In the captain's cabin, the video played at full blast as the crew, with Captain Castorf at their center, watched the latest TV reports about their Volksbühne; it was the hottest talk of Berlin town.

Dramaturgists Matthias Lilienthal and Carl Hegemann sipped their beer; a glance into Lilienthal's office revealed dusty files from the Volksbühne's venerable archives strewn all over the little room. History was being consciously but discreetly recycled into new postmodern performances. Hegemann, an expert on Fichte and a fan of American social interactionism, was producing the theater's rock concerts with the intention of attracting a young audience that would in turn make the cultural elite curious to come and watch what the theater was up to. In addition, he planned a series of events centered on the work of French philosopher Gilles Deleuze. To Hegemann, the Volksbühne was bound to become a real "Media Konzern." In those days in one corner of the captain's cabin also sat the cool, switched-on guitarist Steve Binetti, a real East German who married to get over the wall after an underground career as a GDR punk. Castorf hired him as a stage musician for *A Clockwork Orange*. Binetti did his gig every night in Dracula teeth and with screaming guitar, while Alex hung from his greasy trapeze ten meters above the filthy stage. Castorf explained his strategy of using the underground as a bait for the political establishment that provides the subsidies:

> At the Volksbühne we cooperate with marginal groups, with the homeless and with psychiatric patients. The theater canteen is often more exciting artistically than the stage. We enter into a process of communication, a dialogue which benefits both parties. . . . For this reason it feels good that skinheads come to us, even if we end up fighting them. . . . It's groups like that I want to drag into the theater; the educated middle classes are welcome to come and watch later on.[49]

When the bell rang announcing the third round, the media voted Castorf the art champion of the underground, and Castorf's media victories were about to convince the politicians to continue financing his house. It was as if his postmodern performance were embedded in a new political economy where finance and media took the place of old capitalists and labor politics. Inscribing Castorf's Volksbühne in the Gadamerian model (as in the figure) reveals its function of bridging commerce and culture.

After the Berlin Senate finally granted new subsidies to Castorf's successful house, it was time to expand. Believing that theater is basically a method for making either texts or images work as art and not a profession per se, Castorf did not expand just by adding more of the same. He wanted diversified postmodern performances and began acquiring competence in directing movement out of images and conducting music from texts.

To obtain visual-plastic competence, Castorf derived the means to merge with a ballet under the direction of choreographer Josef Kresnik. Castorf had evaluated Kresnik during two guest productions about Ulrike Meinhof and Rosa Luxemburg. Kresnik gave proof of his ability to cooperate with visual arts by having installation artist Hans Haacke design the scenery for his third Volksbühne ballet, about Ernst Jünger, the darkly conservative anarchist author who had applauded the bloodbath of the First World War and corresponded with Heidegger. Kresnik's provocative choice of Jünger fit Castorf's aggressive media strategy very well.

Like a postmod Mohammed Ali, Dr. Frankentorf immediately recuperated Jünger's terrorism by boasting that Germany needed another *Stahlgewitter*. In the Berliner Ensemble, Brecht's old theater, the West German director Peter Zadek, who was born of Jewish exiles in London, accused his East German colleagues Müller and Castorf of being twin fascistic locomotives on a gloomy art track leading straight back to Auschwitz. How Dr. Rocky Frankentorf loved that! He retorted that he preferred Helmut Kohl to *sozialdemokratische Schlafmützen* (Social Democratic nightcaps). He continued to mount the attack by saying that Wessies would never grasp how an Ossie could share Jünger's desire for

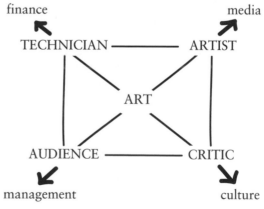

*The Art Firm Blown Up
to Macro Marketing*

intensity: "There I sat, a poor unemployed theatrical person, before the wall came down, in the canteen of the theater in Karl-Marx-Stadt, now Chemnitz once again. I suffered under the GDR, that giant colossus of immobility. Under the weight of that proletarian decadence. Can you really not understand the longing for change, for revolution, for the chance to disrupt the GDR drudge, for a refreshing 'steelbath'"?[50]

Rubbing his hands together, Castorf's smartly dressed financial director moved and grooved like a happy bookmaker. Only two years earlier, Nagel and the Berlin Senate had practically ordered the press scandals, and Castorf thoroughly met Nagel's wildest expectations by constantly delivering mediatic explosions. Underground rock music constantly thudded out of the foyer; Hegemann and Castorf incorporated Neue Slowenische Kunst-Laibach, a group whose heavy-metal fascist sound was already a cult at home in Slovenia. This was postmodern performance music; Laibach made its breakthrough in a truly situationist coup. Under the old regime, they won a Slovenian Communist poster competition with an entry later found to be an old Hitler Youth poster; only the symbols had been changed. When the theater was not hosting rock concerts, poetry readings of dadaist works from the 1920s filled the playbill.

After Kresnik, Castorf incorporated musical composer Christoph Marthaler and splatter-filmmaker Christoph Schlingensief. The former conducted his plays as real concerts, and the latter began his Volksbühne assignment by projecting videos of the vivisection of a kitten at the hands of a slippery neo-Nazi führer from one of Berlin's most unforgiving concrete ghettos. Schlingensief would prove a perfect postmodern match. Assisted by Rock Doctor Hegemann, who now quoted Tom Peters on stage, filmmaker Schlingensief later founded a Hamburg "mission" for homeless people in conjunction with the Salvation Army. In 1997, he burned effigies of Helmut Kohl and organized a political party featuring minorities, the mentally ill, immigrants, and everyone else the media seemed to neglect. The following year, the party Chance 2000 put up candidates in the elections, performed at Documenta and the Berlin Biennial, and set up offices in Austria and Hong Kong.

Ultimately, the project was dropped in favor of Schlingensief's and Hegemann's plan to stage the complete Wagner ring with and for desert bushmen in the German ex-colony of Namibia. Castorf no longer fought alone; Rocky was surrounded by a whole cast of bizarre stage fighters shamelessly vulgarizing flux heritage into mediatic postmodern performance.

After the local victories, the fourth round began in 1995, as Castorf's postmodern performance went on to national export. It was now Bochum's turn to show off Germany's youngest director, Leander Hausmann, an East German actor who had sat in a bath and splashed water in an earlier Castorf performance. It was as if Castorf were franchising the Volksbühne when his disciple Hausmann took over. Soon Bochum copied Berlin to become a brand with a red, potato-print heart as its logo. Neumann gave out flashing electronic badges and stuck up heart posters all over the city.[51]

Castorf's rock concert organizer Hegemann was then recruited as chief dramaturgist. Now Hegemann carried out his job as a full-fledged management consultant for aesthetic event marketing. For the theater in the Ruhr, this meant a total postmodern transformation from a heavy Beckett- and Brecht-like *Grau im Grau* atmosphere. Some years later, Marthaler would establish another Volksbühne dependency in Switzerland when he was appointed head of the Zürich city theater. Rocky won the fourth national round as his boys turned into postmodern performance consultants for German-speaking theaters.

When Castorf's fifth anniversary arrived, the German mass media finally realized that theater is more than just playing Shakespeare. The Volksbühne celebrated their postmodern CEO Frank with a typical trashy buffet of wine, spirits, and beer pouring out of the old dirty marble halls in the chill of Rosa Luxemburg Platz. Photographs taken by the staff were collected for the souvenir album: Kresnik the choreographer surrounded by beautiful brunettes, the composer Marthaler, the splatter-filmmaker Schlingensief, and boxer Frank Castorf himself, dressed up for the party as some sort of vampire. The party was like a decadent rock version of an Otto Dix picture. Castorf's management really lived up to old Heiner Müller's last words to his young Volksbühne friends: "The road hasn't come to an end even though the goal has exploded."[52]

## Stockholmer *Schwung*

Yesterday Berlin, today Germany, and then . . . Sweden. By the end of the summer of 1996, the scenery from Berlin arrived at Stockholm's Stadsteatern. The Swedish technical director thought it extremely interesting, because it looked like giant postmodern designer objects by Alessi: half a fixed globe representing a segment of the earth and two strange movable contraptions, one extremely long bed, and a wave or snake that could be pushed in or out across the earth. The globe leaned and threatened to roll off the stage into the auditorium. The model was on broad display outside the technical director's office long after scenographer Hartmut Meyer and his assistant returned to Berlin.

This was the very same Meyer who had worked with Castorf at the theater in Anklam in East Germany in 1984. Never change a winning team! Then, as today, Castorf and Meyer would have one single piece of cheaply made scenery for a whole play.

This would be the first time Castorf directed anything not in German. He knew it would be tricky, and in vain he tried to bring in some of his German actors, those familiar with his management. Not that the text mattered, since in postmodern performance meaning meant even less than music. Castorf needed routines and habits, however, because what he was good at was conning convention into breaking out of tight bondage. Müller once quoted the installation artist Kounellis as saying that "the less state the more comedy, the more state the more drama."[53] Limited resources and tight control stimulated Rocky-Frank's creativity:

> I cannot cope with freedom; it is nothing to me. If I have a thousand possibilities, I fall apart. But when I am under pressure I develop focused counterpressure; I can not do more than one thing at a time. . . . I need a firm basis from which I can fight. Democracy makes me unhappy. When people start questioning my method to mix triviality with intellectualism in quick Schwung from one to the other, they are questioning me as a whole person, and then I just run away.[54]

Berlin was Castorf's bondage, which made his art work. The Volksbühne, with its old house and limited budget, the city, the Senate, the whole of the FRG and its media—they all worked as his straitjacket. In Stockholm, Hartmut Meyer's sets became his pressure valve. Meyer had long been engaged in shaping the concrete aggressive spaces Castorf's performances craved: a physical space to collide with, slip on, and run your body against, a space tilting toward the auditorium of which it is actually a part.

At the beginning of 1997, immediately after the collation of the production, Meyer and his assistant accompanied the actors to a second-hand clothing store in the wings behind the rehearsal room, where their clothes were already laid out and ready to wear. These were not theatrical costumes, however. They were real second-hand clothes, carefully chosen for their fetish value, their texture, and their appearance. Meyer did not want fresh cloth, and Castorf never let actors rehearse in their own clothes. The usual practice was to dress up in theatrical costumes only in the last week of re-hearsal. But Castorf's postmodern performance did not make art work by thinking or reading or interpreting. This was not exercise in textual repro-duction. It all had to do with ways of embodiment usually thought of as consumption, how an individual turns a dress or a pair of trousers into his or her second skin in the way the actor makes the texts turn into living voices. The German-Russian art philosopher Boris Groys has characterized postmodern performance art as a model for exclusive consumption of the anonymous mass-produced objects that pollute our modern marketplaces.[55]

For Castorf, the postmodern condition is not only an uninhibited way to blend art forms; it experiments with social forms for consumers to recon-quer individual aesthetic spaces in an overmanaged and overmarketed com-mercial organization of culture. Postmodern performance manages given customer conditions. The scenery box was therefore already in place in the rehearsal room, and all actors were dressed up right from the very first re-hearsal. Out of all this stuff and postures, out of this matter and form, peo-ple have to shape their existence.

Castorf, Müller, or Wilson would never appeal to actors by using some suggestive fantasy or psychological plunge into the depth of their private ex-periences. This was what Müller meant when he exhorted actors to differen-tiate between art and what was physical; the actors had to fight in a ring against concrete objects. Castorf's big fight saved the Volksbühne; now he wanted his Swedish actors to put on a similar desperate fight on the Stock-holm stage. If the match showed the slightest sign of being rigged, the audi-ence would become a lynch mob, since postmodern performance is about hard and harsh reality.

Castorf was invited to Stockholm not merely to stage a play. Peter Wahlqvist, the head of the Swedish theater, secretly wished him to sweep away the old Swedish literary and psychological theater as well. Although Wahlqvist had taken over a theater that was the temple of production, he now intuitively felt the new era to be one of marketing and consumption. Castorf was hired as an art consultant and parachuted behind enemy lines to stimulate a shift in paradigm, away from Sjöberg's and Osten's art corpo-ration to postmodern performance.

During the autumn, the workshops of the Stadsteatern worked on producing complete three-dimensional scenery for rehearsal use only. At the same time, considerable tension was brewing in the dramaturgist's office. It had been decided to dramatize one of Strindberg's novels instead of wrestling with Swedish prejudice about how his regular plays ought to be performed. Another work, *Svarta Fanor* (Black Flags), also carried out the theme of the pirate flags Castorf was flying above the Volksbühne. Castorf promised that he would read the book, but the dramaturgists had their doubts. Could he actually be trusted to do it? On a lightning visit before Christmas in 1996, he met the Swedish actors who had answered his call to work on the production. As the start of rehearsals approached, the more nervous everyone became at the total lack of a printed script. At the last moment, a rudimentary dramatization written by a young German playwright appeared. "I'm afraid I didn't have time to do it myself," Castorf apologized during the collation meeting. He moved on to deliver a brilliant and fascinating lecture on aesthetics during which his crew was catapulted from Strindberg via Nietzsche and Kierkegaard to the real source: Schopenhauer revealing the roots of postmodern performance in aesthetic philosophy.

The actors were expectantly nervous. Monica Ohlsson and her assistants were working round the clock to translate the German manuscript during the days before the collation. People who had seen Castorf's plays claimed that he was a radical who did not deem any text sacred. Castorf turned texts into fast food consumption. He stuffed the actors full and had them throw up the junk on the audience. In his own words, he explains:

> In principle I am not against letting the text remain as it is printed. The problem is that I don't believe in the subversive power of language or poetry itself. I destroy a text, but only to put it back together again. If you think that this is just an attack on literature, then you're being a little narrow-minded. I am more interested in reconstruction, in rebuilding something out of the ruins. . . . Literature pretends that it possesses a method for both understanding and controlling the world. I believe that it is extremely difficult to know anything about the world and impossible to control it.[56]

No author or manager had the right to dictate consumption or interpretation of his or her products. The value of wares, as well as of services, must be in the eye and mind of the beholder. This was the postmodern version of Schiller's Schwung, and Castorf served his German cast thin slices of Schiller's play. Here is what was gobbled out of Schiller's *Die Räuber* when Castorf staged it at the Volksbühne:

| Castorf's Scrambled Version of Die Räuber *at the* Volksbühne, *1990* | Materials sampled from Schiller (acts in Roman numerals, scenes in Arabic) |
|:---:|:---:|
| I | I/2 |
| II | I/2 |
| III | I/1 |
| IV | I/1 |
| V | I/3 |
| VI | II/1 |
| VII | II/2 |
| VIII | IV/5 plus II/2 |
| IX | II/3 |
| X | II/3 |
| XI | II/3, V/1, and II/2[57] |

Texts never contain absolute being; therefore the performance constructs the immanent object through acts of aesthetic consumption. Stockholm's Stadsteatern, like most modern firms, had a tradition of work and industry, not of aesthetic consumption. It was difficult to reconcile Castorf's postmodern management with a theatrical work organization based on industrial ideas about "clear scenery" and "agreed time scales and budgets." The Swedes were afraid of how Castorf would manage. Soon it became clear that there was no cause for concern because Castorf combined a postmodern front stage with rather practical backstage methods of efficient aesthetic management. At the same time that his media messages were full of rather obscure statements, his management was making art work as consumption as smoothly as clockwork. Castorf's management style is reminiscent of Russian installation artist Kabakow's stern advice for art managers who want to perform philosophy through organized work. Kabakow explains how one could realize an installation aiming at rather unstructured experiences by concrete organization of museum work:

> I should like to stress the following aspect of the strategic success of any project: precision. Any sign of indecision in your project

will be severely punished. . . . I can give an example from my own work: instead of painting pictures, the first step of an installation project is always a presentation of the project for the institution where it is to be presented. My experience is that the project must be presented in absolutely clear detail, despite the fact that nothing yet exists—neither pictures nor objects. But the precondition must be that your machine does not wake the slightest doubt, and that you can answer any question that is asked. The slightest mistake on your part—for example if someone asks "What happens if we fail to build this ceiling?"—means a failure both for the project and for the person presenting it. There will be such a fiasco that your next project might not even be considered.[58]

When Frank Castorf makes art at work, he follows Ilja Kabakow's practical instruction to the letter. The novelty of the content, the new thing he wanted his actors to perform, was embedded in the secure concrete context of work. In the rehearsal room, the scenery was ready-made. The costumes were ready-made for the actors. This contextual concreteness soaked up any insecurity in the actors as they went about making art work as consumption, as naturally as if they strolled into any shop or supermarket.

Castorf's postmodern management implied other practical changes as well. When the rehearsals for *Svarta Fanor* began in Stockholm, the time from first read-through to premiere was roughly the same as any Stockholm production. At the Volksbühne in Berlin, however, rehearsal times were usually much shorter. Osten, who managed to extend backstage work in the style of Stanislavski, suggested—perhaps out of nostalgia for the 1970s— that the struggle of the 1990s would be about the actors' time, since their calendars were now filling with small gigs to enable them to earn extra money. Long rehearsal times, which were something of the goal for the actors' union struggle, were indeed less appealing to many actors now wishing to do "more intensive, shorter things." Sweden, like the GDR, seemed to be in the managerial process of speeding up, of switching from extensive production to intensive consumption. What went on in most Swedish factories in lean production times was that just-in-time management and other time-cutting methods converged, as they had done twenty years earlier in Osten's work at Stockholm's Stadsteatern. One actor confesses his desire for intensity: "I believe rehearsals could go a hell of a lot faster. I'd rather work quickly. It often gets really slow, drawn out and sticky. If the rehearsals go on for a long time you run out of energy. . . . It's like sport. If you have shorter rehearsals you try harder, it's more intensive. There's more momentum in the work. That would suit me fine."

This change in attitude suited Castorf, whose rehearsal schedule leaves mornings free. He never starts work before twelve and cannot work beyond three in the afternoon. This is not the result of laziness, either; on the contrary, the locomotive from Berlin demands total dedication during the compressed rehearsal periods. The energy he displays in the afternoon sessions means he must have concentrated all morning. After the first week of rehearsals, everyone agrees that three hours with Castorf were far more effective than five with Sjöberg or a weeklong Osten workshop. No one misses the long-winded breaks for coffee, lunch, and chat. They seem antiquated sediments of a fading factory fantasy.

At the stroke of twelve, Frank Castorf would assume his place at the long table in front of Hartmut Meyer's set, complete with the Alessi bed and wave. At the same table sat the dramaturgist Monica Ohlsson and her assistant Jenny, along with the prompter and representatives from the sound and lighting departments. For most of the rehearsals, scenographer Hartmut Meyer and his assistant, Kerstin Laube, were also present. The table was like a shop counter. All of Castorf's directions, simultaneously translated from German by Ohlsson, came from over the counter. Not once during the rehearsals did Castorf enter the territory of the actors or technicians. He would always sit or stand behind his table. Physical space, the shopping mall for art consumption, had to be left free for consumer movement; no intruders should disturb the customers.

Rehearsals assumed their time, with a natural rhythm developing musically. The pattern usually began hesitantly, subdued, and then suddenly accelerated until it exploded in an orgiastic climax of action. Frank showered his actors with cascades of pep talk, while they worked on sculpting their scenes. He encouraged the actors to wrestle with props and setting, even while they were still reading their parts from the script. Frank acted like Rocky frontstage, and backstage he coached his team to box up to a title fight. The rehearsal room was actually transformed from a shop environment and took on something of the atmosphere of a gym.

Castorf followed the chronological order of scenes in the script; every day, one new scene was rehearsed. The gym workout sessions were rather sweaty, since the sloping floor of the stage made the usual relaxed positions impossible and the second-hand clothes inhibited the actors' personal behavior. Actors had no time to feel their way into their parts or even into the play itself. Castorf consciously scrambled any of their attempts to memorize the material. He wanted to block out all possibilities for their being themselves and telling their own story, since in postmodernity narration and epic lost any modern authority. Rather, parts had to be recorded physically, with all the shortcomings and idiosyncrasies of such tactile and vocal recollection. No chance existed for polishing an act. It was as if the aesthetic intensity of Castorf's art work conjured acting into a passion instead of a job. His actors were devouring art, not working or crafting any more. This was not a job. It was an addictive passion imbued with sublime and dark desires. The French philosopher Alain Badiou suggests it is completely wrong "when people like to describe actors as normal 'workers,' interested in professional training, beneficial wage negotiations and confronted by the hard realities of making a living—as if they were interchangeable with . . . bank employees. . . . But we all however know . . . that an actor is irredeemably unique, and that his profession really is not one at all."[59]

The aim of Castorf's aesthetic management was to make rehearsals unique. Even though rehearsals in French are called *repetitions,* Castorf's management consciously blocked all opportunities to "repeat" anything. The German word for rehearsing is *proben,* meaning to "test" or "try on." Castorf actually had his actors try on their parts in a very concrete fashion. He had them try on artifacts and fictions, things and situations, which released an energy he would flash-freeze on the spot while it was fresh. This was far easier than it might sound. Every day, Castorf simply had his technicians throw in new objects, which made the actors' bodies, preconditioned by dress and box bondage, flow forward. One day the crew arranged old newspapers on the stage and turned on a huge fan. The actors, against a strong headwind, had to pick up the papers that were flying around the stage. Another day, a woman was shut inside an oil drum. One of her colleagues sat on the lid, and she had to fight her way out. On another occasion, an old Christmas tree that had dropped its needles ended up on stage. The heavy head of an elk stood in as a dumbbell. The actors were made to wear raincoats while a stream of water splattered the plastic. One woman was placed on a pile of designer clothes and had to root about among Armani, Dior, and Kenzo gear. They were given cups with tea bags in them and had to throw the bags at the scenery and make them stick on the walls.

A dish of asparagus arrived; the actors had to grab a piece and suck on it. They had to jump into oil drums, roll the drum around the stage, embrace the Christmas tree, throw the clothes on, and lift the elk's head. In addition to such artifacts, Castorf would throw in artifictions like evocations of mass media clips floating around in the heads of all contemporary consumers. Castorf's artifacts and the artifictions were as different and varying as all the gear and experiences an individual runs into in shops, boutiques, second-hand stores, malls, or showrooms of commercial consumer culture. Postmodern performance, as Groys has claimed, really made art work as a strange aesthetic education of consumers.

Castorf had many ways of summoning artifictions. He might shout, "Imagine climbing Everest, and your oxygen is running out!" or "Do you remember the murderers in Tarantino's *Pulp Fiction?*" or "Pretend you're Dr. Jekyll turning into Mr. Hyde!" He also used music: extracts from a Laibach record, pieces of a Piazzola Argentine tango, or an aria from a Verdi opera. He might suddenly assign extracts from Strindberg's *A Madman's Manifesto* to portions of *The Communist Manifesto,* text out of its context, for an actor to declaim. On a whim, he might ask an actress to sing a sentimental Irish ballad.

Antoine used texts, Lugné paintings; now Castorf bombarded his actors with objects, pictures, songs, and texts. Artifacts and artifictions were made to work in a direct, physical sense. Whenever Frank felt that *hier brauchen wir ein Bruch* (here we need a break), *etwas muss uns einfallen* (we have to come up with something), he would throw his artifact/artifiction to his actors as a zookeeper would throw meat to tigers in a cage. Artifacts and artifictions solved the problem when Frank was at a loss and wondering what to do next. His problems were never intellectual questions addressed to the actors; he was not asking for his colleagues' brilliant ideas or wise suggestions. Making art work was not a matter of rational thought; Castorf was far from directing like Sjöberg lecturing his cast, or Osten conducting rehearsals as a therapy workshop. The stuff he threw to his actors was neither prop nor representation. They were the real objects of consumption: Armani clothes, a stuffed elk's head, a Christmas tree, and an oil drum. These props possessed physical, fetishistic energy that made *ein Raum entstehen,* a space emerge, with its own inevitable and inescapable *nouveau realisme.* Castorf sensed that this is the only way to manage under a postmodern condition that, according to Ilja Kabakow, is completely lacking any universal system of taste, nor a common universal system for cultural identification valid for the entire society. As a result, your own personality, your interests, your psychic reactions must co-operate with the reactions of your own concrete network of relations—this is a way to organise of an almost biological, erotic nature. Nowadays eroticism is practically the only effective method of socialisation; all other methods have long since collapsed. This is why purely bodily characteristics play such an important role.[60]

The eroticism of Castorf's transfigurative postmodern management occasionally collided with the still-dominant Swedish consensus model based on hopes in transcendental common values. By two o'clock the afternoon

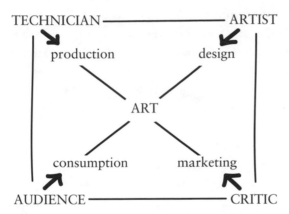

*The Art Firm Zooming In on Micro Management*

of February 4, 1997, the props manager had still not managed to find the greasy oil drum Castorf needed to throw in as an artifact, so Frank simply canceled the session and went out into the city. The next day the drum was in place, and creation flowed anew.

Castorf introduced a way of looking at management that was akin to the economy the media began speaking of during the same period. This was a time when managers developed the habit of presenting themselves as artists and their firms as art. Castorf's postmodern version of aesthetic play and its players were indeed approaching new ways of marketing by events, having design reflect art, speeding up production, and looking upon consumers as creative art audiences. Postmodern management in the new economy was no longer regulated as old-time factory work.

In terms of the Gadamerian model, the connection between making art and business can be summarized as in the figure.

As the premiere approached, the atmosphere was more one of concentration than of nervousness. Robert Wilson had recently landed, as another of

Wahlqvist's international guests, at Stockholm Stadsteatern. Frank Castorf did not attend Wilson's first lecture. He was out on the town with Hartmut getting drunk in a Hungarian café that reminded him of his youth in Budapest. Sometimes he would go to Zorba for a beer with Nisse and the other lads from the technical team. Nice and serious, he nevertheless drank like a real GDR pro. During a Stockholm visit, a colleague reported "I only heard him laugh once, when he heard that the labor union was meeting to discuss the appointment of a new theatre director in two years' time. 'We didn't have that nonsense even in the GDR. Union members were only good for running the company sauna!'"

The pressure mounted during the last week of rehearsal. Everyone was walking around like a zombie trying to recall how the play was to run. They had been through everything at least a few times by then, and Castorf had glued all the single scenes together into a *Klebewerk,* a collage. The usual production routine at the Stadsteater was to test it out on the stage at least a week before the dress rehearsal; many wondered, "When the hell are we going down?"

Castorf, however, did not wish to indulge in production and reproduction. He did not want his boxers to feel comfortable. Art is situational skunk work, neither industrial work nor outmoded craft. Castorf wanted everyone to be on watch. Industrial management avoids risk by planning; postmodern management seeks out risks and lets danger generate sublime energy. The day before the great fight, the cast rushed through the performance, and Frank made some small concluding remarks, a comment or two about timing and tempo. Draw out that line, increase the volume here, scream at the end! Bodies were fit and trim, and craft management was about at perfection.

Gina Rowlands once advised actors to "overprepare, underrehearse, and then just do it." Castorf may have canceled the dress rehearsal to make the press take in the real audience reaction as much as the play itself. Since letting off steam before the premiere was not advisable, everyone went home for a good night's sleep.

"What a premiere!" exclaimed Nisse in the smoke-filled room where Peter Wahlqvist was serving strong Swedish schnapps, icy beer, and herring sandwiches at his customary first-night party. "They all laughed and thought it was good," said one happy actor. Striking a slightly crass note, the technicians muttered that it was a very cheap production, with just the one set and only second-hand clothes.

"Did you see that some people left during the performance?" Castorf had even succeeded in getting the blood of the tame Swedish audience to its collective boiling point. With a bit of luck, the conventional Swedish Strindberg fanatics would protest against the cuts, the rearrangements, and the willful misrepresentation of the book. A scandal, like the ones Strindberg himself once loved to provoke, would prove that Castorf had made old art work again. The audience had eaten art right in pace with the frenzied performance on stage.

At the Schnapps party on March 8, 1997, Castorf's whole German family was present. Like a postmod Jacques-Louis David, the Robespierre-like Kresnik, the giant Lilienthal-Mirabeau, and the Danton dramaturgist Dr. Hegemann surrounded him. That evening, the German press was in the audience, and the vision of a European art firm seemed real. The politically astute Wahlqvist's enthusiasm also indicated that Castorf's postmodern performance had wider societal importance. The European political pendulum had swung back from its widest neolib extreme. The Nobel Prize in Economics had already been awarded to Douglas North for showing the general importance of institutions in a market economy. In Great Britain, Tony Blair had taken over for Mrs. Thatcher by aestheticizing leftist politics into what some called "designer socialism." When Anthony Giddens somewhat later helped him steep philosophical content into his social democracy, he metaphysically baptized Blair's new deal the "third way."[61] There was Schwung also in the Swedish air, so Wahlqvist proposed a toast in aquavit for this Schillerian management consultant to Sweden. "Thank you, Frank, for your wonderful gift to all of us [who are] all fighting against text theatre. What a gift to us all longing for performances making images and music work as art. You have shown us a new radical third way of performing."

# 10

## Dionysus Inc.—
## Extending the Art Firm

### Aesthetic Management and Metaphysical Marketing

#### The Dualism—Aesthetic Management
#### Against Totality and Banality

It was the fall of 2000, and the World Trade Center still towered over its section of Manhattan. Without any prescience of the enormous hit that the global community would take a year later, the world's business climate was already bleak and grim following the dot com information technology crash of the new economy. In one corner of the globe, inspired by Tony Blair's campaign for rebranding Britain with creative industries and publicity efforts by MIT's art-connected media tech lab, the Swedish ministries of trade and industry still flirted with the idea that cool, trendy design and popular entertainment might be used as a relatively low-cost stimulation to the languid business environment.

While the startup boo.com, an artsy vaporware-producing dot com company founded by two Swedes and promoted to venture capitalists by J. P. Morgan,[1] burst like a bubble, rumors romped across the continent. By cleverly coordinating the management of the "media-robust" French, Italian art-connected firms were moving from exclusive traditional crafts to global spectacular corporations raising new capital on international stock markets. It was more than two years before Vivendi-Universal and luxury shopping would be hit by the gloomy post-WTC recession, so managers were still impressed by these success stories. They latched on to the idea that maybe the immediate thrill of the theater stage, rather than e-commerce mediated over the World Wide Web screen, held the key to survival for their business too. Curious about the possibility, organizers of an "experience economy" conference in Stockholm secured Joseph Pine, a management consultant from Ohio and a graduate of MIT's Sloan School of Management, to serve as a keynote speaker at their meetings. Pine and colleague James H. Gilmore had recently published a book entitled *The Experience Economy: Work Is Theatre and Every Business a Stage.*[2]

Pine came across as a superstraight cowboy consultant packaging his mechanical rhetoric in a standard PowerPoint presentation. The gist of his self-evident, down-to-earth message was that a successful business no longer makes money by selling goods and services but rather by charging high prices for *experiences* staged as an attractive context for the product or star. To escape the kind of cutthroat competition that seems inevitable for mature industries with rationalized production, corporations would now need to contribute a surplus value of emotional experience to standard "commodified" goods and services. Only this new type of value added would enable them to beat out stiff competition. That's why "business is theater," Pine exclaimed, underlining his statement with "and I certainly don't mean this metaphorically, but literally."

Toward the end of his presentation, Pine related how he had taken his family to the American Girl show in Chicago to experience the marketing of AG products. They ate dinner in the American Girl Café, seated next to their newly acquired dolls perched in special doll chairs. Responding as anticipated, the Pines left the doll manufacturer (now turned experience economy firm) with lots of props purchased as souvenirs. The Pine family "experience" was a personal illustration of how global businesses stage memorable local happenings and charge hefty fees for them. "Today," added the speaker, "we are willing to pay for ranch work we earlier got paid for, or buy tickets to marketing events that yesterday were free of charge."

Pine set out to domesticate aesthetic energy to generate better business in new art firms. But when he was preaching about the experience economy, he did not come off as someone who had really mastered aesthetic management. He certainly felt the force, but just as certainly he missed the real source of aesthetic energy. He wandered off the road to the third realm and never got close to the aesthetic power of avant-garde enterprises, artistic companies, art corporations, flux firms, and postmodern performances. Something was obviously missing.

Later, in early 2001, an incident occurred which once again recalled Pine's theoretical shortcomings. Protesters against globalization organized violent demonstrations in Seattle, Nice, and Quebec, and now they besieged the annual economic summit in Davos, Switzerland, launching Puerto Allegre as a Brazilian alternative summit.

One of the protest's initiators, Ignacio Ramonet, lectured at the University of Stockholm. Literally and figuratively, Ramonet's appearance at the university set a striking contrast to Pine's earlier one in the same venue. Pine dressed as the stereotypical businessman, totally correct but thoroughly bland in his Brooks Brother business suit and big flowery necktie. Ramonet, on the other hand, wore a pair of Levi 501s above heavy black leather boots. His smart jacket covered a black shirt, and he wore an Italian silk cravat.

Ramonet was the intellectual editor-in-chief of the French newspaper *Le Monde Diplomatique,* globally diffused in translated local editions; Pine was the typical American management consultant. Ramonet hinted at Hegel, delivering his *Weltanschauung* as an ex-rock star rebel; Pine cited Adam Smith, preaching like a reverend on a sunny Sunday morning. But their analyses of the world situation for the new millennium converged as much as their respective policy recommendations diverged. Both agreed that only 10 percent of the global economy is about production of material goods and services, since today the bulk of transactions handle immaterial and symbolic messages in texts and images. Pine worried on behalf of competing corporations, while Ramonet warned about the few concentrated experience providers such as Vivendi-Universal, Bertelsmann, Twentieth Century Fox, and AOL—all manipulators of global emotional information.

To shore up producers, Pine suggested emotional entertainment as a way to increase profit margins and differentiate against cutthroat competition. To protect citizens, Ramonet promoted education as a weapon against the same entertainment that Pine prescribed for total emotional involvement of the experience economy consumer. Ramonet agitated for a popular resistance movement against media moguls flooding the culture with childish entertainment and treating grown-up, highly educated consumers as stupid kids. At the same time (when, incidentally, Rev. Robert Schuller was on U.S.

television casting Mikhail Gorbachev as a true Christian), Pine was proposing exciting Las Vegas conventions for corporate clients, with invitations extended via glittery e-mail. No wonder Ramonet, who built his barricades by
editing a journal full of long intellectual articles craving—yes, even demanding—much effort and patience of readers, was hailed by Fidel Castro as one
of the last true Cuban comrades in 2002.

Ramonet firmly believed that the days of Pine's experience economy were
as numbered as those of capitalistic production once were to Karl Marx; his
credo was that the knowledge industry had to replace superficial entertainment. On the other hand, Pine's idol was Walt Disney, and his favorite hang-
out was the Rainforest Café. In early 2001, Ramonet cheered the demonstrations of Mexican Subcomandante Marcos, who, riding on horseback,
masked, heavily armed, and drawing on his pipe, led his populist attack
against the transformation of his beloved Lacandona jungle of Chiapas into
some global Rainforest Café à la Pine. Pine wanted to rescue the world economy by manufacturing pleasing special effects, a smoke-and-mirrors routine
of exciting events to rejuvenate boring brands. Ramonet had faith that the
coming reign of universal and collective truth would replace egotistic individual pleasure seeking.

Together, these gentlemen produced an interesting amalgam. Ramonet
adhered to the creed of rational knowledge with authority rooted in logical
reasoning; like many rational revolutionaries, he wanted to extend scientifically the intensity of a single passionate revolt—the Bastille in 1789, or Paris
in 1968—into an everlasting social reform. Put in Pine's jargon, Ramonet
wanted the exciting events of revolt to be politically branded as permanent
revolution. He was the rational positivistic planner, constantly on the outlook for scientific brand-stretching devices for stone-dead revolutions and
lost utopias.[3] Ramonet lived up to his ideal by quoting economist and Nobel
laureate James Tobin, although Tobin repeatedly refused to be connected in
any way with Ramonet's "Attac" movement. Pine, on the other hand, took
on the role of the "irrationalist," emotionally engineering boring everyday
business into intensive passionate experiences in attractive atmospheres[4]
with spectacular auras.[5]

Pine and Ramonet are clearly bipolar partners. Interestingly enough, however, general management theory also advocates this dualism. Speaking of
the two-faced Janus manager, Sven Erik Sjöstrand recommends the "radical

position . . . to deny the possibility of rationalizing the 'irrational.' To recognize the simultaneous presence of both the rational *and* the 'irrational' is an important achievement."[6]

Dualistic perspective had been used increasingly to give meaning to successful but untraditional management practices characterizing the museum-boom heroes of the 1980s and 1990s: Thomas Hoving at the Metropolitan Museum of Art, Tom Armstrong of the Whitney Museum of American Art, Jean Christoph Amann at the Museum for Modern Art in Frankfurt am Main, and Nicholas Serrota at London's Tate Gallery. Most conspicuous among them was Thomas Krens, who in the 1990s turned the Guggenheim into a global art franchise in order to finance investments in his museum.[7] Krens, like Robert Wilson, holds two degrees, in art history and in business administration, a fact illuminated by Sjöstrand's Janus theory. This dualistic perspective is seen also throughout the basic recipe for successful art management prescribed by media and entertainment mogul Strauss Zelnick of Twentieth Century Fox:

> A rule of thumb is: If the business side of the company is run effectively and the creative side of the company is run poorly, then you will fail. If the creative side of the company is run well and the business side of the company is run poorly, you will succeed. And if both sides run well, you will succeed greatly.[8]

The Pine-Ramonet dualism presented no simple either-or solution either. The pros and cons of their respective politico-economic arguments and suggestions swayed in limbo. Ramonet presented no hard fact that the rational administration of cheerful revolts would efficiently block remakes of the gulag empire; Pine himself admitted that the seductive attraction fades quickly, leaving the experience economy with rapidly diminishing returns. After glitzy shows, the props—the products and services—inevitably drop from their unique event-marketing pedestal and fall into the relativity of dull market competition.

Pine saw just one way of guaranteeing the return of first-time consumers visiting Eurodisney, Euroguggenheim, Rainforest Café, or Nike Town. He ended his lecture at Stockholm University sadly conceding that the "been there, done that" effect had to be reckoned with, after which he had the glowing eyes of a New Age experience evangelist embarking on a capitalistic crusade for consumers:

Next after experience economy comes something very different: the transformation economy. In a way you can see my book as a Trojan horse for this Transformation economy. I am Christian, you see, and moving over from experience to transformation is what I feel would benefit people most. Transformation is beyond the public and private, for it operates on the person itself. It may start by buying a golf trainer that helps you achieve a lower handicap. Then the sky is the limit. For you as a consumer become the material worked on by the transformation. With transformations we change each other inside. Transformations are the only things that I can honestly guarantee never to be commodified for we cannot commodify human beings.

In other words, what turns "ordinary products into extraordinary experiences,"[9] to quote Pine and Gilmore's Harvard disciples Lasalle and Britton, is that the consumer in spectacular capitalism gets an individual transformative brainwashing instead of being transcended to Kant's public—something Tom Peters and Charles Handy, two gurus of new cool managerialism, had already prophesied when writing on "a brand called you" and "existential companies" managed by "new alchemists."[10] Pine's simple inversion of Ramonet's Marxian faith in a communism resting on the enlightenment of man by rational education echoes an essay from the end of the 1980s in which Guy Debord draws his conclusions for a world after the Big Bang of Berlin's geopolitical bipolarity.

In 1967, Debord's situationist manifesto *La Société du Spectacle*[11] defined a bipolarity of two "spectacles" alienating the modern world from authentic life. The state-run capitalism of the Soviet Union was one pole; here party bureaucracy enslaved workers. In the West, at the other extreme, the management ideology of individual capitalism pacified the population in a hurly-burly banal spectacle of private consumption. In 1968, the hermetically sealed Society of Spectacle became the subversive bible of Parisian students and a blueprint for postmodern ideas of simulacra first copied by Jean Baudrillard.

For Debord, the choice between Eastern totalitarianism and Western banality was a Hobson's choice between cholera and plague. In the old bipolar world, temporary in-between mixes might only be shaped by subversively snatching bits and pieces from the two poles and recycling them as performances during short intensive situations. Debord uses the term *detournement,* which he "borrowed without permission" from Rumanian avant-gardist Is-sidore Issou,[12] to describe his situationist robberies for pataphysical col-lages. After 1989, once the dual system imploded into what Debord saw as the Hegelian horror story of Lyotard's postmodern condition,[13] no hope re-mained for creatively coping with the morass of the integrated spectacle. There were no systems left to steal from; no in-between undergrounds re-mained where the loot could be creatively rearranged into situationist utopias.[14] When totality and banality folded, spontaneous human life was simply squeezed out of the entire globe. It would have suited his argument to see both the Twin Towers collapse and hear Pentagon spokesperson Victoria Clarke emphasize to her CNN audience in March 2003 that the "shock and awe" operation in Iraq, with its Hollywood-designed press lounge and well-directed embedded journalists, was "not a game" and "not a show." Long before, however, Guy Debord lost hope in even the minimal situationist kind of third way subversion and performed the last nihilistic act remaining for a true dualistic desperado: suicide.

## The Third Metaphysics of Art Work

In the early 1990s, about the same time that Debord, the pessimist utopian, committed suicide, Heiner Müller voiced a somewhat more optimistic and realistic trust in the third and in a renaissance for art extended to society at large: "When reasoning has ended up in a cul-de-sac there is suddenly one possibility opening up—it has to do with the indissoluble union of art and philosophy. . . . When enlightenment is dead, only art remains."[15]

Müller's contemporary credo of art as philosophy echoes Schopenhauer. When all hope is gone, he clings to a trust in the third, and the creation of the third depends on dualisms created for the specific purpose of conquering anew an in-between workplace for art. Philosophers Gilles Deleuze and Felix Guattari, also late-twentieth-century followers of the old aesthetic tradition, define philosophy as a third enterprise distinct from but still connected with subjective private reflection and the objective study of public opinion forma-tion. Dualism must be maintained by regular realistic updates because philos-ophizing cannot go on if the dichotomy collapses into monotony, as it did in Debord's fatal depressive worldview. That was why Kant squeezed in a third critique between his first two and why Schiller argued for play between form and matter. It was to highlight the same aesthetic purpose of maintaining du-alism to promote and protect the third that Deleuze and Guattari minted their somewhat eccentric term *schizoanalysis*. French philosopher Alain

Badiou suggested that aesthetic philosophy was a strange pistol of poetry which shot open holes of truth in compact tissues of knowledge, while social philosopher Dany-Robert Dufour saw "wars of paranoia and destruction" in the absence of trinitary human.[16]

Aesthetic philosophers are not the only ones to grasp that aesthetic management is all about making art work as metaphysics in the third realm. Ingmar Bergman's comment on a crisis in a Swedish city theater in 1997 serves as a good illustration of an artist's intuitive understanding of what makes art work:

> This theatre only has itself to blame, as it was financially and artistically mismanaged for many years. What automatically follows, which all is very sad, is that politicians and management consultants move in and take over. And then all hell breaks loose. . . . The only remedy is to get hold of an artistic leader able to unite and motivate everyone for new achievements.[17]

As the previous historical cases of aesthetic management illustrate, the creative development of theater in the direction of art and philosophy implied a pendulum Schwung between dualisms in specific historic epochs. Antoine founded his avant-garde enterprise as a rupture from entertainment mise en scène, and Lugné was doing his art swinging away from the didactic dramaturgy that Antoine's previous breakaway movement had landed in. Wilson makes art work as passage from American banal entertainment, and Müller did his art work as a dissident from the pole of GDR totalitarian propaganda. The case of Pine, the consultant entertainer, and Ramonet, the public educator, illustrates another history-bound dualism serving the purpose of managing aesthetic Schwung.

The tactics of aesthetic management illustrated in these detailed examples are created for the passage between the poles Schiller called form and matter. Long before Schwungs from Wagner to Wilson made pictures, texts, images, and signs work, antagonistic structures were opposing each other in theater. On one hand, there was the image-based French tradition called mise en scène; on the other, text-based German *dramaturgie*.[18]

Guilbert de Pixérécourt (1773–1844) developed French mise en scène to produce the melodrama that still works as a standard for Hollywood films, television soaps, and Joseph Pine Disneyfied entertainment. A critic contemporary of Pixérécourt deplored the "sad truth that literature" has fled a stage "increasingly seeking the assistance of painting like David's picture of

Leonidas."[19] Mise en scène turned images into motion pictures long before silver screen innovators such as Alfred Hitchcock, Jacques Tati, or David Lynch used paintings and their framing as a source of inspiration. On the Boulevard du Crime, Parisians strolled to Pixérécourt's theme park. His shows at the Ambigu and the Gaité illustrated stories based on books whose authors were reduced to the position of simply being suppliers remunerated according to rules of the Société des Auteurs et Compositeurs Dramatiques, an initiative of the very same Pixérécourt in 1805. He was a stage painter and theater architect who mastered a complex technical palette of coloring including costumes, scenery, special effects, musical interludes, and ghostly lighting. Before living on mise en scène, he actually earned money painting ladies' fans.[20] French mise en scène was fixated on the front stage; Pixérécourt loved to parade outside his playhouse, arrayed in his luxurious velvet coat, his *Légion d'honneur* clearly visible on his lapel to advertise his public status.

French mise en scène focused on making motion out of pictures; its aesthetic antipode, German dramaturgy, concentrated on turning texts into music. The father of German dramaturgy was the poet Gotthold Lessing (1729–1781), to whom any musical instrument seemed clumsy and artificial compared to a well-educated actor's voice performing "this natural music to which our individual heart will not fail to open up, because it immediately recognizes that music thus elevated to art must also stem from the nature of all hearts. . . ."[21]

Reading was not enough for "playing a text." Musical skills were needed in declamation (a reality that Schiller painfully experienced as his second play was refused because of his heavy Schwabian accent). Lessing—the poet turned in-house critic at the Hamburg playhouse—called his written remarks *Dramaturgie*. Through these pieces, he proposed to safeguard the life of a performance; maintain its poetic musicality; critically uncover poor translations and corrupted verses; and above all fight the dogmatically dominant French literary conventions that had, in Lessing's view, overlooked the poetical musicality of texts.

Lessing regarded painting as considerably inferior to poetry. When confronted with pictures by Rembrandt or van Eyck, he would wonder whether or not painting had ever contributed anything of aesthetic value.[22] To Lessing, making art work meant to make music out of texts, since this was how poetry might serve the cause of morally educating human emotions. In France, this view was basically shared not by theater directors but by musicians such as Lully (who composed opera recitatives inspired by the singing diction of Madame Champmeslé, an actress famous for her Racine interpretation).[23] So in 1820, at the time that Pixérécourt was pushing mise en scène to its visual extreme in Paris, Goethe, experimenting in the opposite direction, was busy conducting his actors' musical pitch and rhythm to the appropriate voice melody in Weimar. Instead of a *Vorstellung* directing movement in space, the Weimar poet managed, in the tactics of a Vortrag, to conduct vocal music in time:

> He managed the rendering using a method of rehearsing similar to that used for producing an opera. He alone made the decisions of the tempo, the fortes and pianos, the crescendos and diminuendos and so on, and was extremely careful to control that his decisions were executed with precision. . . .[24]

Pixérécourt and Lessing never went for the third in between. Rather, they overkilled their respective methods by pushing them to the edge where art explodes to banality or implodes in totality. In 1835, during a technical rehearsal of special lighting effects, a projection screen suddenly caught fire and instantly destroyed the entire Gaité theatre. Three people died in the blaze. To pay the fees of lawyers who defended him against the charge of causing the fire, Pixérécourt had to put his collection of rare vellum-bound first editions up for sale. He sacrificed the texts on the altar of colorful images.

In Hamburg, the actors did not seem to appreciate Lessing's dramaturgy. They even took umbrage at his criticism, whereupon the printer stopped publishing his comments. Lessing retreated to a bookworm's life and returned to texts, ultimately accepting a post as a librarian.

It was between those two extremes that aesthetic management subsequently invented new tactics for making art work and have text and image schwung into motion and music. By the middle of the nineteenth century, a third in-between realm was delineated where aesthetic managers from Wagner to Wilson could make art work. By then, according to theater historian Gösta Bergman, "a professional director surfaced as both a stage designer and personal instructor after a half-century long struggle between the two traditions."[25]

In the manner of Bayreuth, a number of European art institutions have been conceived to protect the third realm from the surrounding two. That's where Schwungful aesthetic play provides creativity along the lines of Kant and Company. This explains why, in a recent treatise on the value of art, *Über das Neue*, [26] Boris Groys treats the phenomena of creativity and innovation as a modern version of Schiller's Schwung. Groys explains innovation as *transvaluation* that dislocates something from one area to another. He claims that art and artists today are the best illustration of such innovations. Aesthetic value is an artist's reward for successful transvaluation by crossing the borders of the profane and the cultural. As an example, Groys explains that after having been snatched from the profane domain of Parisian hardware stores, Marcel Duchamp's ready-mades were assigned aesthetic value by dislocation into a cultural sphere. Duchamp transvaluated what he bought on the market by schwunging it into culture. Groys goes on to define culture as what is stored up in the historical memory of public collections. To him, the profane are products listed in company sales catalogues and kept in business stocks. Collection-based cultural organizations such as museums draw value from the past. Catalogue-based corporations such as IKEA or Disney establish shareholder value by capitalizing on future sales expectations.[27]

Since transvaluation can move both ways between culture and the profane, Groys's theory of creativity and innovation—also used in the understanding of technological change[28]—actually updates both the classics of Kantian transcendence and Arthur Danto's idea of transfiguration. Kantians focused on Schwung from the subjective into the objective, making strictly personal experience acquire universal value. Aesthetics was to realize, by a kind of transcendental catapult, that an inner unique experience is shared with all humankind and therefore equal to objective knowledge. Groys calls it "profanation." *Cultivation* is his term for what Danto calls transfiguration of the commonplace.[29] Schwung in this direction gives things from the objective sphere of the global marketplace subjective meaning, something Danto considers to be pop art's contribution to philosophy.[30] This is how Warhol gave his exact copy of the mass-consumption Brillo box value to an individual art collector. Transfiguring cultivation reverses the catapulting effect of aesthetic transcendence profanation into a bungee jump deep down to subjective meaning. It makes the individual value the special in the common, where Kant was mainly interested in uplifting the individual to fathom the common sense in what he or she personally experienced.

Political transcendence is probably what Ignacio Ramonet sought while Joseph Pine looked for ways of transfiguring commodities by spectacular event marketing. The problem with both of them was that they wanted the *extensive* to end up in the *intensive*, or vice versa, for good. However, it takes *becoming* to philosophize *being*. Had they possessed aesthetic awareness, they rather would have enjoyed the metaphysical ride, the catapulting or bungee-Schwung itself. What makes art work and generate aesthetic energy is the flight over the third realm, not landing at the destination by crashing into some sort of new managerialism as governmental bureaucratic banality[31] or cool and hip corporate totalitarianism.[32] In both cases, it means bankruptcy for art firms; to paraphrase Kant, metaphysics of the third is about the "feeling of feeling" and a "knowing of knowing," or in the new-economy jargon of dot com entrepreneur Jim Clark, "the *new* new thing,"[33] which may be the closest anyone ever comes to the thing-in-itself.

## The Embedded Art Firm and Its Aesthetic Players

### Technicians Torn Between Production and Finance

In the attempt to update the aesthetic problems in avoiding totality and banality by opting for the third realm, it would seem productive to use the insight from theater studies to try to find the aesthetic players originally identified by Kant, Schelling, Dewey, and Nietzsche. Maybe businesses "out there" already operate like art firms without even being aware of it.

To explore embedded aesthetics, I joined a friend on a business trip to a glassworks deep in the enchanted forests in the south of Sweden, a region known as the Kingdom of Glass. It is where glassworks attract a growing number of tourists. The Kosta Boda glassworks was housed in low buildings bordering a four-sided yard. As I was standing in middle of this yard, the glassworks factory hall was to my left; to the right was the building where the designers had their studios and the marketing department its offices. The house to the far end of the yard was the technical production department. On a lower level was the showroom and store; this early morning, the coaches of visiting tourists were already lining up out in front. Even the quadratic layout of the plant seemed set to make my Gadamer model a map for discovering whether the four aesthetic players—technicians, artists, critics, and audience—were embedded in this potential art firm.

We were there on a Thursday, and even though it was a weekday, tourist coaches queued up outside the factory hall where production, or more rightly the "performance," was to happen. Pairs of glass masters conducted trained teams of five men in the rhythmic blowing of glass. An aura of aesthetic effectiveness and precision was conjured up by the graceful movements of the blowpipe, the gestures of the tools, and the elegant addition of the handle of a jug or cup or the foot of a fruit bowl to a glowing glass artifact. Production here looked like a kind of Nietzschean Schwungdance, which added that touch of the medieval guild often alluded to by tour guides diffusing the regional marketing myth of the Kingdom of Glass. Just as a public theater, a Volksbühne, or a Stockholm Stadsteatern, enhances the public atmosphere of a city downtown, this show consciously refined and recycled a bundle of myths to make the culture of this private firm serve the common good of a whole region. The glassblowers' Schwungdance contributed the same Dionysian energy to their respective aesthetic plays as for drivers of a Formula One race. Glassworks visitors also seemed impressed by the performance of an ancient craft infused with the spirits of old masters who long ago traveled north from the heartlands of Bohemia and prophetically selected their worthy successors from towheaded local boys.

It was not only folklore or heritage, however. A sign saying Glass School at the far end of the great hall signaled another public mission of this private firm. It pointed in the direction of a smaller workshop, where the company trained apprentices in a publicly financed education project aimed at keeping local craft alive. High-quality craft supplies a demand for skilled craftsmen, even in high-wage countries. In France, the corporation LVMH, now holding the capital of brands such as Dior and Hermès, supports new craft schools for reasons similar to those of the Swedes who invest tax money in glass craft training. This is far from a Nike Town outlet selling outsourced manufactured products by entertainment illusion. The technique embedded in this glass work is more about anchoring an abstract immanent thing—the value of glass—in concrete bits of the past. Like lava erupting from a Dionysian volcano, glass pours out of the furnace to be tamed by the Nietzschean technicians.

The process of acquiring Dionysian skills has a history as well. Once upon a time, only a few lucky lads were initiated into the mysteries of the art of glassmaking. At that time, training was a private concern to the factory itself. The education of glassworkers performing to the audience in the hall today is now of public concern and linked to regional economic policy. Skilled craft labor is needed to make art work. In a Kantian way, technicians defined a public realm by putting on fascinating glass works shows. When one makes art work, however, one has to abandon all totalitarian temptations for a pure, aesthetically cleansed existence. Hannah Arendt, another philosopher convinced that theater is a model for making art work, pointed out that life may contain a metaphysical essence that art can make us aware of, but life itself cannot be treated as an art work in its totality.[34] In real life, as in the glassworks, the difficult-to-grasp aesthetic competence is inevitably embedded in forms of professionalism that constantly threaten, as polarities, to obscure the work of art.

As I left the factory hall on my way to the production engineering office, I passed by a group of youths probably having a class in their glass school. It smelled of Swedish coffee. A proud gentleman told me that this was where the machines I had heard whirring in a closed hall next to the open glassblower's location were designed and built. One of these machines spits out candlesticks shaped like crystal balls twenty-four hours a day. Another great glass press industrially produces dishes decorated with mechanical impressions of lobsters and crayfish. The first hall was like an intensive black box theater with glassblowers acting frontstage as acrobats and magicians. The machines of mass production were kept locked up in the back stage of a separate industrial building.

The production engineer reluctantly took me into the locked factory hall. This was industry with no sign of art! No aesthetic energy! Bored operators stood amid the noise, catching dishes with long tongs as they rolled off the production line. While we strolled back to his production office, the engineer talked cost reduction, environmental lead-free methods, and industrial rationalization, thereby distancing himself from the aesthetic discourses that glassblowers might inspire. Modern glassmaking, postulated the frank engineer, ought to be a matter of efficient technology rather than of outmoded craft. Glassblowing, when it comes right down to it, is not that complicated or difficult, he pronounced. I hear an echo of Nemirovic first advising Stanislavski to skip his experiments and set his studio aside, disconnecting it from regular everyday operations, and how the great actor Got urged Antoine to join show biz and quit his Montmartre experiment. In fact, said the bespectacled engineer soberly, anyone can pick up the technique fairly quickly. It was as if he were implying that the craftsmen are bluffing when they make us believe art and aesthetics to be essential to business.

Then he spoke of his own industrial dream. With a sad sigh, he confessed that he longed to launch a new machine; it was more than ten years since the last machine of mass production had been designed. Companies cannot hold on to good engineers when all they do is maintain and repair pieces of old equipment, he pointed out. It would be much more stimulating to work for a real factory where formal planning of industrial production is taken seriously! I held my tongue. Thinking of how companies like German Volkswagen, Austrian Swarovski, and French Malongo present technology as staged production in museums and opera house-like factories, I wanted to add ". . . unless you have a love of art and some Nietzschean understanding of the Dionysian aspects of technique."

This production engineer would probably have never thought of Stanislavski or Diaghilev in connection with his own factory work. His discourse was rather Apollonian. He certainly admired the Swedish mass-marketing firms such as IKEA and H & M, masterminds of subcontracted manufacturing, for their financial success. What seemed to count for him—the ultimate legitimating of his obsession with formal industrial planning—was most certainly profitability and shareholder value. The engineer seemed thoroughly ready to sacrifice Dionysian technique for outsourcing.

The IKEA strategy of inauthentic copying may appear to mark an end for classical metaphysics, which in turn is part and parcel of the condition Lyotard diagnosed as postmodern.[35] In a commercial world of matter and form, however, where technology reproduces self-referring clones, copies, or imitations of products and services, the eternal human search for essence and foundation can now be undertaken only as a metaphysical in-between project. The postmodern condition gives rise to a philosophical desire for existential meaning that makes up a market for a transcended metaphysics of the irreproducible surprise Deleuze relabeled "la pataphysique" in homage of the theatrical innovator Alfred Jarry.[36]

Maybe by now the postmodern condition and its demand for metaphysics have found their way into the Swedish forest too, since in the glassworks the attitude of the production engineer is hardly dominant. On the contrary, technology begs for a new meaning; it is no longer satisfied with its role as an instrument for multiplying stolen ideas. Technology seeks its aesthetic roots of Nietzschean technique. The production engineer is forced to consume gallons of coffee in his struggle against the boredom of repetitive routines that no longer seem commercially synonymous with profitability. He actually seems to envy the passion and intensity of the other departments, where technique has enough inherent life to resist technology. I began to re-call how a technician I met in a Swedish theater expressed the seductive Dionysian power of work intensity: "It's like sitting on an express train rush-ing towards the premiere. We in the theater are a bit jealous of film produc-tion. There everyone knows that they've been chosen because they're the best. There's a fantastic group dynamic and feeling of pride. If anyone mucks up they'll never be chosen again. And everyone is there at the same time. A concentrated, well-oiled machine for which nothing is impossible. An eroti-cally attractive idea of immersion, I imagine it's like this working on a sub-marine crew."

On my way out of the factory hall, I tripped on still another sign of aes-thetic consciousness. A strange, dusty machine rested in a corner; a glass-blower nearby explained that some inventive company engineer, to replace the apprentices transporting the glass between the ovens, had constructed an intricate conveyor belt. Why pay wages when a machine could do the job, he declared, adding that without those lads, there would be no steady in-house supply of new glass workers. The fact that the machine was put aside after realizing how rationalization would empty the craft of its youth-ful candidates indicated that technology had limited use in an art firm. Sud-denly, something I had heard from a sound technician in the Stockholm Stadsteatern came to mind: "I'm probably one of the old school of techni-cians who only like technique that plays an active part on stage. All the tech-nicians here at the theater are interested in art. I suppose we all also had a technical interest first, in the equipment and so on, for what they're worth. But you shouldn't add effects, like the musicals that put technical wizardry center stage. Look at the chandelier in *Phantom of the Opera*. I don't think you can *save* a production with special effects. Simplicity is best. You rather must learn to remove effects, even if they've cost a lot of money. A lack of money has never stopped good art, but too much money can sometimes lower the quality. No, we're really not technical freaks here in the sound de-partment. I myself actually haven't even got a stereo at home."

A machine functional to a production engineer can nevertheless be inap-propriate in an art firm. In the glassworks, it would have limited the oppor-tunity for masters to pull in new recruits. It might even have given senior glassblowers a fairly good reason to quit the art firm and set up small opera-tions of their own in the surrounding forest. Technology for its own sake may threaten what holds the players together in this brittle network of aesthetic play. This is especially true when a $100,000 investment barely covers construction of a nice little kiln on your own piece of land so that you can start selling to passing tourists. The real technicians of the aesthetic play are the craftsmen; if they leave and let engineers alone run the show, the art firm would soon become a deserted playhouse.

Again, this vague feeling out in industry found its explicit articulation in the words of a production planner with a feeling for Dionysian technique in the Stockholm City theater: "I shall never forget a trip we made from Stockholm to East Berlin many years ago. They showed us how they had centralized all the theaters' workshops in a huge complex that resembled a real factory. The blokes building the scenery never knew what play they were working on, or even in which theater it was to be performed. Everything was delivered at night, rationally enough, in huge containers. At that time, we Swedes were in rapture about it all; this was in the sixties and scientific management was even popular within theaters. We were so fond of economies of scale and rationalization. Back then we delocalized workshops for the Opera far out in the suburbs. Soon we regretted that move, and now the Opera has moved their workshops back to the city. If you turn theater into a factory, you kill it stone-dead."

## Artists Halfway Between Design and Media

I turned to the right, went across the courtyard, and approached two buildings. In the first were the designers' studios. I was curious about whether or not they were Schelling's artists, the symbol makers of the firm. The company traditionally employed in-house designers in the manner of a European theater with a fixed company. Regular salaries were pretty low in both locations, but those who managed to design a market success were entitled to a bonus on a contracted royalty base. They all seemed to dream of the great hit, the wine glass or fruit bowl that would give them a bread-and-butter, steady source of income. If a designer were lucky, one single design could become a steady low-cost, high-price cash cow like Chanel No. 5 or the Kelly bag for Hermès.

As long as designers didn't work for the competition, they were encouraged to take on outside assignments. It seemed as if this kind of arrangement stimulated designers to maintain international contacts, acquire renown, and stay on top of global competition. Extra odd jobs were indeed a way to have designers themselves finance avant-garde research that might result in future products for their mother company. An obvious parallel can be drawn between these designers and celebrities attracting audiences to the stage by their name value as entertainers on television and in the movies, or fashion makers who are encouraged to open their own fashion house in addition to holding down a job for an established brand. Companies figure that the media coverage independent artists get might exceed by far what they are able to pay for completely incorporated talents.

As we sat down for a drink in a studio, I got the impression that these people traveled a lot. They seemed both gallery hoppers and museumgoers who regularly commuted to the capital to visit their alma mater, the Royal College of Arts and Crafts. In that respect, this art firm was not a local company going international but rather a local promoter of national and international artists.

The visit to the designers' studio also communicated a feeling for what making art work means in real practice. The white studios sparkled with reflections from multicolored glass artifacts, whispering in Matisse's and Dufy's French, Chagall's Yiddish, Miró's Catalan. Long-necked carafes paraded with artfully designed stoppers; they looked as though they were hats on a Paris catwalk or strange birds on a Dali canvas. As is the case in a

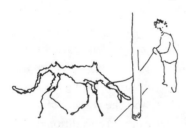

Diaghilev company, the real artist inside a glasswork designer should be able to have a Giacometti sculpture inspire a wine glass, or a Dubuffet canvas, a salad bowl. Artists dig secret tunnels into art history, just as flipped-out Dr. Frankentorf postmodernly sucks off old Erwin Piscator's legacy. The heavy feet of the voluptuous newly designed schnapps glasses are hidden references to their forerunners crafted for the mansions of the 1700s.

Crafted copies were more a matter for technicians across the courtyard, while the designers as artists used art history in a more aesthetic way. They worked beyond heritage and folklore, letting old art and artists inspire their new Schwung as Antoine, Lugné, Diaghilev, and Wilson did. When the real art firm artist makes art work, when he profanates materials from cultural collections, he performs a constructive version of the visual consumption of art that consumers also perform.[37] Perhaps that is why artful designers get the spontaneous approval and sympathy of the market.

What the market accepts may still meet resistance from those who have not yet found their identity as aesthetic players within the embedded art firm. Relationships between the craftsmen-glassblowers and the designers, for example, could be as tense as those of production engineers and glass-blowers. Craftsmen who have not defined themselves as aesthetic techni-cians strive to live up to their work history and demonstrate technical per-fection by resisting crazy whims far from the glass tradition. What really belongs to a tradition and what does not is constantly under debate in an art firm wanting to make old art work without relapsing in historicism or dusty museality.

The debate that seemed present in the glassworks is constantly spelled out in theaters. A stage technician from Stockholm touches upon the issue in this way: "Many directors alternate between film and theater. Almost all scenographers and directors today approach us with ideas from film. They want fast editing and effects that look like music videos. When they talk about their ideas, we realize that this is something for MTV or the Internet. But is it anything for modern theater? And when the ideas come from mid-dle-aged blokes, you can't help but wonder if they're trying to use imagery that isn't really theirs. It can easily go wrong and look pathetic. Sometimes modern theater seems desperate to attract youth with a pair of tight leather pants and some chains."

Glassblowers lean toward conventions, while designers experiment with novelty. New form confronts old matter. A designer wanted glassblowers to insert air bubbles in his designs, yet it had taken craftsmen at least three generations of handicraft to finally eliminate such "defects" in glassware. Production engineers often can't see the point of constantly letting designers add new experimental models to the assortment, and the respect of glass-blowers for designers sometimes seems as meager as that of traditional ma-sons for avant-garde architects. At the same time, designers—like many ar-chitects and fashion makers—increasingly tend to look upon themselves as artists leaving their industrial assignment of making prototypes for series production. In fashion, most designers want to become eccentric artists by creating unique models that infuse a brand with luxurious intensity for unique catwalk events. Today a standard luxury marketing textbook refers to the teaching of both Baudrillard and Bourdieu, maintaining that designer objects should be as "inaccessible" as a Van Gogh painting at Sothebys or Kant's Ding an sich, even to a happy few ultrahigh-net-income buyers.[38] When designers turn artists, their products neither belong to a subject nor are objects; they are closer to the immanent Genettian things consumers have to extrapolate between manifestations and notations. They are the inaccessible immanent essence manifest in an art collection or on show in a museum and notated in the descriptions and depictions in the texts of the museum bookstores. Bernard Arnault, French polytechnician and CEO of the luxury corporation LVMH, explains appointing a rebel artist as head of Dior, against the recommendations of traditional fashion consultants:

> John Galliano is not primarily interested in showing dresses you can buy on the catwalk. He really wants to expose a process of innovation pushed to its extreme and signalling the new ideas that will subsequently mark commercialised clothing. That is his message . . . what we show them are not necessarily something you can dress up in but—again let me [Arnault] emphasize this— ideas pushed to the extreme.[39]

Arnault is an art firm visionary in scandal management, because as early as 1984 Galliano had already cast himself as a trendy taliban when titling one of his first fashion shows Afghanistan Repudiates Western Values. This type of promotion, as scandalous as Diaghilev's use of Nijinsky in tsarist public relations, gave LVMH a key position between finance and media power. The art firms, in between, seem to link commerce with culture in a creative way. Art, be it in the form of catwalk pantomimes or spacey concept cars, is made to work as metaphysical meaning for prêt-a-porter, perfumes, or regular vehicles, and their accessories have one thing in common: a very high profit margin. It also spins off into media culture with an impact far more efficient than regular (and much more expensive) advertising. In the contemporary media-finance nexus, art firms able to maintain their autonomy can thrive in the way economic entrepreneurs did before, as smart middlemen between labor and capital. When Nan Golding gets $2,000 from Camel for a drawing on a cigarette package, when Siemens Kulturprogram offers an established artist 20,000 DM for an installation, or when the German firm Dornbracht asks an artist to make a "statement," both artist and corporate curators seem more than happy with the deal. The latter realize that they are getting an incredible value for the money, while the former are happily unaware that they are earning the trifling stipend of a mediocre management consultant. Artists may erroneously believe that this is the price they pay for autonomy, while corporations, on the other hand, claim the credibility capital of art work.

When a designer complained that he was having trouble keeping glass-blowers from embellishing his sober design with additional intricate decorations, it was a sign of her managing the autonomy of art versus crafts. It recalled Antoine's and Stanislavski's problems with those stage-strutting actors who found it necessary to flatter their audience in quest of success and stardom. To be sure, there were designers who had found their own original ways of managing the autonomy of their third realm. According to one report, a designer successfully upstaged glassblowers when he presented his objects to visitors by telling fascinating stories relating glass to Nordic mythology in a way Schelling would have appreciated. That designer acted somewhat like Sjöberg when he lost his patience and then began writing criticism of his own plays, or when Castorf teamed up with the dramaturge author Hegemann and image maker Meyer to fight for an inner-directed theater company.

Designers are also split between finding new inspiration from the outside and introverted reflection on the essence of art. In their oscillation between the surface and the depth, some designers work with glass painting while others engage in almost chemical glass experiments. The frontstage Diaghilevs versus the backstage Stanislavskis, I thought, after running into one designer who was sitting all alone by his desk, like a wise old monk groaning under the weight of crystal sculptures. The roof of his studio seemed as high as a church, glittering with sacred crystal classics. First, he scolded designers who only look for new ideas. Then he held up a pure prism to the last rays of the winter sun and began philosophizing about the *bleibende Wahre*,[40] the absolute truth that Gadamer, in the footsteps of Master Heidegger, meant only Art can evoke:

> Matter, not form, interests me. The spectrum, optical illusions, physical experiments with the possibilities of craftsmanship. I have no formula for what actually happens. For what actually happens when I get the signal. When the sun shines in a certain way, that's when the miracle happens. You never forget that. The play of light releases an artless beauty. When the sun shines in the right way, I see birds of paradise flying on my walls.

## Critics from Marketing Toward Culture

My company tour was coming to an end, and once again I was at the marketer's small building next to the invitingly open gate through which all the visitors pass. My Gadamerian map indicated that I might find Dewey's critics hidden in the marketing department. The marketers were sitting among posters and catalogues. Samples of beautiful glass objects surrounded them. They were gossiping about the large retail customers who buy up entire production runs for their chain stores. Some prided themselves on being able to forecast which designs would sell. Their speculations led to decisions of series production that in turn might make a lucky designer win his sought-after regular royalty. Some marketers said they took careful notes of "talk trends" in the glass shops and then used these opinions to inform their discussion with designers.

Also evident was the traditional sales attitude whereby salesmen hold that their authority is based on the fact that they are representatives of some average consumers, spokesmen of real common people with everyday needs. To Dewey, however, critics were not prescribers. Their task is not telling artists what to do, like a Nemirovic lecturing a Stanislavski or a Lord Rothermere advising a Diaghilev. A salesperson from the Stockholm theater commented on the practice of the patrons of her theater who signed up for seasonal subscriptions one year in advance: "They can call us whenever they like. If there are any changes to the program we call them at home and tell them directly. Recently we sat here phoning all weekend. But it's quite rewarding. They're pleased we take the trouble to talk to them in person. Maybe our productions are no better or worse than other theaters', but our customers and subscribers get the best service. Often they ask why we don't put on *Hamlet* again. But I don't think they really mind what's on the repertoire. And to tell the truth, there are some productions that we would like to cancel at once, thinking about the customers. Sometimes you're as embarrassed by what's on the stage as you are when the audience behaves badly in the auditorium."

The same sort of double embarrassment of the front stage when the back stage does not meet expectations, or vice versa, or when the audience can't "behave" during the performance, is found among marketers in the glass works. It has something to do with the fixation on total success that mass marketers suffer, their longing for transcendental beauty unifying all mankind in a global humanity like David's revolutionary feasts. They seemed on an eternal search for the blockbusting hot product. They longed for the popular, the people's darling design. Marketing research however has never, ever predicted success, and if this sort of marketing attitude dominated, artists would have little chance of surviving in any company.

A different kind of marketing mind-set, perhaps more in tune with Danto's transfiguration, was also evident, however. Many marketers seemed proud to work for a firm connected to art. They spoke a lot about special editions, the limited series individually signed by each designer; they loosely referred to avant-garde icons like Duchamp ready-mades. Those marketers were more after detecting cool ideas than controlling sales success. Hot populism versus the conquest of cool sophistication, popular universality versus cultivated individuation, seemed to define the divide between marketers. The latter position is reflected clearly in the company advertising outsourced to an agency whose office looks like that of an opera impresario. No products or catalogues are displayed, but the walls are full of designer portraits in black and white, mimicking Brassai's well-known icons of the stars of modern art. The signatures of the individual designers replace the collective company brand, and company history gives way to artists' biographies. The commercial task is neither a matter of selling "glass wares" nor of marketing "designer glass." Marketers become curators offering museum pieces or collectors' items to special glass-art galleries. They work hard for edited products to acquire their art aura by being exhibited in some nonprofit museum. As good critics, they present the artists in art publications; such marketing directly replicates what critics do in art firms.[41]

Designers become artists who make art work as much for their own purpose and history as for that of their art firm brand. Marketing, passing through the process of criticism, evolves into corporate curating of culture documented in the coffee-table volumes sold in museum bookstores.[42] When marketing events turn into culture staged in museum spaces, they are also subjected to harsh art criticism, something that Armani experienced in the New York Guggenheim show and Versace in his London show in the Victoria and Albert Museum in 2002. The marketing consultant of the main sponsor of the German Biennale Pavilion in Venice 2001 actually presented himself as a curator and maintained that branding is no longer a task for marketing but a matter of culture. The company clearly signaled its awareness of art firm criticism linking marketing to culture by hosting a seminar investigating art criticism. Between the power of opinion and the use of the media at the 2002 Cologne Art Fair, its corporate curator even managerialized Hannah Arendt, stating that all firms must regard themselves as organically involved in the context of "LIFE," managerially defined as Love, Intelligence, Freedom, and Evolution.[43]

In the tensions between marketing and culture fermenting within embedded art firms, players can take a midposition of the critic minding both the institutional context and its cultural content. The marketing director of the Swedish theater discussing such issues in regular business terms well illustrates this blurring of business and art:

> I like to keep central control over the marketing budget. Internally we might be working on different projects and on different stages, but externally we have to have a common brand. I reorganized and centralized marketing when there was talk a few years back about diversification. And we were worried that our public subsidies would be drastically cut by the year 2000. Would we still be able to produce theater in the same way? Perhaps we'll have more visiting productions in the future, more people from outside who rent our premises for other purposes than theater. In this case, it will be all the more important to create a brand of a unified civic theater.
>
> It's like when the old department stores turned into malls. They still produce their own adverts where Armani, Prada, Boss, and others are in slightly smaller print, under their common umbrella. We're maintaining our brand by images, that is, graphically with typeface and layout. We are all part of the same family, so advertising and campaigns have to be coordinated to protect and enforce our brand. But this is far from simple; many of our stages feel they should do the marketing job themselves in order to build up their new avant-garde look! We want to be as famous as any consumer goods company, but they feel that underground coolness depends on being exclusive and selective!

## Audience of Half Consumers and Half Managers

Kant's public audience remain the one aesthetic player to identify in its contemporary guise. In recent years, there has been spectacular growth in direct sales in the store next to the hall where the glassblowers perform. No longer is this an anonymous factory out in the boondocks, shipping its wares to urban consumers. The growing direct sales and the everyday contacts with vast numbers of customers has fostered a tolerance for distinction rather than standardization. The anonymous mass market situated somewhere far away seems to be an obsolete myth, as abstract as the revolutionaries' notion of "the people" used by Ramonet or the global idea of a universal "mankind" underlying Pine's general populist advice to managers of the experience economy. The market has dissolved into numerous minor segments and groups having a variety of tastes and preferences.

In the Stockholm theater, an actor once put this in terms resonating with both Joseph Beuys and Joseph Pine: "I am not really sure about this bit about customers—I mean looking upon members of our audience simply as buyers. It's about a deeper level of contact than that, about theater transforming things. We actually transform the audience's world, too."

The rapid museum boom of the 1980s and 1990s, in 2002 alluded to as "the museum bubble," has shifted its meaning. Today it is closely connected to the processes of managing something seemingly commonplace to a level which is special to individual consumers. Managers now want to learn how art can be made to work in that direction. This was theoretically captured by Danto's transfiguration; practically, it is manifested in the Duchampian ready-made.

The direct sales in glasswork had nothing to do with the old company store selling rejected wares or even the wholesale factory outlet marketing slightly out-of-fashion products. The visit to the Kosta Boda glasswork was something very different from a regular company tour. It was a pilgrimage for a new art firm audience composed of consumers who behaved like culture shoppers in a museum store, not as greedy buyers in some crowded bargain basement. The museum boom of the 1980s and 1990s has taught middle-class kids of the pop-music generation how to make art work. Today they buy certified Picasso and Miró T-shirts out of Barcelona museum shops, they choose a dress inspired by Guggenheim's Armani exhibition staged by Robert Wilson, they drive Picasso cars or they acquire a signed Beuys photograph along with furniture bought in a Habitat store. For the postmod middle class, fine arts have definitely turned pop.

During the 1980s, the pioneer cultural consumer, dressed in black, began to float around in his or her postmodern condition, like a weightless embryo in an aestheticized economy frowned upon by his or her culture-radical parents. The offspring were as artsy as their parents were high-tech or radical chic.

Boris Groys claims that contemporary artists such as Wilson or Castorf are actually models for this new kind of cultural consumption when they present their installations and performances.[44] They have taught the audience-consumers to arrogantly sample texts and pick images, to steal whatever signs and colors they fancy from the mediatic glut and make it work as art. Wherever the new cultural consumer vagabonds on the planet, he feels at home in the local museum making global art work locally. With the sophisticated gaze of the cultural connoisseur, anyone in this vast audience feels confident in greeting Picasso or Warhol, Beuys or Boltanski, as if he were an old chum.

Even industrial rationalization and functionalism have lost their strictly utilitarian Bauhaus meanings and hybridized with art like Yves Klein's patented blue color, Armani's procedure of accumulations, Caesar's technique of compressions, Ben's calligraphic graffiti, and Christo's wrapping architecture into an aesthetic style. Since U.S. president Ronald Reagan and British Prime Minister Margaret Thatcher, assisted by business-art clubs such as the BCA and the ABSA, reoriented art funding toward the corporate world, Damien Hearst and Jeff Koons have replaced Coca Cola and McDonald's as the brands for this new audience of privatized U.S. and British cultures.[45] After inspecting the objects in the galleries, they shop for the aesthetic philosophy on sale in the museum bookshop. Huge monographs can be diluted with easily consumed posters to decorate their white-cubicle Zen homes. When they buy gifts for their partners at Agnès B, they may also pick up a catalogue of the Gilbert and George exhibition sponsored by the shop. (Just next door, by the way, Agnès B runs an art gallery of her own, and she makes arty movies too.) They push their way through Japanese tourists in APC's clothing store to buy a CD freshly pressed in the shop's own recording studio. They enjoy performances at Starbucks and listen to lectures in the auditorium of Apple's Prince Street sales point. They admire the generosity of empty spaces as they watch classic paintings projected on screens or listen to poetry read from the stage of the Prada shop installed in the ex-Guggenheim Soho space redesigned by star architect Rem Koolhaas.[45]

They feel no need to go to Eurodisney in Paris when they can go to Euroguggenheim in Bilbao. In Las Vegas, they prefer Guggenheim to trashy casinos, and in Chicago both the American Girl and Rainforest Café seem tacky and dated compared to the Art Institute or the Gucci shop. Instead of watching CNN, they have critical curators like Okwui Enwezor or Daniel Birnbaum brief them on global issues in the Documenta 11 at Kassel or Venice Biennale. They see no reason to read the *Harvard Business Review* or *Le Monde Diplomatique* when there is the *New York Review of Books*, *Wallpaper*, *Du*, *Brandeins*, *Domus*, and *Art Forum*. They feel the business cases of art history like Warhol's factory, Oldenburg's store, Damien Hearst's

pharmacy, and Andreas Gursky's supermarket picture constitute a much more profound reflection than any textbook in retailing or marketing.[46] The nomadic middle class seems almost addicted to an art they thank their metaphysical space of existence for. When they turn entrepreneurs, they recall European lessons by Hugo Boss, Giorgio Armani, or Miuccia Prada and start aping *Vogue* or *Wallpaper* by setting up fancy magazines to connect art with commerce. They market their products like rare paintings in some art gallery. They hire their staff from Cambridge and Oxford as they prefer working with arty intellectual kids instead of computer geeks or finance nerds with an uncool business school MBA.

These new markets are pluralistic, a fact well known to the great number of audience experts employed to run today's shops of art firms as museums. They dispatch an array of cultural goods so cleverly derived out of art that they would have made both Diaghilev and Coco Chanel very jealous. The specialists in art commerce have broadened the field of knowledge about audiences considerably.[47] When an art firm like Beaubourg in Paris, for instance, knows that three quarters of their visitors are business groups, they can no longer talk of a singular "market." Beyond the simplified demographic and sociological categories of market surveys, which differentiate only in old-economy terms, art firms directly experience and take into account a multitude of desires of, say, a group of school kids or busloads of

Japanese tourists collecting postcards in packs of fifty. Observant museum curators note that visitors ask for high-quality art-derived products instead of the tacky souvenirs of yesterday. They start merchandising objects inspired by their exhibitions or offer better products at lower prices than regular interior design stores.

They also know that an educated audience, those who have enjoyed a good audio tour, for example, stay longer in the art space and buy more in the shop. Well-run art-firm stores are aesthetic education centers that have the same cultural impact as the museums built to attract audiences with spectacular architecture. They invite their audiences to make art work in new ways. This made French theologian Michel de Certeau spot new art institutions as places of worship for modern spiritualism. In the 1970s, he identified Beaubourg as such an in-between space. He defended it against attacks from the left by Bourdieu, claiming the new museum totalized old class culture, and from the right by Baudrillard, to whom the Pompidou Center was another banalized anti-intellectual shopping mall.[48] There is no doubt that the audience in Kosta Boda glassworks actually recycles a century of European avant-garde in the Swedish wilderness. Helped by technicians, artists, and critics of the art firm, they absorb old art and make it work anew. Their efforts to think locally and act globally have changed. Frank Castorf tapped old Piscator much more consciously when putting on a show for the kids in the Volksbühne than did Sid Vicious when recycling Issidor Issou and Guy Debord in the Sex Pistols songs that entertained their parents.[49]

In that sense, the Swedish glassworks is only a minor example of a European trend headed by companies such as the German Vitra with its Gehry-drawn design museum; the Deutsche Bank's Guggenheim art spaces in Berlin, Bilbao, and Las Vegas; or the Alessi museum in northern Italy.

The Italian firm Alessi is a typical case of how aesthetic development can extend the intensive experience of nice design into time and defeat fads and fashions of media trends by making art work. It has taken the patience and love of the whole Alessi family to let art-loving brother Alberto Alessi slowly but surely transform the family factory in Crusinallo. Their efforts have changed their production from formerly simple tin cutlery into the famous Alessi brand featuring the Memphis Group architects on coffee-table stages all over the world.

As is the case in many other invisible art firms, the investment of Alberto Alessi has taken so long to pay off that no shareholder would be patient enough to ride out the time. Only patient brothers might, for instance, stand the loss incurred when Salvador Dali bullied young Alberto into spending a fortune designing a "metaphysical comb" (which never materialized, of course). Relating a firm to art is equal to opting for a long-term strategy which carries with it significant aesthetic risks, and although there are no quick fixes, there are rewards in extending the intensity of aesthetic experience into long-term operations. Art firms hope to achieve the amazing effect of a Christo, who succeeds in repeating the same wrapping over and over again yet still surprises and impresses his audience, even if it is only with his perseverance. Designers for an art firm like Alessi are regarded as family friends in the same way that artists were once part of renaissance courts. It becomes obvious how envious big industrial corporations are of such a long-term art strategy when a car designer on a television commercial states he wants to create not useful products but "eternal sculptures," or that he wishes in his old age to walk with his son "through a museum where this car is parked and say, 'Hey, I was part of this.'" Art made to work surfaces even as a magic source of eternal life.

Consumers making up this new kind of art firm audience can no longer be regarded as old-time buyers. In contemporary socioeconomic terms, art firms of the nineties were positioned in between the two worlds of finance-management and media-culture, replacing capital and labor in the old political economy. The audience shifted to audiovisual consumers shopping in a multitude of media-cultural markets. In the eighties and nineties, audiences were identified as yuppies, DINKs (dual incomes, no kids), HNWI (high-net-worth individuals), in the pre-WTC economy, a rapidly growing group of individuals owning more than $1 million or the ultra-HNWI, the 55,000 people in the world who owned more than $30 million in 1999 before the stock markets crashed.[50] The latter segments were speculators that spend on art firms the money they have earned on finance-management highly dependent on a media-culture that in turn was fueled circuitously and constantly by art firm creativity. Goodwill was the gold that corporate alchemists tried to squeeze out of their art firm investments. During this period, therefore, art firms, so it seems, positioned themselves in the public consciousness as linking and distancing our two socioeconomic sectors of contemporary formalism and materialism: capitalistic financial management and media-controlled culture. Bernard Arnault and François Pinault, two successful French art-collecting, luxury-brand investors, have increased the value of their art firms to all French investors eager to support national heritage.[51] This new version of the good old in-between art firm seemed to offer audiences a possibility for distancing and reflecting on their double identity as media-culture consumers and finance-managing investors. This new role of art firms is taking on importance as aesthetic educators of a new in-between class presenting itself more as a managerial than a middle class.

What then does the art firm offer those pretending to be members of a managerial class? In art firms, consumers find something apart from the dominating shareholder value of a corporate world focused on short-term trading. The contemporary countertypes of yesterday's courtly artists do not survive only in family art firms. In the dot com era, venture capitalists were frequently exposed to theatrical sales pitches by high-performing storytellers in the service of investment bankers. Many management scholars turned away from producing knowledge and began diffusing their stories to large corporations as real stage performers. Professors Steven Brown, Kjell Nordström, and Franz Liebl offered their consultancy clients stand-up comedy, hard rock, and techno-rave. Brown, who argued that postmodern marketing is romanticism revisited, is himself a top entertainer in his own Irish tradition; the Swede Nordström acts out his Viking-funky business on stage to the joy of all overaged Harley Davidson fans in his manager audience (as a board member of the dot com Spray, he mounted shows which were instrumental in spurring the enthusiasm of venture capitalists). Signaling a growing trend in Germany and France, management consultants brought in theater companies to stage plays for an insider audience of employees.[52] Service industries, consultants, managers looking for higher pay, all sorts of start-ups and upstarts, began systematically flirting with art and artists in a quest for new events, competencies, metaphors, and products.[53] Art firms seemed to have the quality of not threatening the corporate power structure while at the same time remaining critical to power. To a captive corporate audience of managers, they made art work to defreeze locked-in power positions and frankly address internal conflicts, a trend that promises to make way for the processes of creative problem solving. Corporations such as Siemens brought in artists to visualize future economic trends in art and economy and produced a show at the Hamburg Deichtorhalle in the spring of 2002; Daimler Chrysler has in-house artists moderating high-tech product development projects. Business excellence and managerial performance are increasingly seen as the fruits of artful creation in organizations that make value in ways similar to the strategies used by aesthetic players in making art work. Such artlike businesses are more clan-like and gift-based than traditional models of industry or trade firms.[54]

Art-aware management researchers have found that artistic virtuosity similar to that found in theatrical companies or music groups is a key competence of "hot groups" in high-performing businesses and projects.[55] This of course represents a modernized incorporated version of medieval jesters and companies of comedians in ancient courts. The glassworks Kosta Boda, for example, has itself actually worked for an audience of managers made up of the board of its owners. The corporate owners of the Swedish glassworks totally enjoyed flying to New York with their designers, since, among other things, together they went gallery hopping.

Such fringe benefits may explain why big corporations tend to act as patrons to art firms. Although Kosta Boda profits were pretty low, as is the case of most art firms, this Swedish glassworks was nevertheless, according to reports, a favorite subject of its boardroom conversations. One browsed quickly through the dull factories of the financial portfolio to devote time to this tiny firm in the Swedish forest. It would seem that finance professionals had less to learn from discussing regular industrial cash cows than from posing as engaged art firm patrons. On the other hand, perhaps art firms had the quality of considerably widening the communication among the inside audience of managers in the courtly boardroom theater.

Yesterday's art firms were connected to state power and incorporated in their political economy, as the cases of the Berlin Volksbühne and Stadsteatern in Stockholm have shown. The stakeholders of art and culture had once been politicians and their citizen-voters. Now finance corporations feudally truffle their portfolios with corporate collections, art awards, art spaces, gourmet restaurants, fashion shops, and even cute little glassworks deep in the Swedish fairy-tale forest in much the same way that the Grand Duke helped Diaghilev run his opera tour to Paris. In the current trend of cultural privatization, successful museum curators compete to replace the nobility, academics, and old money of their boards of trustees with cool CEOs of global corporations eager to promote their cultural image on attractive new markets. Today, this new cultural managerial elite is under the same suspicion of clinching juicy private deals on the art markets the same way that insiders do on the market for stocks. Although private gain might occur, the main reason for increasing corporate audiences seems to be that the truffle might mushroom into something of value even to the balance sheet.

In the early 1900s, a prince from the Swedish Royal Court launched the glassworks of Småland nationwide. At that time, the Swedish royal family comprised a poet prince, a painter prince, and an avant-garde designer prince. Today progressive CEOs prefer running their own little art firms, while the king of Sweden has to inaugurate dull trade fairs and sweaty sport events. Posing in front of contemporary art these days are not royalty but Europe's top politicians and CEOs. This manager-audience likes to profile itself as being as innovative and unconventional as the avant-garde artist.[56] They even pick art historians to write up their manager biographies.[57] The reason they like their pieces of art, at least according to art historian Wolfgang Ullrich,[58] is that it is something that takes time to appreciate and is difficult to understand. Art helps reinvent space in the virtual void of high-tech work and slows down speedy stress in fast firms, but it is not simply another media or means of efficient communication. There is actually no guarantee that an individual will ever grasp what a piece of art is about. A person must take the risk of making it work, must be open to its metaphysical aspects. Joining the audience of an art firm, in a confusing role between that of a cultural consumer and a financial manager, might be interpreted as publicly making a statement critical of too-simple managerial methods and quick fixes in a shareholder value-dominated fast economy. By stepping down from a position of manager and up from that of media consumption, a person expresses philosophical awareness of being human. I recall the excitement of managers having listened to how Christo Javacheff argued for the "urgency of pure aesthetics" with "no strings attached" being "the most useful thing in the world" of "highest priority for mankind" because "only art makes us different from the animals." They shamefully admitted that Christo represented creative management and an entrepreneurial risk taking they had long given up struggling for inside their own corporations. For the managerial-class audience, art worked as aesthetic inspiration to manage a publicly meaningful economy in the true Kantian sense, to step down from empty abstractions of new managerialism and slowly make aesthetics, in a true Schillerian sense, regain our faith in the common senses and playful joy of human life.[59]

## An Emerging Art Firm: Pistoletto's Aesthetic Play

Arthur Schopenhauer extended philosophy into a new market for metaphysics where art could work. Joseph Beuys extended art into society. Now the time has come to expand the art firm from the third realm of theaters to business on a vast aesthetic field and make the dream of Dionysus Inc., mentioned in the Preface, come true. Managers themselves feel the need to go beyond sponsorship and really embed art into business. Success is no longer measured by the invention of new products or application of the latest IT but by being as artistically creative with given hardware as theaters have been using texts and images, signs and colors to make art work. Managerial lessons from Kant to Gadamer have filtered through two centuries of aesthetic practice, and today they are diffused through MBA textbooks into everyday business practice, thanks to the growing aesthetic awareness of postmodern management scholars as well as their students.[60] The rapidly increasing number of business-aesthetics connections treated by contemporary art may well erode differences between art and business schools in the future.[61]

The return of Dionysus Inc. inspired a group of people from both art and business to gather for a joint art show seminar in Berlin.[62] Little did I suspect how close business and aesthetics had come and how much managers had in common with artists at the time that a couple of friends and I were arranging this meeting late in 2001.

During deep and sincere discussions, young artists and managers met to deconstruct mutual clichés of the ideal-type executive and the idealist artist. It seemed clear that artists had moved far beyond the stereotypical "show us the money" attitude[63] about business and that managers familiar with performance art saw art as something to make work in ways other than boasting status by hanging on a gallery wall or as financial collateral deposited in a bank vault. Some managers had an art school background, and many artists cooperated with firms in projects ranging from pure event marketing to creativity coaching for corporate personnel. Gone were the neat old distinctions between art and working life; the third realm was widening into an aesthetic field for mutual projects.

One management consultant claimed marketing was about to cure its Don Giovanni complex of seducing as many buyers as possible; her partner saw the advent of new firms basing their success on an inner ethos attracting an audience much as Kandinsky wanted spiritual art to do.[64] A trendy marketer insisted that what he was doing was best called "curating" and that Krishnamurti had more to say to marketing managers than Philip Kotler did. Henrik Schrat, a German concept artist, introduced a "manager-in-residence" to his English art school.

To Michelangelo Pistoletto, the grand old man of Italian conceptual art and founder of Fondazione Pistoletto in Biella, the competence of contemporary artists is precisely such an autonomous cultivation of inner values that forces them to express the true necessities other people forget about in their everyday muddle. Carl Hegemann of the Volksbühne called the real "new economy a true economy," adding that those who had a feel for doing business are risk-taking entrepreneurs with more in common with anarchosyndicalists than with the big corporations practicing an imperialism as obsessed with control as the central committee of the communist party under Stalin. What other than some Schopenhauerian desire for the absolute can explain why people would turn down high pay in show-biz entertainment or high media exposure in some TV reality show for making art work, as old Piscator did, instead of playing educative museum-theater in a high-status institution? Hegemann would claim that it's the same irrational desire for actionist metaphysics that makes an individual an entrepreneur. He proves his point by reciting the names of his favorite avant-garde rebel agitators: Joseph Pine, Gary Hemel, and, of course, Tom Peters.[65]

The revolutionary art firm has to take up the struggle for metaphysics in reality. The business of art is as embedded in reality as any firm in the market. To Hegemann, however, the creative challenge for artists as well as for entrepreneur is to produce *in* the market but not *for* the market. Art must remain free but refrain from staying pure or isolated. Making art work takes daredevils who surprise their audiences, assume risks, and cleverly negotiate liberties that no established advertising agency selling success under the pressure of big budgets ever dares. Hegemann mentions that a Calvin Klein ad for public tax money investment in art firms, copied from a Volksbühne concept, generates a media creativity that, when it works, is immediately stolen by private businesses and diffused by commercial culture. The publicly financed art firm is not the proper vehicle for dispersing party propaganda or for handling power struggles. It does not produce to order, only on speculation. Therefore the art firm performs a kind of societal skunk works by stubbornly situating itself in the third realm. Only art firms, in other words, can inject economic energy into a market democracy.

When I look back at a decade of study of the Volksbühne art firm, I realize the amazing consequence of Castorf's long-term aesthetic strategy for his art firm. Ever since the fall of the wall, the Volksbühne has obviously been motivated by its aim of radiating art into the surrounding culturescape. The work with the homeless people in the early nineties, the confrontations with right-wing hooligans, all the Schlingensief performances like the Chance 2000 party or the bizarre Namibian Wagner project, the Deleuze event, "Mille Plateaux," the rock concerts, readings, and debates in the two Volksbühne cafés, the installation of the "Volksbutik" in 1996, the guest performances in the 1997 Documenta, and finally, the 2002 "Neustadt," when Bert Neumann transformed the whole house on Rosa Luxemburg Platz into a complete townscape—all of this was geared at escaping isolated totalitarianism toward banality and carefully avoiding pure kitsch in the process. In 2003, when the news circulated that Wolfgang Wagner, Richard Wagner's grandson, had called in Christoph Marthaler and Christoph Schlingensief, two sons of the Volksbühne, to stage "Tristan" and "Parsifal" at Bayreuth, the Schopenhauerian art firm connection was again made obvious.[67]

During the same period, other art firms adopted a similar long-term strategy to move in the opposite direction. During the late nineties, the Italian fashion firm Prada built an empire by acquiring such brands as Miu-Miu, Helmut Lang, Jil Sander, and Azzedine Alaïa. In consequence, its once-strong signature was threatened with banality by this cocktail of different styles. Prada has, however, cleverly used a number of projects to regain some of its early transcendence. By 1993, they founded an art space in Milan, and they also moved into an ex-art space in Soho and organized a seminar on "Hope" in 2002. The setting was a Milan prison; the seminar featured radical social philosophers Toni Negri and Gianni Vattimo. At the thematic art show *Shopping* in a Frankfurt museum, Andreas Gursky presented three giant photos—Prada I, II, and III—discreetly repositioning their New York outlet as a museum piece rather than a point of sale. In 2002, the first issue of the art magazine *Tate International Arts and Culture* presents Miuccia Prada, owner of the art firm, as a Ph.D. in political science, agreeing that the time has come to return to the universal values of classical beauty.

Thanks to the presence of Michelangelo Pistoletto and his team in Berlin, I stumbled upon another example of a strikingly well-managed emerging art firm. Fondazione Pistoletto has emerged in a way similar to Robert Wilson's Watermill Foundation, Marina Abramovic's retreat estate, Hermann Nitsch's Prinzendorff manor and the art firms of other successful senior artists who have invested in places for making art work.[66] In 1993, after a period as a professor at the Vienna Art Academy, Pistoletto got the idea of investing his earnings from the international art market in Cittadellarte, a project for his foundation situated in his hometown of Biella in northern Italy. By selling traditional pieces of art, he earned the money to transform the concept of art into that of an art firm. Pistoletto's explanation of the name Cittadellarte contains his conception of a third realm: "The name *Cittadellarte* incorporates two meanings: that of a citadel, a protected and defended area, and that of a city, which suggests a dynamics of extension and of complex interrelations with the world."[67]

Biella is a monument to the industrial revolution, where a dynamic textile industry, including the internationally famous family firms Fila, Emilio Zegna, and Nino Cerrutti, operate in an historical landscape of old abandoned mills. In Cittadellarte, housed in one of Biella's oldest factory compounds, Pistoletto has created UNIDEE, a university for ideas, which arranges workshops and seminars for young artists residing in Cittadellarte during the summer months. The art students, who benefit from various scholarships granted by international partners, are selected on the basis of a presentation of a socially responsible art project.

Pistoletto arrived in Berlin with his wife, Maria, and two collaborating young artists, Omi and Theresa. Their passionate account of their art firm was so exciting that I soon found myself in Biella. On the train, I read the twenty-second letter in Schiller's book from 1792 that I always carry. I anticipated that the trip to Biella would shed light on one of its more enigmatic statements: "The more general the mood and the less limited the bias produced in us by any particular art, or by any particular product of the same, then the nobler that art and the more excellent that product will be."[68]

While some friends and I were enjoying a nice risotto prepared by Maria Pistoletto, her daughter, a designer who had just completed her master's thesis on museum shops; a son-in-law, who now managed the economy of the Fondazione after a time as head of finance in an international aviation company; and Michelangelo presented the art firm. He appeared like a philosophical patriarch at the end of a light glass table with his back to a large window overlooking the inner courtyard of Cittadellarte. It was a crystal-cold winter day, and the sun hit the whitewashed façade of the old newly restored factory.

"People come to me like to a witch or magician," Michelangelo began. "They want me to tell them the future. I tell them that I know the future. I am a magician, but a magician who does not like to manipulate his clients like a cheap consultant. I want to share my tricks with people, so I ask them to sit down at my table. OK, you want to know the future. It's easy because the future is what we decide to make together. Let's talk about what we want. Then let's do a project—that's what Cittadellarte is here for! That is how I conceive my project—and mind you, it is a project and not a visionary utopia. I don't declare that I want to change the world all by myself. I propose a cooperation."

"But what is art to you, Michelangelo?" I asked stupidly, and I heard John Dewey laugh at me in the back of my head.

"Bah, I sell my paintings for as much I can get in the U.S. to invest here in Biella. Art collectors are in a sense the bankers of my art firm. You see, I regard pieces of art as traces of an artist's philosophical education. To do art in that narrow sense helps you articulate and define your own message. I myself worked a lot with mirrors, and this gave me my outlook on reality, being neither purely subjective nor purely objective. Very early, I also worked with groups making theater, creating performances in the village where we spent the summer. But now I don't want to make art but make art work. So, first of all, in order to understand my kind of art firm, you need to completely forget what you think art is, you need to completely erase all your ideas about art. What is needed is a clearing out of the mind. An open mind. A responsive and responsible mind. This place is free, open, and responsive, like a free, open, and responsive mind. Art to me is such freedom, a clearing in the chaotic world. That is how it can become a massive generator, a generator of energy."

"And the artist, who is the artist then, Michelangelo?" I asked my question as a crazy chorus of Beuys, Kandinsky, Wilson, and Müller cautioned "Shut up, you fool" deep inside my skull.

"Well, today the artist is just someone who has one single great privilege in society. The artist is autonomous, and her only job is to formulate her inner message as clearly as possible. We accept this extreme autonomy only for artists. They are able to reject the social world, and in doing so, they actually perform the most social action conceivable. Only artists can reach this zero point from which art as an autonomous field will grow."

"So UNIDEE is a way to make artists develop art into an open space?"

As I said this, I saw strange figures floating in the air above the brightly shining white building outside the window behind Michelangelo. Their wings were as long as old coats, and their eighteenth-century wigs glimmered in the sunshine. One after the other, Immo Kant, Freddy Schiller, and Arty Schopenhauer landed on the red tile roof of Cittadellarte as aesthetic guardian angels.

"Indeed so! Today there is a conflict between opposite poles, the catastrophic contrasts in the world, clearly visible to everyone and in one way or other experienced by everyone. But bang! The Berlin Wall fell in 1989, and crash! The WTC collapses in 2001. Opposite forces are no longer represented by the twentieth-century East-West ideological conflict. Now the bipolar clash is between the increasingly gigantic globalization systems and more minute fragmentation of sociocultural individualities, between the economic and technological peaks and depths of human degradation proliferating in the world. Art must operate in between, because energy always manifests itself as the meeting or clash of two opposite poles, between the positive and negative."

"How do you conceive of this meeting/clash, Michelangelo?" I finally asked, all the time aware of the aesthetic angels on the factory roof, happy philosophical hummingbirds merrily singing in the sunshine.

"I am funding Cittadellarte, because I want to get things going! I don't care about big cars or luxury housing. I want to further concrete action for a new kind of socially responsive-responsible art. You can see my art firm as a modern version of the studios of Renaissance artists where science, production, and economy were inextricably bound up with imagination, philosophy, and spirituality. I have always worked like that, which caused problems in the short run but was good in the long run. By chance I got my first gallery when I left school. An art dealer in Turin, who showed artists like Giacometti, Magritte, and Bacon, liked a painting that had won me first prize at a Milan art show. He paid me to paint a set for his gallery, but I started to experiment with mirrors instead. This made him so disappointed that I ran away on the opening night of my show! I preferred to visit Paris— I had never been there—instead of getting criticized at home in Turin.

"In Paris, I ran into a small American with a dog. His show had arrived, a set of strange pictures of soup cans, hamburgers, and cartoons. I gave the guy one of my mirror paintings, and soon after Sonnabend came to Turin and bought up the whole show on the recommendation of his wife's former husband, Leo Castelli. I next found myself as the only European in the pop art scene in New York. Then this lust to do new things took over again.

Sonnabend got angry that I could never settle for a stable marketable style of production as the others in his art firm could. The final straw came when he declared that I should become an American citizen, using the argument that the point of his art firm was to revert the stream of cultural trade. I went back home and set up my own team of young artists, which we branded 'Arte Povera.' It worked so well that the man with the dog came over to invite us back to the States. I prefer to run my own art firm independently, though, so I stayed here. I want to be free to develop new ideas.

"Then I began doing performances with a group called Zoo. As a professor, I enjoy working with young students and have set up my own university too. Next, I would like to set up some sort of party . . . perhaps we should call it 'Love Difference'! What do you think? Do you want to help us found this?"

I did not answer right away. Inspired by his rhetoric, I doodled in surreal ecriture automatique on my paper napkin. I was playing with the 2002 update of the Gadamerian model:

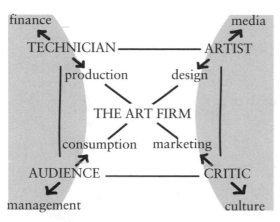

*Economic Embeddedness of the Art Firm*
*and its Aesthetic Players*

If this is how the art firms of tomorrow would emerge out of their embeddedness into a new finance-managerial and media-cultural bipolarity, Dionysus Inc. would then find its third position between media-culture and finance-management. No doubt this splitting up would stir up creativity by loosening couplings between media, finance, management, and culture. Now one world would become two, connected by a third, with this strange thing called art in the middle position as an art firm.

Artists like Michelangelo made it possible to clearly discern players out there ready to join in the aesthetic play if only they were encouraged. I drew arrows like vectors of totality imploding into the drudgery of heavy managerial control and banality exploding art in the nihilistic volatility of media and finance. Over time, businesses may make strategic use of art firms to widen their scope from a micro world of material production to a macro atmosphere of media-finance. Such was the shift of Paris fashion where some ten remaining fashion houses today employ fewer than one thousand to produce catwalk events for a thousand international fashion journalists; in the 1950s, fifty houses paid forty thousand workers to produce luxury garments for some three thousand customers. In a reverse strategic move, other businesses may have art-firm skills zoom in from macro mediatic culture to influence micro manufacture of new design, thus adding the mundane senses of touch, taste, and smell to the standard audio-visuality of art. I imagined how marketing might leave a stick product placement perspective and develop into a new kind of critique with the ability to maintain this focus and not evaporate into a general commercial culture. I realized that this development would have good support when marketing departments of business schools become increasingly interested in art. The most popular courses for higher education at the turn of the millennium seem to be related to aesthetics and art. In the future, consumers might be transformed into philosophizing audiences while managers might escape the pressure of finance, finding relief in art spaces taking on the traits of the old family firm complete with its aesthetic-ethic vision. Maybe the durable legacy of an ephemeral new economy is an aesthetic sensitivity to the spiritual in modern organizations,[69] and art firms might conceivably serve as models for helping firms generate aesthetic energy by stimulating technicians, artists, critics, and audiences to maintain Schwung in aesthetic play. With this in view, I myself was instrumental in launching a new international education for turning curators into such aesthetic organizational change agents.[70]

All this made me curious to find out about Michelangelo's own background, but when I asked him which art school he had attended, he explained.

"Dad was an artist, you know, but he took the job of an art restorer in order to feed us after the war. When the lad from the local art academy proved to be no good, he took me on as a helper and taught me all the old painting techniques. Mom, on the other hand, was anxious to give me a good start in modern society, so she enrolled me in a school of commerce and advertising where I first encountered cubism, surrealism, dadaism, expressionism, and other styles useful for making ads. Even before I graduated, I was single-handedly running an ad agency after the teacher who owned it asked me take over when he moved to Milan. That job was OK, but I needed something else. I wanted to express *something*; I really did not know what.

"My father had taught me the craft and traditions of old art, and Mother had had me schooled in the commercial communication of the future. Now I had to explore the in between of aesthetics on my own. I began spending nights painting, and one of my first paintings was awarded first prize at an art fair in Milan. By sheer luck, I had entered a field that I had been indirectly prepared for in ways an art academy could not have done."

Michelangelo's art firm is clearly the product of an extremely talented and energetic entrepreneur, who is able to extend his energy to even the most conservative industrialists and make them enthusiastic and cooperative. Slowly but surely, he is involving both the regional authorities and local businesses in the Biella Chamber of Commerce in his art firm. Without his intense inner-directedness, which made him work on mirrors when paintings had been asked for, do performances when mirrors were in demand, or work on art late at night even though his ad agency was thriving, the art firm would have never materialized, and "socially responsible art" would have been reduced to just another legitimating social issue.

Today's development clearly shows in the popularity of businesses with a value base of their own. The aesthetic turn, of which Pistoletto's art firm is a good example, has the power to make volatile financial dealers and heavy production engineers more prone to evince their Dionysian qualities. Sports events staged by big industry and finance already aim for that aesthetic effect in Dionysian techno-theatres such as Monza, Monte Carlo, and Wimbledon. Designers and media professionals then might be encouraged to bring out the artists they have inside.

This is what happens at good schools of design and communication—St. Martins, the Pratt Institute, Parsons School of Design, the Rhode Island School of Design—where aesthetic coaches such as Pistoletto try to rescue socioeconomic dynamics by redesigning dull jobs into playful artistry with a clear public mission.

As if he had read my thoughts, Michelangelo carried on: "But it is important that we have fun too. The art firm must be joyful and gay. Our latest project therefore is called the 'big social game.' We look upon social transformation as a game where only art and artists can change the rules while at the same time playing. Economy is play, and so is politics. The play of plays,

the one we constantly stage in my theatre of Cittadellarte, is aesthetic, and its outcome is art with social impact and responsibility."

I could no longer hear what Michelangelo was saying. His voice had fused with that of my aesthetic philosophers singing in homage to an art firm manifesting aesthetic play in the third realm. I even saw my old father waving to me from the rooftop. Maybe it was the good wine with which we washed down Maria's risotto and lovely sweet fruit salad. No, I am sure this was more a Nietzschean Rauch, an aesthetic euphoria rushing through my veins as warm aesthetic energy. Michelangelo, this new Dionysus incarnated to save the new millennium, summoned us all, as he put it, "to found art firms managing work that must be done together. It is called civilization. This place is the atelier, the studio, and the laboratory of that art."

"Michelangelo," I heard myself saying to this Dionysus behind whose imposing stature the bright white façade of his art firm radiated outside the big glass window, "Michelangelo, your art firm reminds me of a surrealist painting by Giorgio de Chirico. . . . "

"I know exactly which one you mean," responded Dionysus gently.

*La Metafisica.* . . .

# Notes

### Chapter 1

1. Johannes Stüttgen, *Zeitstau* (Stuttgart: Urachhaus, 1988), 15. (author's translation)
2. Claus-Otto Scharmer, *Asthetik als Kategorie Strategischer Führung* (Stuttgart: Urachhaus, 1991).
3. Friedrich Schiller, *On the Aesthetic Education of Man* (Oxford: Oxford University Press, 1982), 217.
4. Walter Hoyer, ed., *Schillers Leben dokumentarisch* (Köln: Kiepenhauer & Witsch, 1967), 410.
5. Schiller, 217.
6. Ibid., 219.
7. Hoyer, 385–86. (author's translation)
8. Schiller, 157.
9. Ibid., 145.

### Chapter 2

1. Friedrich Burschell, *Friedrich Schiller in Selbstzeugnissen und Bilddokumenten* (Hamburg: Rowohlt Taschenbuch, 1975), 119. (author's translation)
2. Immanuel Kant, *Werkausgabe in zwölf Bänder* (Frankfurt am Main: Suhrkamp, 1990), II, 833.
3. Benedetto Croce, *Aesthetics* (Boston: Nonpareil, 1983), 244.
4. Kant, II, 833.
5. Gernot Böhme, *Kants Kritik der Urteilskraft in neuer Sicht* (Frankfurt am Main: Suhrkamp, 1999), 28.
6. Arsenij Gulyga, *Immanuel Kant* (Göteborg: Daidalos, 1991), 188.
7. Kant, X.
8. Ibid., 87.
9. Ibid., 218.
10. Ibid., 153.
11. Ibid., 130–31.
12. Böhme, 119.
13. Ibid., 187.
14. Ibid., 204.
15. Richard Kearny, *The Wake of the Imagination—Towards a Postmodern Culture* (Minneapolis: University of Minnesota Press, 1988), 106–113.
16. Kant, X, 215.
17. Ibid., 211.
18. Ibid., 226–27.
19. Kant, *The Critique of Judgment* (Oxford: Clarendon Press, 1991), 39.
20. Kant, *Werkausgabe*, X, 110.
21. Kant, *Critique*, 39.
22. Kant, *Werkausgabe*, X, 252.
23. Ibid., 242.
24. Ibid., 245.
25. Ibid., 249.

26. Ibid., 279–82.
27. Ibid., 191.
28. Jochen Kirchhoff, *Schelling* (Hamburg: Rowohlt Taschenbuch, 1988), 29.
29. Ibid., 27–8. (author's translation)
30. Georg W. F. Hegel, *Werke in 20 Bänder* (Frankfurt am Main: Suhrkamp, 1970), XIII, 25.
31. Ibid., XIII, 26. (author's translation)
32. Friedrich Schelling, *Ausgewählte Schriften in 6 Bänder* (Frankfurt am Main: Suhrkamp, 1985), 691. (author's translation)
33. Hegel, "Earliest System-Programme of German Idealism: Berne, 1796," translated by H. S. Harris, in *Hegel's Development: Toward the Sunlight 1770–1801* (Oxford: Clarendon, 1972), 510–12.
34. Schelling, IV, 544. (author's translation)
35. Ibid., I, 685.
36. Ibid.
37. Ibid., II, 291–99.
38. Hoyer, *Schillers Leben*, 656. (author's translation)
39. Schelling, II, 172.
40. Ibid., I, 686. (author's translation)
41. Schelling, "Construction of the Content of Art," in *The Philosophy of Art* (Minneapolis: University of Minnesota Press, 1989), II, 71.
42. Ibid., 35.
43. Schelling, *Ausgewählte,* II, 223.
44. Schelling, "Construction," II, 59.
45. Schelling, *Ausgewählte,* II, 260.
46. Ibid., II, 253.
47. Ibid., II, 239.
48. Ibid., IV, 489.
49. Ibid., IV, 477.
50. Ibid., IV, 499.
51. Ibid., IV, 503.
52. Ibid., IV, 553.
53. Ibid., IV, 501.
54. Ibid., II, 175. (author's translation)
55. Ibid., IV, 557.
56. Ibid., IV, 523.
57. Kirchhoff, 87.
58. Karl Jaspers, *Schelling Grösse und Verhängnis* (München: Piper, 1955).
59. Schelling, *Ausgewählte,* II, 599.
60. Kirchhoff, 28. (author's translation)
61. John Dewey, *Art as Experience* (New York: Putnam, 1958).
62. Ibid., 325.
63. Ibid.
64. Ibid., 299.
65. Ibid., 308.
66. Ibid., 307.
67. Ibid., 302.
68. Ibid., 324–25.
69. Ibid., 277.
70. Ibid., 83.
71. Richard Shusterman, *Pragmatist Aesthetics* (Oxford: Blackwell, 1992), 124.
72. Martin Seel, *Die Kunst der Entzweiung: Zum Begriff der ästhetischen Rationalität* (Frankfurt am Main: Suhrkamp, 1985), 267.
73. Dewey, 83.
74. Ibid., 214.
75. Ibid., 131.
76. Karl Bohrer, *Plötzlichkeit: Zum Augenblick des ästhetischen Scheins* (Frankfurt am Main: Suhrkamp, 1981).
77. Dewey, 181.
78. Ibid., 198.
79. Ibid., 181.
80. Ibid., 16.
81. Ibid., 14.
82. Ibid., 183.
83. Ibid., 163.
84. Ibid., 249.
85. Umberto Eco, *Das offene Kunstwerk* (Frankfurt am Main: Suhrkamp, 1973).
86. Dewey, 51.
87. Ibid., 178.
88. Ibid., 134.
89. Ibid., 177.
90. William James, *Le pragmatisme* (Paris: Ernest Flammarion, 1917), 11.
91. William James, *Pragmatism* (New York: New American Library, 1974), 113.
92. Ibid., 46.
93. Ibid., 162.
94. Ibid., 113.
95. Rafael Ramirez, *The Beauty of Social Organization* (München: Accedo, 1991), 38–41.
96. Margaret Rose, *Marx's Lost Aesthetic* (Cambridge: Cambridge University Press, 1989), 81.
97. George Santayana, *The Sense of Beauty* (New York: Dover, 1955), 110–12.
98. Dewey, 224.
99. Ibid., 348.
100. Ibid., 195.

101. James, *Pragmatism*, 137.
102. Georg Simmel, *Philosophy of Money* (London: Routledge and Kegan Paul, 1982).
103. Israel Scheffler, *Four Pragmatists: A Critical Introduction to Pierce, James, Mead, and Dewey* (London: Routledge and Kegan Paul, 1986), 191.
104. Dewey, 199.
105. Friedrich Nietzsche, *The Birth of Tragedy*, translated by Francis Golffing (Garden City, N.Y.: Doubleday Anchor, 1956), 23.
106. Ibid., 37.
107. Friedrich Nietzsche, *Werke in sechs Bänder* (München: Carl Hanser, 1980), I, 37.
108. Nietzsche, *Birth*, 42.
109. Nietzsche, *Werke*, I, 52.
110. Nietzsche, *Birth*, 56.
111. Arthur Danto, *Nietzsche as Philosopher* (New York: Macmillan, 1965), 65.
112. Nietzsche, *Werke*, I, 79.
113. Ibid., I, 127.
114. Ibid., I, 103.
115. Ibid., I, 126.
116. Nietzsche, *Birth*, 138.
117. Frederick Copleston, *Friedrich Nietzsche—Philosopher of Culture* (London: Search Press, 1975), 8.
118. Nietzsche, *The Birth*, 124.
119. Josef Chytry, *The Aesthetic State* (Berkeley: University of California Press, 1989), 299.
120. Roger Hollinrake, *Nietzsche, Wagner and the Philosophy of Pessimism* (London: Allen and Unwin, 1982), 226.
121. Nietzsche, "Richard Wagner in Bayreuth," in *Thoughts Out of Season*, 3rd ed., vol. IV, 1, translated by Anthony M. Ludovici (London: T. N. Foulis, 1910), 172.
122. Nietzsche, *Werke*, IV, 1045.
123. Carl von Clausewitz, *Geist und Tat* (Stuttgart: Alfred Körner, 1941), 153–78.
124. Ibid., 156.
125. Clausewitz, *Om Kriget* (Stockholm: Bonniers Fakta förlag, 1991), 112.
126. "Art of War or Science of War," in Clausewitz, *On War*, translated by O. J. Matthijs Jolles (New York: Random House, 1943), 85.
127. Azar Gat, *The Origin of Military Thought From the Enlightenment to Clausewitz* (Oxford: Clarendon Press, 1989).
128. Ibid.
129. Clausewitz, *Om Kriget*, 235.
130. Ibid., 59.
131. Clausewitz, "The Genius for War," in *On War*, 43.
132. Clausewitz, *Om Kriget*, 71.
133. Paul Virilio, *La machine de vision* (Paris: Editions Galilée, 1988), 63. (author's translation)

## Chapter 3

1. Remy Saisselin, *Le bourgeois et le bibelot* (Paris: Albin Michel, 1990).
2. Gerard-Georges Lemaire, *Les cafés litteraires* (Paris: Henri Veyier, 1987).
3. Jules Humbert and Henri Berguin, *Histoire illustrée de la literature grecque* (Paris: Henri Didier, 1947), 129–31.
4. Søren Kierkegaard, *Antingen eller och begreppet ångest* (Stockholm: Wahlstrom and Widstrand, 1989), 40–48.
5. Hans-Georg Gadamer, *Wahrheit und Methode* (Tübingen: J.C.B. Mohr, 1960).
6. Gadamer, "Play as the Clue to Ontological Explanation," in *Truth and Method*, 2nd ed., translated revisions by Joel Weinsheimer and Donald G. Marshall (New York: Crossroad, 1989), 116.
7. Gadamer, *Wahrheit*, 104.
8. Ibid., 132.
9. Ibid., 134–35.
10. Ibid., 118.
11. Paul Virilio, *Esthetique de la disparition* (Paris: Editions Galilée, 1989).
12. Gadamer, *Wahrheit*, 122.
13. Gadamer, "Play," 128.
14. Luigi Pareyson, *Conversations sur l'esthetique* (Paris: Gallimard, 1992), 52–53. (author's translation)
15. Gadamer, *Philosophische Lehrjahre* (Frankfurt am Main: Vittorio Klostermann, 1995), 215.
16. Rüdiger Safranski, *Ein Meister aus Deutschland* (Müchen: Carl Hanser, 1994), 306.
17. Martin Heidegger, "The Origin of the Work of Art" in *Poetry, Language, Thought*, translated by Albert Hofstadter (New York: Harper and Row, 1971), 77.
18. Gadamer, *Philosophische*, 217.
19. Bernard-Henri Levy, *Le siècle de Sartre* (Paris: Grasset, 2000).

20. Michael Zimmerman, *Heidegger's Confrontation with Modernity: Technology, Politics and Art* (Bloomington: Indiana University Press, 1990).
21. Ernst Jünger, *Der Arbeiter* (Hamburg: Hanseatische Verlag Sanstalt, 1932), 67.
22. Ibid., 218.
23. Zimmerman, 99.
24. Ibid., 100.
25. Octavio Paz, "En filosofs elände," in *Moderna Tider,* June–July 20/21, 3 (Stockholm 1992), 68–73.
26. Igor Golomstock, *Totalitarian Art in the Soviet Union, the Third Reich, Fascist Italy, and the People's Republic of China* (London: Collins Harvill, 1990), 9.
27. Ibid., 18.
28. Stephen Bann, ed., *The Tradition of Constructivism* (New York: DaCapo, 1974), 35.
29. Golomstock, 62.
30. Ibid., 67.
31. Pierre Guillet de Monthoux, *Action and Existence* (Chichester: Wiley, 1983), 39–56.
32. Richard Kearny, *The Wake of the Imagination* (Minneapolis: University of Minnesota Press, 1988), 134.
33. Boris Groys, *Staline oeuvre d'art totale* (Nimes: Editions Jacqueline Chambon, 1990), 24.
34. Ibid., 85
35. Golomstock, 51.
36. Ingemar Karlsson and Arne Ruth, *Samhället som teater* (Stockholm: Liber förlag, 1983).
37. Hans Christian Andersen, *Sagor och berättelser* (Malmö: Bokförlaget Norden, 1937), 113.
38. Ibid., 108.
39. *Leipzig Illustrierte Zeitung: Kultur-Sonderausgabe 1944: Der europäische Mensch,* 1944, 30–36.
40. Ibid., 28. (author's translation)
41. Guillet de Monthoux, *The Moral Philosophy of Management* (Armonk, NY: M. E. Sharpe, 1993), 241–58.
42. Luc Ferry, *Homo aestheticus* (Paris: Bernard Grasset, 1990) 285–89.
43. Witold Gombrowicz, *Ferdydurke,* translated by Eric Mosbacher (London: Marion Boyars, 1979), 85.
44. Barbara Czarniawska-Joerges and Gideon Kunda, *Socialisation into Modernity,* working paper (Department of Business Administration, Lund University, Sweden, 1992).
45. Sanna Axelsson, "En Blöjbebis historia," article in *CupidZero, Stockholm, 1992.*
46. Howard Becker, *Art Worlds* (Berkeley: University of California Press, 1982).
47. Joseph Beuys, *Kunst = Kapital* (Wangen, Germany: FIU, 1992), 48. (author's translation)
48. Pat Hackett, ed., *The Andy Warhol Diaries* (New York: Warner, 1989).

## Chapter 4

1. Adam Smith, *The Theory of Moral Sentiment* (Oxford: Clarendon, 1979), 183.
2. Ibid., 185.
3. Rüdiger Safranski, *Schopenhauer und die wilden Jahre der Philosophie* (Hamburg: Rowohlt, 1990), 43.
4. Arthur Schopenhauer, *Die Welt als Wille und Vorstellung* (Leipzig: Brockhaus, 1888), I, 517.
5. Ibid.
6. Ibid., I, 530.
7. Ibid., I, 496. (author's translation)
8. Ibid., I, 43–62.
9. Ibid., I, 323.
10. Ibid., I, 69.
11. Curt Janz, *Friedrich Nietzsche* (München: Carl Hanser, 1993), I, 196.
12. Schopenhauer, I, 201.
13. Ibid., I, 118; Schopenhauer, *The World as Will and Idea* (London: Dent, 1997), 31.
14. Ibid., 27.
15. Schopenhauer, *Die Welt,* I, 201.
16. Schopenhauer, *The World,* 32.
17. Ibid., 35.
18. Schopenhauer, *Die Welt,* I, 122.
19. Safranski, 166.
20. Jacqueline Lichtenstein, *La couleur éloquente* (Paris: Flammarion, 1989), 25–26.
21. Johann Goethe, "Zur Farbenlehre," in *Sämtliche Werke* (Stuttgart: Cottaschen Buchhandlung, 1869), III, 644.
22. Ibid. (author's translation)
23. Ibid.
24. Johannes Volkelt, *Arthur Schopenhauer* (Stuttgart: Fr. Frommanns, 1900), 117.

25. Schopenhauer, *Die Welt*, I, 321.
26. Volkelt, 121. (author's translation)
27. Schopenhauer, *Die Welt*, I, 220.
28. Ibid., 232.
29. Schopenhauer, *The World*, 103.
30. Schopenhauer, *Die Welt*, I, 211.
31. Schopenhauer, *The World*, 108.
32. Schopenhauer, *Die Welt*, I, 280.
33. Schopenhauer, *The World*, 153.
34. Schopenhauer, *Die Welt*, I, 276.
35. Ibid., 249.
36. Schopenhauer, *The World*, 172.

## Chapter 5

1. Lore Lucas, *Die Festspiel-Idee Richard Wagners* (Regensburg: Gustav Bosse, 1973), 19.
2. Richard Wagner, *Oper und Drama* (Berlin: Felix Gross, 1852), 79.
3. Ena Carlborg-Mannberg and Eva Hjertstrand-Malmros, *Gustaf den III:s skötebarn* (Stockholm: Carlsons, 1991), 74.
4. Lucas, 16.
5. Dominique Leroy, *Histoire des arts du spectacle en France* (Paris: L'Harmattan, 1990), 238.
6. Wagner, *Mein Leben* (München: List, 1969), II, 643.
7. Lucas, 57. (author's translation)
8. Hans Mayer, *Richard Wagner in Bayreuth* (Stuttgart: Belser A.G., 1976), 40.
9. Curt Janz, *Friedrich Nietzsche* (Munchen: Carl Hanser, 1978), I, 723.
10. Lucas, 75. (author's translation)
11. Ibid., 68.
12. Mayer, *Richard Wagner* (Hamburg: Rowohlt, 1976), 80.
13. Erich Kuby, *Richard Wagner & Co.* (Hamburg: Nannen, 1963), 61.
14. Wagner, *Oper*, 103. (author's translation)
15. Schopenhauer, *Die Welt als Wille und Vorstellung*, I, 358. (author's translation)
16. André Antoine, *Mes souvenirs sur le théâtre libre* (Paris: Arthéme Fayard, 1921).
17. Ibid., 29.
18. Jean Chothia, *André Antoine* (Cambridge: Cambridge University Press, 1991), 82.
19. Antoine, 51. (author's translation)
20. Aurelien Lugné-Poe, *Le sot du tremplin* (Paris: Librairie Gallimard, 1930), 94.
21. Chothia, 3.
22. Gilles Quéant, *Encyclopédie du théâtre contemporain* (Paris: Les publications de France, 1957), 34.
23. André Degaine, *Histoire du theatre* (Paris: Nizet, 1993), 287.
24. Chothia, 107.
25. Antoine, 20.
26. Jacques Robichez, *Le symbolisme au theatre* (Paris: L'Arche editeur, 1957), 113.
27. Marvin Carlson, *The French Stage in the Nineteenth Century* (Metuchen, N.J.: Scarecrow Press, 1972), 212.
28. Lugné-Poe, *Acrobaties* (Paris: Gallimard, 1931), 55.
29. Ibid., 59.
30. Ibid., 62.
31. Degaine, 313.
32. Lugné-Poe, *Acrobaties,* 159.
33. Ibid., 182. (author's translation)
34. Chothia, 185.
35. Ibid., 28.
36. Daniel-Henri Kahnweiler, *Juan Gris, sa vie, son oeuvre, ses écrits* (Paris: Gallimard, 1946), 106.
37. Kahnweiler, *Confessions esthétiques* (Paris: Gallimard, 1963), 23.
38. Kahnweiler, *Juan Gris*, 106.
39. Pierre Assouline, *L'Homme de l'art D.-H. Kahnweiler 1884 -1979* (Paris: Ballard, 1988), 155.
40. Kahnweiler, *Confessions*, 24.
41. Assouline,126.
42. Calvin Tomkins, *Duchamp* (New York: Henry Holt, 1996), 59.
43. Kahnweiler, *Confessions*, 29.
44. Ibid., 38.
45. Kahnweiler, *Juan Gris*, 107.
46. Lichtenstein, *La couleur éloquente*, 98.
47. Richard Kerney, *The Wake of Imagination* (Minneapolis: University of Minnesota Press, 1988), 106.
48. Lichtenstein.
49. Nelson Goodman, *Languages of Art: An Approach to a Theory of Symbols* (London: Oxford University Press, 1969).
50. Goodman, "The Way the World Is," *Review of Metaphysics,* Sept. 14, 1960, *14*(l), 53.
51. Goodman, *Languages*, 32–33.
52. Ibid., 88.
53. Ibid. 69.
54. Ibid., 110–11.

55. Wolfgang Brückner, "Der Blaue Reiter und die Entdeckung der Volkskunst," in Gottfried Boehm and Helmut Pfotenhauer, eds., *Beschreibungskunst—Kunstbeschreibung* (München: Wilhelm Fink, 1995), 530.

56. Jean-François Lyotard, *Signé Malraux* (Paris: Grasset, 1996), 92, 144.

57. Georgia Illetschko, *Kandinsky und Paris* (München: Prestel, 1997), 76.

58. Sixten Ringbom, *The Sounding Cosmos* (Åbo: Åbo Akademi, Finland, 1970).

59. Vassily Kandinsky, *Concerning the Spiritual in Art* (New York: Dover, 1977) 15.

60. Ibid., 30.

61. Boehm and Pfotenhauer, *Beschreibungskunst—Kunstbeschreibung* (München: Fink, 1995), 27.

62. Lichtenstein, 191–92.

63. Kandinsky, 31.

64. Ibid., 25.

65. Lichtenstein, 163.

66. Ibid., 170.

67. Ibid., 174. (author's translation)

68. Benedetto Croce, *Aesthetics* (Boston: Nonpareil, 1983), 220–34.

69. Arthur Danto, "Abbildung und Beschreibung," in Gottfried Boehm, ed., *Was ist ein Bild?* (München: Wilhelm Fink, 1994), 125–47.

70. Ray Monk, *Ludwig Wittgenstein—The Duty of a Genius* (London: Vintage, 1991).

71. Goodman, "The Way."

72. Danto, 125–47.

73. Peter Cassirer, *Huvudlinjer I retorikens historia* (Lund, Sweden: Studentlitteratur, 1997).

74. Lichtenstein, 85.

75. Guillet de Monthoux, *Action and Existence.*

76. Boehm and Pfotenhauer, *Beschreibungskunst,* 27.

77. Rose-Lee Goldberg, *Performance Art* (London: Thames and Hudson, 1995), 121.

78. Richard Schechner, *Performance Theory* (London: Routledge, 1988).

79. Ibid., 40.

80. Pierre Bourdieu, *Les régles de l'art—genèse et structure du champs littéraire* (Paris: Les editions du Seuil, 1992), 74.

81. Jacqueline Martin, *Eloquence Is Action* (Stockholm: Stifelsen för utgivning av teatervetenskapliga studier, 1987), 11.

82. Gérard Genette, *L'Œuvre de l'art* (Paris: Seuil, 1994), 230.

83. Marianne Alsne, *Koreografi och upphovsrätt* (Hallberg, Sweden: Närke-Tryck AB, 1988), 194.

## Chapter 6

1. Marie-Catherine Sahut and Régis Michel, *David, l'art et le politique* (Paris: Gallimard, 1989), 19.

2. Robert Herbert, *David, Voltaire, Brutus and the French Revolution* (London: Penguin, 1972).

3. Sahut and Michel, 52–53.

4. Noelle Guibert and Jacqueline Razgonnikoff, *Le journal de la Comédie Française 1787–1799* (Paris: Sides, 1989), 125–26.

5. Judith Chazin-Bennahum, *Dance in the Shadow of the Guillotine* (Carbondale: Southern Illinois University Press, 1988).

6. Sahut and Michel, 150. (author's translation)

7. Stéphane Marchand, *Les Guerres du Luxe* (Paris: Fayard, 2001), 65.

8. Charles Saunier, *Louis David* (Paris: Henri Laurens editeur, 1964), 64; Sahut and Michel, 143.

9. Daniel-Henri Kahnweiler, *Confessions,* 141, 142, 144. (author's translation)

10. Konstantin Stanislavski, "On Various Trends in Theatrical Art," in *Konstantin Stanislavsky: Selected Works*, compiled and translated by Olga Shartze (Moscow: Raduga, 1984), 161.

11. Stanislavski, "The Studio on Povarskaya," in *My Life in Art,* translated by J. J. Robbins (NY: Meridian Books, 1966), 434.

12. Pavel Rumjantsev, *Stanislavkij repeterar Rigoletto* (Göteborg: Bo Ejeby Förlag, 1933), 6.

13. James Roose-Evans, *Experimental Theatre* (London: Routledge, 1989), 11.

14. Jean Benedetti, *Stanislavski* (London: Methuen Drama, 1988), 60, 175.

15. Claudine Amiard-Chevrel, *Le theatre artistique de Moscou* (Paris: Editions du Center National de Recherché Scientifique, 1979), 40.

16. Ibid., 41.
17. Stanislavski, "Duncan and Craig," in *Konstantin Stanislavski: Selected Works*, 223.
18. Amiard-Chevrel, 41.
19. Dieter Hoffmeier, *Stanislavskij: Auf der suche nach dem Kreativen im Schauspieler* (Stuttgart: Urachhaus, 1993), 57.
20. Benedetti, 143.
21. Stanislavski, "Duncan and Craig," 223.
22. Goldberg, *Performance Art*, 45.
23. Stanislavski, "Studio," 437.
24. Amiard-Chevrel, 60.
25. Stanislavski, *Mitt liv i konsten* (Stockholm: Fröléen & Comp., 1951), 526.
26. Ibid., 538. (author's translation)
27. Stanislavski, *Skuespillerens ydre teknik* (Köpenhavn: Nyt nordisk Förlag Arnold Busck, 1991), 236. (author's translation)
28. Ibid., 246. (author's translation)
29. Ibid., 96. (author's translation)
30. Ibid., 96.
31. Stanislavski, *En skuespillers arbejde med sig selv* (Köpenhavn: Nyt nordisk Förlag Arnold Busck, 1988), 51. (author's translation)
32. Ibid., 26. (author's translation)
33. Brian Johnston, *Text and Supertext in Ibsen's Drama* (University Park: Pennsylvania State University Press, 1989), 55.
34. Stanislavski, *En skuespillers,* 55. (author's translation)
35. Ibid., 87. (author's translation)
36. Richard Buckle, *Diaghilev* (London: Weidenfeld and Nicolson, 1979), 74.
37. Stanislavski, *Mitt liv i konsten,* 505.
38. Lynn Garafola, *Diaghilev's Ballets Russes* (New York: DaCapo, 1989), 14.
39. Buckle, 41.
40. Garafola, 45.
41. Buckle, 87.
42. Ibid., 143.
43. Garafola, 180.
44. John Drummond, *Speaking of Diaghilev* (London: Faber and Faber, 1997), 87.
45. Buckle, 206.
46. Ibid., 529.
47. Drummond, 168.
48. Garafola, 223.
49. Ibid., 253.
50. Kahnweiler, *Juan Gris,* 277. (author's translation)
51. Garafola, 306.

52. Bengt Häger, *Ballets suedois* (Stockholm: Streiffert & Co Bokförlag, 1989), 57.
53. Garafola, 177–200.
54. Buckle, 513.
55. Garafola, 325. (author's translation)
56. Sahut and Michel, 58.
57. Edouard Pommier, *L'art de la liberté* (Paris: Editions Gallimard, 1991), 40.
58. Mona Ozouf, *La fête révolutionnaire* (Paris: Editions Gallimard, 1976), 250.
59. Jean Starobinski, *L'invention de la Liberté* (Geneve: Skira, 1987), 100. (author's translation)
60. Ibid. (author's translation)
61. Sahut and Michel, 156. (author's translation)
62. Ozouf, 256.
63. Sahut and Michel, 154. (author's translation)
64. Ozouf, 257.
65. Ibid., 138.
66. Ingvar Holm, *Politik som teater* (Stockholm: Carlsons, 1991), 100.
67. Pommier, 298. (author's translation)
68. Ibid., 81.
69. Holm, 119–28.
70. Pierre Bourdieu, *Raisons pratiques* (Paris: Éditions du Seuil, 1994) 37–58.
71. Saisselin, 101–42.
72. Bourdieu, *Les règles de l'art.*
73. Saisselin, 55–72.
74. Pierre Legendre, *Dieu au miroir* (Paris: Fayard, 1994).
75. Legendre, *Jouir du pouvoir* (Paris: Editions du Minuit, 1976), 114.
76. Legendre, *L'amour du censeur* (Paris: Editions du Seuil, 1974), 206.
77. Romain Laufer, "Généalogie de la notion de service," in Anne Jacob and Hélène Verin, *L'inscription sociale du marché* (Paris: L'Harmattan, 1995).
78. Gunnar Olsson, *Lines of Power, Limits of Language* (Minneapolis: University of Minnesota Press, 1991), 137.
79. Legendre, *Dieu,* 55.
80. Ibid., 174–75. (author's translation)
81. Rafael Ramirez, *The Beauty of Social Organization* (München: Accedo, 1991).
82. Legendre, *Dieu,* 73.
83. Gilles Deleuze and Felix Guattari, *Anti-Oedipus* (London: Athlone Press, 1983), 362.

84. Legendre, *Dieu,* 242.
85. Yves Thoret, *La théâtralité* (Paris: Dunod, 1993), 25.
86. Ibid.
87. Legendre, *Dieu,* 123.
88. Vaslav Nijinsky, "Letter to Serge Diaghilev," translated by Kyril FitzLyon in *The Diary of Vaslav Nijinsky,* edited by Joan Acocella (New York: Farrar, Straus and Giroux, 1999), 254–61.

### Chapter 7

1. Pauline Brunius, *Brev från öst och väst* (Stockholm: Albert Bonniers Förlag, 1934), 29.
2. Jean-Louis Deotte, *Oubliez, les ruines, l'Europe, le musée* (Paris: L'Harmattan, 1994), 101.
3. Patrick Devaux, *La Comédie Française* (Paris: P.U.F., 1993), 41.
4. André Degaine, *Histoire du theatre* (Paris: Nisbet, 1993), 302.
5. Jean Caune, *La culture en action* (Grenoble: P.U.G., 1992), 81.
6. Georges Banu, *Les cités du Theatre d'art de Stanislavski à Strehler* (Paris: Éditions Theatrales, 2000), 23.
7. Heinrich Braulich, *Die Volksbühne* (Berlin: Henschel, 1976), 34. (author's translation)
8. Ibid., 56.
9. Ludwig Hoffman, *Erwin Piscator, Theater Film Politik* (Berlin: Henschel, 1980), 336. (author's translation)
10. Knut Boeser and Renata Vatkova, *Erwin Piscator, eine Arbeitsbiographie in 2 Bänden* (Berlin: Edition Hentrich, 1986), I, 45.
11. Ibid., I, 41. (author's translation)
12. Ibid.
13. Ibid., I, 65. (author's translation)
14. Ibid., I, 282.
15. Braulich, 213. (author's translation)
16. Ibid., 211. (author's translation)
17. Ibid., 213.
18. Harald Swedner and Björn Egeland, *Teatern som social institution* (Lund: Studentlitteratur, 1974), 288–89.
19. *Skådebanans Årsbok,* Stockholm, 1927–1929.
20. Ann Mari Engel, *Teatern I Folkets Park 1905–1980* (Stockholm: Akademilitteratur, 1982), 95.

21. Lars Östman, *Ordens finansiella villkor* (Stockholm: School of Economics manuscript, 2000).
22. Claes Rosenqvist, *Den svenska nationalscenen* (Lund: Wiken, 1988).
23. Engel, 62–84.
24. Swedner and Egeland, 294.
25. Katja Waldén, ed., *Teatern I centrum* (Borås: Atlantis, 1990), 204. (author's translation)
26. Rosenqvist, 212. (author's translation)
27. Waldén, 211. (author's translation)
28. Ibid., 83.
29. *Teaterns kostnadsutveckling 1975–1990* (Stockholm: SOU, 1991), 71, 326.
30. Alf Sjöberg, *Teater som besvärjelse* (Stockholm: P.A. Norstedt och Söner, 1982), 127.
31. Gunnar Lundin and Jan Olsson, *Regissörens roller—samtal med Alf Sjöberg* (Lund: Bo Cavefores Förlag, 1976), 127.
32. Ibid., 128.
33. Sjöberg, 72. (author's translation)
34. Ibid., 243.
35. Lundin and Olsson, 52–53.
36. Sjöberg, 26–27. (author's translation)
37. Lundin and Olsson, 23. (author's translation)
38. Sjöberg, 193.
39. Lundin and Olsson, 101.
40. Sjöberg, 81. (author's translation)
41. William Baumol and William Bowen, *Performing Arts: The Economic Dilemma* (Cambridge, Mass.: Twentieth Century Fund, 1966).
42. Gösta Bergman, *Regi och spelstil under Gustaf Lagerbielke* (Stockholm: P. A. Norstedt och Söner, 1946), 135–37.
43. Sjöberg, 246. (author's translation)
44. Ibid., 81. (author's translation)
45. Citations from rehearsals of *Enemies* from field records in Pierre Guillet de Monthoux, *Ordning, röra, reda: Alf Sjöbergs uppsätting av Gorkijs Fiende* (Stockholm: K.T.H. working paper from the department of industrial economics and organization, 1974). Quotations attributed to Alf Sjöberg and others in the section "Dramaturgical Products" are from the author's unpublished interviews with Sjöberg and his actors in 1973.
46. Sjöberg, 20.
47. Ibid., 52. (author's translation)

48. Ibid., 65. (author's translation)
49. Lundin and Olsson, 18–19. (author's translation)
50. William Sauter, *Teaterögon* (Stockholm: Liber Förlag, 1986).
51. Lundin and Olsson, 122.
52. Sjöberg, 66. (author's translation)
53. Sjöberg, unpublished letter to the author, Jan. 2, 1974.
54. Ibid.
55. Ingmar Bergman, *The Magic Lantern,* translated by Joan Tate (New York: Viking, 1988), 199.
56. Ibid., 198.
57. Per Ringby, *Avantgardeteater och modernitet* (Gideå, Sweden: Vildros,1995) 105, 152.
58. Ibid., 125. (author's translation)
59. Ibid., 130.
60. Waldén, 75.
61. Ibid., 83.
62. Vivica Bandler, in Waldén, 77. (author's translation)
63. Suzanne Osten and Helena von Zweigbergk, *Barndom, feminism och galenskap—Osten om Osten* (Hässleholm: Alfabeta Bokförlag, 1990), 54–55. (author's translation)
64. Ibid., 56. (author's translation)
65. Ibid., 108. (author's translation)
66. Ibid., 129. (author's translation)
67. Monica Sparby, *Unga Klara: barnteater som konst* (Stockholm: Gidlund, 1986), 96.
68. Ibid., 127.
69. Ibid., 66. (author's translation)
70. Osten and von Zweigbergk, 132.
71. Ibid., 120. (author's translation)
72. Suzanne Osten, in Waldén, 124. (author's translation)
73. Sparby, 50–67.
74. Ibid., 127.
75. Suzanne Osten, in Waldén, 123. (author's translation)

## Chapter 8

1. Beuys, *Kunst = Kapital,* 43–44. (author's translation)
2. Carin Kuoni, ed., *Joseph Beuys in America* (New York: Four Walls Eight Windows, 1990), 125–26.
3. Johannes Stüttgen, *Zeitstau* (Stuttgart: Urachaus, 1988), 113. (author's translation)
4. Cornelia Wagner, "Le cas Joseph Beuys," in *Colloque conservation and restauration des oeuvres d'art contemporain* (Nancy: La documentation Française, 1994).
5. Calvin Tomkins, *Duchamp: A Bibliography* (New York: Henry Holt, 1996), 354.
6. Stüttgen, 113. (author's translation)
7. Beuys, 48.
8. Stüttgen, 117. (author's translation)
9. Ibid. (author's translation)
10. Beuys, 48. (author's translation)
11. Ken Friedman, "Rethinking Fluxus" in *Catalogue for Fluxus Show* (Brisbane, Australia: Institute of Modern Art, 1990).
12. Beuys, 91–92. (author's translation)
13. Friedman.
14. Kuoni, 169.
15. Beuys, 48, 37, 46. (author's translation)
16. Kuoni, 176.
17. Ibid., 151.
18. Stüttgen, 104.
19. Ibid., 70.
20. Ibid., 71. (author's translation)
21. Jean Sellem, "Interview with Bengt af Klintberg," *Lund Art Press,* 1990, 2(2), 67.
22. Thierry de Duve, *Kant After Duchamp* (Cambridge, Mass.: MIT Press, 1996), 288–89.
23. Kuoni, 10.
24. Stüttgen, 158–63.
25. Stephan von Borstel, Dieter Neubert, Irina Rosentreter, Rhea Thönges-Stringaris, eds., *Die unsichtbare Skulptur* (Stuttgart: Urachaus, 1989), 25. (author's translation)
26. Georg Simmel, *On Individuality and Social Forms* (Chicago: University of Chicago Press, 1971), 7.
27. Werner Beierwaltes et al., *Die Kunst gibt zu Denken* (Münster: Schriftenreihe der staatliche Kunstakademie Düsseldorf, 1981), Heft 7, 100.
28. Simmel, *Philosophie des Geldes* (Frankfurt am Main: Suhrkamp, 1989), 615. (author's translation)
29. Simmel, *Das individuelle Gesetz* (Frankfurt am Main: Suhrkamp, 1987), 74.
30. Ibid., 71. (author's translation)
31. Georg Simmel, in Dieter Henrich and Wolfgang Iser, eds., *Theorien der Kunst*

(Frankfurt am Main: Suhrkamp, 1987), 255. (author's translation)

32. Ibid., 254.

33. Ibid. 256–57. (author's translation)

34. Max Weber, *Wirtschaft und Gesellschaft* (Tûbingen: J.C.B. Mohr, 1976).

35. Pierre Bourdieu and Hans Haacke, *Free Exchange* (Stanford, Calif.: Stanford University Press, 1995),108–9.

36. Friedman.

## Chapter 9

1. Jean-Francois Lyotard, *La condition postmoderne* (Paris: Les Editions de Minuit, 1979).

2. Ibid., 107.

3. *Teaterns roller* (Stockholm: SOU, 1994), 52, 252.

4. Johan Fornäs, *Nio år efter tältprojektet* (Göteborg: Stencil musikvetenskapliga institutionen, 1986).

5. Mats Lindqvist, *Is i Magen* (Stockholm: Natur Och Kultur, 2001).

6. Suzanne Osten, in Waldén, *Teatern I centrum*, 124. (author's translation)

7. Boeser and Vatkova, *Erwin Piscator,* I, 103.

8. Ibid., 104.

9. Siegfried Wilzopolski, *Theater des Augenblicks* (Berlin: Zentrum für Theaterdokumentation, 1992), 157.

10. Ibid., 191, 265. (author's translation)

11. Sybille Weber, "Wo verläuft die Front," in *Theater der Zeit,* Aug.–Sept. 1993, 26. (author's translation)

12. Wilzopolski, 290. (author's translation)

13. Ivan Nagel, *Überlegungen zur Situation der Berliner Theater* (Berlin: Senat report, 1991), 15. (author's translation)

14. Article in *Die Zeit,* Jan. 27, 1995.

15. Wilzopolski, 290.

16. Hans-Dieter Schütt, *Die Erotik des Verrats—Gespräche mit Frank Castorf* (Berlin: Dietz, 1996), 66.

17. Wilzopolski, 76. (author's translation)

18. Ibid., 84. (author's translation)

19. Author interview with Frank Castorf.

20. Schütt, 106. (author's translation)

21. Schütt, 103–4. (author's translation)

22. Michael Töteberg, "Medienmaschine," in *Text + Kritik. Zeitschrift für Literatur,* 1997, III, 191. (author's translation)

23. Ibid., 190.

24. Dirk Baecker, *Postheroisches Management* (Berlin: Merve, 1994).

25. Heiner Müller, *Krieg ohne Schlacht— Leben in zwei Diktaturen* (Köln: Kiepenheuer und Witsch, 1994), 173.

26. Ibid., 180, 181, 184. (author's translation)

27. Ibid., 290–91. (author's translation)

28. Moderna Museet catalog, *Rörelse i konsten* (Stockholm, 1961).

29. Thomas Schober, *Das Theater der Maler* (Stuttgart: Metzlersche Verlagsbuchhandlung, 1994), 71.

30. Ibid., 304.

31. Serge Guilbaut, *Comment New York vola l'idée d'art moderne* (Nimes: Editions Jacqueline Chambon, 1989).

32. Roselee Goldberg, *Performance Art* (London: Thames and Hudson, 1995), 130.

33. Nick Kaye, *Art into Theatre* (Amsterdam: Harwood, 1996), 23.

34. Per Ringby, *Avantgardeteater och modernitet* (Gideå: Vildros, 1995), 103.

35. Christopher Innes, *Avant-Garde Theatre 1892–1992* (London: Routledge, 1996), 204.

36. Marvin Carlson, *Performance—A Critical Introduction* (London: Routledge, 1996), 110.

37. Holm Keller, *Robert Wilson* (Frankfurt am Main: Fischer Taschenbuch, 1997), 63.

38. Ibid., 103. (author's translation)

39. Ibid., 96. (author's translation)

40. Wilzopolski, 146.

41. Schütt. 103 (author's translation)

42. Wilzopolski, 210. (author's translation)

43. Schütt, 123. (author's translation)

44. Hoffman, 33. (author's translation)

45. Nagel, 16. (author's translation)

46. Berndt Sucher, "Ohne Rücksicht auf Verluste," in *Theater der Zeit,* Aug.–Sept. 1993.

47. Schütt, 73, 103. (author's translation)

48. Müller, *Germania 3. Gespenster am toten Mann* (Wien: Akademitheater, 1997), 91. (author's translation)

49. "Frank Castorf Interview," *Theater der Zeit,* Aug.–Sept. 1993, 23. (author's translation)

50. Castorf, in *Der Zeit,* Jan. 13, 1995, 3. (author's translation)

51. Judith Wilske, *Die Vaterlosen—ein Intendantwechsel am Schauspielhaus*

*Bochum* (Witten: Auslandsarbeit Universität Witten Herdecke, 1996).

52. Schütt, 7.
53. Müller, *Krieg*, 112. (author's translation)
54. Schütt, 156. (author's translation)
55. Boris Groys, in Andreas Grosz and Daniel Delhaes, *Die Kultur AG* (Munchen: Carl Hanser, 1999), 19–26.
56. "Castorf Interview," 20. (author's translation)
57. Wilzopolski, 246.
58. Ilja Kabakow and Boris Groys, *Die Kunst der Installation* (München: Carl Hanser, 1996) 41. (author's translation)
59. Alain Badiou, *Rhapsodie pour le Théâtre* (Paris: Imprimerie national, 1990), 79. (author's translation)
60. Kabakow and Groys, 58.
61. Anthony Giddens, *The Third Way* (Oxford: Polity Press, 1998).

#### Chapter 10

1. Ernst Malmsten, Erik Potanger, and Charles Drazin, *BooHoo: A Dot Com Story from Concept to Catastrophe* (London: Random House Business Books, 2001).
2. B. Joseph Pine II and James H. Gilmore, *The Experience Economy* (Cambridge: Harvard Business School Press, 1999).
3. Guillet de Monthoux, *Action and Existence*.
4. Gernot Böhme, *Atmosphäre* (Frankfurt am Main: Surhkamp, 1995).
5. Ivar Björkman, *Sven Duchamp expert på auraproduktion* (Stockholm: doctoral dissertation, University of Stockholm, 1999).
6. Sven Erik Sjöstrand, *The Two Faces of Management* (London: Thomson Business Press, 1997), 197.
7. Hilmar Hoffmann, ed., *Das Guggenheim Prinzip* (Köln: Dumont, 1999), 42–55.
8. Richard Ohmann, *Making and Selling Culture* (Hanover: University Press of New England, 1996), 19.
9. Diana Lasalle and Terry Britton, *Priceless: Turning Ordinary Products into Extraordinary Experiences* (Cambridge: Harvard Business School Press, 2002).
10. Thomas Frank, *One Market Under God* (New York: Anchor, 2000), 228–29. Charles Handy, *New Alchemists* (London: Hutchinson, 1999).

11. Guy Debord, *La société du spectacle* (Paris: Editions Gallimard, 1992).
12. Anselm Jappe, *Guy Debord* (Marseilles: Via Valeriano, 1998).
13. Debord, *Commentaires sur "La société du spectacle"* (Paris: Editions Gallimard, 1992).
14. Vincent Kaufmann, *Guy Debord* (Paris: Fayard, 2001).
15. Katharina Keim, "Vom Theater der Revolution zur Revolution des Theaters," in *Text + Kritik Zeitschrift für Literatur*, 1997, III, 100.
16. Alain Badiou, *Manifeste pour la philosophie* (Paris: Editions du Seuil, 1989) 18, 60; Dany-Robert Dufour, *Les mystères de la Trinité* (Paris: Gallimard, 1990); François Dosse, *L'empire du sense, l'humanisation des sciences humaines* (Paris: La Découverte, 1997), 151–9.
17. Ingmar Bergman, interviewed in *Dramat* (Stockholm, 1998), I, 18. (author's translation)
18. Gösta Bergman, *Regihistoriska studier* (Stockholm: Norstedt, 1952), 152. (author's translation)
19. Gösta Bergman, *Regi och spelstil under Gustaf Lagerbielke* (Stockholm: Norstedt, 1946), 69. (author's translation)
20. Paul Marcoux, *Guilbert de Pixérécourt* (New York: Peter Lang, 1992), 25.
21. Gotthold Lessing, *Werke in sechs Bänden* (Leipzig: Hesse, 1899), IV, 32. (author's translation)
22. Alf Ahlberg, *Gotthold Ephraim Lessing* (Stockholm: Natur och Kultur, 1963), 40.
23. Michel Poizat, *L'opera ou le cri de l'ange* (Paris: Editions A. M. Métailié, 1986), 92.
24. Bergman, *Regihistoriska studier*, 124. (author's translation)
25. Ibid., 152. (author's translation)
26. Groys, *Über das neue* (München: Carl Hanser, 1992).
27. Jean-Marie Messier, *j6m.com* (Paris: Hachette littérature, 2000), 90.
28. Thomas Knoblauch, *Die möglichkeit des neuen* (Stuttgart: M&P Verlag für Wissenschaft und Forschung, 1996).
29. Danto, *The Transfiguration of the Commonplace* (Cambridge: Harvard University Press, 1981).

30. Danto, *Philosophizing Art* (Berkeley: University of California Press, 1999).

31. Robert Protherough and John Pick, *Managing Britannia—Culture and Management in Modern Britain* (Corbridge: Brynmill Press, 2002).

32. Frank.

33. Michael Lewis, *The New New Thing* (London: Hodder & Stoughton, 1999).

34. Hannah Arendt, *Men in Dark Times* (New York: Harcourt Brace, 1955), 109.

35. Daniel Birnbaum, *Lebensraum—or IKEA and the end of metaphysics,* catalogue for show at Nordiska museet in Stockholm, 1999.

36. Gilles Deleuze, *Critique et clinique* (Paris: Les editions du minuit, 1993), 118.

37. Jonathan Schroeder, *Visual Consumption* (London: Routledge, 2002).

38. Danielle Allères, *Le Luxe—strategies de marketing* (Paris: Economica, 1999).

39. Bernard Arnault, *La passion creative* (Paris: Plon, 2000), 76.

40. Gadamer, *Wahrheit und methode,* 106.

41. Björkman.

42. See Silvio SanPietro and Ico Migliore, *New Exhibits Made in Italy* (Milano: Edizione L'Archivolto, 1998); Silvio SanPietro and Paola Gallo, *New Shops Made in Italy* (Milano: Edizione L'Archivolto, 2000); and Pablo Soto, *Vetrine* (Barcelona: Loft, 2003).

43. Mike Meire, lecture at exhibition-seminar on art work consulting (Berlin: Haus am Lützowplatz, 2000).

44. Andreas Grosz and Daniel Delhaas, *Die Kultur AG* (München: Carl Hanser, 1999), 19–27.

45. Chin-tao Wu, *Privatising Culture* (London: Verso, 2002), 301.

46. For more details on art-inspired shop design, see Chuihua Chung, Jeffrey Inaba, and Rem Koolhaas, eds., *Harvard Design School Guide to Shopping* (Köln: Taschen, 2000); Otto Riewolt, *Retail Design* (London: King, 2000); Aurora Cuito, *Shop Design* (Barcelona: Loft, 2001).

47. Max Hollein and Christoph Grunenberg, *Shopping: A Century of Art and Shopping Culture,* catalogue for art show *Shopping* (Frankfurt am Main: Ostfildern-Ruit: Hatje Cantz, 2002).

48. Denis Bayart and Pierre-Jean Benghozi, *La tournant commercial des musées* (Paris: La documentation Française, 1993).

49. Francois Dosse, *Michel de Certeau, la marcheur blessé* (Paris: Éditions de la Decouverte, 2002) 465.

50. Greil Marcus, *Lipstick Traces* (Cambridge: Harvard University Press, 1989).

51. Stéphane Marchand, *Les guerres du luxe* (Paris: Fayard, 2001) 120.

52. Airy Routier, *L'ange exterminateur* (Paris: Albin Michel, 2003); Olivier Toscer, *Argent public, fortunes privées* (Paris: Éditions DeNoel, 2002).

53. Georg Schreyögg and Robert Dabitz, *Unternehmenstheater* (Wiesbaden: Gabler, 1999). Judith Wilske, Theater für Unternehmenein Gestltungsentwurf für das Paradox der Unternehmensberatung, Witten, Germany, Diplomarbeit im Fach Betreibswirtschaftslehre Universität Witten-Herdecke, 1997

54. Lotte Darsö and Michael Dawids, *Art in Business* (working paper; Copenhagen: Learning Lab Denmark, 2002).

55. See Robert Austin, Artful Making: *What Managers Need to Know on How Artists Work* (New York: Prentice Hall, 2002): Keith Grint, *The Art of Leadership* (Oxford: Oxford University Press, 2000); John Dobson, *The Art of Management and the Aesthetic Manager* (Westport: Quorum, 1999); Eve Chiapello, *Les modes de controles des organizations artistiques* (Paris: doctoral thesis, Université Paris IX Dauphine, 1994); Lawrence Hyde, *The Gift: Imagination and the Erotic Life of Property* (New York: Vintage, 1983).

56. Jean Lipman-Blumen and Harold Levitt, *Hot Groups: Seeding Them, Feeding Them to Ignite Your Organization* (New York: Oxford University Press, 1999); Mark Marotto, Bart Victor, Johan Roos, *Collective Virtuosity—Aesthetic Experiences in Groups* (working paper 6B; Lausanne: Imaginations Lab, 2000).

57. Emma Stenström, *Konstiga företag* (Stockholm: doctoral dissertation, Stockholm School of Economics, 1999).

58. Pierre Daix, *Francois Pinault* (Paris: Editions de Fallois, 1998).

59. Wolfgang Ullrich, *Mit dem Rücken zur Kunst* (Berlin: Verlag Klaus Wagenbach, 2000).

60. Protherough and Pick.

61. Steven Brown, *Postmodern Marketing* (London: International Thomson Business Press, 1995); Fuat Firat, Nick Dholakia, and Alladi Venkatesh, "Marketing in a Postmodern World," *European Journal of Marketing*, 1995, 29(1), 40–56; Antonio Strati, *Aesthetics and Organization* (London: Sage, 1999); Rafael Ramirez, *The Beauty of Social Organization* (München: Accedo, 1991); Pierre Guillet de Monthoux and Antonio Strati, eds., special journal issues on *Aesthetics* in *Consumption, Markets, and Culture*, 2002, 5, 1, 2; Strati and Guillet de Monthoux, eds., special journal issues on *Aesthetics* in *Human Relations*, 2002, 55, 7; Laurent Lapierre, *Imaginaire et leadership* (Montreal: Editions Presses Hec); Derrick Chong, *Arts Management* (London: Routledge, 2001); Giep Haggort, *Art Management-Entrepreneurial Style* (Delft: Eburon, 2000); Richard A. Peterson, *Creating Country Music: Fabricating Authenticity* (Chicago: University of Chicago Press, 1997).

Parallel to the mushrooming of articles on aesthetics and art in academic management journals and management research units working in the crossover field of art and management (such as the European Centre of Art and Management, known as ECAM, operating in Sweden, France, and Switzerland; the Centre for Art and Leadership at Copenhagen Business School and Learning Lab, both in Denmark; and the Imagination Lab in Lausanne, Switzerland), there are active scholarly arts management associations such as the International Association for Art and Management (AIMAC), the Association for Cultural Economics International (ACEI), Art and Business Council, Inc., and the European Research Institute for Comparative Cultural Policy and the Arts (ERICARTS www.ericarts.org) that publish relevant research on arts management in the *International Journal of Arts Management*, the *Journal of Cultural Economics*, and newsletters such as the Arts and Business Newsletter (info@AandB.org.uk), the Arts Management Newsletter (www.artsmanagement.net), and the ACEI newsletter. The dialogue seminar fuses art and reflection on work and technology according to a Wittgensteinian model for tacit knowledge (see Bo Göranzon, *The Practical Intellect,* London: UNESCO-Springer Verlag, 1991; and "Beyond All Certainty: Wittgenstein and Turing, an Account of a Philosophical Dialogue on Skill and Technology," in Elinor Schaffer, ed., *The Third Culture,* Berlin: Walter de Gruyter, 1998). The *Pink Machine* project under the direction of Professor Claes Gustaffson at the Royal Institute of Technology, Stockholm, investigates the importance of frivolity, improvisation, and play in industrial engineering. A growing number of European studies explore the similarities and differences between management of art and general management. See Eve Chiapello, *Les modes de contrôle des organisations artistiques* (Paris: doctoral dissertation, Université Paris, 1994); Grete Wennes, *Skjönnheten og udyret* (Bergen: doctoral dissertation, Norwegian School of Business, 2002); Emma Stenström, *Konstiga företag* (Stockholm: doctoral dissertation, Stockholm School of Economics, 2000); Annsofi Köping, *Den Bunda Friheten* (Stockholm: Arvinius, 2003); Katja Lindquist, *Exhibition Enterprising* (Stockholm: doctoral dissertation, Stockholm University, 2003); Björkman, *Sven Duchamp: Expert på auraproduktion* (Stockholm: doctoral dissertation, Stockholm University, 1999); Marja Soila-Wadman, *Kapitulationens estetik* (Stockholm: Arvinius, 2003); Nina Koivonen, *Leadership in Orchestras* (Tampere, Finland: Tampere University Press); Ruth Bereson, *The Operatic State* (London: Routledge, 2001); Jeanette Wetterström, *Stor opera små pengar* (Stockholm: Carlssons Förlag, 2001). For an international overview of current research in the area, see also proceedings in two volumes of the 2nd workshop on "Aesthetics, Art and Management—Towards New Fields of Flow," held in Gattieres, France, July 20–23, 2003, Brussels: EIASM, Place de Brouckére 31 B.

62. Loredana Parmesani and Alexandra Mir list these artists, artist groups, and art firms as having developed art work as an aesthetic commentary on corporate models during the 1990s: Banca di Oklahoma S.r.l., Technotest S.r.l., Premiata Ditta S.a.s., Name Diffusion, Coop Romagnola Int. Fi$h-handel Servaas & Zn., Ingold Airlines, Kostabi World, Philippe Cazal (all mentioned in Loredana Parmesani, *Business Art Business,* Milan: Flash Art Books, 1993), Andy Stillpass, Jennifer Nelson, Carey Young, Superflex, Daniel Pflumm, Peter Persson, Thomas Bayrle, Icelandic Love Corporation, Mejor Vida Corporation, Daniel Knorr, Chris Saunders, Fabryka Cokierkow, Dejanov & Heger, Claude Closky, Riga Dating Agency, Alexandra Mir, Björn Nörgaard, Bonk Business Inc., Landfill Andrea + Philippe, Atelier van Lieshout, Gardar Eine Einarsson/Matias Faldbakken, Volker Eichelmann/Ruth Maclennan, Jens Haaning, Paola Pivi, Laird Borelli on ChanSchatz, Bernadette Corporation, Purple Institute, Florian Zeyfang, Kathrin Böhm/Stefan Saffer, Chris Evans, Leif Elggren/Thomas Liljenberg, Kelly Kuvo, Melissa Longenecker, Matthieu Laurette, Henrik Schrat, Ola Pehrson, Gareth James, Mark Lombardi, Sandy Nicholson, Tuija Lindström (presented in Alexandra Mir, *Corporate Mentality,* New York: Lukas and Sternberg, 2003). ECAM has initiated an international masters course at Stockholm University to develop new corporate and cultural curating founded on art history and management (see www.arthistory.su.se/curator). ECAM will soon launch an international project named "LIEDERSHIP" to stimulate artwork and aesthetic energy for managerial rejuvenation and industrial transformation. Both projects, which aim at a closer cooperation between artists and managers for mutual creativity, have received financial support from the Tercentenary Foundation of the Swedish National Bank.

63. Art work consulting curated by Karin Pott, Dagmar Reichert, and Pierre Guillet de Monthoux at Haus am Lützowplatz, with support of project "Fields of Flow," financed by the Swedish National Bank Tercentenary Foundation, Berlin Nov. 23, 2001–May 1, 2002. See review in *Kunstforum,* Jan.–Mar. 2002, Heft 158; and *Frankfurter Allgemeine Zeitung,* Dec. 18, 2001, no. 294.

64. For a review of artists preoccupied with subtle reflections on money and finance, see for example the journal *Kunstforum,* Jan.–Mar. 2000, Band 149; and catalogue for show *art&economy,* Felix Zdenek, Beate Hentschel, and Dirk Luckow, eds. (Hamburg: Hatje Cantz, 2002).

65. Simonetta Carbonara and Christian Votava, from Realise in Karlsruhe.

66. Carl Hegemann, "Das revolutionäre Unternehmen," *Frankfurter Allgemeine Zeitung,* Aug. 25, 2001.

67. "Getting Wieder at Bayreuth," article in *International Herald Tribune,* June 24, 2003; Bryan Magee, *Wagner and Philosophy* (London: Penguin, 2000).

68. Guillet de Monthoux, "Performing the Absolute: Marina Abramovic Organizing the Unfinished Business of Arthur Schopenhauer," *Organization Studies,* 2000, *21*(special issue), 29–51.

69. Michelangelo Pistoletto, information leaflet for Cittadellarte in Biella, 2000.

70. Schiller, *On the Aesthetic Education of Man* (Oxford: University Press, 1982), 151–59.

71. Guillet de Monthoux, "The Spiritual in Organizations," in Stephen Laske and Stefan Gorbach, *Spannungsfeld personalentwicklung* (Wien: Manzsche Verlags-Und Universitätsbuchhandlung, 1993); "Herr Hulot Meets Monsieur Simmel," *Simmel Studies,* 2003, *13*(1), 73-83.

72. See www.arthistory.su.se/curator.

# Index